Lecture Notes in Computer Science 2361

Edited by G. Goos, J. Hartmanis, and J. van Leeuwen

Springer
Berlin
Heidelberg
New York
Barcelona
Hong Kong
London
Milan
Paris
Tokyo

Johann Blieberger   Alfred Strohmeier (Eds.)

Reliable
Software Technologies –
Ada-Europe 2002

7th Ada-Europe International Conference
on Reliable Software Technologies
Vienna, Austria, June 17-21, 2002
Proceedings

Springer

Series Editors

Gerhard Goos, Karlsruhe University, Germany
Juris Hartmanis, Cornell University, NY, USA
Jan van Leeuwen, Utrecht University, The Netherlands

Volume Editors

Johann Blieberger
Technical University Vienna, Institute of Computer-Aided Automation
Treitlstraße 1-3, 1040 Vienna, Austria
E-mail: blieb@auto.tuwien.ac.at

Alfred Strohmeier
Swiss Federal Institute of Technology Lausanne (EPFL)
1015 Lausanne, Switzerland
E-mail: alfred.strohmeier@epfl.ch

Cataloging-in-Publication Data applied for

Die Deutsche Bibliothek - CIP-Einheitsaufnahme

Reliable software technologies : proceedings / Ada Europe 2002, 7th Ada
Europe International Conference on Reliable Software Technologies, Vienna,
Austria, June 17 - 21, 2002. Johann Blieberger ; Alfred Strohmeier (ed.). -
Berlin ; Heidelberg ; New York ; Barcelona ; Hong Kong ; London ; Milan ;
Paris ; Tokyo : Springer, 2002
    (Lecture notes in computer science ; Vol. 2361)
    ISBN 3-540-43784-3

CR Subject Classification (1998): D.2, D.1.2-5, D.3, C.2.4, C.3, K.6

ISSN 0302-9743
ISBN 3-540-43784-3 Springer-Verlag Berlin Heidelberg New York

Springer-Verlag Berlin Heidelberg New York
a member of BertelsmannSpringer Science+Business Media GmbH

http://www.springer.de

© Springer-Verlag Berlin Heidelberg 2002
Printed in Germany

Typesetting: Camera-ready by author, data conversion by Boller Mediendesign
Printed on acid-free paper   SPIN: 10870279   06/3142   5 4 3 2 1 0

Foreword

The Seventh International Conference on Reliable Software Technologies, Ada-Europe 2002, took place in Vienna, Austria, June 17–21, 2002. It was sponsored by Ada-Europe, the European federation of national Ada societies, in cooperation with ACM SIGAda, and it was organized by members of the Technical University of Vienna.

The conference on Reliable Software Technologies provides the forum for researchers, developers, and users to share their research results, present tools, report on experiences, and discuss requirements that have recently arisen from the ever-changing application domains. As in past years, the conference comprised a three-day technical program, during which the papers contained in these proceedings were presented, along with vendor presentations. The technical program was bracketed by two tutorial days, when attendees had the opportunity to catch up on a variety of topics related to the field, at both introductory and advanced levels. On Friday a workshop on "Standard Container Libraries" was held. Further, the conference was accompanied by an exhibition where vendors presented their reliability-related products.

This year's conference had a specific focus on embedded systems which resulted in a special session. In addition, other sessions were related to embedded systems and several tutorials concentrated on problems and solutions for embedded systems.

Invited Speakers

The conference presented four distinguished speakers, who delivered state-of-the-art information on topics of great importance, for now and for the future of software engineering:

- Embedded Systems Unsuitable for Object Orientation
  Maarten Boasson, University of Amsterdam, The Netherlands
- On Architectural Stability and Evolution
  Mehdi Jazayeri, Technical University of Vienna, Austria
- Encapsulating Failure Detection: From Crash to Byzantine Failures
  Rachid Guerraoui, Swiss Federal Institute of Technology, Lausanne, Switzerland
- Contextware: Bridging Physical and Virtual Worlds
  Alois Ferscha, Universität Linz, Austria

We would like to express our sincere gratitude to the invited speakers, well-known to the community, for sharing their insights and information with the audience and for having written down their contributions for the proceedings.

Submitted Papers

A large number of papers were submitted. The program committee worked hard to review them, and the selection process proved to be difficult, since many papers had received excellent reviews. Finally, the program committee selected 24 papers for inclusion in the proceedings, and one contribution for presentation only. The final result was a truly international program with authors from Australia, Austria, Belgium, Canada, China, France, Germany, Greece, Israel, Japan, Malaysia, The Netherlands, Portugal, Russia, Spain, Switzerland, the United Kingdom, and the USA, covering a broad range of software technologies: Embedded Systems, Distributed Systems, Real-Time Systems, OO Technology, Case Studies, Ada Language Issues, Tools, High Integrity Systems, Program Analysis, Libraries, APIs, and Bindings.

Tutorials

The tutorial program featured international experts presenting introductory and advanced material on a variety of subjects relevant to software engineers:

- SPARK, an "Intensive overview", *Peter Amey & Rod Chapman*
- MaRTE OS: Bringing Embedded Systems and RT POSIX Together, *Michael González Harbour & Mario Aldea*
- Principles of Physical Software Design in Ada 95, *Matthew Heaney*
- Implementing Design Patterns in Ada 95, *Matthew Heaney*
- CORBA 3 and CORBA for Embedded Systems, *S. Ron Oliver*
- Using Open Source Hardware and Software to Build Reliable Systems, *Joel Sherrill & Jiri Gaisler*
- Cleanroom Software Engineering: An Overview, *William Bail*
- Exceptions – What You Always Wanted to Know about Exceptions, But Were Afraid to Ask, *Currie Colket*

Workshop on Standard Container Libraries for Ada

At the initiative of Ehud Lamm a half day workshop was held on "Standard Container Libraries for Ada". Since both contemporary dominant general purpose programming languages, Java and C++, come equipped with a standard set of reusable containers, such as Maps and Sets, and since there are quite a few Ada libraries for these purposes, the need of standard container libraries for Ada was discussed.

There is little agreement on the exact details of a standard container library. There is however a general feeling, as could be witnessed during discussions on comp.lang.ada, that such a library is important for Ada's future. A standard container library is important for achieving many of Ada's goals, top among them the use of reusable components for efficient software engineering. Other important goals that can be served by a standard container library are educational uses and efficient implementation of common algorithms and data structures, which is important for real-time systems. Designing a useful standard container library for Ada is a difficult task, as the language is used in a wide variety of different domains, with different and at times conflicting demands. Hence the need for debating and elaborating the issues among a group of interested Ada users.

The workshop was confined to container library issues, and did not address more general questions regarding the Ada standard library. The library designed is intended to be a collection of abstract data types, data structures (i.e., concrete data types), and common algorithms, useful for sequential programming. Possible candidates for inclusion in the library were judged according to this mission statement. Concurrent versions of the containers were considered to the extent that their inclusion does not interfere with the mission statement, either by complicating the design, or by imposing unacceptable run-time overhead.

Acknowledgments

Many people contributed to the success of the conference. The program committee, made up of international experts in the area of reliable software technologies, spent long hours carefully reviewing all the papers and tutorial proposals submitted to the conference. A subcommittee comprising Johann Blieberger, Bernd Burgstaller, Erhard Plödereder, Jean-Pierre Rosen, and Alfred Strohmeier met in Vienna to make the final paper selection. Some program committee members were assigned to shepherd some of the papers. We are grateful to all those who contributed to the technical program of the conference. Special thanks to Ehud Lamm for organizing and holding the workshop.

We would also like to thank the members of the organizing committee. Gerhard H. Schildt and Johann Blieberger were in charge of the overall coordination and took care of all the clerical details for the successful running of the conference. Helge Hagenauer supervised the preparation of the attractive tutorial program. Thomas Gruber worked long hours contacting companies and people to prepare the conference exhibition. Bernd Burgstaller supported the paper submission and review process and together with Dirk Craeynest he created most of the brochures and the Advance and Final Program of the conference. Bernhard Scholz was a great help in finding sponsors and organizing social events.

Last but not least, we would like to express our appreciation to the authors of the papers submitted to the conference, and to all participants who helped to achieve the goal of the conference, to provide a forum for researchers and practitioners for the exchange of information and ideas about reliable software technologies. We hope they all enjoyed the technical program as well as the social events of the 7th International Conference on Reliable Software Technologies.

June 2002

Johann Blieberger
Alfred Strohmeier

Organizing Committee

Conference Chair
Gerhard H. Schildt, TU Vienna, Austria

Program Co-chairs
Johann Blieberger, TU Vienna, Austria
Alfred Strohmeier, Swiss Fed. Inst. of Technology Lausanne (EPFL), Switzerland

Tutorial Chair
Helge Hagenauer, University of Salzburg, Austria

Exhibition Chair
Thomas Gruber, ARC Seibersdorf research GmbH, Austria

Publicity Chair
Dirk Craeynest, Offis nv/sa & K.U.Leuven, Belgium

Local Organization Chair
Bernd Burgstaller, TU Vienna, Austria

Ada-Europe Conference Liaison
Alfred Strohmeier, Swiss Fed. Inst. of Technology Lausanne (EPFL), Switzerland

Program Committee

Ángel Álvarez, Technical University of Madrid, Spain
Lars Asplund, Uppsala University, Sweden
Neil Audsley, University of York, UK
John Barnes, UK
Guillem Bernat, University of York, UK
Maarten Boasson, University of Amsterdam, The Netherlands
Ben Brosgol, ACT, USA
Bernd Burgstaller, TU Vienna, Austria
Ulf Cederling, Vaxjo University, Sweden
Roderick Chapman, Praxis Critical Systems Limited, UK
Paolo Coppola, INTECS HRT, Italy
Dirk Craeynest, Offis nv/sa & K.U.Leuven, Belgium
Alfons Crespo, Universidad Politécnica de Valencia, Spain
Peter Dencker, Aonix GmbH, Germany
Raymond Devillers, Université Libre de Bruxelles, Belgium
Brian Dobbing, Praxis Critical Systems Limited, UK
Wolfgang Gellerich, IBM, Germany

Table of Contents

High-Integrity Systems

Ada Language

Program Analysis

Tools

Distributed Systems

Libraries, APIs, and Bindings

Object-Orientation

Author Index 367

Embedded Systems Unsuitable for Object Orientation

Maarten Boasson

Kruislaan 403, 1098 SJ Amsterdam, The Netherlands
boasson@science.uva.nl

Abstract. It is argued that the current focus on object technology is detrimental to progress in embedded systems. The core of the problem is that object orientation is fine for analysis but does not answer the design needs. Solutions for shortcomings are sought within the OO dogma, making things worse. This paper will outline a different approach and will discuss benefits of that approach relative to object orientation.

1 Introduction

"Could you please forget about object orientation and get back to real technology?" was the recent plea from the senior vice president and general manager of the Global Software Group of Motorola, expressed during an informal after-dinner speech at the COMPSAC 2001 conference. His main reasons for making this strong request were the incredible size of the executables and the poor performance of OO-based programs. For a company dealing in embedded systems where both size and performance are essential ingredients for success one can understand the need for technology that does not waste those scarce resources.

If this were the only such plea, it could easily be dealt with by calling the mobile phone application too specific for considering a change in both education and research directions, but there are many more such statements and therefore one cannot lightly disregard the growing doubt about the usefulness of object orientation.

Unfortunately, very little is documented about bad experiences resulting from the use of object technology: first, companies are not generally very forthcoming with details on projects that were not successful, and second, it is hardly possible to get anything published that questions the usefulness of object technology.

2 Object Technology

Object technology has a long history. Essentially it goes back to the days that the great pioneers in computer science began thinking about formalization of abstraction. One abstraction that received a great deal of attention and (consequently?) became very popular was "abstract data types". The reasoning behind it was that by abstracting away implementation details of functions, it would become much easier to locally change implementations and thus would improve modularity and everything that entails from that. Indeed, as long as the interface and the associated semantics of

J. Blieberger and A. Strohmeier (Eds.): Ada-Europe 2002, LNCS 2361, pp. 1-12, 2002.

a function remain unchanged, the actual implementation of that function is irrelevant, and different versions with different characteristics can thus be exchanged without concern for the integrity of the program in which it is embedded. Clearly, since all data access is necessarily achieved through procedural interfaces, the programming model adopted for this type of abstraction naturally became the client-server paradigm.

In addition, it turns out that the algebraic techniques available at the time were powerful enough to begin to reason formally about properties of abstract data types. Formal reasoning about programs had until then not been possible, and this new ability seemed to indicate a path to introducing mathematical techniques into programming. It is therefore not surprising that abstract data types were seen as the basis for future software engineering.

From a different perspective the concept of objects was promoted as well. The intuitive analogy between objects and real-world entities strongly suggested that the great design gap between the real world and its artificial effigy could be dramatically reduced by designing with objects. This would then both improve the quality of a design and significantly reduce the required effort for design, and thus should be a major step towards solving the software crisis. Needless to say, before long the entire community, academic and industrial, had turned to object technology, forgetting and ignoring essentially everything else. Such behavior is typical of the immaturity of the field of software engineering, and has been observed in a number of different guises (e.g. the unrealistic expectations of so-called Integrated Programming/Project Support Environments; the shift from technology to process, as embodied in CMM).

The analogy between objects and real-world entities was first explored and exploited by Simula [see for a good overview e.g. http://java.sun.com/people/jag/SimulaHistory.html], even though the term object had not yet been coined yet. Simula provided a powerful simulation tool, and later full programming language, that, unfortunately, never became very popular. The power of Simula for simulation, however should not be taken as an indication that this type of technology will be successful in all of computing. Indeed, simulation is a special case in which the aim is to build an artifact that displays behavior analogous to that of the real world, and it is therefore not a great surprise that objects can be of great help.

Related to the usefulness of objects in modeling, is the benefit obtained from their use in analysis. Analyzing complex system requirements is a non-trivial exercise and the structure induced by object hierarchies can greatly help in reducing the effort needed for understanding such requirements.

3 Object Technology Revisited

Thus far we have elaborated on the benefits of OO technology, as seen from the modeler's and analyst's perspectives. The step to adopting this technology for design seems a small one, but in fact is a major one and represents a very serious error of judgement. The difference between analyzing a system and designing one is enormous: during analysis, the focus is on understanding the various functional components of a system and their interactions, whereas designing is about implementing the desired functionality under the constraint that all quality goals for the system are achieved. Quality goals in this context refer to what are often called non-functional properties, such as performance, fault-tolerance, scalability, etc. Implementing the required functionality, difficult as it may be in some cases, is trivial if no quality goals are formulated. The major design problem is to structure the design in such a way that a workable compromise is reached in which an acceptable quality level is achieved.

There is no theory and very little experience today to help designers in this endeavor. Essentially, all elements of an engineering discipline are missing: there are no guidelines to ensure progress in the design process, and neither is there theory that permits verification of the result of the design process against the specifications. Thus, in spite of close to 30 years of research, the art of software system design is still largely an art and hardly understood at all. In such circumstance to claim that any particular paradigm is the solution to all design problems is like advocating the use of a hammer for the design of a perpetual motion machine.

Consider the problem of designing a large distributed embedded software system, say hundreds to thousands of functional components, with all sorts of real-time, availability, performance and scalability requirements. Since this is an embedded system, it will have to interact with its environment, and it would appear natural to consider mapping entities from that environment onto software constructs: clearly a case for the application of object technology. However, object technology forces the software to be structured in a particular way that establishes relationships between objects that do not necessarily reflect the way real-world entities are related. In essence, the programming model of object orientation is client-server, where asymmetry exists between caller and callee (the convention of calling a *procedure call* a *method invocation* in object parlance does not change this, of course). In the real world, the entities that have been modeled in the system very often have no hierarchical relationships, but have their own autonomous behavior. This results in awkward programming constructs necessary for overcoming the idiosyncrasies of the object paradigm.

4 Example

Suppose we want to develop a system for simulating driving behavior on multi-lane highways in real-and continuous time. Even though this is not really an embedded system, requirements can be made very similar to those typical for embedded systems. From the large number of design options to be explored we will elaborate briefly on the most important ones.

1. The classical approach to this problem is to develop a simulation engine that can handle the required number of cars and the appropriate road topology. Then, running the simulation simply involves creating, initializing and updating the desired number of data structures, each one representing a single car with its behavioral parameters and actual state.

2. Another approach could be to use objects to represent cars, i.e. to package the data structures representing the state of a car with the procedures that operate on them. The activity of the car objects could then be controlled in one of two ways: (2a) the

objects can either be made active and base their processing on simulation time directly, or (2b) a central controller could invoke the relevant methods.

An important design issue is how the different car objects learn about the state of other cars, knowledge which is vital for adapting the behavior to the situation on the road. Here again, there are several possibilities:

3. Car objects directly interact: a car needing to find out about another car invokes a method of that other object and thus obtains the required information; or
4. Status information of all cars in the simulation is maintained by a coordination object that obtains the information from the car objects and makes it available upon request.

Analysis of these approaches shows that (1) is hardly object oriented. (2a) and (2b) can both be seen as OO, although the active objects of (2a) depart from the original object model. (3) is a solution in pure OO style, but has many problems that cannot easily be dealt with. Addressing these problems in the OO paradigm creates significant additional complexity, that one would like to avoid if possible [3]. (4) in essence departs from the OO model, in that it externalizes the status information that is essentially private data of the object. In many ways this is the most elegant solution, which in addition (and in contrast to the others) can be made to perform and scale well.

The interesting observation to be made is that the only solution that is acceptable in terms of the quality constraints to be met, is the one that departs the most from the object model. The example given is sufficiently similar to a large number of real applications, that this observation should be taken seriously; the question then arises whether other paradigms are possible that more directly correspond to the solution hinted at in (4). This is indeed the case, and a growing number of people is recognizing the importance of such paradigms, to the extent that efforts are underway of integrating at least one such programming model in both CORBA [www.omg.org] and OpenWings [www.openwings.org]. It remains to be seen whether such integration is possible without compromising too much, and moreover whether the OO flavor adds anything useful to the paradigm.

5 An Alternative Programming Model

We will now describe an alternative programming model to the object model, that has proven its benefits in real applications since at least 10 years. One of the more convincing demonstrations was the recent integration of some 1000 software components that were designed according to the model we will describe and that were developed in a multi-vendor, multi-country setting: the very first time the integration of all components was attempted the system actually worked correctly![1]

---

[1] This result was obtained by Hollandse Signaalapparaten B.V. (now Thales Nederland B.V.) with their propriety architecture SPLICE, which is in the process of being commercialized.

5.1 Preliminaries

Recently coordination models and languages have become an active area of research [6]. In [7] it was argued that a complete programming model consists of two separate components: the computation model and the coordination model. The computation model is used to express the basic tasks to be performed by a system, i.e. the system's functionality. The coordination model is applied to organize the functions into a coherent ensemble; it provides the means to create processes and facilitates communication. One of the greater merits of separating computation from coordination is the considerably improved modularity of a system. The computation model facilitates a traditional functional decomposition of the system, while the coordination model accomplishes a further de-coupling between the functional modules in both space and time. This is exemplified by the relative success of coordination languages in the field of distributed and parallel systems.

Since the early 80's we have developed and refined a software architecture for large-scale distributed embedded systems [2], that is based on a separation between computation and coordination. Below, we first present the basic software architecture, after which we shall focus on the underlying coordination model. We demonstrate how the basic coordination model can be gradually refined to include non-functional aspects, such as distributed processing and fault-tolerance, in a modular fashion. The software architecture has been applied in the development of commercially available command-and-control, and traffic management systems. We conclude with a discussion of our experiences in the design of these systems.

A software architecture defines the organizational principle of a system in terms of types of components and possible interconnections between these components. In addition, an architecture prescribes a set of design rules and constraints governing the behavior of components and their interaction [4]. Traditionally, software architectures have been primarily concerned with structural organization and static interfaces. With the growing interest in coordination models, however, more emphasis is placed on the organizational aspects of behavior and interaction.

In practice, many different software architectures are in use. Some well-known examples are the Client/Server and Blackboard architectures. Clearly, these architectures are based on different types of components - clients and servers versus knowledge sources and blackboards - and use different styles of interaction: requests from clients to servers versus writing and reading on a common blackboard.

The software architecture that we developed for distributed embedded systems basically consists of two types of components: applications and a shared data space. Applications are active, concurrently executing processes that each implement part of the system's overall functionality. Besides process creation, there is no direct interaction between applications; all communication takes place through a logically shared data space simply by reading and writing data elements. In this sense this architecture bears strong resemblance to coordination languages and models like Linda [5], Gamma [1], and Swarm [9], where active entities are coordinated by means of a shared data space.

5.2 The Shared Data Space

The shared data space is organized after the well-known relational data model. Each data element in the shared data space is associated with a unique sort, that defines its structure. A sort definition declares the name of the sort and the record fields the sort consists of. Each record field has a type, such as integer, real, or string; various type constructors, such as enumerated types, arrays, and nested records, are provided for building more complex types.

Sorts enable applications to distinguish between different kinds of information. A further differentiation between data elements of the same sort is made by introducing identities. As is standard in the relational data model, one or more record fields can be declared as key fields. Each data element in the shared data space is uniquely determined by its sort and the value of its key fields. In this way applications can unambiguously refer to specific data elements, and relationships between data elements can be explicitly represented by referring from one data element to the key fields of another.

5.3 Applications

Essentially, applications interact with the shared data space by writing and reading data elements. The architecture does not provide an operation for globally deleting elements from the shared data space. Instead, data can be removed implicitly using an overwriting mechanism. This mechanism is typically used to update old data with more recent values as the system's environment evolves over time. Additionally, applications can hide data, once read, from their view. This operation enables applications to progressively traverse the shared data space by successive read operations. By the absence of a global delete operation, the shared data space models a dynamically changing information store, where data can only be read or written. This contrasts the view where data elements represent shared resources, that can be physically consumed by applications. Thus an existing (sequential) programming language is extended with coordination primitives for creating processes and for interacting with the shared data space.

The overwriting mechanism that is used when inserting data elements into the shared data space potentially gives rise to conflicts. If at the same time two different applications each write a data element of the same sort and with the same key value, one element will overwrite the other in a nondeterministic order. Consequently one of the two updates will be lost. In applications where this type of nondeterministic behavior is considered undesirable, the architect should impose the design constraint that for each sort at most one application shall write data elements with the same key value.

6 Refinement of the Architecture

The shared data space architecture is based on an ideal situation where many non-functional requirements, such as distribution of data and processing across a computer network, fault-tolerance, and system response times, need not be taken into account. We next discuss how, through a successive series of modular refinements, a software architecture can be derived that fully supports the development of large-scale, distributed embedded systems.

6.1 A Distributed Software Architecture

The first aspect that we consider here is distribution of the shared data space over a network of computer systems. The basic architecture is refined by introducing two additional components: heralds and a communication network.

Each application process interacts with exactly one herald. A herald embodies a local cache for storing data elements, and processing facilities for handling all communication needs of the application processes. All heralds are identical and need no prior information about either the application processes or their communication requirements. Communication between heralds is established by a message passing mechanism. Messages between heralds are handled by the communication network that interconnects them. The network must support broadcasting, but should preferably also support direct addressing of heralds, and multicasting. The interaction with heralds is transparent with respect to the shared data space model: application processes continue to operate on a logically shared data space.

The heralds are passive servers of the application processes, but are actively involved in establishing and maintaining the required inter-herald communication. The communication needs are derived dynamically by the collection of heralds from the read and write operations that are issued by the application processes. The protocol that is used by the heralds to manage communication is based on a subscription paradigm, where the subscribing herald maintains a cache for data received from publishing heralds..

Each subscribing herald stores all transferred copies into its local cache, overwriting any existing data of the same sort and with the same key value. During all transfers a protocol is used that preserves the order in which data elements of the same sort have been written by an application. This mechanism in combination with the design constraint that for each sort at most one application writes data elements with the same key value, guarantees that overwrites occur in the same order with all heralds. Otherwise, communication by the heralds is performed asynchronously.

The search for data elements matching the query associated with a read request is performed locally by a herald. If no matching element can be found, the operation is suspended either until new data of the requested sort arrives or until the specified timeout has expired.

As a result of this protocol, the shared data space is selectively replicated across the heralds in the network. The local cache of each herald contains data of only those sorts that are actually used by the application it serves. In practice the approach is viable, particularly for large-scale distributed systems, since the applications are generally interested in only a fraction of all sorts. Moreover, the communication pattern in which heralds exchange data is relatively static: it may change when the operational mode of a system changes, or in a number of circumstances in which the configuration of the system changes (such as extensions or failure recovery). Such changes to the pattern are rare with respect to the number of actual communications using an established pattern. It is therefore beneficial from a performance point of view to maintain a subscription registration. After an initial short phase each time a new sort has been introduced, the heralds will have adapted to the new communication requirement. This knowledge is subsequently used by the heralds to distribute newly produced data to all the heralds that hold a subscription. Since subscription registration is maintained dynamically by the heralds, all changes to the system configuration will automatically lead to adaptation of the communication patterns.

Note that there is no need to group the distribution of a data element to the collection of subscribing heralds into an atomic transaction. This enables a very efficient implementation in which the produced data is distributed asynchronously and the latency between actual production and use of the data depends largely on the consuming application processes. This results in upper bounds that are acceptable for distributed embedded systems where timing requirements are of the order of milliseconds (depending on the properties of processors and communication technology used, obviously).

6.2 Temporal Aspects

The shared data space models a persistent store: data once written remains available to all applications until it is either overwritten by a new instance or hidden from an application's view by execution of a read operation. The persistence of data decouples applications in time. Data can be read, for instance, by an application that did not exist the moment the data was written, and conversely, the application that originally wrote the data might no longer be present when the data is actually read.

Applications in the embedded systems domain deal mostly with data instances that represent continuous quantities: data is either an observation sampled from the system's environment, or derived from such samples through a process of data association and correlation. The data itself is relatively simple in structure; there are only a few data types, and given the volatile nature of the samples, only recent values are of interest. However, samples may enter the system at very short intervals, so sufficient throughput and low latency are crucial properties. In addition, but to a lesser extent, embedded systems maintain discrete information, which is either directly related to external events or derived through qualitative reasoning from the sampled input.

This observation leads us to refine the shared data space to support volatile as well as persistent data. The sort definition is extended with an additional attribute that indicates whether the instances of a sort are volatile or persistent. For persistent data the semantics of the read and write operations remain unchanged. Volatile data, on the other hand, will only be visible to the collection of applications that is present at the moment the data is written. Any application that is created afterwards, will not be able to read this data.

The subscription-based protocol, that manages the distribution of data in a network of computer systems, can be refined to exploit the distinction between volatile and persistent data. Since volatile data is only available to the applications that are present at the moment the data is written, no history needs to be kept. Consequently, if an application writes a data element, it is immediately forwarded to the subscribing heralds, without storing a copy for later reference. This optimization reduces the amount of storage that is required. Moreover, it eliminates the initial transfer of any previously written data elements, when an application performs the first read operation on a sort. This enables a newly created application to integrate into the communication pattern without initial delay, which better suits the timing characteristics that are typically associated with the processing of volatile data.

6.3 Fault Tolerance

Due to the stringent requirements on availability and safety that are typical of large-scale embedded systems, there is the need for redundancy in order to mask hardware failures during operation. Fault-tolerance in general is a very complex requirement to meet and can, of course, only be partially solved in software. In his architecture, the heralds can be refined to provide a mechanism for fault-tolerant behavior. The mechanism is based on both data and process replication. By making fault-tolerance a property of the software architecture, the design complexity of applications can be significantly reduced.

In this paper we only consider failing processing units, and we assume that if a processor fails, it stops executing. In particular we assume here that communication never fails indefinitely and that data does not get corrupted.

If a processing unit in the network fails, the data that is stored in this unit, will be permanently lost. In order for the data still to be available for the system, copies of each data element are stored across different units of failure. The subscription-based protocol already implements a replicated storage scheme, where copies of each data element are stored with each of the consumers. The basic protocol, however, is not sufficient to implement fault-tolerant data storage in general.

The solution is to store a copy of each data element in at least one other unit of failure. The architecture is extended with an additional type of component: a persistent cache. This component executes a specialized version of the subscription protocol. On start-up a persistent cache broadcasts the name of each persistent sort on the network. As a result of the subscription protocol that is executed by the collection of heralds, any data element of a persistent sort that is written by an application, will be automatically forwarded to the persistent cache. There can be any number of instances of the persistent cache executing on different processing units, dependent on the required level of system availability. Moreover, it is possible to load two or more persistent caches with disjoint sets of sort names, leading to load distribution related to the storage of persistent data.

When a processing unit fails, the applications that are executed by this unit will be lost. The architecture can be refined to support both passive and active replication of applications across different processing units in the network.

Using passive replication, only one process is actually executing, while one or more back-ups are kept off-line, either in main memory or on secondary storage. When the processing unit executing the active process fails, one of the back-ups is activated. In order to be able to restore the internal state of the failed process, it is required that each passively replicated application writes a copy of its state to the shared data space each time the state is updated. The internal state can be represented by one or more persistent sorts. When a back-up is activated, it will first restore the current state from the shared data space and then continue execution.

When timing is critical, active replication of processes is often a more viable solution. In that case, multiple instances of the same application are executing in parallel, hosted by different processing units; all instances read and write data. Typically, active replication is used when timing is critical and the failing component must be replaced instantaneously. The subscription-based protocol can be refined to support active replication transparently. If a particular instance of a replicated application performs a write operation, its herald attaches a unique replication index as a key field to the data element. The index allows the subscribing heralds to distinguish between the various copies that they receive from a replicated application. Upon a read request, a herald first attempts to return a matching element having a fixed default index. When, after some appropriate time-out has expired, the requested element is still not available, a matching element with an index other than the default is returned. From that moment on it is assumed that the application corresponding to the default index has failed, and the subscription registration is updated accordingly. The index of the actually returned data element now becomes the new default.

6.4 System Modifications and Extensions

In the embedded systems domain requirements on availability often make it necessary to support modifications and extensions while the current system remains on-line. There are two distinct cases to be considered.
– The upgrade is an extension to the system, introducing new applications and sorts but without further modifications to the existing system.
– The upgrade includes modification of existing applications.

Since the subscription registration is maintained dynamically by the heralds, it is obvious that the current protocol can deal with the first case without further refinements. After installing and starting a new application, it will automatically integrate.

The second case, clearly, is more difficult. One special, but important, category of modifications can be handled by a simple refinement of the heralds. Consider the problem of upgrading a system by replacing an existing application process with one that implements the same function, but using a better algorithm leading to higher quality results. In many systems it is not possible to physically replace the current application with the new one, since this would require the system to be taken off-line.

By a refinement of the heralds it is possible to support on-line replacement of applications. If an application performs a write operation, its herald attaches an additional key field to the data element representing the application's version number. Upon a read request, a herald now first checks whether multiple versions of the requested instance are available in the local cache. If this is the case, the instance having the highest version number is delivered to the application - assuming that higher numbers correspond to later releases. From that moment on, all data elements with lower version numbers are discarded. In this way an application can be dynamically upgraded, simply by starting the new version of the application, after which it will automatically integrate and replace the older version.

7 Conclusion

Due to the inherent complexity of the environment in which large-scale embedded systems operate, combined with the stringent requirements regarding temporal behavior, availability, robustness, and maintainability, the design of these systems is an intricate task. Coordination models offer the potential of separating functional requirements from other aspects of system design. We have presented a software architecture for large-scale embedded systems that incorporates a separate coordination model. We have demonstrated how, starting from a relatively simple model based on a shared data space, the model can be successively refined to meet the requirements that are typical for this class of systems.

Over the past years the architecture adumbrated above has been applied in the development of commercially available command-and-control, and traffic management systems. These systems consist of some 1000 applications running on close to 100 processors interconnected by a hybrid communication network. Experience with the development of these systems confirms that the software architecture, including all of the refinements discussed, significantly reduces the complexity of the design process [3]. Due to the high level of decoupling between processes, these systems are relatively easy to develop and integrate in an incremental way. Moreover, distribution of processes and data, fault-tolerant behavior, graceful degradation, and dynamic reconfiguration are directly supported by the architecture

Comparing the presented solution with the attempts at achieving similar (or even less) performance in the object community, one cannot escape wondering about the staggering complexity and size of that effort. Whereas a full CORBA implementation, including support for fault tolerance, real-time behavior etc. can only be described in many volumes of specification and requires hundreds of megabytes of code, the architecture presented here is implemented in less than a megabyte.

Experiments conducted by the Institute for Defense Analyses of the USA DoD indicate that the performance ratio of our approach and CORBA for an air defense system is around 50.

In some sense, the architecture presented here can be considered to be truly object oriented: the distributed shared data space is one object, and the application processes are each active objects. Although this is correct from a syntactic perspective, it only leads to loss of meaning for the term "object orientation". In fact the relationship between application processes in this architecture is based on sharing of data, which strongly violates the OO paradigm.

References

1. J.-P. Banatre, D. Le Metayer, "Programming by Multiset transformation", Communications of the ACM, Vol. 36, No. 1, 1993, pp. 98-111.
2. M. Boasson, "Control Systems Software", IEEE Transactions on Automatic Control, Vol. 38, No. 7, 1993, pp. 1094-1107.
3. M. Boasson, "Complexity may be our own fault", IEEE Software, March 1993.
4. M. Boasson, Software Architecture special issue (guest editor), IEEE Software, November 1995.

5. N. Carriero, D. Gelernter, "Linda in Context", Communications of the ACM, Vol. 32, No. 4, 1989, pp. 444-458.
6. D. Garlan, D. Le Metayer (Eds.), "Coordination Languages and Models", Lecture Notes in Computer Science 1282, Springer, 1997.
7. D. Gelernter, N. Carriero, "Coordination Languages and their Significance", Communications of the ACM, Vol. 35, No. 2, 1992, pp. 97-107.
8. K. Jackson, M. Boasson, "The importance of good architectural style", Proc. of the workshop of the IEEE TF on Engineering of Computer Based Systems, Tucson, 1995.
9. G.-C. Roman, H.C. Cunningham, "Mixed Programming Metaphors in a Shared Dataspace Model of Concurrency", IEEE Transactions of Software Engineering, Vol. 16, No. 12, 1990, pp.1361-1373.

On Architectural Stability and Evolution

Mehdi Jazayeri

Technische Universität Wien
jazayeri@tuwien.ac.at

Abstract. Many organizations are now pursuing software architecture as a way to control their software development and evolution costs and challenges. A software architecture describes a system's structure and global properties and thus determines not only how the system should be constructed but also guides its evolution. An important challenge is to be able to evaluate the "goodness" of a proposed architecture. I suggest stability or resilience as a primary criterion for evaluating an architecture. The stability of an architecture is a measure of how well it accommodates the evolution of the system without requiring changes to the architecture. As opposed to traditional predictive approaches to architecture evaluation, I suggest retrospective analysis for evaluating architectural stability by examining the amount of change applied in successive releases of a software product. I review the results of a case study of twenty releases of a telecommunication software system containing a few million lines of code to show how retrospective analysis may be performed.

Keywords: software architecture, software evolution, architecture evaluation, architectural stability, retrospective analysis, software visualization

1. Introduction

After many years of research on software architecture, interest in software architecture seemed to suddenly explode in the latter half of the 1990s. Both industry and academic interest in software architecture has been intense, as witnessed by the many books, conferences and workshops on software architecture. Some of the recent milestone publications are the paper by Perry and Wolf [Perry92] that proposed a systematic framework for the study of software architecture, Shaw and Garlan [Shaw96] that tried to present software architecture as a systematic discipline, Kruchten[Kruchten96] that proposed a model of software architecture that enlarged the view of software architecture from dealing only with static structure to consisting of four different aspects.

Prior to these works, Parnas had laid the foundations of software architecture in a number of seminal papers. The problems he addressed in these papers in the 1970s and 1980s took two decades to be recognized as real problems by the software industry. Parnas not only identified the key problems, he also developed a set of related architectural concepts for addressing these problems. These concepts are still fundamental for understanding and solving the problems of software construction. I

J. Blieberger and A. Strohmeier (Eds.): Ada-Europe 2002, LNCS 2361, pp. 13-23, 2002.
© Springer-Verlag Berlin Heidelberg 2002

will review some of these concepts here because they form the underpinnings of any work on software architecture, including this one.

The most fundamental of these ideas was the principle of "information hiding" [Parnas72]. This principle gives the designer a concrete method for decomposing a design into modules. The modularization is on the basis of design decisions. Each module protects, or encapsulates, or "hides" an important design decision. The motivation behind the method is that if important design decisions are encapsulated in separate modules, then changing a design decision in the future will affect only the associated module and not require changes that are scattered throughout the software. The same motivation is behind the development of object-oriented development, but information hiding is a more fundamental and basic notion.

The problem of *change* is a key challenge to software engineering. The ideas of "design for change" and "anticipation of changes" [Parnas79] were the motivations for Parnas's work and information hiding was a concrete design method to implement them. Parnas also proposed a set of relations and structures as a basis for designing and documenting a system's architecture. The "uses" relation [Parnas74] describes a relationship among modules of a system. A module M1 uses module M2 if a working copy of M2 must be present for module M1 to satisfy its specification. This fundamental relationship supports the design of software structures that are organized as a hierarchy of modules. One important implication of such a design is that it makes it possible to define working subsets of the hierarchy. This means that we can not only build the software incrementally, but also that we can build potentially useful subsets of the software.

The subsettable software designs and information hiding lead almost naturally to the idea of a family of designs. In [Parnas76], Parnas describes the reasons for designing families of programs rather than single programs and gives a concrete approach for doing it. The idea is to clearly identify the design decisions that are common to family members and those that distinguish among family members. Naturally, design decisions can be hidden by appropriate modules and we can build the right family member by using the module that captures the right decision. The idea of program families was inspired by the IBM System 360 architecture, which indeed billed itself as a family architecture. The architecture was shared by all the members of the family. Particular "realizations" of the architecture exhibited different properties, primarily in terms of performance. Today, the concept of program families is pursued under the topic of software product families or product-line architectures.

2. Architecture and Evolution

Despite the concern with "change" and accommodating changes, most of the early definitions of software engineering focus explicitly on construction and only implicitly, if at all, with the phenomenon of software "evolution." By and large, software processes and design techniques concentrate on construction. Yet we know from experience that evolution is a key problem in software engineering and exacts huge costs. Anecdotal evidence even hints that companies spend more resources on maintenance (i.e. evolving their software) than on initial development. Probably the earliest work to deal explicitly with software evolution is that of Lehman[Lehman80,

Lehman85]. Even Parnas finally got to deal explicitly with the issue of evolution in his paper on software aging [Parnas94], where he posits a set of hypotheses and insights on why software needs to evolve and how we can deal with the challenges. Recently, Bennett and Rajlich[Bennet00] proposed a software development process that considers the evolution and retirement of software as explicit phases in the software lifecycle.

We can argue that, as Parnas foresaw in his early work on "change," evolution is the underlying, if implicit, motivation for much of the recent software development research. For example, product-line architectures are a systematic approach to controlling software evolution. They try to anticipate the major evolutionary milestones in the development of the product, capture the properties that remain constant through the evolution and document the variability points from which different family members may be created. The approach gives a structure to the product's evolution and possibly rules out some unplanned evolutions, if the architecture is respected. Incremental software processes, such as the unified process, are also ways to structure the software's evolution through prescribed steps. The assumption is that evolution is helped by the feedback gained from releases of the early increments.

3. The Role of Software Architecture

There are many definitions for software architecture. Definitions usually concentrate on structural properties and the kinds of decisions that an architect must make. A common view is that architectural decisions are those that have to be made before concurrent work on the system can be started. That is, the architectural decisions span the system components and determine their overall relationships and constraints. Once these decisions have been made, work on the individual components may proceed relatively independently. The architectural decisions determine many of the significant properties of the system and are difficult to change because they span the whole system. Therefore, one of the major implications of a software architecture is to render particular kinds of changes easy or difficult, thus constraining the software's evolution possibilities. Despite the importance of evolution, and the impact of the software architecture on evolution, it is surprising that most definitions of software architecture do not explicitly mention evolution. In fact, it can be argued that the primary goal of a software architecture is to guide the evolution of the system, the construction of the first release of the system being only the first of many milestones in this evolution.

4. Architecture Evaluation and Assessment

Because of the key role that architecture plays in the life of a system, it is important to evaluate or assess a system's architecture. Reviews and inspections are accepted evaluation methods in software engineering. In such an evaluation, we have to decide what factors we are evaluating and what the goals of the evaluation are. Depending on the definition of software architecture and its goals, it is possible to define an evaluation procedure. Typically, such an evaluation is qualitative and is itself difficult to evaluate.

A representative architecture evaluation method is the Architecture Tradeoff Analysis Method (ATAM), developed at the Software Engineering Institute [Kazman99]. ATAM tries to help elicit the goals of the architecture and then evaluates the architecture against those goals. The procedure is said to take 3 or 4 calendar days. It is aimed at evaluating how well the architecture meets its quality goals such as performance, reliability, security, and modifiability.

We call such kinds of evaluations *predictive*. They try to anticipate how well an architecture will perform in the future. While useful, predictive evaluations suffer from inherent uncertainty. How do we know what to assess? Even if we did know, how do we assess it? How sure can we be of the results?

A way to answer these questions is to apply *retrospective* evaluation. I will describe retrospective evaluation here in the context of evolution. First, we start with the assumption that the software architecture's primary goal is to guide the system's evolution. Retrospective evaluation looks at successive releases of the product to analyze how smoothly the evolution took place. Intuitively, we want to see if the system's architectural decisions remained intact throughout the evolution of the system, that is, through successive releases of the software. We call this intuitive idea "architectural stability."

There are many ways we can perform such an analysis but all rely on comparing properties from one release of the software to the next. This implies that some architectural information must be kept for each release. For example, we might compare the uses relation in successive releases. If the relation remains substantially unchanged, we can conclude that it was a stable (or robust) architecture that supported evolution well. There are virtually any number of quantitative measures we can make depending on what aspect of the architecture we are interested in evaluating.

Retrospective analysis can have many uses. First, we can empirically evaluate the software architecture's stability. Second, we can calibrate our predictive evaluation results. Third, we can use the results of the analysis to predict trends in the system's evolution. Such predictions can be invaluable for planning the future development of the system. For example, a manager may use previous evolution data of the system to anticipate the resources needed for the next release of the system, or to identify the components most likely to require attention, or to identify the components needing restructuring or replacement, or, finally, to decide if it is time to retire the system entirely. In the next section, we describe a case study that shows some simple examples of retrospective analyses.

5. Case Study

We have applied three different kinds of retrospective analyses to twenty releases of a large telecommunication software system. In the first, we compared simple measures such as module size, number of modules changed, and the number of modules added in the different releases. In the second, we tried to detect coupling among modules by discovering which modules tend to change in the same releases, and in the third, we used color visualization to "map out" the system's evolution. In this section, we give an overview of these experiments. The details may be found in [Gall97, Gall98, Gall99].

The telecommunication system under study consists of over ten million lines of code. The system is organized into *subsystems*, each subsystem consists of *modules*, and each modules consists of *programs*. We had access to a database that contained information about the system but not the code itself. The size of components is recorded as the number of subcomponents it contains. For example, the size of a module is the number of programs it contains.

5.1   The First Analysis: Simple Metrics

In the first set of analyses, we simply plotted various basic size-related metrics according to releases. For example, Fig. 1 shows the growth in the number of programs in the system. It shows a steady but stabilizing growth of the system. It appears to show a stable system, possibly approaching a dormant state, getting ripe for retirement.

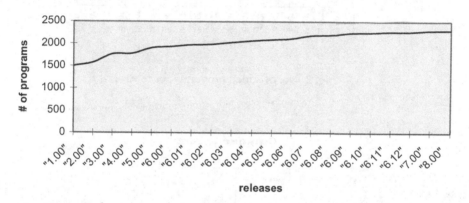

Fig. 1 Growth of the system in size

Fig. 2 shows the number of *added* programs. Here we see that a decreasing number of programs are added at each release, with a curiously higher number in every other release. This phenomenon could be due to the way the releases were planned. The manager of the project should be able to interpret the result and decide whether it was expected. In any case, the fact that the number of additions is decreasing also points to a stabilization of the system.

Fig. 3 plots two related numbers: the percentage of programs added and the percentage of programs changed in each release. The figure seems to indicate that in one release "many" programs are added and in the next "many" are changed. We don't know if there is any correlation between the programs added and those changed in the next release. But the figure certainly invites many questions that should be of interest to the manager.

Finally, in Fig. 4 we show the growth in size of three different modules. We see that two of the modules are relatively stable while the third is growing significantly. This figure indicates that it is not enough to study the data only at the system level. It is possible that undesirable phenomena at a lower level, in this case at the module level, mask each other out at the system level. Certainly the growth of Module A compared to the other modules should ring an alarm bell to the manager.

These figures show how simple metrics plotted along the releases of a system can reveal interesting phenomena about the evolution of the system. Unusual and anomalous evolutions of components can be easily spotted. Any deviations from expectations should be investigated.

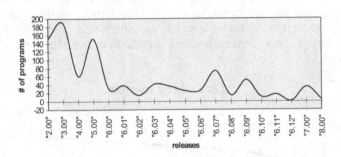

Fig. 2. No. of added programs per release

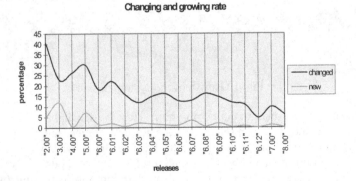

Fig. 3. No. of changed and added programs per release

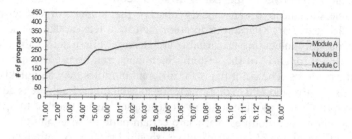

Fig. 4. Growth of size of modules in one subsystem

5.2   The Second Analysis: Hidden Module Coupling

In the second experiment, we tried to uncover potential (hidden) dependencies among modules or programs of the system. The idea was to discover if there are certain modules that always change during the same release. For example, Table 1 shows two particular programs that are changed in nine releases together. In the two other releases, one is changed but not the other. We developed a number of analysis techniques for discovering and correlating "change sequences". If two modules are always changed in the same sequences of releases, it is likely that they share some possibly hidden dependencies. The longer the sequence, the higher is the likelihood of cross-dependencies. Such analysis can be easily performed and can reveal a great deal about the architecture. In fact, the goal of the architecture is to minimize such dependencies so that change and evolution is isolated in different modules. If changes are required in many modules, the architecture suffers from lack of stability.

Table 1. Coupling among subsystems A and B

SUB_2=<1 2 3 4 6 7 9 10 14>										
A.aa.111	1	2	3	4	6	7	9	10	14	17	19
B.ba.222	1	2	3	4	6	7	9	10	14	16	18

5.3   The Third Analysis: Color Visualization

In this study our goal was to make the results of retrospective study more apparent and easy to grasp. We used visualization techniques to summarize the large amount of data that could be plotted and displayed. In particular, we explored the use of color in such visualizations. Due to the need for color, the reader is urged to look at an on-line version of this paper to view the figures in color. We use color percentage bars to display a history of a release. For example, Fig. 5 represents a module by a bar in each release. The bar contains different colors. The colors represent different version numbers of programs in the module. For example, in the first release, when all programs are at version 1, the bar is a single color. By comparing the bars for different releases, the eye can quickly observe the amount of changes from one release to the next. Large variations in color indicate a release that is undergoing lots of change, possibly indicating an unstable architecture. Fig. 6 shows the change maps for modules A through H of the system. Such maps can be used to quickly identify problematic modules. The color maps for different modules may be quickly compared to get a sense of how module evolutions relate to each other. Such maps could be used as a "fingerprint" of a module to show its evolution. It is possible to spot different types of evolution and modules that share certain patterns of evolution. A predictive evaluation of the architecture, if effective, should be able to anticipate the kind of fingerprint a module should produce during its evolution.

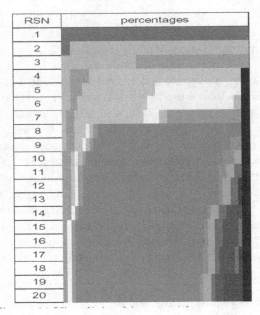

Fig. 5. Visualizing evolution with percentage bars

6. Retrospective Analysis

The case studies of the previous section show a glimpse of how retrospective analysis may be applied and exploited. The information from retrospective analysis may be used for forward engineering as well, primarily by using the information from the past to predict the requirements of the future, for example, in answering questions such as how much code changes the next release will entail and how much it will cost.

The tools we have used are simple and require very little information to be kept for each release of the software. Yet, such data is not commonly maintained, analyzed, or exploited. The key point is that the tools must maintain data across releases to enable the reasoning and analysis about the software's evolution. This means that software reengineering tools must be enhanced to deal with releases explicitly to be able to support retrospective evolution analysis. Because of the huge amount of data involved, visualization techniques seem to be useful.

An example tool that can be used for evolution analysis is the Evolution Matrix [Lanza01] which visualizes the evolution of classes in an object-oriented system. The evolution of various metrics about a class may be displayed. Size and color are used to represent the metrics. The evolution analysis applied to a large number of classes has led to classifying different types of classes based on their evolution patterns. Lanza [Lanza01] has observed classes that he categorizes as supernova (suddenly explodes in size), pulsar (grows and shrinks repeatedly), white dwarf (shrinks in size), red giant (continues being very large), and idle (does not change). Such a tool can be a powerful aid in retrospective analysis. For example, a large number of idle classes would indicate a stable architecture. (Clearly, idle classes could also indicate dead code so analysis had to be done carefully.)

7. Summary and Conclusions

We have argued that a primary goal of a software architecture is to guide the evolution of a software product. To evaluate how well a software architecture achieves this goal, we can analyze the architecture for adherence to certain rules that we believe support evolution. But there is more that we can do. Using appropriate analysis tools, we can try to evaluate an architecture's "stability" or "resilience" by observing the actual evolution of the associated software product. We call this kind of analysis "retrospective" because it looks back on the software product's releases. We have shown the results of some simple tools that can help in retrospective analysis. These tools combine simple metrics and visualization to summarize in a compact form the evolution patterns of a system, thus enabling the engineer or manager to check the reality against the expected results.

In principle, predictive analysis and retrospective analysis should be combined. Perfect predictive evaluations would render retrospective analysis unnecessary. If we are not sure of perfection, however, retrospective analysis is necessary to validate our predictions and detect deviations from plans.

Acknowledgments

I would like to acknowledge the support of Harald Gall who has been a close collaborator on all this work, particularly on the case studies.

This work was supported in part by the European Commission within the ESPRIT Framework IV project no. 20477 ARES (Architectural Reasoning for Embedded Systems). We would like to thank our partners in this project. Many of the results of the ARES project are presented in [Jazayeri00].

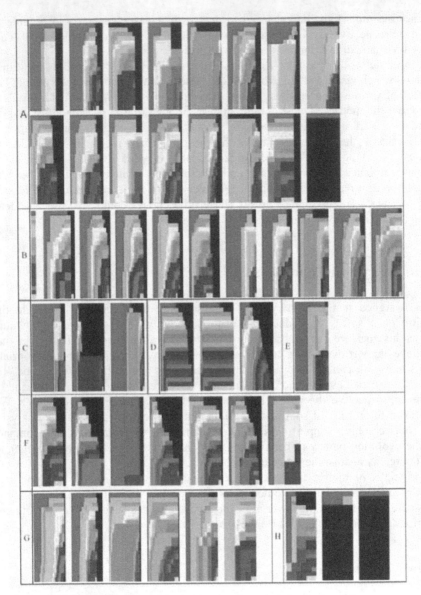

Fig. 6. Evolution of modules A through H in terms of programs

8. References

[Bennett00] K. Bennett and V. Rajlich, "A staged model for the software lifecycle," *Computer* 33(7): 66–71, July 2000.

[Gall97]   H. Gall, M. Jazayeri, R. Klösch, and G. Trausmuth, "Software Evolution Observations Based on Product Release History," Proceedings of International Conference on Software Maintenance (ICSM '97), Bari, Italy, IEEE Computer Society Press, Los Alamitos, CA, September 1997.

[Gall98]   H. Gall, K. Hajek, and M. Jazayeri, "Detection of logical coupling based on product release histories," Proceedings of International Conference on Software Maintenance (ICSM '98), Washington, DC, IEEE Computer Society Press, Los Alamitos, CA, November 1998.

[Gall99]   H. Gall, M. Jazayeri, and C. Riva, "Visualizing software release histories: the use of color and third dimension," Proceedings of International Conference on Software Maintenance (ICSM '99), pp. 99–108, Oxford, UK, IEEE Computer Society Press, Los Alamitos, CA, September 1999.

[Jazayeri00] M. Jazayeri, A. Ran, and F. van der Linden, Software Architecture for Product Families: Principles and Practice, Addison-Wesley, Reading, 2000.

[Kazman99] R. Kazman, M. Klein, and P. Clements, "Evaluating software architectures for real-time systems."

[Kruchten95] P. B. Kruchten, "The 4+1 view model of architecture," IEEE Software, 29(11): 42–50, November 1995.

[Lanza01]   M. Lanza, "The Evolution Matrix: Recovering Software Evolution using Software Visualization Techniques," Proceedings of IWPSE (International Workshop on Principles of Software Evolution), 2001, Vienna.

[Lehman80] Lehman M.M., "Programs, life cycles and laws of software evolution," Proceedings of the IEEE, pp. 1060-1076, September 1980.

[Lehman85] Lehman M.M. and Belady L. A., Program evolution, Academic Press, London and New York, 1985.

[Parnas72]   D. L. Parnas, "On the criteria to be used in decomposing systems into modules," Communications of the ACM, 15(12): 1053–8, December 1972.

[Parnas74]   D. L. Parnas, "On a buzzword: hierarchical structure," Proceedings IFIP Congress (1974), North-Holland, Amsterdam, 1974.

[Parnas76]   D. L. Parnas, "On the design and development of program families," IEEE Transactions on Software Engineering, 2(2): 1–9, March 1976.

[Parnas79]   D. L. Parnas, "Designing software for ease of extension and contraction," IEEE Transactions on Software Engineering, 5(2):128–138, March 1979.

[Parnas94]   D. L. Parnas, "Software aging," Proc. International Conference on Software Engineering (ICSE 94), Sorrento, May 1994, pp. 279-287.

[Perry92]   D. E. Perry and A. L. Wolf, "Foundations for the study of software architecture," ACM SIGSOFT Software Engineering Notes, 17(4): 40–52, October 1992.

[Shaw96]   M. Shaw and D. Garlan. Software architecture: perspectives on an emerging discipline. Prentice Hall, Englewood Cliffs, NJ, 1996.

Encapsulating Failure Detection: From Crash to Byzantine Failures

Assia Doudou*, Benoît Garbinato**, and Rachid Guerraoui

Distributed Programming Laboratory,
Swiss Federal Institute of Technology, Lausanne.

Abstract. Separating different aspects of a program, and encapsulating them inside well defined modules, is considered a good engineering discipline. This discipline is particularly desirable in the development of distributed agreement algorithms which are known to be difficult and error prone. For such algorithms, one aspect that is important to encapsulate is failure detection. In fact, a complete encapsulation was proven to be feasible in the context of distributed systems with process crash failures, by using *black-box* failure detectors. This paper discusses the feasibility of a similar encapsulation in the context of *Byzantine* (also called *arbitrary* or *malicious*) failures. We argue that, in the Byzantine context, it is just impossible to achieve the level of encapsulation of the original crash failure detector model. However, we also argue that there is some room for an intermediate approach where algorithms that solve agreement problems, such as consensus and atomic broadcast, can still benefit from *grey-box* failure detectors that partially encapsulate Byzantine failure detection.

1 Introduction

Agreement problems are at the heart of reliable distributed computing, in particular transactional and real-time distributed systems. A canonical form of such problems is the well-known *consensus* problem that has been extensively studied in the literature (See [7] for a survey). Designing agreement algorithms and proving them correct is particularly difficult because of the possibility of partial failures. Roughly speaking, to reach agreement despite failures, processes need some plausible hints about which process is faulty and which process is correct. In a completely asynchronous system, where process relative speeds and message transmission delays are unbounded, obtaining any meaningful hint is impossible. One might never be able to distinguish a process that is faulty from one that is very slow. Consequently, even under the assumption that at most one process may crash, and even in its simplest form, consensus cannot be solved [6]. This fundamental result is known in the literature as the *FLP* impossibility result.

Some timing assumptions about the system are needed in order to solve agreement. The traditional approach consisted in building agreement algorithms

---

* Currently with Kudelski, Lausanne, Switzerland.
** Currently with Sun Microsystems, Gland, Switzerland.

J. Blieberger and A. Strohmeier (Eds.): Ada-Europe 2002, LNCS 2361, pp. 24–50, 2002.

that directly manipulate timing parameters to detect process failures, e.g., using timeouts and clock synchronization protocols [5]. Direct handling of timing assumptions makes the resulting (agreement) algorithms very hard to prove and error prone. Adding a simple instruction can for instance cancel the validity of a complicated proof.

A more modular approach was proposed recently [2]. The idea is to encapsulate the timing assumptions inside specific modules called *failure detectors* and specified through precise axiomatic properties. With this approach, an agreement algorithm does not need to directly handle timing assumptions. It just needs to interact with a failure detector through a simple and well defined interface. Obeying the tradition of good practices in software engineering, once a failure detector is specified and implemented, the algorithms that use it only need to know its interface. As long as the properties of the failure detector are ensured, one can freely change its implementation and, for instance, optimize it according to the network topology.

However, so far, the failure detector approach of [2] was only shown to be feasible in the context of *crash* failures: the simplest form of failures. A process that crashes is simply supposed to halt all its activities. In practice, processes might exhibit more complex behaviors. They may stop only *some*, but not all of their activities, e.g., within the same process, some threads are indefinitely blocked while others are not. Because of software bugs or malicious behaviors, processes may even send messages that have nothing to do with those they are supposed to send. In short, processes can exhibit so-called *Byzantine* failures [12] (sometimes called *arbitrary* or *malicious* failures). Solving agreement in this context is harder than in the crash-failure model, and one obviously needs timing assumptions here as well.

A question is now in order: does the modular failure detector approach of [2] apply to the context of Byzantine failures? To address this question, we proceed in four steps. In each step, we consider one of the fundamental modularity aspects of the original crash failure detector approach of [2], and we discuss the extent to which this aspect remains valid in the context of hypothetical Byzantine failure detectors. The aspects we consider are the following.

- *Specification orthogonality.* The specification of crash failure detectors is independent from the algorithms using such failure detectors. In the Byzantine context, no failure detector specification can feature this aspect. We show that this is due to the inherent nature of Byzantine failures. We propose however an intermediate approach where only part of the Byzantine behaviors is captured by the failure detector, namely *muteness* failures. This approach enables us to capture a tricky part of Byzantine failures inside well defined modules (muteness failure detectors), hence restricting the dependency between the algorithm and the failure detector.

- *Implementation generality.* Due to the specification orthogonality of crash failure detectors, their implementation can be made independent from the algorithms using them. This makes it possible to view a failure detector as a black-box of which implementation can change without any impact on the algorithms that use it, as long as it complies with its specification, i.e., it ensures its axiomatic properties. Since Byzantine failure detectors cannot be specified orthogonally to the algorithms using them, it is not surprising that their implementation depends somehow on those algorithms. We show that this dependency even restricts the set of algorithms that can make a meaningful use of failure detectors. We suggest a *grey-box* approach with a parameterized implementation of a muteness failure detector that is sufficient to solve consensus in a Byzantine environment.

– *Failure Encapsulation.* In [2], all aspects related to failure detection are encapsulated inside the failure detector module. Consequently, the only places where the algorithm deals with failures is by interacting with the failure detector. In a Byzantine context, failures have many faces, some of which can simply not be encapsulated inside the failure detector. We dissect the tricky issues underlying this problem and we present a consensus algorithm that relies on some additional modules to handle those issues. Besides muteness failure detectors, we make use for instance of echo broadcast and certification protocols.

– *Failure Transparency.* Because of the simple nature of crash failures, one can mask them. For example, using a consensus algorithm as an underlying black-box, one can build on top an atomic broadcast algorithm that simply ignores failures, i.e., it does not even need to interact with the failure detector module (the latter is used as sub-module by the consensus algorithm). We argue that this transparency aspect is simply impossible in a Byzantine context. We present however an atomic broadcast algorithm where some failures are masked by the consensus algorithm, whereas others are handled directly.

By discussing these four aspects, this paper contributes to better understanding the applicability of a failure detector approach in a Byzantine environment. We discuss a new failure detection notion and we introduce two Byzantine-resilient agreement algorithms to illustrate our point: a consensus and an atomic broadcast. To simplify the presentation of the paper, the correctness proofs of the algorithms are left to the appendices.

2   Specification Orthogonality

The specification of crash failure detectors is independent from the algorithms using these failure detectors. We call this nice aspect *specification orthogonality*. Achieving the same level of specification orthogonality in a Byzantine environment is not possible, but there is room for an intermediate approach based on a notion of *muteness failure detectors*.

2.1   Failure Detector Specification in a Crash Model

Intuitively, a crash failure is a physical event that causes a process to halt all its activities. A failure pattern is represented by a function that describes crashes that occur in the system, and the failure detector is a distributed oracle that provides hints about the failure pattern [2]. A process p typically consults the failure detector to know whether a given process q has crashed or not. Several classes of failure detectors were defined in [2], each one characterized by a *completeness* and an *accuracy* property. Completeness expresses the ability of a failure detector to eventually detect failures, while accuracy expresses its ability to eventually avoid false suspicions. For instance, the class $\Diamond \mathcal{S}$ (*Eventually Strong*) gathers failure detectors which satisfy two fundamental properties: (1) (Strong Completeness) eventually, every process that crashes is permanently suspected by every correct process; and (2) (Eventual Weak Accuracy) eventually, some correct process is never suspected by any process. These axiomatic properties capture the timing assumptions that are sufficient to solve the consensus problem [1].

Defined this way, crash failures are *context-free*, i.e., they are defined independently of what is executed by the processes on which they occur, e.g., a consensus algorithm. So, crash failure detectors are specified in a completely orthogonal manner with respect to the algorithms using them.

2.2   Two Flawed Approaches

A Naive Approach. It is very tempting to define Byzantine failure detectors in an analogous way to crash failure detectors. This would mean however defining Byzantine failure events in an analogous way to crash failure events. However, when a process commits a crash event, it stops *all* its activities with respect to *all* other processes in the system. This is clearly not the case in the Byzantine failure model. In such a model, a faulty process might not have necessarily halted, but might for instance send messages that have nothing to do with those it is supposed to send in the context of its algorithm, or it might arbitrarily decide to stop sending any messages (without halting though). In fact, a Byzantine process is a process that arbitrarily decides to deviate from the specification of its algorithm. To illustrate this point, consider a process q that is part of a set Ω of processes trying to agree on some value. Suppose now that q executes agreement algorithm $\mathcal{A}$, which is proven to be correct, whereas all other processes in Ω execute a different agreement algorithm $\mathcal{A}'$, also proven to be correct. With respect to processes executing $\mathcal{A}'$, q is viewed as a Byzantine process, that is, a *faulty* process (although it executes correct algorithm $\mathcal{A}$). In fact, a Byzantine process q might exhibit an incorrect behavior with respect to some process p but behaves correctly with respect to another process p'. For instance, q might be executing $\mathcal{A}$ against process p and $\mathcal{A}'$ against process p.

The specification of Byzantine failures is hence intimately related to a specific algorithm and to a specific process. Therefore, Byzantine failures are not context-free, unlike crash failures. Consequently, a Byzantine failure detector specification cannot be, unlike a crash failure one, orthogonal to the algorithm using it. In short, trying to specify a failure detector that tracks all Byzantine failures introduces too much dependency with the algorithm aimed at using that failure detector.

A Conservative Approach. A different approach consists in separating crash failures from other kinds of Byzantine failures, and in using crash failure detectors to detect the former while leaving the latter to the algorithm itself. The rationale behind this approach is to keep intact the modularity of the original model of [2] and deal with failures that are of a more malicious nature at a separate level, e.g., within the agreement algorithm itself.

Unfortunately, this conservative approach does not make sense either, and this is because crash failure detectors are inherently defined to track physical crashes and not logical failures. To better understand this point, assume that an algorithm designer is provided with a perfect crash failure detector in a Byzantine environment [2]. Such a failure detector guarantees (1) (Strong Completeness) eventually, every process that crashes is permanently suspected by every correct process; and (2) (Strong Accuracy) no process is suspected before it crashes.

Such a failure detector guarantees that every process that crashes is eventually suspected by all processes, and that no process is suspected unless it crashed. The malicious thing about Byzantine processes however is that they can stop participating in the algorithm without crashing. From a more practical point of view, this means that these processes can for instance send *heartbeat* messages in a timely manner (in order not to be suspected to have crashed), yet do not send any message related to the actual algorithm. According to the definition of a perfect failure detector, these are correct processes and there is no reason to suspect them. In some sense, such Byzantine processes do not *physically* crash but they *algorithmically* crash. From the perspective of a correct process however, either behavior can lead to the same problem if the faulty process is not properly detected: the progress of correct processes cannot be guaranteed and even a perfect crash failure detector is useless here.

2.3   An Intermediate Approach: Muteness Failure Detectors

As an alternative to the two flawed approaches sketched above, we suggest an intermediate one that focuses on the notion of *muteness* failures. These can be viewed as special case of Byzantine failures, yet are more general than crash failures (see Figure 1). Such failures encompass what we above referred to as physical *and* algorithmic crashes. Interestingly, adequately defined, muteness failure detectors encapsulate a sufficient level of synchrony to solve the consensus problem in the Byzantine failure model, as we discuss in Section 4. The specification of muteness failure detectors is not orthogonal to the algorithms using them, but it introduces a well-defined dependency relation with the algorithms. Below, we formally define the notions of *muteness failure* pattern and *muteness failure detector*.

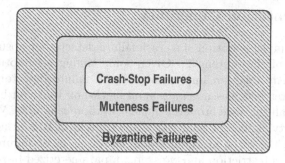

Fig. 1. Inclusion relation between different types of failures

Formal Definitions. Each algorithm $\mathcal{A}$ can be made to generate a set of messages that have some specific syntax, i.e., a syntax that is specific to $\mathcal{A}$. We say that a message m is an $\mathcal{A}$ message if the syntax of m corresponds to the syntax of the messages that may be generated by $\mathcal{A}$. Note that a message m sent by a Byzantine process that carries a semantical fault but has a correct syntax is considered to be an $\mathcal{A}$ message. Based on this definition, we define a *mute* process as follows. A process q is *mute*, with respect to some algorithm $\mathcal{A}$ and some process p, if q prematurely stops sending $\mathcal{A}$ messages to p. We say that process q fails by *quitting algorithm $\mathcal{A}$ with respect to process p*. A muteness failure pattern $F_{\mathcal{A}}$ is a function from $\Omega \times \mathcal{T}$ to 2^{Ω}, where $F_{\mathcal{A}}(p, t)$ is the set of processes that quit algorithm $\mathcal{A}$ with respect to p by time t. By definition, we have $F_{\mathcal{A}}(p, t) \subseteq F_{\mathcal{A}}(p, t+1)$. We also define $quit_p(F_{\mathcal{A}}) = \bigcup_{t \in \mathcal{T}} F_{\mathcal{A}}(p, t)$ and $correct(F_{\mathcal{A}}) = \Omega - \bigcup_{p \in \Omega} quit_p(F_{\mathcal{A}})$. We say that q is *mute to p for $\mathcal{A}$* if $q \in quit_p(F_{\mathcal{A}})$, and if $q \in correct(F_{\mathcal{A}})$, we say q is *correct* for $\mathcal{A}$. We define a *muteness failure detector history* as a function $H_{\mathcal{A}}$ from $\Omega \times \mathcal{T}$ to 2^{Ω} where $H_{\mathcal{A}}(p, t)$ denotes the set of processes suspected by process p to be mute at time t. A *muteness failure detector* is then a function $\mathcal{D}_{\mathcal{A}}$ that maps each failure pattern $F_{\mathcal{A}}$ to a set of failure detectors histories.

We define a class of muteness failure detectors, denoted by $\Diamond M_{\mathcal{A}}$, by introducing the *mute $\mathcal{A}$-completeness* and *eventual weak $\mathcal{A}$-accuracy* properties, which should be satisfied by any failure detector $\mathcal{D}_{\mathcal{A}} \in \Diamond M_{\mathcal{A}}$. These properties are stated as follows:

Mute $\mathcal{A}$-Completeness. There is a time after which every process that is mute to a correct process p, with respect to $\mathcal{A}$, is suspected by p forever.

Eventual Weak $\mathcal{A}$-Accuracy. There is a time after which a correct process p is no more suspected to be mute, with respect to $\mathcal{A}$, by any other correct process.

3   Implementation Generality

Intuitively, the implementation of a crash failure detector encapsulates the (partial) synchrony of the system [2]. Given some timing assumptions about the underlying system, one can implement a crash failure detector. Once implemented, the latter becomes a very *general* black-box that can be used by *any* algorithm. We call this nice property *implementation generality*. We argue below that this property cannot be achieved in the context of Byzantine failures. One needs to restrict the set of algorithms that can use a given failure detector. We discuss below this restriction and we sketch a parameterized implementation of a muteness failure detector in a partial synchrony model.

3.1   Algorithmic Restrictions

As we pointed out, the specification of a Byzantine (or a muteness) failure detector is context sensitive: it depends on the algorithm using that failure detector. Not surprisingly, the implementation of any failure detector of class $\Diamond M_{\mathcal{A}}$ is tightly related to the algorithm $\mathcal{A}$ that uses it. A natural question is now in order: can we devise an implementation of a muteness (or Byzantine) failure detector where the dependency with the algorithm using the failure detector would be captured by a generic parameter? This would mean that *any* algorithm could use such an implementation, provided an adequate instantiation of that generic parameter.

The answer is *no*, as we discuss below in the context of $\Diamond M_{\mathcal{A}}$. Basically, there are algorithms for which no implementation of $\Diamond M_{\mathcal{A}}$ does make sense. These are algorithms $\mathcal{A}$ in which the expected correct behavior of a process can be confused with an incorrect one, i.e., where the set of correct processes overlaps the set of mute processes. Imagine for example that a correct process p, to respect the specification of $\mathcal{A}$, must become mute with respect to all processes. Then *Mute A-Completeness* requires the processes to suspect p while *Eventual Weak A-Accuracy* requires the processes to eventually stop suspecting p. So, the two properties of the muteness failure detectors become in contradiction. To circumvent this problem, we impose some restrictions on algorithms that can use failure detectors of class $\Diamond M_{\mathcal{A}}$. Interestingly, such restrictions do not exclude useful algorithms that solve hard problems like consensus (next section).

Roughly speaking, we require from such algorithms that they have a regular communication pattern, i.e., each correct process communicates regularly (to prevent the case where muteness is viewed as a correct behavior). More precisely, we define a class of algorithms, named $\mathcal{C}_{\mathcal{A}}$, for which the use of $\Diamond M_{\mathcal{A}}$ does indeed make sense. We characterize $\mathcal{C}_{\mathcal{A}}$ by specifying the set of attributes that should be featured by any algorithm $\mathcal{A} \in \mathcal{C}_{\mathcal{A}}$. We qualify such algorithms as *regular round-based* and we define the attributes that characterize these algorithms as follows.

Attribute (a). Each correct process p owns a variable $round_p$ that takes its range $\mathcal{R}$ to be the set of natural numbers $\mathbb{N}$. As soon as $round_p = n$, we say that *process p reaches round n*. Then, until $round_p = n + 1$, process p is said to be *in round n*.

Attribute (b). In each round, there is at most one process q from which all correct processes are waiting for one or more messages. We say that q is *a critical process of round n* and its explicitly awaited messages are said to be *critical messages*.

Attribute (c). Each process p is critical every k rounds, $k \in \mathbb{N}$ and if p is correct then p sends a message to all in that round.

Intuitively, Attribute (a) states that $\mathcal{A}$ proceeds in rounds, while Attribute (b) defines the notion of critical process and restricts the number of such processes to one in each round. Finally, Attributes (c) expresses, in terms of rounds, the very fact that a correct process is critical an infinite number of times, and that it should therefore not be mute. It is important to notice here that the period of interest of this attribute is the duration of an algorithm, i.e., infinity actually means in pract ice until the algorithm using the failure detector terminates. Interestingly, many agreement algorithms that we know of feature these three attributes. In particular, the consensus algorithm of [2] using $\Diamond\mathcal{S}$ is of class $\mathcal{C_A}$ (as well as all variants of that algorithm that were devised later). They trivially feature Attributes (a), (b) and (c), since they proceed in asynchronous rounds and rely on the rotating coordinator paradigm; in particular, they feature $k = N$ for Attribute (c).

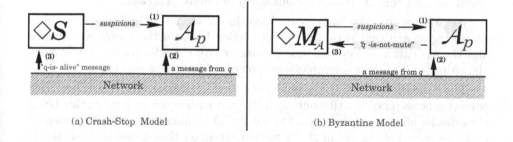

(a) Crash-Stop Model   (b) Byzantine Model

Fig. 2. Algorithm and failure detector modules interaction

3.2   Failure Detector Implementation in a Partial Synchrony Model

To implement a crash failure detector that solves an agreement problem like consensus, one needs to make some timing assumptions about the underlying system model. [1]

---

[1] A crash failure detector that would solve consensus, and yet be implementable in an asynchronous model, would obviously contradict the FLP impossibility result [6].

In the partial synchrony model of [5] for example, one can provide a timeout-based implementation of $\Diamond\mathcal{S}$ [2] (see Figure 2.a). Roughly speaking, this model assumes that δ, the bound on communication delays, and ϕ, the bound on process relative speeds, do exist but that they are either unknown, *or* known but they hold only after some *Global Stabilization time* (GST) that is itself unknown. The implementation of $\Diamond\mathcal{S}$ (in [2]) is based on timeouts and proceeds in the following way. Every process p periodically sends "p-is-alive" messages: these *heartbeat* messages are completely separated from those generated by the consensus algorithm (or by whatever algorithm using the failure detector). This independence is made possible because a crashed process stops sending all kinds of messages, no matter whether they are generated by the algorithm or by the local failure detector module. Therefore, from the non-reception of "p-is-alive" messages, any crashed processes is eventually suspected by all correct processes. The existence of GST plus the periodic sending of "p-is-alive" messages allow to eventually stop suspecting any correct process. So, this implementation meets the required accuracy and completeness properties of $\Diamond\mathcal{S}$.

Consider the case of a mute process that stops sending algorithm messages without crashing, but keeps sending other messages, in particular those related to the failure detector implementation. The process plays by the rule as far as messages "p-is-alive" are concerned, and at the same time, stops sending all other messages. So, the periodic reception of messages from the remote failure detector module of some process p is no longer a guarantee that an algorithm message will eventually arrive from p. Consequently, an implementation of $\Diamond M_A$ based on independent messages cannot capture mute processes.

We still assume the same partial synchrony model as in [2], and we suggest an approach that captures the interaction between the muteness detector and the algorithm within a generic parameter. We consider *regular round-based* algorithms and we give an implementation of $\Diamond M_A$ in this context.

The basic idea of our $\Diamond M_A$ implementation is sketched in Figure 2.b. Each correct process p holds a timeout Δ_p initialized with some arbitrary value being the same for all correct processes. The value of Δ_p is increased at the beginning of each new round of algorithm $\mathcal{A}_p$ by some function g_A that depends on $\mathcal{A}$ (this is the parameter of our implementation). Besides Δ_p, each failure detector module $\Diamond M_A$ maintains a set $output_p$ of currently suspected processes. Each time an $\mathcal{A}$ message is received from some process q (arrow 2), algorithm $\mathcal{A}_p$ delivers "q-is-not-mute" to $\Diamond M_A$ (arrow 3) and q is removed from $output_p$ in case it was previously suspected. A newly suspected process q is added to $output_p$ (arrow 1) if p does not receive a "q-is-not-mute" message for Δ_p ticks (arrow 3).

Proving the correctness of this implementation is not straightforward because, rather than approximating the delay between two "p-is-alive" messages (as done for $\Diamond\mathcal{S}$ in [2]), our implementation approximates the delay between two $\mathcal{A}$ messages. This task is particularly difficult because the delay between two $\mathcal{A}$ messages could be function of the timeout. For example, each time the timeout increases, the delay between two $\mathcal{A}$ messages could also increase. This would lead to the impossibility of approximating this delay. In [3], we prove the correctness of our implementation by assuming (1) a partially synchronous model, and (2) timing properties on $\mathcal{A}$ that hold after GST. Those timing properties state a set of necessary conditions on the timeout function, i.e., g_A, and the existence of a function expressing the progress of any correct process.

In short, we have argued in this section that the implementation of Byzantine (or muteness) failure detectors (like $\Diamond M_A$) does not make sense for any arbitrary algorithm $\mathcal{A}$. We suggested some realistic restrictions on the algorithms that would make such implementation possible. Even given those restrictions, we have pointed out the very fact that it is not enough to make timing assumptions about the system model to implement a Byzantine failure detector. One needs to make timing assumptions about $\mathcal{A}$ as well.

4   Failure Encapsulation

Crash failure detectors encapsulate all aspects related to failures. Consequently, a failure detector module acts as a black-box of which only the interface needs to be known by the algorithms that use it. We call this nice aspect *failure encapsulation*. Achieving the same level of failure encapsulation in a Byzantine environment does not seem to be possible, but there is room for an intermediate approach as we discuss in this section. We illustrate our point in the context of the consensus problem: each process proposes a value and the correct processes need to decide the same value among the set of proposed values.

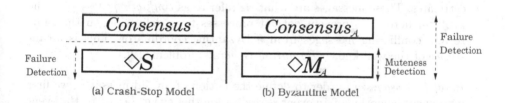

Fig. 3. Failure detection encapsulation

4.1   Failure Encapsulation in the Crash Model

In the consensus algorithm of [2] using $\Diamond \mathcal{S}$, all issues related to failures are encapsulated within the failure detector (see Figure 3.a). The algorithm is based on the rotating coordinator paradigm. It proceeds in asynchronous rounds, in a sequential manner (from the perspective of any given process). Each round has exactly one coordinator process. When they reach a given round, the processes wait for the coordinator of that round to propose a value. They wait until they suspect the coordinator of that round to have crashed. If they receive the proposal of the coordinator, they adopt that proposal and acknowledge that adoption. The coordinator decides its value if a majority of processes have adopted that value, and in that case broadcast the decision message to all. In the case where a process in a given round suspects the coordinator of that round, the process moves to the next round.

The critical point in such algorithm is when all processes wait for an estimate from the coordinator. A possible crash of the coordinator might prevent the correct processes from progressing. Each correct process hence consults the output of its failure detector to get hints about possibly crashed processes. From the perspective of the consensus algorithm of [2], the failure detection mechanism is completely hidden within the failure detector module, i.e., within $\Diamond S$.

4.2   Failure Encapsulation in the Byzantine Model

When considering a Byzantine model, obviously a complete encapsulation of failures cannot be provided. We illustrate this point in the context of consensus in a Byzantine model augmented with $\Diamond M_A$ instead of $\Diamond S$. Indeed, $\Diamond M_A$ can only cope with the muteness failures, while leaving other Byzantine behaviors undetected (see Figure 3.b). More precisely, the other failures are the following:

- *Conflicting Messages.* The consensus algorithm of [2] is based on the rotating coordinator paradigm, i.e., in each round, the current coordinator communicates its estimate to all processes. Considering this algorithm in the context of Byzantine failures raises a new problem: a Byzantine coordinator, rather than sending a unique estimate to all processes, may send them different estimates. These messages are what we refer to as *conflicting* messages. The problem here is to prevent correct processes from delivering, in the same round, conflicting messages from a Byzantine coordinator. This is an instance of the well-known *Byzantine Generals* problem [12].

- *Invalid Messages.* In order to define the notion of invalid messages, we first introduce the notion of an event *preceding* another event. Let $e1$ be the event of receiving a set of messages $m1$ at a process p, and let $e2$ be the event of sending some message $m2$ by the same process p. We say that $e1$ *precedes* $e2$, noted $e1 \prec e2$, if the event $e2$ of sending $m2$ is conditioned by the event $e1$ of receiving set $m1$ (see Figure 4). From an algorithmic viewpoint, this definition can be translated as follow: If receive $m1$ then send $m2$. In a trusted model, i.e., one that excludes malicious behaviors, when some process performs some event $e2$, such that $e1 \prec e2$, it is trivially ensured that (1) $e1$ happened before $e2$, and (2) if the computation of message $m2$ depends on set $m1$ then $m1$ is correctly taken into account to compute $m2$. In contrast, this is no longer true in a Byzantine model. A Byzantine process may perform $e2$ either without hearing about $e1$, or without taking into account the occurrence of $e1$. The resulting message $m2$ sent by the Byzantine process is referred to as an invalid message.

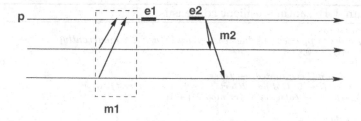

Fig. 4. *e*1 precedes *e*2

- *Missing Messages.* A *Missing* message is a message that was voluntary skipped by some incorrect process, while this process is still sending other messages.

4.3   Solving Consensus in the Byzantine Model

In the absence of a way to completely encapsulate the detection of Byzantine failures into a single module, we propose an intermediate approach that aims at dealing with the malicious failures stated above via a modular strategy.

Our algorithm is obtained by transformation of the crash-resilient consensus algorithm of [2]. The main adaptations can be summarized as follows: (1) replacing $\Diamond \mathcal{S}$ by $\Diamond M_A$ to cope with muteness failures, (2) applying an *echo broadcast* mechanism in order to cope with conflicting messages, (3) appending a *certificate* to some messages in order to cope with invalid messages, and (4) detecting skipped messages. We also assume that f, the maximum number of Byzantine processes in a run, is less than two thirds of the total number of processes N, i.e., the processes involved in consensus. Since the need of adaptation (1) has been extensively discussed in Section 2, we restrict our discussion to adaptations (2) to (4). Note also that, in our adaptation, we found it convenient to consider a decentralized variant of the original consensus algorithm of [2]: when it receives an estimate from the coordinator, every process acks that estimate to all other processes directly, instead of going back to the coordinator; Similarly, when a process suspects the coordinator, it informs all other processes about the suspicion and then moves to the next round.

Each one of those adaptations is discussed below, while the full version of our algorithm is given in Algorithm 1; the corresponding correctness proofs are given in Appendix A. In this algorithm, we construct a local predicate for any other process q at every process p and denoted $Byzantine_p(q)$. Initially this predicate is *false*. As soon as p detects some misbehavior exhibited by q, like sending invalid messages or skipping expected messages, p sets its local predicate $Byzantine_p(q)$ to true.

Echo Broadcast Protocol. To cope with conflicting messages, we use an *echo broadcast* protocol [17, 15]. The echo broadcast forces the coordinator to prove

---

Algorithm 1 Byzantine-resilient consensus

1: **function** $propose(e_i)$
2:   {$Every\ process\ p_i\ executes\ the\ Task\ 1\ and\ Task\ 2\ concurrently$}
3:   $InitialCertif_i \leftarrow \emptyset$;
4: **loop**   { $Task\ 1$}
5:     $CurrentRoundTerminated_i \leftarrow false$;
6:     $ReadyCertif_i \leftarrow \emptyset$; $GoPhase2Certif_i \leftarrow \emptyset$; $DecideCeritf_i \leftarrow \emptyset$;
7:     $coordSuspect_i \leftarrow false$; $c_i \leftarrow (r_i\ mod\ N) + 1$;

8:     **if** $c_i = i$ **then**
9:         $send_{all}\ E_i(Initial, p_i, r_i, e_i, InitialCertif_i)$

10:     **while** not $(CurrentRoundTerminated_i)$ **do**
11:         **when** receive Valid $E_j(Initial, p_j, e_j, InitialCertif_j)$ from p_j
12:             **if** $(j = c_i) \wedge$ (no Echo message was sent in r_i by p_i) **then**
13:                 send to p_{c_i} $E_i(Echo, p_i, r_i, e_j)$;

14:         **if** $c_i = i$ **then**
15:             **when** receive $(N - f)$ messages $E_j(Echo, p_j, r_i, e)$ for the same value e
16:                 $ReadyCertif_i \leftarrow \{E_j(Echo, p_j, r_i, e) : p_i\ received\ E_j(Echo, p_j, r_i, e)from\ p_j\}$;
17:                 $send_{all}\ E_i(Ready, p_i, r_i, e, ReadyCertif_i)$;

18:         **when** receive Valid $E_j(Ready, p_j, r_i, e, ReadyCertif_j)$
19:             $DecideCertif_i \leftarrow DecideCertif_i \cup \{E_j(Ready, p_j, r_i, e, ReadyCertif_j)$;
20:             **if** (First Ready message received) $\wedge$ $(i \neq c_i)$ **then**
21:                 $ReadyCertif_i \leftarrow ReadyCertif_j$;
22:                 $e_i \leftarrow e$;
23:                 $send_{all}\ E_i(Ready, p_i, r_i, e_i, ReadyCertif_i)$;
24:             **else if** $(N - f\ Ready\ messages\ received)$ **then**
25:                 $send_{all}\ E_i(Decide, p_i, r_i, e, DecideCertif_i)$;
26:                 $return(e)$;

27:         **if** $(p_{c_i} \in \Diamond M_{\mathcal{A}} \vee Byzantine_i(c_i)) \wedge (not\ coordSuspected_i)$ **then**
28:             $send_{all}\ E_i(Supicion, p_i, r_i)$;
29:             $coordSuspected_i \leftarrow true$;

30:         **when** $(receive\ N - f\ messages\ E_j(Supicion, p_j, r_i)) \wedge (phase_i = 1)$
31:             $GoPhase2Certif_i \quad\quad \leftarrow \quad\quad \{E_j(Supicion, p_j, r_i)\quad\quad :$
$p_i\ received\ E_j(Supicion, p_j, r_i)\ from\ p_j\}$;
32:             $send_{all}\ (E_i(GoPhase2, p_i, r_i, e_i, ReadyCertif_i), E_i(GoPhase2Certif_i))$;

33:         **when** receive Valid $(E_j(GoPhase2, p_j, r_i, e_j, ReadyCertif_j), E_j(SuspectProof_j))$
34:             **if** $phase_i = 1$ **then**
35:                 $phase_i = 2$;
36:                 $InitialCertif_i \leftarrow \emptyset$;
37:                 $send_{all}\ (E_i(GoPhase2, p_j, r_i, e_i, ReadyCertif_i), E_i(SuspectProof_j))$;
38:             $InitialCertif_i \leftarrow InitialCertif_i \cup (E_j(GoPhase2, p_j, r_i, e_j, ReadyCertif_j)$;
39:             **if** $(N - f\ GoPhase2\ messages\ received)$ **then**
40:                 $(e_i, ReadyCertif_i) \leftarrow Last\_Successfully\_EchoBroadcast(InitialCertif_i)$;
41:                 $currentRoundTerminated_i \leftarrow true$;
42:                 $r_i \leftarrow r_i + 1$

43: **when** receive Valid $E_j(Decide, p_j, r, e, DecideCertif_j)$ {$Task2$}
44:     $send_{all}\ E_j(Decide, p_j, r, e, DecideCertif_j)$;
45:     $return(e)$;

---

that it does not send conflicting messages to correct processes. The coordinator of some round r, say process q, initiates the echo broadcast by sending its estimate v in an *Initial* message to all processes. When a correct process p receives this *Initial* message, it *echoes* v to q by sending it a signed *Echo* message including v; any additional message it receives from q is ignored by p. Once process q receives

$N - f$ signed *Echo* messages for v, it sends a *Ready* message that carries the set of received *Echo* messages. No correct process p delivers v until it receives the *Ready* message that carries the $N - f$ expected *Echo*.[2] The echo broadcast is illustrated in Figure 5.

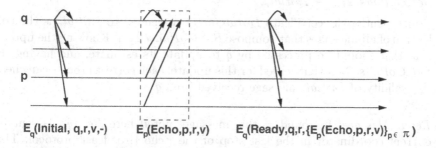

$E_q(\text{Initial, q,r,v,-})$ $E_p(\text{Echo,p,r,v})$ $E_q(\text{Ready,q,r,}\{E_p(\text{Echo,p,r,v})\}_{p \in \pi})$

Fig. 5. Echo broadcast protocol

Message Certification.   To cope with invalid messages, we introduce the notion of *certificate*. The aim of a certificate is to prove the *validity* of some message $m2$ such that $m1 \prec m2$. Such a validity is proved by exhibiting, in the certificate appended to $m2$, the very fact that the reception of $m1$ has indeed occurred. Then, based on the set associated to $m1$, any correct process can check if $m1$ was correctly taken into account to compute $m2$. Therefore, the structure of any certificate consists in the collection of all signed messages that compose $m1$.[3]

In the following, we detail four kinds of messages in our algorithm that require the use of certificates. The first two are *Initial* and *Ready*: these messages are introduced by the Echo Broadcast protocol. The last two are *Decide* and *GoPhase*2.

- *Initial Message.* In round r, this message, noted here $Initial_r$, carries the estimate proposed by the current coordinator. This message is validated by a certificate named $InitialCertif$.

  For the first round ($r = 1$), since no rounds happened before, $Initial_r$ does not need its certificate to be validated. That is, in this round, the certificate $InitialCertif$ is empty and any estimate proposed by the current coordinator, say q, is considered valid.

---

[2] Lemma 1 in Appendix A shows how this algorithm prevents correct processes from delivering, in the same round, conflicting estimates that may be sent by a Byzantine coordinator.

[3] Theorem 3 in Appendix A shows how the notion of certificate enables to preserve consensus agreement across rounds.

For all other rounds ($r > 1$), the estimate proposed by q must be selected during Phase 2 of round $r - 1$. During this phase, process q should wait for $N - f$ GoPhase2 messages, according to which it updates its estimate. We note this set of ($N - f$) GoPhase2 messages $Set\_GoPhase2_{r-1}$. Since $Initial_r$ must be sent after the reception of $Set\_GoPhase2_{r-1}$, we have that $Set\_GoPhase2_{r-1} \prec Initial_r$.

Consequently, the certificate $InitalCertif$ appended to $Initial_r$ is the collection of all messages that compose $Set\_GoPhase2_{r-1}$. Knowing the update rule that should be processed by q to update its estimate, and having set $Set\_GoPhase2_{r-1}$ that served for this update, each correct process can check the validity of $Initial_r$ message received from q.

- *Ready Message.* In round r, this message, noted here $Ready_r$, is sent by current coordinator in the last step of the Echo Broadcast protocol. This message is validated by a certificate named $ReadyCertif$.

  In round r, the current coordinator should wait for $N - f$ similar $Echo$ messages before sending $Ready_r$. We note this set of ($N - f$) $Echo$ messages Set_Echo_r. Since $Ready_r$ must be sent after receiving Set_Echo_r, we have that $Set\_Echo_r \prec Ready_r$. Consequently, the certificate $ReadyCertif$ appended to $Ready_r$ is the collection of all messages that compose Set_Echo_r.[4]

- *GoPhase2 Message.* In round r, this message, noted here $GoPhase2_r$, can be sent by any process q. This message is validated by a certificate named $GoPhase2Certif$.

  In round r, any process should have received at least $N - f$ $Suspicion$ messages before sending $GoPhase2_r$. We note this set of ($N - f$) $Suspicion$ messages $Set\_Suspicion_r$. Since $GoPhase2_r$ must be sent after the reception of $Set\_Suspicion_r$, we have that $Set\_Suspicion_r \prec GoPhase2_r$. Consequently, the certificate $GoPhase2Certif$ appended to $GoPhase2_r$ is the collection of all messages that compose $Set\_Suspicion_r$.

- *Decide Message.* In round r, this message, noted here $Decide_r$, can be sent by any process q. This message is validated by a certificate named $DecideCertif$.

  In round r, any process should have received at least $N - f$ $Ready_{r'}$ messages from the same round $r' \leq r$ before sending $Decide_r$. We note this set of ($N - f$) $Ready$ messages $Set\_Ready_{r'}$. Since $Decide_r$ must be sent after the reception of $Set\_Ready_{r'}$, we have that $Set\_Ready_{r'} \prec Decide_r$. Consequently, the certificate $DecideCertif$ appended to $Decide_r$ is the collection of all messages that compose $Set\_Ready_{r'}$.

---

[4] When a coordinator builds this certificate, we say that it has *successfully echo certified* its estimate.

Detecting Missing Messages. The detection of such misbehaviors is based on the FIFO property of our communication channels and on the following properties of our algorithm:

- In every round r, a correct process p sends only a bounded number of messages to some other process q. We denote this bound by n_{round};

- A message m sent by a correct p while in round r should include the value r.

To illustrate how these two properties are used to detect *Missing* messages, consider the correct process p waiting, in round r, for some specific message m' from process q:

- As soon as p has received a message from q with round number $r' > r$, process p detects that q has skipped the expected message;

- As soon as p has received more than $r \cdot n_{round}$ messages from q, process p detects that q has skipped the expected message.

5   Failure Transparency

In the crash failure model, building a consensus black-box on top of failure detectors has the advantage of fully encapsulating all failure-related issues and providing a powerful abstraction for solving other agreement problems [2, 9, 8]. So, for an agreement algorithm that is built on top of consensus, failure management is completely invisible (see Figure 6.a). We call this nice aspect *failure transparency*. Achieving the same level of failure transparency in a Byzantine environment is not possible, but again there is room for an intermediate approach. We illustrate here this issue on a well-known agreement problem, namely, the atomic broadcast problem that was solved in the crash model by a simple and elegant reduction to the consensus [2], i.e., it is built using consensus as an underlying building block.

5.1   Reducing Atomic Broadcast to Consensus

In atomic broadcast, correct processes have to agree on the delivery order of messages and every message broadcast by a correct process should eventually be delivered by every correct process. T can be very useful for instance to implement a replicated service [4]; the specification of atomic broadcast is recalled in Appendix B. In [2] an atomic broadcast algorithm is built on top of a consensus black-box, i.e., atomic broadcast is *reduced* to consensus. Roughly speaking, the reduction algorithm proposed in [2] aims at transforming atomic broadcast into a sequence of consensus instances. Each consensus instance is responsible for atomically delivering a batch of messages.

Now, let us assume that the consensus black-box used for the reduction is resilient to Byzantine failures (e.g., our algorithm proposed in the previous

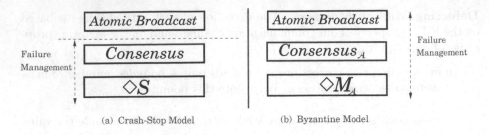

(a) Crash-Stop Model   (b) Byzantine Model

Fig. 6. Failure transparency

section). Does the reduction of [2] still works in the Byzantine model? The answer is *no*.

In a consensus algorithm, nothing prevents the processes from deciding on a corrupted value proposed by a Byzantine process. In fact, the decided value has only to be a value proposed by **some** process (not necessary a correct one). As a consequence, when executing a sequence of consensus, each one may return a corrupted batch proposed by some Byzantine process. This can lead correct processes to always decide on batches containing only corrupted messages. In others words, with such a non-restrictive consensus validity, the validity of the atomic broadcast can be violated, i.e., messages from correct processes might never be delivered. In fact, the Byzantine behaviors may appear at every level of our stack of algorithms (see Figure 6.b).

5.2 Atomic Broadcast in a Byzantine Model

In the following, we propose a wy to adapt the reduction of [2] to the Byzantine model, by incorporating some of the failure management in the atomic broadcast algorithm itself, i.e., outside of the consensus box. As in [2], we also use an underlying *reliable broadcast* algorithm, used by correct processes to send and receive messages. This algorithm provides two primitives $R\_broadcast$ and $R\_deliver$ that allow correct processes to broadcast and deliver messages according to the semantics of the reliable broadcast; the specification of reliable broadcast is recalled in Appendix B.

Reduction Algorithm. The full version of our reduction algorithm is given in Algorithm 2, while the correctness proofs are given in Appendix B. The atomic broadcast interface is defined by two primitives: $A\_broadcast$ and $A\_deliver$, which allow correct processes to broadcast and deliver messages according to the semantics of the atomic broadcast.

Let us now see more precisely how this algorithm proceeds. First, an $A\_broad-cast$ of a message m is performed through $Task$ 1, by invoking the primitive $R\_broadcast$ with message m. Second, a correct process $A\_delivers$ the received

---

Algorithm 2 Byzantine-resilient atomic broadcast with consensus

1: {*Every correct process p executes the following*}
2: **Initialization**
3:   $R\_delivered \leftarrow \emptyset$
4:   $A\_delivered \leftarrow \emptyset$
5:   $k \leftarrow 0$
6: {*Task1, Task2 and Task3 can be executed concurrently*}
7: **procedure** $A\_broadcast$ {*Task 1*}
8:   $R\_broadcast(m)$

9: **procedure** $A\_deliver$
10:   **when** $R\_deliver(m)$ {*Task2*}
11:     $R\_delivered \leftarrow R\_delivered \cup \{m\}$
12:   **when** $R\_delivered - A\_delivered \neq \emptyset$ {*Task3*}
13:     $k \leftarrow k + 1$
14:     $A\_undelivered \leftarrow R\_delivered - A\_delivered$
15:     **for** $i = 1$ **to** $i = N$ **do**
16:       $VectPropose[i] \leftarrow null$
17:     $send_{all} E_p(p, k, A\_undelivered)$
18:     **when** received $(f + 1)$ $E_q(q, k, A\_undelivered_q)$ from different processes
19:       $VectPropose[q] \leftarrow E_q(q, k, A\_undelivered_q)$
20:     $propose(k, VectPropose)$
21:     **wait until** $decide(k, VectDecide)$
22:     $A\_deliver^k \leftarrow \cup_{l=1}^{l=f+1} VectDecide[l] - A\_delivered$
23:     atomically deliver all messages in $A\_deliver^k$ in some deterministic order
24:     $A\_delivered \leftarrow A\_delivered \cup A\_deliver^k$

---

messages through *Task* 2 and *Task* 3. These tasks manipulate three sets of messages:

- *R_delivered*. This set contains the messages *R_deliver*ed to process *p*. So, in *Task* 2, each time a correct process *p* *R_deliver*s a message *m*, it inserts *m* into *R_delivered* set.

- *A_delivered*. This set contains messages that have been *A_deliver*ed to process *p*.

- *A_undelivered*. This set contains the messages that have been *R_deliver*ed, but not yet *A_deliver*ed.

In *Task* 3, when a correct process *p* notices that the set *A_undelivered* is not empty, it starts constructing a vector of propositions with which it launches a new instance of consensus. Let k be a sequence number that disambiguates between different concurrent executions of consensus instances. Before launching the kth consensus instance, each correct process *p* sends to all processes a signed message $(p, k, A\_undelivered)$. Then, *p* waits for $f + 1$ signed messages of the form $(q, k, A\_undelivered_q)$ from different processes. These messages are collected in a vector $VectPropose$, where $VectPropose[q] = (q, k, A\_undelivered_q)$ if p received a message from q, and $VectPropose[q] = null$ otherwise. Once the construction of $VectPropose$ is completed, p launches the kth consensus instance with $VectPropose$ as its initial value.

The goal here is to make sure that any initial value proposed by some process (correct or not) is of the form $VectPropose$: for the kth consensus instance, the initial value of any process should be a vector of $f + 1$ signed messages of the form $(q, k, A\_undelivered_q)$. Then, if a Byzantine process proposes an initial value that does not respect this format, its value is considered to be corrupted and is not accepted by correct processes. Thanks to the required $VectPropose$ format, we ensure that, in the presence of at most f Byzantine processes, any decided value contains at least one batch of messages proposed by a correct process.

Finally, once the kth consensus instance has been launched, process p waits for the kth decision, which is carried by $VectDecide$. Having the decision vector $VectDecide$, each correct process takes the union of all messages that appear in this vector, except the ones that have been already $A\_delivered$, and then delivers them in some deterministic order.

6   Related Work

Beside our work, we know of two research efforts that aimed at extending the notion of crash failure detectors to Byzantine models, and solving consensus using such detectors. Malkhi and Reiter considered a system model where all messages are exchanged using a causal-order reliable broadcast primitive [13]. They defined the notion of *quiet process*, which is close to our notion of muteness. Based on this notion, they introduced a failure detector, noted $\Diamond S$ (bz), which satisfies *Strong Completeness* and *Eventual Weak Accuracy* properties. The aim of $\Diamond S$ (bz) is to track processes that prevent the progress of the algorithm using it.

In [11], Kihlstrom et al. defined the Eventual Weak Byzantine failure detector $\Diamond W$ (Byz). Contrary to the specification of [13], and contrary to the one we propose, this class of failure detectors captures all *detectable* Byzantine behaviors.[5] The set of failures captured by $\Diamond W$ (Byz) include those that prevent the progress of the algorithm, i.e., muteness.

None of [13] or [11] gave a precise definition of their failure detectors. Consequently, they did not have to face the issue related to the *non-orthogonality* of the specification (Section 2). This issue obviously applies to their work as well. Because none of them tried to provide an implementation of failure detectors in a Byzantine environment and prove it correct, they did not have to face the *non-generality implementation* issue either (Section 3). However, without restricting the class of algorithms that can make use of such failure detectors, we can easily

---

[5] These include all failures, except those related to the application, such as cheating on an initial value.

end up with contradicting failure detectors properties, as we have pointed out in this paper. In fact, in [11], the authors presented a failure detector implementation that roughly aims at inserting a timeout mechanism in the branch of the algorithm where there are some expected messages. None of those papers has exhaustively addressed the issue of approximating an interval between algorithmic messages, which is a complex task that does not depend only on the synchrony assumptions of the system.

Both [13] and [11] described also consensus algorithms in a Byzantine environment. The aim of our approach was not to describe a consensus algorithm that is more efficient or more resilient than previous ones, but rather to focus on the modularization of such algorithms, and hence address the more general problem of *failure encapsulation* (Section 4). Similarly, several byzantine resilient atomic broadcast algorithms have been proposed [15, 10, 14]. By trying to follow the original reduction of [2], we suggested a simple and more modular approach that illustrates the issue of *failure transparency* (Section 5).

7   Conclusion

Devising distributed algorithms is difficult because of the possibility of partial failures. To help factorize this difficulty, Chandra and Toueg suggested a modular approach where failure detection is encapsulated inside a specific oracle called a *failure detector* [2]. They have shown how this modular approach simplifies the reasoning about the correctness of agreement algorithms.

Since the original failure detector approach was proposed in the context of crash-failures, a natural question comes to mind: does it make sense to follow a similar approach in the context of Byzantine failures? In other words, is there a notion of *Byzantine failure detector* that also enables a nice modularization?

To answer this question, we have considered four nice modularity aspects of crash failure detectors, and we have argued that none of those aspects can be completely kept as it is in a Byzantine context. The fundamental reason is the inherent nature of Byzantine failures: it is just impossible to completely separate Byzantine failure detectors from their context, i.e., from the algorithms using failure detectors. Roughly speaking, this is because the very definition of a Byzantine failure is itself context sensitive: a process commits a Byzantine failure if it deviates from its *specification*. Simply giving up the failure detector approach in a Byzantine context would however not be very constructive, because an algorithm designer would be left with the alternative of mixing failure detection with all other aspects of distributed processing in an ad hoc manner.

We have suggested an intermediate approach that preserves part of the modularity of the original failure detector approach. Other intermediate approaches might be possible and the objective of this paper was not to advocate one approach in particular. As we pointed out however, coming out with a sound failure detector notion in a Byzantine environment is fraught with the danger of proposing specifications that are, either useless, or impossible to implement even in completely synchronous systems.

Acknowledgments

We are very grateful to Jean-Michel Helary and Mike Reiter for their constructive comments on this work, and to Sidath Handurukande and Corine Hari for their help in improving the presentation of this paper.

References

[1] T. D. Chandra, V. Hadzilacos, and S.Toueg. The weakest failure detector for solving Consensus. *Journal of the ACM*, 43(4):685–722, July 1996.

[2] T. D. Chandra and S. Toueg. Unreliable failure detectors for reliable distributed systems. *Journal of the ACM*, 43(2):225–267, March 1996.

[3] A. Doudou. *Abstractions for Byzantine-Resilient State Machine Replication.* PhD thesis, Swiss Federal Institute of Technology, Lausanne (EPFL), 2000.

[4] A. Doudou, B. Garbinato, and R. Guerraoui. Abstractions for Byzantine Resilient State Machine Replication. In *Symposium on Reliable Distributed Systems.* IEEE, October, 2000.

[5] C. Dwork, N. Lynch, and L. Stockmeyer. Consensus in the presence of partial synchrony. *Journal of the ACM*, 35(2):288–323, apr 1988.

[6] M. Fischer, N. Lynch, and M. Paterson. Impossibility of Distributed Consensus with One Faulty Process. *Journal of the ACM*, 32:374–382, April 1985.

[7] M. J. Fischer. The consensus problem in unreliable distributed systems (A brief survey). In *Proceedings of the International Conference on Foundations of Computations Theory*, pages 127–140, Borgholm, Sweden, 1983.

[8] R. Guerraoui. Non-blocking atomic commit in asynchronous sytems with failure detectors. *Distributed Computing*, 15(1), January 2002.

[9] R. Guerraoui and A. Schiper. The generic consensus service. *IEEE Transactions on Software Engineering*, 27(14):29–41, January 2001.

[10] K. P. Kihlstrom, L. E. Moser, and P. M. Melliar-Smith. The secure protocols for securing group communication. In *Proceedings of the 31st Hawaii International Conference on System Sciences*, volume 3, pages 317–326. IEEE, January 1998.

[11] K. P. Kihlstrom, Louise E. Moser, and P. M. Melliar-Smith. Solving consensus in a Byzantine environment using an unreliable fault detector. In *Proceedings of the International Conference on Principles of Distributed Systems (OPODIS)*, pages 61–75, December 1997.

[12] L. Lamport, R. Shostak, and M. Pease. The Byzantine Generals Problem. *ACM Transactions on Programming Languages and Systems*, 4(3):382–401, July 1982.

[13] D. Malkhi and M. Reiter. Unreliable Intrusion Detection in Distributed Computations. In *Proceedings 10th Computer Security Foundations Workshop (CSFW97)*, pages 116–124, June 1997.

[14] L. E. Moser, P. M. Melliar-Smith, and D. A. Agrawala. Total ordering algorithms. In *ACMCSC: ACM Annual Computer Science Conference*, 1991.

[15] M. K. Reiter. Secure Agreement Protocols: Reliable and Atomic Group Multicast in Rampart. In *Proceedings of the 2nd ACM Conference on Computer and Communications Security*, pages 68–80, November 1994.

[16] R. L. Rivest, A. Shamir, and L. Adleman. A method for obtaining digital signatures and public-key cryptosystems. *Communications of the ACM*, 21(2):120–126, February 1978.

[17] S. Toueg. Randomized Byzantine Agreements. In *Proceedings of the 3rd ACM Symposium on Principles of Distributed Computing*, pages 163–178, August 1983.

Appendix A: Correctness of the Consensus Algorithm

We prove in this section that Algorithm 1 solves consensus in the presence of less than one third of Byzantine processes (the rest must be correct) using failure detector $\Diamond M_{\mathcal{A}}$. We first recall below the properties of consensus and detail the assumptions underlying our proofs.

Consensus Problem Specification. The problem consists for a set of processes to *decide* on some common value among a set of *proposed* values [2]. The agreement must be reached despite the presence of Byzantine processes. Formally, the processes need to satisfy the following properties:

- **Validity:** if a correct process decides v then v was proposed by some process.
- **Agreement:** no two correct processes decide differently.
- **Termination:** every correct process eventually decides.

System Assumptions. The system is composed of a finite set $\Omega = \{p_1, ..., p_N\}$ of N processes, fully interconnected through a set of reliable FIFO communication channels. The maximum number f of Byzantine processes is less than $N/3$. Hereafter, we assume the existence of a real-time global clock outside the system: this clock measures time in discrete numbered ticks, which range T is the set of natural numbers $\mathbb{N}$. It is important to notice that this clock is not accessible to processes: it is solely used to reason about runs. The timing assumptions that are accessible to the processes are encapsulated within $\Diamond M_{\mathcal{A}}$. We assume that the channels and the messages are authenticated. Any correct process can authenticate the sender of each message, and messages have signatures such as RSA [16]. Roughly speaking, the authentication prevents an Byzantine process from changing the contain of some message it relays, or sending some message and claiming to have received this message from another process. In the following, the context of every lemma and theorem is Algorithm 1.

Lemma 1 *In any round r, the coordinator (correct or not) of r cannot successfully echo certify two different values v and w.*

PROOF: The proof is by contradiction. Assume that in round r the coordinator, say process p, successfully echo certified two value v and w. Consequently, process p constructs: (1) a *Ready* message for v, with a *ReadyCertif* composed of $N - f$ messages $E_j(Echo, p_j, r, v)$, and (2) a *Ready* message for w, with *ReadyCertif* composed of $N-f$ messages $E_j(Echo, p_j, r, w)$. Therefore, in round r, two sets of $N - f$ processes sent *echo* messages for two distinct values v and w. In presence of less than $N/3$ Byzantine processes, the previous statement is correct only if at least one correct process sent two conflicting *echo* messages. Since, each correct process sends at most one *echo* message, then no two different messages can be successfully echo certified in the same round: a contradiction. □

Lemma 2 *Let r be the smallest round for which at least $f + 1$ correct processes deliver an estimate v that was successfully echo certified. Then, no other value $w \neq v$ can be successfully echo broadcast in any subsequent round r' (i.e., $r' \geq r$).*

PROOF: The proof is split in two cases.

Case 1 ($r = r'$) : Immediat from Lemma 1.

Case 2 ($r' > r$): The proof is by contradiction. Assume that l is the first round for which the lemma does not hold. Thus, at least one correct process receives, in round l, a valid *Ready* message that carries an estimate w different than v. A valid *Ready* message implies that the appended certificate *ReadyCertif* is a set of $N - f$ messages $E_q(Echo, q, l, w)$. So, at least $f + 1$ correct processes sent an *Echo* of w to the coordinator of round l, say process p. Therefore, at least $f + 1$ correct processes find the message *Initial*, sent by process p and carrying w, valid. A valid *Initial* message implies that the appended certificate *InitialCertif* is a set of $N - f$ messages $E_q(GoPhase2, q, l - 1, e_q, ReadyCertif_q)$ such that, among these $N - f$ messages, w corresponds to the last value successfully echo broadcast. On the other hand, by assumption we know that the lemma holds for all rounds k such that $r \leq k < l$. Consequently, until round $l - 1$, no value different than v was successfully echo certified, and there is at least $f + 1$ correct processes that delivered v. To construct its certificate *InitialCertif$_p$*, the coordinator p of round l needs the participation of at least $N - f$ processes that sent to p their *GoPhase2* message from round $l - 1$. Therefore, there is at least one correct process q that has delivered v in round $l - 1$, which has its *GoPhase2* in *IntialCertif$_p$*. Therefore, the last value successfully echo certified that appears in *InitalCertif$_p$* is v. Thus w could not be validated by *InitialCertif* of p: a contradiction. $\square$

Theorem 3 *No two correct processes decide differently (Agreement).*

PROOF: The proof is by contradiction. Assume that two correct processes, say p and q, decide on two different values, v and w respectively, during rounds r and r' such that $r \leq r'$. In order to decide, each correct process must receive at least $N - f$ *Ready* messages for the same estimate (if it either decides in Task 1 or Task 2). Therefore, when p decides on v, in round r , there is at least $f + 1$ correct processes that deliver the same value v in some round $k \leq r$. Consequently, from Lemma 2, there is no other value w different than v that could be successfully echo certified in any round $r' \geq k$. Consequently, the correct process q could not decide on some $w \neq v$. This contradicts our assumption, i.e., q decides $w \neq v$. $\square$

Lemma 4 *If one correct process decides, then every correct process eventually decides.*

PROOF: Let p be a correct process that decides either in Task 1 or Task 2. In both cases, p sends a valid *Decide* message to all before deciding. By the assumption of reliable channels, every correct process that has not yet decided eventually receives the valid *Decide* message, which is handled by Task 2, and then decides. $\square$

Lemma 5 *If no correct process decides in round r, then eventually all correct processes proceed to round $r + 1$.*

PROOF: The proof is by contradiction. Let r be the smallest round for which the lemma does not hold: no correct process decides in round r, and some correct process never reaches round $r + 1$. As r is the smallest of such rounds, each correct process eventually reaches round r. We show the contradiction by proving the following successive results:

1) At least one correct process eventually reaches Phase 2 of round r.
2) Each correct process eventually reaches Phase 2 of round r.
3) Each correct process eventually reaches Phase 1 of round $r + 1$.

Proof of 1): Assume that no correct process decides in round r, and no correct process reaches Phase 2 of round r. We consider two cases: the coordinator p_c of round r (a) sends at least one valid *Ready* message to some correct process, or (b) does not send any valid *Ready* message to any correct process.

Case (a): process p_c sends at least one valid *Ready* message to some correct process p. So, p receives this valid *Ready* message and relays it to all. Each correct process q is by assumption in Phase 1. So, q delivers the valid *Ready* message received from p and then, reissues the message to all. By the assumption of reliable channels and $f < N/3$, all correct processes eventually receive $N - f$ valid *Ready* messages. Thus eventually some correct process receives at least $N - f$ messages *Ready* and then decides in round r: a contradiction with the fact that no correct process decides in round r. So only case (b) remains to be considered.

Case (b): process p_c does not send any valid *Ready* message to any correct process p. This means that either (1) p_c is *Mute* to p, and by the mute $\mathcal{A}$-completeness of $\Diamond M_{\mathcal{A}}$ process p eventually suspects p_c, or (2) p_c sends a non valid *Ready* message to p, or p_c skips the *Ready* message, which leads in both cases the predicate $Byzantine_i(p_c)$ to become true. In any case, each correct process eventually suspects p_c and sends a *Suspicion* message to all. Thus, at least one correct process p receives $N - f$ *Suspicion* messages. Then, p sends a *GoPhase2* message and proceeds to Phase 2: contradiction with the fact that no correct process reaches Phase 2 of round r. $\square$

Proof of 2): By (1), at least one correct process, say p, eventually reaches Phase 2 of round r, after sending to all a valid *GoPhase2*. Every correct process still in Phase 1 receives this message and, in turn, reaches Phase 2.

Proof of 3): By (2), all correct processes reach Phase 2 of round r. Then each correct process sends a valid *GoPhase2* message to all. Thus each correct process receives at least $N - f$ messages *GoPhase2*. This allows Phase 2 of round r to be completed. Consequently, each correct process proceeds to next round, i.e., $r + 1$. $\square$

Theorem 6 *Eventually every correct process decides (Termination).*

PROOF: By the eventual weak $\mathcal{A}$-accuracy property of $\Diamond M_{\mathcal{A}}$, there is a time t after which some correct process p is not suspected by any correct process to be mute. Let r be a round such that (1) p is the coordinator of r, and (2) every correct process enters round r after t (if such a round does not exist, then by Lemma 5, one correct process has decided in a round $r' < r$, and so, by Lemma 4 every correct process decides, and the termination property holds). As $f < N/3$ and no correct process suspects p in round r. Thus no correct process ever proceeds to Phase 2 of round r. Process p sends its valid *Initial* message. As p is correct, each correct process eventually receives and delivers its *Initial* message and then sends an *Echo* for the received message. So, p eventually receives $N - f$ messages *Echo* message needed to successfully echo certified its estimates. By the reliable channel assumption, each correct process receives a valid *Ready* message and then relays it to all. Therefore, every correct process will receive enough valid *Ready* messages to decide. $\square$

Theorem 7 *The decided value is a value proposed by some process (Validity).*

PROOF: Trivially ensured since any decided value is some value proposed by a coordinator, i.e., some process. $\square$

Appendix B: Correctness of the Atomic Broadcast Algorithm

We prove in the following that Algorithm 2 solves the atomic broadcast problem in the presence of Byzantine failures and two third of correct processes. We make here the same assumptions as in Appendix A. Algorithm 2 relies in addition on the properties of both consensus and reliable broadcast. The reliable broadcast specification is given below:

- **Agreement:** if a correct process $R\_delivers$ a message m, then all correct processes eventually $R\_deliver$ m.
- **Validity:** if a correct process $R\_broadcasts$ a message m, then it eventually $R\_delivers$ m.
- **Integrity:** for any message m, every correct process $R\_delivers$ m at most once, and if the sender of m is some correct process p then m was previously $R\_broadcast$ by p.

Before going into the proofs, we first recall the specification of atomic broadcast.

Atomic Broadcast Specification. We define the interface of the atomic broadcast by two primitives: $A\_broadcast$ and $A\_deliver$, which allow correct processes to broadcast and deliver messages according to the semantics of the atomic broadcast. This semantics guarantees that (1) all correct processes deliver the same set of messages (Agreement), (2) all correct processes deliver messages in the same order (Total order), (3) the set of delivered messages includes all the messages broadcast by correct processes (Validity), and (4) no spurious messages are delivered from correct processes (Integrity). The intuitive properties presented above can be formalized as follows:

- **Agreement:** if a correct process $A\_delivers$ a message m, then all correct processes eventually $A\_deliver$ m.
- **Total order:** if two correct processes p and q $A\_deliver$ two messages m and m', then p $A\_delivers$ m before m' if and only if q $A\_delivers$ m before m'.
- **Validity:** if a correct process $A\_broadcasts$ a message m, then it eventually $A\_delivers$ m.
- **Integrity:** for any message m, every correct process $A\_delivers$ m at most once, and if the sender of m is some correct process p then m was previously $A\_broadcast$ by p.

In the following, the context of every lemma and theorem is Algorithm 2.

Lemma 8 *Consider any two correct processes p and q, and any message m, if $m \in R\_delivered_p$, then we eventually have $m \in R\_delivered_q$.*

Proof: Trivially follows from the agreement property of reliable broadcast.   □

Lemma 9 *For any two correct processes p and q, and any $k \geq 1$:*

1) *If p executes $propose(k, *)$, then q eventually executes $propose(k, *)$.*
2) *If p $A\_delivers$ messages in $A\_deliver_p^k$ then q eventually $A\_delivers$ messages in $A\_deliver_q^k$, and $A\_deliver_p^k = A\_deliver_q^k$.*

Proof: The proof is by simultaneous induction on 1) and 2).

Lemma part 1, $k = 1$: we prove that if p executes $propose(1, *)$ then q will eventually execute $propose(1, *)$. Since $A\_delivered_p$ is initially empty, $R\_delivered_p$ must contain some message m, when p executes $propose(1, *)$. Then by Lemma 8, m is eventually in $R\_delivered_q$ for any correct process q. Since $A\_delivered_q$ is initially empty for any process q, $R\_delivered_q - A\_delivered_q \neq \emptyset$ eventually holds. So, each process q eventually executes $send_{all}E_q(q, 1, *)$. in the presence of at most f incorrect processes, each process q constructs its vector $VectPropose$ and hence executes $propose(1, *)$.

Lemma part 2, $k = 1$: we prove that if p $A\_delivers$ a messages in $A\_deliver_p^1$, then q eventually $A\_delivers$ messages in $A\_deliver_q^1$ such that $A\_deliver_p^1 = A\_deliver_q^1$. If p $A\_delivers$ messages in $A\_deliver_p^1$, then it has previously executed $propose(1, *)$. By part 1 of Lemma 9, each correct process eventually executes $propose(1, *)$. By termination, validity and agreement properties of consensus, all correct processes eventually decide on the same vector of messages $VectDecide^1$. Since $A\_delivered_p^1$ and $A\_delivered_q^1$ are initially empty, and $VectDecide_p^1 = VectDecide_q^1$ then $A\_deliver_p^1 = A\_deliver_q^1$.

Lemma part 1, $k = n$: We assume that the lemma holds for all k such that $1 \leq k < n$. We prove that if p executes $propose(n, *)$ then eventually q executes $propose(n, *)$. If p executes $propose(n, *)$, then there is some message $m \in R\_delivered_p$ and $m \notin A\_delivered_p$. Thus, m is not in $\cup_{k=1}^{n-1} A\_deliver_p^k$. By, the induction hypothesis, for all k we have $A\_deliver_p^k = A\_deliver_q^k$. So, m is not in $\cup_{k=1}^{k-n-1} A\_deliver_q^k$. Since m is in $R\_delivered_p$, by Lemma 8 m is eventually in $R\_delivered_q$. Therefore, for any process q $R\_delivered_q - A\_delivered_q \neq \emptyset$ eventually holds. So, each process q eventually executes $send_{all}E_q(q, n, *)$. In presence of at most f Byzantine processes, each process q constructs its vector $VectPropose$ and hence executes $propose(n, *)$.

Lemma part 2, $k - n$: We prove that if p $A\_delivers$ messages in $A\_deliver_p^n$ then q eventually $A\_delivers$ messages in $A\_deliver_q^n$ such that $A\_deliver_p^n = A\_deliver_q^n$. If p $A\_delivers$ messages in $A\_deliver_p^n$ then, p has previously executes $propose(n, *)$. By part 1 of this lemma each correct process executes $propose(n, *)$. By termination, validity and agreement properties of consensus, all correct processes eventually decide on the same vector of messages $VectDecide^n$. Consequently, we have $VectDecide_p^n = VectDecide_q^n$. By the induction hypothesis for all $1 \leq k < n$ we have $A\_deliver_p^k = A\_deliver_q^k$. Hence, the set of messages $A\_deliver_p^n$ delivered by p is equal to the set of messages $A\_deliver_q^n$ delivered by q.

$\square$

Theorem 10 *All correct processes deliver the same set of messages in the same order (agreement and total order).*

Proof: Immediate from Lemma 9 and the fact that all correct processes deliver the messages in the same deterministic order. $\square$

Theorem 11 *If some correct process $A\_broadcasts$ a message m, then it eventually $A\_delivers$ m (validity).*

Proof: The proof is by contradiction. We assume that a correct process p $A\_broadcasts$ a message m and never $A\_delivers$ m. Thus, by Lemma 10 no correct process $A\_delivers$ m.

By Task 1 of Algorithm 2, we know that to $A\_broadcast$ a message m a correct process p executes $R\_broadcast(m)$. Therefore, thanks to validity and agreement properties of reliable broadcast, eventually every correct process q $R\_delivers$ m in Task 2, i.e., eventually $m \in R\_delivered_q$. on the other hand, by assumption we state that no correct process q never $A\_delivers$ m, so no process q inserts m in $A\_delivered_q$.

From Algorithm 2, there exist a constant k, such that for all $l \geq k$, every correct process q has $m \in R\_delivered_q^l - A\_delivered_q^l$, i.e., $m \in A\_undelivered_q^l$. Then, each process q executes $send_{all}E_q(l, q, A\_undelivered_q)$ and builds its $VectPropose$ with which it launches its lth consensus. By termination and agreement properties of consensus, we infer that all correct processes eventually decide on the same $VectDecide^l$. Furthermore, by our restriction in Algorithm 2 on initial values format and the validity property of consensus, we ensure that any decision $VectDecide^l$ returned by l^{th} consensus is a vector of $(f+1)$ signed messages $E_s(s, l, A\_undelivered_s)$ from different processes. So, in the presence of at most f Byzantine processes, there is at least one message $E_s(s, l, A\_undelivered_s)$ from some correct process s. Consequently, we have $m \in A\_undelivered_s$. Since the decision is on the union of all messages in $VectDecide^l$ except those which are already $A\_delivered$, m is eventually $A\_delivered$ by all correct processes: a contradiction. □

Theorem 12 *For any message m, every correct process $A\_delivers$ m at most once, and if the sender of m is a correct process p, then m was previously $A\_broadcast$ by p (integrity).*

Proof: Suppose that a correct process p $A\_delivers$ a message m, p inserts m in its set of delivered messages $A\_delivered_p$. So, from Algorithm 2 p delivers m at most once.

Now, if a correct process p $A\_delivers$ a message m then, it has previously decided on $VectDecide^k$ for some k, such that $m \in VectDecide^k$. By the restriction imposed in Algorithm 2 on initial values format and the validity property of consensus, we ensure that $VectDecide^k$ is composed of $f + 1$ signed messages $E_q(k, q, A\_undelivered)$. If m belongs to a batch of messages $A\_undelivered_q$ such that q is Byzantine, we cannot infer that some processes has effectively executed $A\_broadcast(m)$. Otherwise, i.e., if m belongs to a batch $A\_undelivered_q$ such that q is correct then we infer that q has executed in Task 1 $R\_deliver(m)$. Then, by the integrity property of reliable broadcast, if the sender of m, say p, is a correct process, then p $R\_broadcasts$ message m, which means that p has $A\_Broadcast$ message m in Task 1. □

Contextware: Bridging Physical and Virtual Worlds

Alois Ferscha

Institut für Praktische Informatik
Universität Linz
ferscha@soft.uni-linz.ac.at

Abstract. Today a variety of terms – like Ubiquitous Computing, Pervasive Computing, Invisible Computing, Ambient Intelligence, Sentient Computing, Post-PC Computing, etc. – refers to new challenges and paradigms for the interaction among users and mobile and embedded computing devices. Fertilized by a vast quantitative growth of the Internet over the past years and a growing availability of wireless communication technologies in the wide, local and personal area, a ubiquitous use of "embedded" information technologies is evolving. Most of the services delivered through those new technologies are services adapted to *context*, particularly to the person, the time and the place of their use. The aim for seamless service provision to anyone (personalized services), at any place (location based services) and at any time (time dependent services) has brought the issues of software *framework design* and middleware to a new discussion: it is expected that context-aware services will evolve, enabled by wirelessly ad-hoc networked, autonomous special purpose computing devices (i.e. *"smart appliances"*), providing largely invisible support for tasks performed by users. It is further expected that services with explicit user input and output will be replaced by a computing landscape sensing the physical world via a huge variety of electrical, magnetic, optical, acoustic, chemical etc. sensors, and controlling it via a manifold of actuators in such a way that it becomes merged with the virtual world. Applications and services will have to be greatly based on the notion of context and knowledge, will have to cope with highly dynamic environments and changing resources, and will need to evolve towards a more implicit and proactive interaction with users.

In this paper we explore the software engineering issues, challenges and enabling technologies associated with the provision of context aware services able to:

(i) describe, gather, transform, interpret and disseminate context information within ad-hoc, highly dynamic and frequently changing computing environments,

(ii) dynamically discover, inspect, compose and aggregate software components in order to identify, control and extend context, as well as overcome context barriers (like time, position, user preference, etc.),

(iii) allow for dynamic interactions among software components in a scalable fashion and satisfying special requirements such as fidelity, QoS, fault-tolerance, reliability, safety and security,

(iv) integrate heterogeneous computing environments and devices with different functionality, ability, form factor, size and limited resources wrt. processing power, memory size, communication, I/O capabilities, etc.

(v) support the adaptation of novel forms of sensitive, situative, non-distracting user interfaces not limited to particular modes and styles of interaction, input- output devices or service scenarios.

J. Blieberger and A. Strohmeier (Eds.): Ada-Europe 2002, LNCS 2361, pp. 51–64, 2002.

In an analogy to the term "middleware" – generally understood as software technologies that serve to mediate between two or more separate (and usually already existing) software components – we introduce the term "*contextware*" as the core of software technologies mediating services and the context of their use, thus bridging virtual and physical worlds.

Keywords: Software Frameworks, Context Awareness, Embedded Systems, Ubiquitous Computing, Pervasive Computing, Mobility.

1. Future Pervasive Computing Environments

The vision of a future pervasive computing landscape [Bana 00] is dominated by the ubiquity of a vast manifold of heterogeneous, small, embedded and mobile devices, the autonomy of their programmed behaviour, the dynamicity and context-awareness of services and applications they offer, the ad-hoc interoperability of services and the different modes of user interaction upon those services. This is mostly due to technological progress like the maturing of wireless networking, exciting new information processing possibilities induced by submicron IC designs, low power storage systems, smart material, and motor-, controller-, sensor- and actuator technologies, envisioning a future computing service scenario in which almost every object in our everyday environment will be equipped with embedded processors [Arno 99], wireless communication facilities and embedded software to percept, perform and control a multitude of tasks and functions. Since many of these objects will be able to communicate and interact with each other, the vision of "context aware" appliances [ELMM 99] and spaces [MIT] [Essa 99] [RoCa 00] – where dynamically configured systems of mobile entities by exploiting the available infrastructure and processing power of the environment – appears close to reality. We can hypothesize that the individual utility of mobile communication, wireless appliances and the respective mobile Internet services will be greatly increased if they were *personalized*, i.e. user centered and dynamically adapted to user preference, *location aware*, i.e. multimodal and multifunctional with respect to the environment [AAHL 97], and *time dependent*, i.e. if they were time dynamic and exhibited timely responsiveness (the more recent literature refers to time, space and personal preference as dimensions of a *context*, and *context awareness* as the ability to respect those – and other dimensions – when delivering service to the user [DeAb 99] [Dey 01]. One impacting trend hence will be the evolution of context aware digital environments – often referred to as "smart appliances" or "smart spaces" – that intelligently monitor the objects of a real world (including people), and interact with them in a pro-active, autonomous, souvereign, responsible and user-authorized way. People will be empowered through an environment that is aware of their presence, sensitive, adaptive [Moze 99] and responsive to their needs, habits and emotions, as well as ubiquitously accessible via natural interaction [SATT 99].

The next generation of "pervasive" computing environments hence will be characterised by the following basic elements: (i) *ubiquitous access*, (ii) *context awareness*, (iii) *intelligence*, and (iv) *natural interaction*. Ubiquitous access refers to a situation in which users are surrounded by a multitude of interconnected embedded systems, which are mostly invisible and weaved into the background of the surrounding, like furniture, clothing, rooms, etc., and all of them able to sense the setting and state of physical world objects via a multitude of sensors. Sensors, as the key enablers for implicit input from a "physical world" into a "virtual world", will be operated in a time-driven or event-driven way, and actuators, as the generic means for implicit output from the "virtual" to the "physical world", will respond to the surrounding in either a reactive or proactive fashion (see Figure 1). The way how humans interact with the computing environment will thus fundamentally change towards implicit, ubiquitous access. Context awareness [RCDD 98] refers to the ability of the system to recognise and localise objects as well as people and their intentions. Intelligence refers to the fact that the digital surrounding is able to adapt itself to the people that live (or artefacts that reside) in it, learn from their behaviour, and possibly recognise as well as show emotion. Natural interaction finally refers to advanced modalities like natural speech- and gesture recognition, as well as speech-synthesis which will allow a much more human-like communication with the digital environment than is possible today.

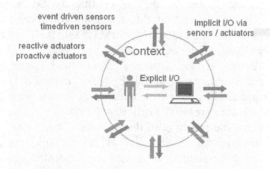

Fig. 1. Contextware: supporting implicit Sensor-Actuator controlled interactions

It appears obvious that the notion of "context" is what will be the driving force for future applications and services using global networks (like the Internet) as backbone communication infrastructure. The context of an application is understood as "any information that can be used to characterize the situation of an entity", an entity being "a person, place or object that is considered relevant to the interaction between a user and an application, including the user and applications themselves" [Dey 01]. A key architecture design principle for context-aware applications (see e.g. [AAHL 99]) will be to decouple mechanism for collecting or sensing context information [SDOA 99] and its interpretation, from the provision and exploitation of this information to build and run context-aware applications [Schi 95]. To support building context-aware applications, software developers should not be concerned with how, when and where context information is sensed. Sensing context must happen in an application independent way, and context representation must be generic for all possible applications [FBN 01].

2. Technology Trends and Contextware Challenges

What was envisioned as the future "pervasive" computing landscape in the previous section follows from technology trend observations in the hardware, software and communications area [HIR 01]. The challenges posed by those trends towards the realization of pervasive computing environments concern a ubiquitous communication infrastructure for devices, the support for user interaction and user mobility, the provision of universal interfaces and the adaptation to individual user needs. One of the most important concerns, however, is to design and develop software components that facilitate ad-hoc networking applications characterized by highly dynamic changes in the environment and the access modes or patterns, and their scalability with respect to the complexity of interactions and the number of involved entities or actors – i.e. the establishment of profound software methods and development processes for contextware. Towards this end, a more integrated view of software design has to be adopted, also considering hardware, communication and access trends.

Ubiquitous access in an embedded pervasive computing environment is promisingly implemented based on a continuous, wireless communication infrastructure involving broadband satellite systems, radio communication (e.g. GSM, GPRS, TETRA, DECT, EDGE, UMTS/IMT2000, G4, Bluetooth, HomeRF, IEEE802.11, HiperLAN, HomeCast, etc.), infrared (IrDA) and ultrasonic communication, wireless sensor networks, power line communications, wireline communications and standards (USB, IEEE1394, HomePNA), etc. The primary "software" challenge here lies in the maintenance of seamless connections as devices move between different areas of different network technology and network connectivity, as well as the handling of disconnects. While communication problems like routing and handover can be handled at the network level, others cannot be solved at his level as they relate to the interaction semantics at the application level [Else 99] [Arno 99]. Device heterogeneity and wide differences in hardware and software capabilities requires a communication infrastructure that maintains knowledge about device characteristics and manages coherent device interactions (e.g. among wearable devices, home appliances and outdoor appliances). Personal area network (PAN) technologies are supposed to address theses issues.

The dynamic interconnection of devices and discovery services [McGr 00] within PANs is approached with network technologies like MobileIP, IPv6, and coordination software systems [OZKT 01] like HAVI [LGDE 00], Java/Jini [Wald 99], JXTA [WDKF 02][Gong 02], Java wireless data, Java-Spaces, the Simple Object Access Protocol [BEKL], Web-OS, XML-RPC, UPnP [ChLa 99], Salutation [Mill 99], Tspaces, etc. While service registration and discovery, lookup services, self organization, caching and differencing methods have working solutions today (see Table 1 for a comparison), context based networking [Esle 99] and the context based coordination of entities and activities must still be considered as research issues.

Table 1. A Comparison of Approaches for "Coordination"

	Jini/Java	UPnP	Salutation	Tspaces
Originator	SUN Microsystems	primarily Microsoft	Industry / Academic consortium	IBM
Register / Announcing Presence:	Unicast/Multicast to Jini lookup service Lease expiry for up to date information	SSDP Protocol, working with or without Proxy Service Unicast/Multicast HTTP - UDP	through a Salutation Manager (SM) works as a service broker	making services available on a Tuple Space
Discovering other devices	Querying lookup services Optionally using an RMI proxy	SSDP (Simple Service Discovery Protocol) used to announce their presence as well as find other devices	queries on SM	Database indexing and query on the TupleSpace
Describing capabilities	Registration Information can have attribute pairs RMI interface with known methods	XML documentation is made available URIs are used	functional units which know features of a service	Java RMI Method invocation interfaces with known methods
Self configuration	not considered	DHCP or AutoIP multicast DNS	not considered, difficult because of transport independence	not considered
Invoking services:	Through the lack of device driver difficult, device must be Java enabled, RMI	Invoking Services via Browser, or direct API calls through applications	flexible, vendor specific, realised through SM	Java RMI framework
Security:	Java Security	not finished yet	allows user authentification	access controls by User
Transports:	TCP/IP – Proxies	TCP/IP – Proxies	transport independent	TCP/IP
Supported Devices	all kind of devices, mobile, household equipment	all kind of devices, mobile, household equipment	printer, FAX, telephone, PDA , computer (of any size) but not limited to them	Printers, PDAs, Computers
Remarks	no self configuration makes it weak RMI Method invocation is difficult to handle + Security	self configuration is considered as the strongest feature of this technology	advantages in the functionality of the SMs, problems with transport independence	enhancement of Linda TupleSpace concept

As far as a "pervasive Internet" is concerned, a major enabling technology is the miniaturization of devices able to accept and to respond to HTTP requests, i.e. the provision of WWW servers to be weaved into arbitrary fabrics of daily use objects. Figure 2 demonstrates popular embedded webserver miniatures (as they are readily available from e.g. HYDRA, Dallas Semiconductors, Tini, Boolean, etc.), envisioning the technological options for e.g. embedded Internet appliances.

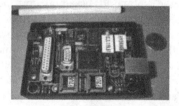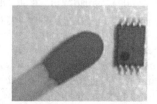

Fig. 2. Miniaturized Embedded and On-Chip Webservers

New output technologies like light emitting polymers (see Figure 3, right), foldable displays, laser diodes, electronic inc, electronic paper etc. together with new materials able to serve as sensors or input technologies for monitoring the environment (digital and analog), appliances like T-shirt computers, finger rings, hot badges, smart rooms and smart environments, interactive workspaces like smart walls, tables, chairs etc., spawn a whole new space for information appliance designs. Implicit input and output in an embedded Internet will generally be realized via sensor and actuator technologies, involving optical and opto-electrical (photodiodes, -conductors, charge coupled devices, light-emitting diodes and polymers, lasers, liquid crystals), acoustic (e.g. acoustic transducers, sonar transducers, surfaces acoustic wave devices), mechanical (metallic, silicon pressure sensors and accelerometers, solid-state displacement transducers, piezoelectric field-effect transducers), thermal (silicon transistor thermometers, diode temperature sensors, pyroelectric and quartz thermometers, integrated temperature transducers), magnetic (magnetoresistors, silicon depletion-layer magnetometers, magneto-injection transistors, MOS magnetic field sensors), chemical sensors, microwave sensors, environmental sensors, etc. A consequence of this multisensory input possibilities is the need for a "continuously present" interface, e.g. continually-worn sensors in a context-aware computing application [SSP 98], the integration of voice-vision-text technologies, gesture, eye- and body-movement recognition etc. (Figure 3 illustrates technologies enabling a "continuous" interface to e.g. an embedded Internet)

Fig. 3. New Materials for a "continuously Present" Interface
(Pyroelectric material (TWO LEFT) , LEP Display (RIGHT))

3. Contextware: Bridging Physical and Virtual Worlds

To build context aware applications [SDA 99], the adoption of a world model (in the sequel referred to as "virtual world") representing a set of objects and their state in a physical (or "real") world (or at least the subworld essential for the specific application) is the common software engineering approach suggested in the literature [DSA 99] [DSAF 99a] [DSAF 99b]. What makes an application context aware is the ability to interact with objects in the real world, requiring adequate models and representations of the objects of interest, and the possibility to sense, track, manipulate and trigger the real objects from within the world model. Several frameworks for such world models have appeared recently [PRM 99] [KBMB 00] [KHCR 00] [FCE], the most prominent ones [HP] identifying *persons*, *things* and *places* as the primary abstract classes for real world objects. People living in the real world, acting, perceiving and interacting with objects in their environment are represented in a "virtual world" by "virtual objects" or "proxies". Proxies of persons, things and places are linked to each other in the virtual world, such that this "linkage" is highly correlated with the "linkage" of physical persons, things and places in the real world. A context-aware application [BBC 97] now monitors the state and activity of the real world objects via *set of sensors*, *coordinates* the proxies according to the rules embodied in the application, and notifies, triggers [Brow 98] or modifies the physical world objects via a *set of actuators*.

We claim that a context-aware application can only be "intelligent" about an object if it can *identify, localize* and track, and *coordinate* with respect to and relative to the other objects around:

(i)   Identification (sensing the identity of or recognizing a real world object),

(ii)   localization (sensing its position and possibly its movement in space), and

(iii)   coordination (relating it semantically to other objects and behavioral rules)

hence are the central issues for embedded pervasive computing applications, and, moreover, are essential to all context-aware applications. They are among the few aspects that are fundamentally different from conventional middleware.

A plenty of ready-to-use technologies for the automated recognition (identification) of real world objects can be accounted: technologies based on optical (barcode and OCR), magnetic (SmartCard), ultrasonic (Active Badge and iButton) sensors, voice and vision based systems, biometrical systems (fingerprint, retina, face recognition), etc.. Many of those are also suitable for short distance positioning and tracking (localization), and are already in use for locator services in many different fields of application. Global positioning technologies based on GSM, GPS, dGPS extend the range of options for long distance localization.

An identification and localization technology with a certain appeal for embedded pervasive computing applications is radio frequency identification (RFID) which is based on radio or electromagnetic propagation, i.e. the ability to allow energy to penetrate certain physical objects and read a tag that is not necessarily visible. Objects can be identified remotely, either in the form of reading an identity code, or more simply just checking for the presence of a tag. An RFID system consists of a tag (or transponder), and a reader device. The transponder as a passive component responds by replying to an interrogation request received from an interrogator. The reader as an active component induces an interrogation request, and receives back some data from the transponder (such as an identity code or the value of a measurement) with virtually zero time delay. Different frequencies of the radio system of the reader result in different reading ranges (10 cm to 1 m) and properties of the system. Commonly available tags have an operating frequency in the range from 60 kHz to 5.8 GHz, 125 kHz and 13,56 MHz being the most prominent frequencies in use today. The reason why transponders have recently started to become major players in the field of electronic identification is their contact-less and powerless operation (no power supply needed in the tag), low cost packaging, "unlimited" lifetime, ISO standard compliance (14443 A/B and 15693-2), a wide choice of qualified packaging (Smart Cards, tags, inlets, smart labels, etc.), short range operation, proximity and vicinity communication with one and the same technology, cryptographic security (i.e. the protection against unauthorised product copies or data modification), and, last but not at least, low investment level for contact-less technology integration.

Coordination [OZKT 01] finally, is the concern of software frameworks providing concerted but autonomous components for object representations of the physical world, such as persons, things and places. Coordination, in its very early understanding addresses to express the interaction among individual, abstract "agents" (humans, processes, services, devices, software objects, etc.) within a coordination model, the linguistic embodiment of which is a coordination language. Such languages have been designed to allow for a description of the dynamic creation and destruction of agents, the flows of control and communication among agents, the control of spatial distribution of agents, and the synchronization and distribution of agent actions over time. Metadata models like the RDF (Resource Description Framework) [RDF 99] for the definition and description of abstract object classes and the operations required by a applications have been successfully applied in context-aware embedded Internet applications [FBN 01]. Generally, such frameworks provide an abstract specification (or a model) of the set of relevant objects and the semantics of the operations to be supported by the application. Concrete implementations by exploiting the mechanisms of inheritance and reuse realize the (i) creation and management of virtual representations of physical objects, (ii) mechanisms for sensing (including identification, localization and tracking) and manipulating such objects, and (iii) mechanisms for the coordinated invocation of object methods.

4. A Context-aware Application Scenario

To illustrate the co-influence of hardware and software engineering issues by an example, we have developed a person/thing/place scenario and have implemented a "context-aware luggage" framework. The framework "models" the physical world as instances of the abstract object classes person, thing and place, and the contextual interrelatedness among those object instances by a set of (bilateral) object relations. Object instances can be created and interrelated at run-time, relations can be updated according to dynamic changes of context (like time, location, etc.) via time-triggered or event-triggered sensors. Figure 4 exemplifies a simple physical world scenario containing a person "ferscha" presently located in town "vienna" as the "owner" of a "suitcase". Upon change of context, like the movement to a different place, inheritance mechanism resolve transitivity of object relations like the "is_in" relation for objects "contained" in a (geographically) moving (physical world) object.

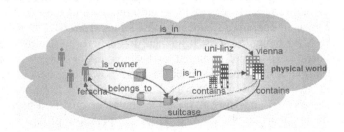

Fig. 4. Objects and their Interrelationship in a Physical World Scenario

Technologically, an embedded personal computer has been integrated into an off-the-shelf suitcase (see Figure 5), executing a standard HTTP services on top of a TCP/IP stack over an integrated IEEE802.11b WLAN adaptor. A miniaturized RFID reader is connected to the serial port of the server machine, an RFID antenna is integrated in the frame of the suitcase so as to enable the server to sense RFID tags contained in the suitcase. A vast of 125KHz magnetic coupled transponders are used to tag real world objects (like shirts, keys, PDAs or even printed paper) to be potentially carried (and sensed) by the suitcase. The suitcase itself is tagged and possibly sensed by readers integrated into home furniture, car or airplane trunks, conveyor belts etc. so as to allow for an identification and localization at any meaningful point in space of the application.

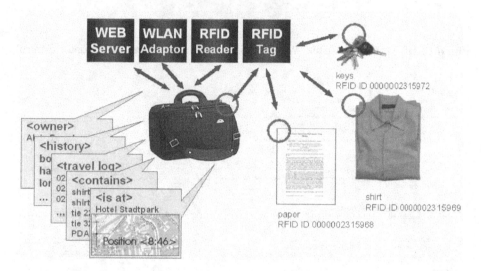

Fig. 5.   "Context-Aware Luggage" as an Application instance of the Context Framework

In our context framework, an application specific abstraction of the real world is generated from three generic classes for persons, things, and places. The reification of physical world objects and their relation among each other is expressed in RDF (see Figure 6). The person object represents the concepts about a person that are necessary to link their physical properties and activities to the virtual world. The thing object encapsulates the basic abstraction for objects relevant to the application and has instances like shirt, bag, etc. The place object is used to represent the essential features of a physical location like an office room or a waiting lounge. Places, things and persons may be related in a manifold of ways.

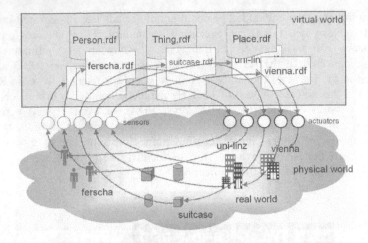

Fig. 6. RDF Model for Virtual World Representation under Sensor/Actuator Control

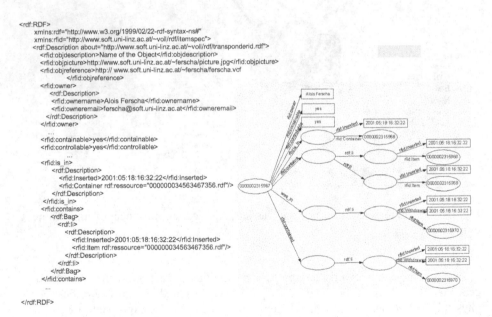

Fig. 7. Relating Physical World Objects with their Virtual Reifications

The RDF in Figure 7 sketches quite a few relations of our context framework: The *owner* relation expresses ownership of a real world object by another, the *contains* and *is_in* relations expresses geometrical containment of an object within another one, the *contained* and *was_in* relations trace the history of containment into RDF bags, the *containable* attribute defines whether an object may contain another one, the *controllable* attribute allows to prevent or enable the modification of an object RDF by the object itself, etc. The unique ID associated with every real world object is the ID encoded in its RFID tag. It is sensed by the RFID reader which triggers a script to update the involved object RDFs (Inserting e.g. the shirt into the suitcase would cause the RFID reader to identify the shirt tag and update (among others) both the shirts RDF relation *is_in*, as well as the suitcases RDF relation *contains* by cross-referring URIs. Figure 7 left presents a snapshot of an RDF of the suitcase after some insert operations.

5. Conclusions

Recent advances in hardware-, communication- and sensor-/actuator technologies envision a whole new area of a situation dependent computing landscape, challenging the classical software design and development principles. Besides the demand for new middleware paradigms and concepts that encompass – besides software issues – also devices, users, interaction, and dynamicity of context, have created new requirements for the **automated** configuration and operation of pervasive computing applications. Central to those is the notion of "**context**", preliminarily defined [DeAb 99][Dey 01] as any information that can be used to characterize the state or situation of an entity and the spectrum of its behaviours. Software architectures and frameworks for context-aware applications [UKC] thus must be concerned with (i) abstract representations of context, (ii) sensing, collecting, interpreting and transforming of context information and (iii) disseminating and making appropriate use of context information to impact the behaviour of the application. The methodological approach today is to employ standardized Web-metadata modelling (like SGML, XML, RDF) to solve (i) [CaDe 00], integrated electrical, chemical, magnetic, optical, acoustic etc. multi-sensor systems for (ii), and integrated multi-actuator systems involving data processors, controllers, motors, filters, etc. for (iii). Given today's global networks as the backbone communication infrastructure, ubiquitous access to this infrastructure demands technological solutions for the "spontaneous" discovery and configuration of devices and services, the selection of meaningful services offered by autonomous software components, the automatic adaptation to mobile and sporadic availability, the interoperability across manufacturers, platforms and services and the scalability with respect to the number of involved activities and entities. On top of **ubiquitous access**, **context-awareness** and issues of **intelligence** (learning, memorizing, planning, forgetting) and knowledge processing are essential for the provision next generation contex-aware applications. A very important aspect is the way how humans **interact** with those applications: requirements towards pro-active (rather than reactive) responsiveness, towards implicit (rather than explicit) input-output and towards continuously (in time and space) available, "naturally occurring" interfaces [CCB 00] will drive their development. The "linking" of real world contexts with their virtual counterparts poses three fundamental problems to be solved in a "co-investigation" of the spectrum of options in hardware for sensors and actuators, and software framework designs are related to (i) *identification* – the automated recognition of the identity of entities – (ii) *localization* and tracking of those entities as they change state in space and time, and (iii) *coordination* – i.e. to bring the autonomous activities of virtual entities to a concerted action that represents the application.

References

[AAHL 97] G. D. ABOWD, C.G. ATKESON, J. HONG, S. LONG, R. KOOPER, M. PINKERTON: Cyberguide: A mobile context-aware tour guide. *ACM Wireless Networks*, Vol. 3, no. 5, pp. 421-433,   1997. http://www.acm.org/pubs/articles/journals/wireless/1997-3-5/p421-abowd/p421-abowd.pdf

[Arno 99] D. ARNOLD ET.AL.: Discourse with disposable Computers: How and why you will talk to your tomatoes. *USENIX Workshop on Embedded Systems*, 1999.

[Bana 00] Banavar, G. et al., "Challenges: An Application Model for Pervasive Computing", *Proceedings 6th Annual Intl. Conference on Mobile Computing and Networking (MobiCom 2000)*, August 2000.

[Brow 98] P. J. BROWN: Triggering Information by Context. *Personal Technologies*, Vol. 2, Nr.1, pp. 18-27, 1998. http://www.cs.ukc.ac.uk/pubs/1998/591/content.html

[BBC 97] P. J. BROWN, J. D. BOVEY, X. CHEN: Context-Aware Applications: From the Laboratory to the Marketplace. *IEEE Personal Communications*, Vol. 4, Nr. 5, pp. 58-64, 1997.

[BEKL] Box, D., Ehnebuske, D., Kakivaya, G., Layman, A., Mendelsohn, N., Frystyk Nielsen, H., Thatte, S. Winer, D. SOAP: Simple Object Access Protocol. http://www.w3.org/TR/SOAP/.

[CaDe 00] D. CASWELL, P. DEBATY: Creating a Web Representation for Places. *Proceedings of the Ninth International World Wide Web Conference*, 2000. http://cooltown.hp.com/papers/placeman/PlacesHUC2000.pdf

[ChLa 99] B. CHRISTENSSON, O. LARSSON: Universal Plug and Play Connects Smart Devices. *WinHEC 99*, 1999. http://www.axis.com/products/documentation/UPnP.doc

[CCB 00] J. L. CROWLEY, J. COUTAZ, F. BERARD: Perceptual user interfaces: Things That See. *Communications of the ACM*, Vol. 43, Nr. 3, pp. 54-64, 2000.

[CZHJ 99] S. E. CZERWINSKI, B.Y. ZHAO, T.D. HODES, A. D. JOSEPH, R. H KATZ: An Architecture for a Secure Service Discovery Service. *Mobicom'99*, 1999. http://ninja.cs.berkeley.edu/dist/papers/sds-mobicom.pdf

[DeAb 99] A. K. DEY, G. D. ABOWD: Toward a Better Understanding of Context and Context-Awareness. GIT, GVU Technical Report GIT-GVU-99-22, June 1999. ftp://ftp.gvu.gatech.edu/pub/gvu/tr/1999/99-22.pdf

[Dey 01] A. K. Dey: Understanding and Using Context. Personal and Ubiquitous Computing, *Special Issue on Situated Interaction and Ubiquitous Computing*, 5(1), 2001.

[DSA 99] A. K. DEY, D. SALBER, G. D. ABOWD: A Context-Based Infrastructure for Smart Environments. *The First International Workshop on Managing Interactions in Smart Environments (MANSE '99)*, Dublin Ireland, 1999. http://www.cc.gatech.edu/fce/ctk/pubs/MANSE99.pdf

[DSAF 99a] A. K. DEY, D. SALBER, G. D. ABOWD, M. FUTAKAWA: The Conference Assistant: Combining Context-Awareness with Wearable Computing. *The Third International Symposium on Wearable Computers (ISWC'99)*, 1999. http://www.cc.gatech.edu/fce/ctk/pubs/ISWC99.pdf

[DSAF 99b] A. K. DEY, D. SALBER, G. D. ABOWD, M. FUTAKAWA: An Architecture to Support Context-Aware Applications. GVU, Technical Report GIT-GVU-99-23, June 1999. ftp://ftp.gvu.gatech.edu/pub/gvu/tr/99-23.pdf

[ELMM 99] K. F. EUSTICE, T. J. LEHMAN, A. MORALES, M. C. MUNSON, S. EDLUND, M. GUILLEN: A universal information appliance. *IBM Systems Journal*, Vol. 38, Nr. 4, 1999. http://www.research.ibm.com/journal/sj/384/eustice.html

[Esle 99] M. ESLER ET.AL.: Next Century Challenges: Data Centric Networking for Invisible Computing. *Proceedings of the 5th Annual International Conference on Mobile Computing and Networking (MobiCom'99), August 1999.*

[Essa 99] I. ESSA: Ubiquitous Sensing for Smart and Aware Environments: Technologies toward the building of an Aware House. *DARPA/NSF/NIST Workshop on Smart Environments*, 1999.
http://www.cc.gatech.edu/gvu/perception/pubs/se99/pp.pdf

[FCE] Future Computing Environments: The Context Toolkit. http://www.cc.gatech.edu/fce/contexttoolkit/

[FBN 01] A. FERSCHA, W. BEER, W. NARZT: Location Awareness in Community Wireless LANs. *Proceedings of the Informatik 2001: Workshop on Mobile internet based services and information logistics, September 2001.*

[Gong 02] L. GONG: Peer-to-Peer Networks in Action. *IEEE Internet Computing*, Vol. 6, Nr. 1, pp. 36-39, *Jan/Feb 2002.*

[HaHo 94] A. HARTER, A. HOPPER: A distributed location system for the active office. *IEEE Network*, Vol. 8, Nr. 1, pp. 62-70, 1994.

[HIR 01] K. HENRICKSEN, J. INDULSKA, A. RAKOTONIRAINY: Infrastructure for Pervasive Computing: Challenges. *Proc. of the Informatik 2001: Workshop on mobile internet based services and information logistics, September 2001.*

[HP] Hewlett Packard: CoolTown Appliance Computing: White Papers.
http://cooltown.hp.com/papers.htm

[KBMB 00] T. KINDBERG, J. BARTON, J. MORGAN, G. BECKER, I. BEDNER, D. CASWELL, P. DEBATY, G. GOPAL, M. FRID, V. KRISHNAN, H. MORRIS, J. SCHETTINO, B. SERRA, M. SPASOJEVIC: People, Places, Things: Web Presence for the Real World. *WWW'2000*, 2000.
http://cooltown.hp.com/dev/wpapers/WebPres/WebPresence.asp

[KHCR 00] F. KON, C. HESS, CHRISTOPHER, M. ROMAN, R. H. CAMPBELL, M. D. MICKUNAS: A Flexible, Interoperable Framework for Active Spaces. *OOPSLA'2000 Workshop on Pervasive Computing*, Minneapolis, MN, 2000.

[LGDE 00] Lea, R., Gibbs, S., Dara-Abrams, A. and Eytchison, E., "Networking Home Entertainment Devices with HAVi", *Computer*, Vol. 33, No. 9, September 2000.

[McGr 00] R. E. MCGRATH: Discovery and its Discontents: Discovery Protocols for Ubiquitous Computing. Department of Computer Science University of Illinois Urbana-Champaign, Urbana UIUCDCS-R-99-2132, March 25, 2000. http://www.cs.uiuc.edu/Dienst/Repository/2.0/Body/ncstrl.uiuc_cs/UIUCDCS-R-2000-2154/pdf

[Mill 99] B. MILLER: Mapping Salutation Architecture APIs to Bluetooth Service Discovery Layer. Bluetooth Consortium 1.C.118/1.0, 01 July 1999.

[MIT] MIT Media Lab: Smart Rooms. http://ali.www.media.mit.edu/vismod/demos/smartroom/

[Moze 99] M. C. MOZER: An intelligent environment must be adaptive. *IEEE Intelligent Systems and Their Applications*, Vol. 14, Nr. 2, pp. 11-13, 1999.
http://www.cs.colorado.edu/~mozer/papers/ieee.html

[OZKT 01] A. OMICINI, F. ZAMBONELLI, M. KLUSCH, R. TOLKSDORF (EDS.): Coordination of Internet Agents. Models, Technologies, and Applications. *Springer Verlag*, Berlin 2001.

[PRM 99] J. PASCOE, N. RYAN, D. MORSE: Issues in developing context-aware computing. In H-W.Gellersen, editor, *Handheld and Ubiquitous Computing*, Nr. 1707 in Lecture Notes in Computer Science, pages 208-221, Heidelberg, Germany, September 1999. Springer-Verlag

[RDF 99] O. LASSILA, R. R. SWICK: Resource Description Framework (RDF): Model and Syntax Specification. Recommendation, World Wide Web Consortium, Feb. 1999.
http://www.w3c.org/TR/REC-rdf-syntax/.

[RoCa 00] M. ROMAN, R. H. CAMPBELL: GAIA: Enabling Active Spaces. In *9th ACM SIGOPS European Workshop*. September 17th-20th, 2000. Kolding, Denmark.
http://choices.cs.uiuc.edu/2k/papers/sigopseu2000.pdf

[SaAb 98] D. SALBER, G. D. ABOWD: The Design and Use of a Generic Context Server. *Perceptual User Interfaces Workshop (PUI '99)*, San Francisco, 1998.
http://www.cs.gatech.edu/fce/contexttoolkit/pubs/pui98.pdf

[SDA 99] D. SALBER, A. K. DEY, G. D. ABOWD: The Context Toolkit: Aiding the Development of Context-Enabled Applications. *The 1999 Conference on Human Factors in Computing Systems (CHI '99)*, Pittsburgh, 1999. http://www.cs.gatech.edu/fce/contexttoolkit/pubs/chi99.pdf

[SDOA 99] D. SALBER, A. K. DEY, R. ORR, G. D. ABOWD: Designing for Ubiquitous Computing: A Case Study in Context Sensing. GVU, Technical Report GIT-GVU-99-29, July 1999. ftp://ftp.gvu.gatech.edu/pub/gvu/tr/1999/99-29.pdf

[Schi 95] W. N. SCHILIT: *A System Architecture for Context-Aware Mobile Computing (Ph. D. Dissertation)*. New York: Columbia University, 1995.

[SATT 99] A. SCHMIDT, K. A. AIDOO, A. TAKALUOMA, U. TUOMELA, K. LAERHOVEN, W. V. VELDE: Advanced Interaction in Context. *HandHeld and Ubiquitous Computing*, Karlsruhe, 1999.

[SSP 98] T. STARNER, B. SCHIELE, A. PENTLAND: Visual Contextual Awareness in Wearable Computing. *The Second International Symposium on Wearable Computers (ISWC'98)*, Pittsburgh, 1998.

[UKC] UKC Mobicomp: Mobile and Context-Aware Computing Research at U.K.C. http://www.cs.ukc.ac.uk/projects/mobicomp/

[Wald 99] Waldo, J., "Jini Technology Architectural Overview", White Paper, Sun Microsystems, Inc., January 1999.

[WDKF 02] ST. WATERHOUSE, D. M. DOOLIN, G. KAN, Y. FAYBISHENKO: Distributed Search in P2P Networks. *IEEE Internet Computing,* Vol. 6, Nr. 1, pp. 68-72, *January/February 2002.*

Evaluating Performance and Power of Object-Oriented Vs. Procedural Programming in Embedded Processors

Alexander Chatzigeorgiou and George Stephanides

Department of Applied Informatics,
University of Macedonia,
156 Egnatia Str., 54006 Thessaloniki, Greece
alec@ieee.org, steph@uom.gr

Abstract. The development of high-performance and low power portable devices relies on both the underlying hardware architecture and technology as well as on the application software that executes on embedded processor cores. It has been extensively pointed out that the increasing complexity and decreasing time-to-market of embedded software can only be confronted by the use of modular and reusable code, which forces software designers to use objected oriented programming languages such as C++. However, the object-oriented approach is known to introduce a significant performance penalty compared to classical procedural programming. In this paper, the object oriented programming style is evaluated in terms of both performance and power for embedded applications. A set of benchmark kernels is compiled and executed on an embedded processor simulator, while the results are fed to instruction level and memory power models to estimate the power consumption of each system component for both programming styles.

1 Introduction

The increasing demand for high-performance portable systems based on embedded processors has raised the interest of many research efforts with focus on low power design. Low power consumption is of primary importance for portable devices since it determines their battery lifetime and weight as well as the maximum possible integration scale because of the related cooling and reliability issues [1]. The challenge to meet these design constraints is further complicated by the tradeoff between performance and power: Increased performance, for example in terms of higher clock frequency, usually comes at the cost of increased power dissipation.

To reduce the system power consumption, techniques at both the hardware and the software domain have been developed. The overall target of the most recent research that is summarized in [2] is to reduce the dynamic power dissipation, which is due to charging/discharging of the circuit capacitances [1]. Hardware techniques attempt to minimize power by optimizing design parameters such as the supply voltage, the number of logic gates, the size of transistors and the operating frequency. Such decisions usually affect performance negatively. On the other hand, software

J. Blieberger and A. Strohmeier (Eds.): Ada-Europe 2002, LNCS 2361, pp. 65–75, 2002.

techniques primarily target at performing a given task using fewer instructions resulting in a reduction of the circuit switching activity. In this case, an improvement is achieved for both performance and power. Moreover, software methodologies normally address higher levels of the system design hierarchy, where the impact of design decisions is higher and the resulting energy savings significantly larger.

The increasing complexity and decreasing time-to-market of embedded software, forces the adoption of modular and reusable code, using for example object oriented techniques and languages such as C++ [3], [4]. The shift of the system functionality to the software domain enables greater flexibility in maintaining and updating an existing application. Object Oriented Programming (OOP), through features such as data abstraction and encapsulation of data and functions, is widely accepted as a methodology to improve modularity and reusability [5], [6]. Equally important, is the integration of hardware description languages and OOP programming languages into a common modeling platform. A promising example of this case is the enhancement of C++ with classes to describe hardware structures in SystemC [7].

In spite of its advantages, the acceptance of OOP in the embedded world has been very slow, since embedded software designers are reluctant to employ these techniques due to the additional performance overhead, in an environment with relatively limited computational power and memory resources. The introduced penalty on the system performance, in terms of execution time and memory overhead, has been demonstrated in the literature [8], [9], [10], [11]. This inherent drawback of object-oriented languages has forced the software community to develop sophisticated compilers, which attempt to optimize the performance of OOP [12], [13], [14]. An open standard defining a subset of C++ suitable for embedded applications has also been initiated [15].

Considering the intense need for low power, the purpose of this work is to investigate the effect of object oriented techniques compared to traditional procedural programming style, in an embedded environment, on both performance and power. Power exploration is not restricted to the processor but also considers the energy consumption of the instruction and data memories, whose power dissipation is a significant component of the total power in an embedded system. Since this is the first study of the power implications of object oriented programming, the aim here is not to evaluate existing compiler techniques in improving the performance of OOP but rather to show that OOP, if not applied properly, affects significantly not only the system performance but also its power consumption.

The target architecture that has been used for comparing object oriented programming style versus procedural programming is the ARM7 TDMI embedded processor core which is widely used in embedded applications due to its promising MIPS/mW performance [16]. Moreover it offers the advantage of an open architecture to the designer [17]. In order to evaluate both programming styles in terms of performance and power, the OOPACK benchmark kernels will be used a test vehicle [18].

The paper is organized as follows: Section II provides an overview of the sources of power consumption in an embedded system. Section III describes briefly the OOPACK benchmarks, while in Section IV the process that has been followed for the comparisons will be presented and the experimental results will be discussed. Finally, we conclude in Section V.

2 Sources of Power Consumption

The sources of power consumption in an embedded system, with varying importance according to the architecture and target application can be categorized as follows:

1. Processor power consumption, which is due to the operation of the processor circuitry during the execution of program instructions. This operation translates to switching activity at the nodes of the digital circuit, which in turn corresponds to charging/discharging the node capacitances, resulting in dynamic power dissipation [1]. To quantify this power component appropriate instruction-level power models have been developed. These models are based on the hypothesis that [19], it is possible by measuring the current drawn by a processor as it repeatedly executes certain instructions, to obtain most of the information required to evaluate the power cost of a program for that processor. This claim has been refined to state that the total energy cost cannot be calculated by the summation of the energy costs of the individual instructions [19], [20], [21]. It has been proved that the change in circuit state between consecutive instructions has to be taken into account in order to establish accurate instruction level power models.

The two basic components of an instruction power model therefore are:

a. *Base Energy Costs*: These are the costs that are associated with the basic processing required to execute an instruction. This cost is evaluated by measuring the average current drawn in a loop with several instances of this instruction. Some indicative base costs for several instruction types and addressing modes for the ARM7 processor core are shown in Table 1.

Type	Instruction	Addressing Mode	Base Cost (mA)
Arithmetic	ADD	LSL Immediate	9.92
	SUB	Immediate	6.67
	CMP	Immediate	6.65
	MOV	Immediate	8.07
Load/Store	LDR	Offset Immediate	10.76
	STR	Offset Immediate	8.55
Branch	B		8.73

Table 1. Base Costs for the ARM7 processor

b. *Overhead Costs*: These costs are due to the switching activity in the processor circuitry and the implied energy consumption overhead resulting from the execution of adjacent instructions. To measure the average current drawn in this case, sequences of alternating instructions are constructed. Some indicative overhead costs between pairs of instructions are shown in the matrix of Table 2, for the addressing modes of Table 1. Overhead costs between instructions of the same kind are significantly smaller.

Therefore, the total energy consumed by a program executing on a processor can be obtained as the sum of the total base costs and the total overhead costs. Thus, energy is given by

$$E_p = \sum_{i=1}^{n} I_{base_i} \times V \times N_i \times t + \sum_{i=2}^{n} I_{ovhd_{i,i-1}} \times V \times t \qquad (1)$$

where I_{base_i} is the average current drawn by instruction #i, $I_{ovhd_{i,i-1}}$ the overhead cost for the sequence of instructions i and i-1, N_i the required number of clock cycles for instruction #i, V the supply voltage and t the clock period. For the results that will be shown next a supply voltage of 5 V and a clock speed of 20 MHz has been assumed.

	ADD	CMP	STR
SUB	1.24	0.13	2.42
MOV	1.35	1.10	2.64
LDR	3.29	2.77	0.80
B	1.25	1.03	2.00

Table 2. Overhead Costs (mA) for pairs of different instructions

2. Memory power consumption, which is associated with the energy cost for accessing instructions or data in the corresponding memories. Energy cost per access depends on the memory size and consequently power consumption for large off-chip memories is significantly larger than the power consumption of smaller on-chip memory layers. This component of the total power consumption is related also to the application: The instruction memory energy consumption depends on the code size, which determines the size of the memory and on the number of executed instructions that correspond to instruction fetches from the memory. The energy consumption of the data memory depends on the amount of data that are being processed by the application and on whether the application is data-intensive, that is whether data are often being accessed. For a typical power model the power consumed due to accesses to a memory layer i, is directly proportional to the number of accesses, f_i, and depends on the size, S_i, and the number of ports, Nr_ports_i, of the memory, the power supply and the technology. For a given technology and power supply the consumed energy can be expressed as:

$$E_i = f_i \cdot F(S_i, Nr\_ports_i) \tag{2}$$

The relation between memory power and memory size is between linear and logarithmic.

An example of a power optimizing approach for data-dominated applications such as multimedia algorithms, is the Data Transfer and Storage Exploration (DTSE) methodology [22] which aims at moving data accesses from background memories to smaller foreground memory blocks, which are less power costly, resulting in significant power savings.

3. Interconnect power consumption, which is due to the switching of the large parasitic capacitances of the interconnect lines connecting the processor to the instruction and data memories. This source of power consumption will not be explored in this study, however, since it depends on the number of data being transferred on the interconnect, it can be considered that a larger number of accesses to the instruction and data memory will result in higher interconnect energy dissipation. Several power reduction techniques have been developed for addressing this source of power consumption of which most important are appropriate data encoding schemes that minimize the average switching activity on the interconnect busses [2].

3 OOPACK Benchmarks

OOPACK is a small suite of kernels [18] that compares the relative performance of object oriented programming in C++ versus plain C-style code compiled in C++. All of the tests are written so that a compiler can, in principle, transform the OOP code into the C-style code. Although the style of object-oriented programming tested is fairly narrow, employing small objects to represent abstract data types, the range of applications to which they are used justifies the performance and power exploration. The four kernels for OOPACK are :

- **Max:** measures how well a compiler inlines a simple conditional.
- **Matrix:** measures how well a compiler propagates constants and hoists simple invariants
- **Iterator:** measures how well a compiler inlines short-lived small objects
- **Complex:** measures how well a compiler eliminates temporaries

The above benchmarks have some desirable characteristics as outlined in [14]: They allow measurements of individual optimizations implemented in the compiler, performance is tested for commonly used language features and are representative of widely used applications (for example matrix multiplication is common in embedded DSP applications).

The *Max* benchmark (OOPACK_1) uses a function in both C and OOP style to compute the maximum over a vector. The C-style version performs the comparison operation between two elements explicitly, while the OOP version performs the comparison by calling an inline function. This benchmark aims to investigate whether inline functions within conditional statements are compiled efficiently.

The *Matrix* benchmark (OOPACK_2) multiplies two matrices containing real numbers to evaluate the efficiency of performing two classical optimizations on the indexing calculations: invariant hoisting and strength-reduction. C-style code performs the multiplication in the following manner :

```
for( i=0; i<L; i++ )
  for( j=0; j<L; j++ )
  {
    sum = 0;
    for( k=0; k<L; k++ )
      sum += C[L*i+k]*D[L*k+j];
    E[L*i+j] = sum;
  }
```

where, for example, the term L*i is constant for each iteration of k and should be computed as an invariant outside the k loop. Modern C compilers are good enough at this sort of optimization for scalars and programmers do not have to bother doing the optimization by hand. However, in OOP style, invariants and strength reduction often concern members of objects. Optimizers that do not peer into objects miss the opportunities. In the above example, the OOP version performs the multiplication employing member functions and overloading to access an element, given the row and the column.

The *Iterator* benchmark (OOPACK_3) computes a dot-product using a common single index in the C-style version and using iterators for the OOP-version. Iterators are a common abstraction in object-oriented programming, enabling the management of a collection class without the client program caring about the underlying structure of the collection. Although iterators are usually called "light-weight" objects, they may incur a high cost if compiled inefficiently. In this benchmark all methods of the iterator are inline and in principle correspond exactly to the C-style code. It has to be noted that the OOP-style code uses two iterators, and good common-subexpression elimination should be expected to reduce the two iterators to a single index variable.

Complex numbers are a common abstraction in scientific programming. The purpose of the *Complex* benchmark (OOPACK_4) is to measure the efficiency of C++ in handling complex arithmetic by multiplying the elements of two arrays containing complex numbers (defined with a class). In C-style the calculation is performed by explicitly writing out the real and imaginary parts while in OOP-style complex addition and multiplication is done using overloaded operations. The complex arithmetic is all inlined in the OOP-style, so in principle the code should run as fast as the version using explicit real and imaginary parts.

4 Results and Discussion

The process that has been set up in order to evaluate each kernel in terms of performance and power is shown in Fig. 1. Each OOPACK code was compiled using the C++ compiler of the ARM Software Development Toolkit v2.50 [17], which provided both the code size and the minimum RAM requirements for the data of each kernel. Next, the execution of the code using the ARM Debugger provided the number of executed assembly instructions as well as the total number of cycles. The ARM Debugger was set to produce a trace file logging instructions and memory accesses. It should be noted that the ARM C++ compiler implements most basic optimizations such as common subexpression elimination, loop invariant motion, live range splitting, constant folding, tail-calling and branch elimination [17].

The trace file is then parsed serially by a separate profiler that has been developed in *C* language, in order to collect information concerning the executed instructions and to obtain the number of data memory accesses. The parser has built-in look-up tables containing physical measurements [23] of the base and overhead energy costs in mA, for all types of instructions and instruction pairs. In this way it is possible by counting all instruction occurrences and assigning to them a base and an overhead energy cost according to the instruction type and addressing mode, to obtain the total energy cost for the processor.

Finally, the number of executed instructions and the code size are used as input to a memory power model in order to calculate the energy consumption of the instruction memory. In the same way, the number of data memory accesses and the minimum RAM size are used to compute the energy consumption of the data memory.

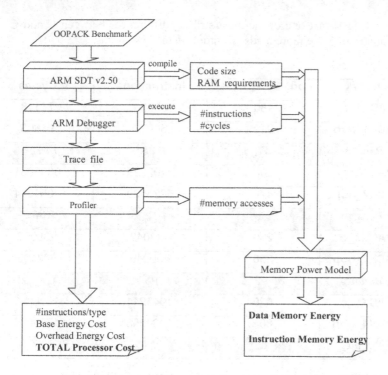

Fig. 1: Experiment set up for evaluating performance and power

Experimental results concerning the code size of each kernel, the number of executed instructions and cycles are given in Table 3 for all OOPACK kernels. As it can be observed, the OOP programming style has a larger impact on the resulting code size than on the number of executed instructions. This is reasonable, since the use of objects increases significantly the code size through the definition of classes, however runtime is not drastically increased mainly due to the use of inline methods. Code size refers only to the kernel size, excluding library functions, since the aim is to illustrate the effect of OOP on the programming style and its consequences. Whether the performance penalty, which can be up to 18%, is considered significant or not, depends on the application. In any case, the results are in agreement with previous studies and clearly demonstrate the so-called abstraction penalty [11] when writing object-oriented code.

Results concerning the required data memory size and the number of data memory accesses are given in Table 4. The RAM (this could be any type of random access memory) size is the same for both programming styles since the read-write data are not altered. For example, in the OOPACK3 kernel, the data memory size corresponds to two tables of *double* with 1000 elements plus a global *double* variable, for both C-style and OOP-style. The number of memory accesses refers only to the benchmark kernel and consequently it reflects the increased data transfers when abstract data types are used, probably due to inefficient use of registers. This is consistent with the observation in [10] that one of the most striking differences between C and C++, is that C++ programs issue more loads and stores than C programs.

Benchmark	code size (bytes)	Instructions	Cycles
OOPACK1_c	180	50536	77118
OOPACK1_oop	212	56032	91605
OOP Penalty	17.78 %	10.88 %	18.79 %
OOPACK2_c	308	5402229	8303851
OOPACK2_oop	424	5625529	9051974
OOP Penalty	37.66 %	4.13 %	9.00 %
OOPACK3_c	260	433042	635096
OOPACK3_oop	356	450049	677103
OOP Penalty	36.92 %	3.93 %	6.61 %
OOPACK4_c	620	1041241	1606642
OOPACK4_oop	804	1084256	1710665
OOP Penalty	29.68 %	4.13 %	6.47 %

Table 3: Performance comparison between C_style and OOP_style for all kernels

Benchmark	RAM size (bytes)	Mem_accesses
OOPACK1_c	8008	8043
OOPACK1_oop		16035
OOP Penalty		99.37 %
OOPACK2_c	21600	1226765
OOPACK2_oop		1555328
OOP Penalty		26.78 %
OOPACK3_c	16008	79063
OOPACK3_oop		95063
OOP Penalty		20.24 %
OOPACK4_c	32000	256992
OOPACK4_oop		304996
OOP Penalty		18.68 %

Table 4: Memory comparison between C_style and OOP_style for all kernels

From a power perspective, this increases energy dissipation even further since according to the physical measurements [23] base and overhead costs for Load/Store instructions are slightly higher than for other instructions. Moreover, increased number of loads/stores results in more data memory accesses, which can be very power consuming when large data memory sizes are used.

In Table 5 the energy that has been calculated using instruction level and memory power models is presented for all system components that have been considered. For the programs under study, the most energy consuming system component is the processor. The overall energy overhead might not be critical for general purpose applications when performance and power constraints are relaxed, but should certainly affect the decision whether to use object-oriented code, when designing high-performance and low power systems, such as portable multimedia processing units.

Benchmark	Processor	Instr. Memory	Data Memory	System
OOPACK1_c	0.220	0.0181	0.0287	0.267
OOPACK1_oop	0.253	0.0206	0.0572	0.331
OOPACK2_c	18.148	2.234	6.882	27.264
OOPACK2_oop	19.534	2.406	8.726	30.666
OOPACK3_c	1.272	0.176	0.388	1.836
OOPACK3_oop	1.382	0.189	0.466	2.037
OOPACK4_c	3.353	0.472	1.724	5.549
OOPACK4_oop	3.632	0.517	2.046	6.195
Avg. OOP Penalty	9.90 %	9.61 %	41.22 %	14.76 %

Table 5: Comparison of energy consumption for all system components (in mJ)

It should be mentioned that the relatively large differences in code size between C-style and OOP-style are partially reflected in the instruction memory energy results due the extremely small-sized applications that have been selected. For real applications, with larger code size a significant increase of the instruction memory energy for the OOP style should be expected, however it should be noted that power dissipation increases sub-linearly with memory size. The results are shown in graphical form in Fig. 2, to provide an overview of each system component contribution to the total energy consumption.

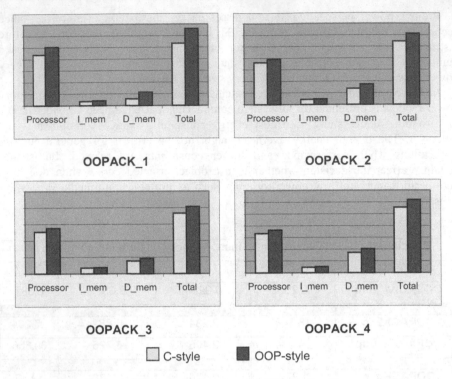

Fig.2 : Energy comparison between C-style and OOP-style for all system components

5 Conclusions

Object-oriented programming is widely accepted as a methodology for writing modular and reusable code. In embedded applications however, designers should consider when taking hardware/software decisions, the performance penalty that is introduced by the use of object-oriented code. In this paper, it has been demonstrated, through the compilation and execution of benchmarks on an embedded processor simulator, that OOP can result in a significant increase of both execution time and power consumption. In embedded systems where low power operation is the primary requirement, object oriented techniques can result in an energy dissipation overhead in all system components such as the processor core, the instruction and data memories. Since compilers usually cannot optimize code to reach the level of procedural programming performance, the number of executed instructions increases, increasing proportionally the instruction level power consumption. Moreover, care should be taken when opting for object oriented style, especially in large programs, since data abstraction can lead to a large code size increase resulting in a significantly higher power consumption of the instruction memory.

References

1. Chandrakasan A. and Brodersen R.: Low Power Digital CMOS Design. Kluwer Academic Publishers, Boston (1995)
2. Benini L. and De Micheli G.: System-Level Power Optimization: Techniques and Tools. ACM Transactions on Design Automation of Electronic Systems, vol. 5, (2000) 115-192
3. Cockx A. J.: Whole program compilation for embedded software: the ADSL experiment. 9th International Symposium on Hardware/Software Codesign (CODES'2001), Copenhagem, Denmark, (2001)
4. Plauger P.J.: Embedded C++. Embedded Systems Conference (ESC'99), Chicago, Illinois, USA, (1999)
5. Sommerville I.: Software Engineering. Addison-Wesley, Harlow (1995)
6. Harrison R., Samaraweera L.G., Dobie M.R., and Lewis P.H.: Comparing Programming Paradigms: an Evaluation of Functional and Object-Oriented Programs. Software Engineering Journal, vol. 11, (1996) 247-254
7. SystemC Homepage, http://www.systemc.org
8. Haney S.W.: Is C++ Fast Enough for Scientific Computing?. Computers in Physics, vol. 8, (1994) 690-694
9. Robinson A.D.: C++ Gets Faster for Scientific Computing. Computers in Physics, vol. 10, (1996) 458-462
10. Calder B., Grunwald D., and Zorn B.: Quantifying Behavioral Differences Between C and C++ Programs. Journal of Programming Languages, vol. 2, (1994) 313–351
11. Robinson A.D.: The abstraction penalty for small objects in C++. Parallel Object-Oriented Methods and Applications Conference (POOMA'96), Santa Fe, New Mexico, (1996)
12. Collin S., Colnet D. and Zendra O.: Type Inference for Late Binding. The SmallEiffel Compiler. JMLC'97, Linz, Austria, (1997), pp. 67-81
13. Zendra O., Colnet D. and Collin S.: Efficient Dynamic Dispatch without Virtual Function Tables. The SmallEiffel Compiler. OOPSLA'97, Atlanta GA, USA, (1997), pp. 125-141
14. Rotithor H., Harris K., and Davis M.: Measurement and Analysis of C and C++ Performance. Digital Technical Journal, vol. 10, (1999) 32-47
15. Embedded C++ Homepage, http://www.caravan.net/ec2plus
16. Furber S.: ARM System-on-Chip Architecture. Addison-Wesley, Harlow (2000)
17. ARM software development toolkit, v2.50, Copyright 1995-98, Advanced RISC Machines.
18. Kuck & Associates (KAI): C++ Benchmarks, Comparing Performance. http://www.kai.com/C_plus_plus/benchmarks/_index.html
19. Tiwari V., Malik S. and Wolfe A.: Power Analysis of Embedded Software: A First Step Towards Software Power Minimization. IEEE Transactions on VLSI Systems, vol. 2, (1994), 437-445
20. Tiwari V., Malik S., Wolfe A. and Lee T.C.: Instruction Level Power Analysis and Optimization of Software. Journal of VLSI Signal Processing, vol. 13, (1996) 1-18
21. Sinevriotis G. and Stouraitis Th.: Power Analysis of the ARM 7 Embedded Microprocessor. 9th Int. Workshop on Power and Timing Modeling, Optimization and Simulation (PATMOS'99), Kos, Greece, (1999), pp. 261-270
22. Catthoor F., Wuytack S., De Greef E., Balasa F., Nachtergaele L, Vandecappelle A.: Custom Memory Management Methodology: Exploration of Memory Organisation for Embedded Multimedia System Design. Kluwer Academic Publishers, Boston (1998)
23. Sinevriotis G. and Stouraitis Th.: SOFLOPO: Low Power Software Development for Embedded Applications. Public Final Report, European Commission, ESD Best Practice: Pilot Action for Low Power Design, (2001)

OMC-INTEGRAL Memory Management

Jose Manuel Pérez Lobato[1] and Eva Martín Lobo[2]

[1] Departamento de Informática, Universidad Carlos III,Leganés, Madrid, Spain
jperez@inf.uc3m.es, http://www.arcos.inf.uc3m.es
[2] I.N.T.A., 28850 Torrejón de Ardoz, Madrid, Spain
martinle@inta.es, http://www.inta.es

Abstract. The management of the memory restrictions imposed by the processor (1750A) was one of the major difficulties found in designing the Software (SW) controlling the Optical Monitoring Camera (OMC) payload of the **International Gamma Ray Laboratory (INTEGRAL) mission of the European Space Agency (ESA)**. This article explains the solutions adopted at high and low level, in order to solve the problems created by this restriction. It also provides a general description of the main functionality of the OMC satellite payload.

1 Introduction

The development of Embedded Real Time SW projects implies the need of using reliable HW and SW, but in the most of times it is not possible use the last generation technology because it is not validated (it is needed a lot of time and money to perform the validation tests to reach this reliability). This must not be seen as a handicap but as a dare to look for solutions to the existing restrictions. This paper shows an interesting application of low-level Ada features to the spacecraft software system focusing on the memory restrictions of the processor used.

The paper comprises the following sections:

- Section 2 describes the system context and the general features of the SW project.
- Section 3 explains the memory restrictions of system.
- Section 4 and 5 describe the solution adopted from the low and high level point of view.
- Section 6 shows the authors conclusions.

2 System Overview

OMC Aplication SW (OMCAS) is one of the software applications (programmed in ADA 83) which is in charge of controlling a payload (OMC) belonging to the INTEGRAL mission (Satellite to study gamma-ray sources). There are other instruments placed in the spacecraft (The Spectrometer (SPI), The Imager (IBIS) and The Joint European X-ray Monitor (Jem-X)).

J. Blieberger and A. Strohmeier (Eds.): Ada-Europe 2002, LNCS 2361, pp. 76–87, 2002.

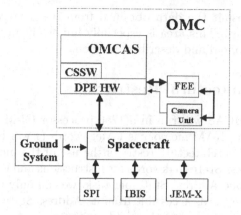

Fig. 1. INTEGRAL-OMC block diagram

OMCAS fits in the INTEGRAL system as depicted in 1. The OMC will be used to obtain sky images of the spectrum visible range and to relate them to the observations provided by the other instruments operating in other ranges.

OMCAS will be put on-board on a Digital Processing Equipment (DPE) unit, which will be in charge of interfacing with the camera unit through the Front End Electronics (FEE), and also with the Command and Data Management Unit (CDMU) through the On Board Data Handler (OBDH) bus. The DPE main board is based on standard **1750 architecture**, using a **1750 microprocessor** plus a **Memory Management Unit** (MMU). The MMU allows the addressing of **2 Mbytes** from which 1840 Kbytes will be available for OMCAS code and data, and the rest will be used to store the ASTRES operating system and the Common Service Software (CSSW). The board will host 128 Kbytes of PROM memory from which 96 Kbytes will be available for OMCAS code. The DPE will interface with the FEE by means of a set of lines (RS-422 serial, High Speed Serial Line (HSSL), Low Speed Serial Line (LSSL), Bi-level, etc.).

OMCAS will interface with the OBDH and with the FEE using the I/O services provided by the CSSW. It will be executed over the CSSW real-time kernel and all the HW resources will be operated using CSSW functions designed for that purpose.

2.1   Software Basics

OMCAS will receive and interpret the telecommands (TCs) generated either on the ground or in the spacecraft that will define the actions to be executed according to the mission. The OMC will be commanded to obtain the images and the housekeeping data, which will be sent to ground through the spacecraft as telemetry(TM) packets.

The main tasks are: *Collect TC, Control OMCGenerate TM* and *Perform Periodic housekeeping.* We have to point out that a shared memory area (RAW

TM) is used to transmit the data obtained from the Charge-Coupled Device (CCD) to the TM task. This area is especially important in the memory management solution adopted and described later on.

3 Logical Architectural Restrictions

As stated above, OMCAS will run in a 1750 processor (N-MA31750) using the A mode. The available RAM memory is 1 Megawords (1 word=16 bits), but the characteristics of this architecture restricts the use of the memory available to 64 Kwords per Address State (64kwords for instructions and 64kwords for data). Therefore if we use one Address State per task, we can only use a maximum of 64kwords of data (the words accessible from its Address State) corresponding to the 16 logical pages associated to this Address State.

To understand this restriction we need to know the processor memory management: The 1750 Memory Management Unit (MMU) has **32 memory areas** or structures (16 for code and 16 for data) for storage. Each one has **16 logical memory addresses (Logical Pages)**. Each logical memory address can be associated to one **physical page** (a page, be it logical or physical, has a size of **4Kwords**. When the processor is executing a specific task in a specific **Address State(AS)**, the "data" memory accessible is just the one associated to the two memory structures of this AS. There are 16 AS, and each one has associated one memory structure for data and one for code. Therefore from one AS we have access to 16 logical pages for data and also 16 pages for code. This is due to the fact that the memory address used by the processor directly is 16-bits long and therefore can only address a maximum of 2^{16} memory words. To allow the access up to 2^{20} memory words, the 4 most significant bits of the memory address provided by the processor are used by the memory unit to select 1 of the 16 logical memory addresses of the memory structure associated to the actual AS. The logical memory address selected provides the 8 most significant bits of the physical address. Therefore these 8 bits plus the 12 less significant bits (4kwords) provided by the processor make up a 20 bits physical address.

This procedure gives the possibility of accessing up to 2^{20} memory words, with the restriction of changing the AS each time to a different one, accessing it from those stored in the current memory structure.

4 Low Level Memory Management

In order to be able to access the full available memory, the first solution is to associate each of the **256 logical pages** (16 AS * 16 logical pages each AS) to a different physical one. Thus, every time we need to access a specific physical page we can change to the AS corresponding to the appropriate logical page. This solution will present some problems:

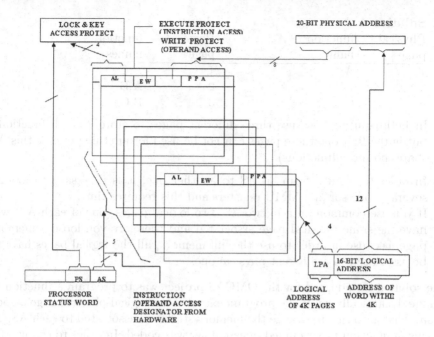

Fig. 2. Expanded memory mapping diagram

1. The code, like the data, is distributed in several AS. This does not mean to say, at least theoretically, that the code is duplicated in several physical pages. For example, if the code size is less than 64 Kwords all the logical pages of all the AS can have the same 16 physical pages associated. Although, if the code does not fit in 16 logical pages, in order to optimize the memory use and to avoid duplication of the same code in the physical memory, the linker (TLD in this case) will divide the code in several pieces. Each one is stored in a page (4Kwords). Each of these code units will contain the code used in several AS. Of course, if the code units shared between several AS are small and cannot be placed in a single page (see example 1), a waste of memory may be produced because the memory pages are not used at full capacity.

Example

Next table shows the name of the functions and the AS where the code is allocated:

Function Name	AS
A	1, 2
B	2, 3
C	1, 3

In this case, there are two possibilities for storing the functions.

Solution 1		Solution 2	
Physical page	function name	Physical page	function names
1	A	1	A,C
2	B	2	A,B
3	C	3	B,C

In both solutions, we use three different pages to store 3 small functions, but in the first one these pages can not be used for anything else (if this AS shares no more functions).

2. In order to change from an AS to another one, it is necessary to modify several processor and MMU registers and this requires time.
3. If you use common data in two AS, two logical pages (one of each AS) will have the same physical page associated and therefore you loose a memory page, because in order to use the full memory, all the logical pages have to be associated to a different physical one.

The solution we adopted for the OMCAS project was to program a function to change dynamically while the program executes the logical-physical page association. That is to say, to change the memory structure associated to each AS. To do this, a function programmed in assembler was coded. In order to change, for example, the association of the logical page 3 of the AS1 to the physical page 6, the aforementioned code is the following:

```
Ra, Rx: machine_code.Register;-- Processor registers
Cmd: machine_code.Io_Cmd;   -- Use to store Machine Code Instr.
dato,phypagenumber: integer;
Begin
-- Processor registers that will be used to change the mem. assoc,
--in order to reestablish the situation, are inserted in the stack.
--  Machine code instructions (pshm) are used
machine_code.epshm (machine_code.R5,machine_code.R6);

-- A var. is defined with the value of the phys. page selected
   (06).
-- The 8 most significant bits of the physical address is 06,
-- these correspond to the 8 less significant bits of the reg.
-- used to store the logical page value.
-- The others 8 bits of the logical page, used to store inf. about
-- the page permissions (access protection, execution (for inst.)/
-- write(for operands)), shall take the value 16#F0#.
with machine_code; use machine_code;

phypagenumber:=16#06#;
change_to_C2 (phypagenumber,dato)
--   dato:=16#F006#; -- dato:= -4090; -- 2s complement
-- put in the logical page 3 of the AS 1 (16#13#) the above
```

```
-- mentioned physical address
--wopr: instruction write operand page register
   Cmd := machine_code.wopr + machine_code.io_cmd(16#13#);
--   Cmd := 16#5213#;
Ra := machine_code.R5;
machine_code.L (machine_code.R5, dato'address, machine_code.SP);
machine_code.L (machine_code.R6, Cmd'address, machine_code.SP);
machine_code.Xio(machine_code.R5, 0, machine_code.R6);
-- I get out the registers from the stack
machine_code.Popm (machine_code.R5,machine_code.R6);

procedure change_to_C2 (np: in integer; dato:out integer) is
-- This procedure receives a page number and calculates the
-- value that must be placed in the page register
x:integer;
begin
-- 2 complement calculation
 x:= 255 -np+1;
-- Add 16#F000# (= 10#3840#) to the result.
x:= -1*(3840 + x);
dato:=x;
end change_to_C2;
```

This solution, once tested, was proposed by the SW development team of the OMC Application Software to the ESA Engineers due to the restriction imposed by the ESA to software developers enjoining them not to use low level functions. The ESA gave its OK to the solution, but taking into account that such a solution could be used for the other INTEGRAL instruments, it was decided that the function would be included as part of the CSSW.

5   High Level Memory Management

5.1   OMC Functional Description

Once it was decided how to use all the memory necessary from one AS, the problem was now the management of the large amount of data that the OMC instrument produces to be telemetered to ground. First we shall give a brief description of the instrument functionality.

The OMC uses a **CCD** of 1024x1024 pixels of visible imaging area. This area is exposed to the sky during the exposure time telecommanded from ground and an image is recorded in its pixels. Afterwards the image is transferred to the storage area of the CCD and from here, once the analog data is converted to digital values, these are sent to the RAM memory of the DPE. The data transferred consist of 16 bits per pixel (1 word): 12 bits with the pixel counts and 4 with value 0.

Around the visible image area of the CCD, there is also an occult area which could be used to detect the dark current. This occult part is also transferred from the image area to the storage area.

OMCAS is in charge of command the transfer from the storage area to the memory, and, in order to command this transfer; OMCAS shall send, via a serial line, the coordinates and the size of the portion of the image (section) from CCD storage area to be transferred. It is also possible to command the binning. That is to say, the number of pixels whose counts (each time that a pixel receives a specific amount of photons the count of the energy received is increased by one) are added in a single word sent to the memory.

The main science capabilities of the instrument are included in the following operation modes:

Normal Mode: This mode is used when it is necessary to extract from the CCD up to 400 portions of image stored in the DPE RAM obtained by SW processing (windows), each one sized from 5x5 to 11x11 pixels. Before extracting the windows from the CCD a centering algorithm is used in order to ensure that the windows extracted are in the correct position. To perform the centering algorithm up to 10 windows of 31x31 pixels window size are extracted. This mode is used if the integration time is higher than 10 seconds, if this time is lower a slightly different mode, the Fast Monitoring Mode, will be used. The only difference between both modes is the above mentioned integration time.

Dark Current (DC) Calibration Mode: This mode is used to extract the left and right borders of the visible imaging area. The maximum section size to be extracted during this mode is a section of 16x1024 pixels.

Flat Field (FF) Calibration Mode: This mode is used to extract large sections from the CCD with or without switching on one of the Light Emitting Diodes (LEDs) in order to calibrate the CCD and detect damaged pixels. The maximum section size to be extracted during this mode is 1064x1033 pixels.

5.2   Memory Solutions Adopted

Different memory management solutions were adopted to manage each of the different images types corresponding to each mode:

Normal and Fast Monitoring Modes: The following data structures will be used in these modes:

1. To store the data extracted from the CCD an array is used. It stores 8 lines of the CCD (CCD FIFO size) in 2 consecutive logical pages associated to 2 consecutive physical pages.

   ```
   type T_VAR_HSL is array (1..8,1..1024) of T_UNSIGNED_16;
   ```

2. To store the pixels of the windows the T_WINDOWS structure is used. It contains the data of 40 windows and is stored in 1 page. The variable fits in 1 logical page and is associated dynamically to 10 different physical pages to achieve a total window storage size of 400 different windows. OMCAS extract all the pixels of each line (1024 pixels, 16 bits per pixel) from the CCD. Afterwards the pixels forming part of the selected windows are stored in the array (T_WINDOW) of the corresponding window. As the pixels provide a value between 0 and $2^{12} - 1$, only 12 of the 16 bits of each pixel have a useful value and therefore, in order to save memory, there remaining four bits will not be used and just 12 bits are stored:

```
type t_pixels_compressed is record
  pixel1: CSSW_COMMON_TYPES.T_UNSIGNED_12;
  pixel2: CSSW_COMMON_TYPES.T_UNSIGNED_12;
  pixel3: CSSW_COMMON_TYPES.T_UNSIGNED_12;
  pixel4: CSSW_COMMON_TYPES.T_UNSIGNED_12;
 record;
for t_pixels_compressed use
 record
  pixel1 at 0 range 0..11;
  pixel2 at 0 range 12..23;
  pixel3 at 0 range 24..35;
  pixel4 at 0 range 36..47;
end record;
for t_pixels_compressed'size use 48;

type T_WINDOW is array (1..31) of t_pixels_compressed;
for T_WINDOW'size use  1488;

type T_WINDOWS is array (1..40) of T_WINDOW;
```

3. To synchronize the Normal task (which extracts the pixels from the CCD) and the TM task (which sends them to ground) the following structure is used:

```
type T_R_WIN_NORMAL is record
        tar_rank : integer;
        type_tar : CSSW_COMMON_TYPES.T_UNSIGNED_2;
        x_tar : CSSW_COMMON_TYPES.T_UNSIGNED_11;
        y_tar : CSSW_COMMON_TYPES.T_UNSIGNED_11;
        tar_size_tc : CSSW_COMMON_TYPES.T_UNSIGNED_2;
        tar_size : CSSW_COMMON_TYPES.T_UNSIGNED_4 ;
        phys_page: CSSW_COMMON_TYPES.T_UNSIGNED_8;
        status: CSSW_COMMON_TYPES.T_UNSIGNED_3;
end record;

type T_V_WIN_NORMAL is array (1..400) of T_R_WIN_NORMAL;
```

This data is shared between the Science task and the TMSC task because the latter needs this data to build the science TM packets. The phys_page defines the physical page where the NORMAL task has stored previously the window and is used by the TM task to perform the logical-physical association. The status field is used to synchronize both tasks and define the three different possibilities of a window filling:

- full (all the pixels of the window have been extracted from the CCD and therefore it can be telemetered)
- half full or empty (some pixels or none of the window pixels have been extracted from the CCD)
- sent (the window has been telemetered to ground).

The following basic algorithm will be used during the Normal and Fast Monitoring (FM) modes:

1. Obtain the TC information concerning the windows to be extracted
2. Order the windows to be extracted by row,the low row value first
3. When the integration is finished:
   (a) Extract an 8Kwords section (the lower 8 rows of the CCD) in the T_VAR_HSL structure
   (b) Select the pixels of the T_VAR_HSL structure that are part of the windows to be extracted and store them in the T_WINDOWS structure and change the status field of the T_V_WIN_NORMAL.
   (c) Repeat step 3a until all the windows are extracted.

At the same time, the TM task is executing itself, looking for full windows in the T_V_WIN_NORMAL data structure. Obviously, the windows will be filled in the order in which they are stored in the structure, therefore, usually, all the windows stored in an AS are filled before changing to the next one and so the number of AS changes are reduced.

DC Calibration Mode: To store the pixels of the windows extracted from the CCD two possibilities are considered:

1. To use a variable stored in 4 logical pages (and 4 physical pages) as follows: To store the pixels of the windows extracted the following structure is used.

```
type T_WINDOW_DC is array (1..4096) of t_pixels_compressed;
```

To store two windows, two variables of this type will be used.
2. To use a variable stored in 1 logical page and 4 physical pages and dynamically change the logical¡-¿physical association:

```
type T_WINDOW_DC is array (1..1024) of t_pixels_compressed;
```

To store two windows, two variables of this type will be used.

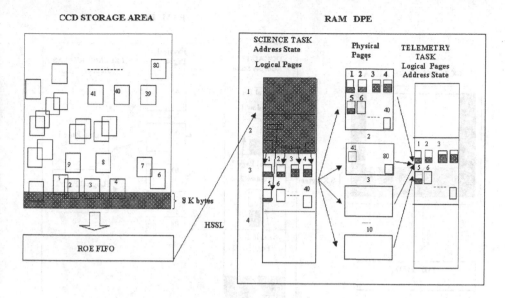

Fig. 3. Normal and FM science modes

The first option will be used if there are enough logical pages free in the AS. The following basic algorithm will be used during the DCCalibration mode:

1. Command the integration and wait until it is finished.
2. Extract 8 lines of the CCD section in the T_VAR_HSL structure.
3. Obtain pixels corresponding to windows to be extracted from the T_VAR_HSL structure and store them in the T_WINDOW_DC structure
4. Repeat 2 until both windows are completely extracted.

FFCalibration Mode: To store the pixels of the window the following structures are used:

```
type T_V_FF_STATUS_PHYS_PAGES is array (1..50) of
CSSW_COMMON_TYPES.T_UNSIGNED_2;

type T_V_FF_ADDRESS_PHYS_PAGES is array (1..50) of
CSSW_COMMON_TYPES.T_UNSIGNED_16;

type T_WINDOW_FF is array (1..4,1..1024) of
CSSW_COMMON_TYPES.T_UNSIGNED_16;
```

The T_WINDOW_FF structure is used to store the pixels read. One variable and is stored in a Logical Page and associated dynamically to different physical pages. The T_V_FF_STATUS_PHYS_PAGES array is used to store the status of each physical page: half full (blocked), full, half included in a TM packet or

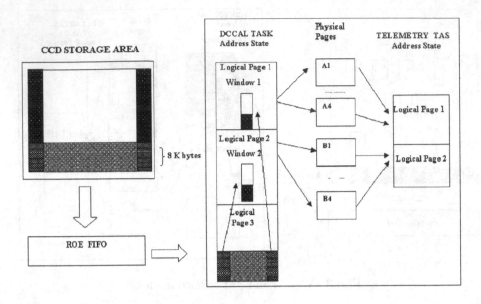

Fig. 4. Dark current calibration mode

free. OMCAS will reuse the physical pages for storing new data when they are sent to ground. The T_V_FF_ADDRESS_PHYS_PAGES array is used to store the address of the corresponding physical pages.

The following basic algorithm will be used during the FFCalibration mode:

1. Command the integration and wait until it is finished.
2. Obtain a section of the window to be extracted not greater than 4Kpixels and with a integer number of lines in the T_WINDOW_FF structure associated to a free physical page and afterwards change the page status and the logical¡-¿ physical page association to the next free physical page.
3. Repeat 2 using the free physical pages until the window is completely extracted.

6   Conclusions

To solve the problem we have to face up, not only the high level problems but also the low level details.

While the high level design was performing, it was necessary to test some low level implementation details, that could be problematic, trying to solve them as soon as possible because the solution adopted could affect the general design. Our

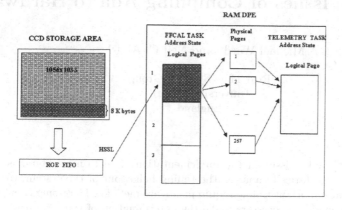

Fig. 5. FFCalibration mode

system shows that some times is not possible to perform a top-down approach and it is necessary to mix it with low level subjects.

Although theoretically the low level questions have to be managed in the detail design phase, it is obvious that real time applications require to pay especial attention to the implementation details, not only those related to time restrictions, but also, as in our case, to those related to memory management.

Moreover, it should be taken into account that this type of SW, which requires the use of old technologies, implies to adopt imaginative solutions that are not necessary when there are surplus HW resources.

We expect our solution could be useful to solve this kind of memory management problems.

References

1. TLD Systems LTD: Reference Document for the TLD Run Time System
2. TLD Systems LTD: Reference Document for the TLD Macro Assembler, Linker and Utilities
3. TLD Systems LTD: Reference Document for the TLD Debugger
4. J.G.P.Barnes: Programacion en ADA ISBN:84-86251-52-4. EDICIONES Diaz de Santos.
5. Karl A. Nyberg: The Annotated Ada Reference Manual ANSI/MIL-STD-1815-1983 (Annotated)

Language Issues of Compiling Ada to Hardware

Michael Ward* and Neil C. Audsley

Real Time Systems Group
University of York
England

Abstract. A key issue in the implementation of real-time systems is the ability to statically analyse the timing behaviour of the system, to ensure that important timing requirements are met. The increasing complexity of modern processors make the determination of the worst-case execution time of software difficult via analytical means.
This paper discusses the compilation of Ada programs directly to hardware circuits, so removing the need for a processor. The solution is discussed in terms of Ada (specifically a Ravenscar / SPARK subset). The contributions of the paper are twofold. Firstly, the compilation of Ada to hardware (Field-Programmmable Gate Arrays) is described. Secondly, issues with the Ada language are addressed. These relate to processor concepts (eg. interrupts, representation clauses) that are embodied in the language that need to be modified for compilation to hardware.

1 Introduction

Real-Time Systems are those where the timing of an output is as important as the accuracy of its value. Often, these types of systems have to be proved correct in both the functional and time domains. Confidence in the timing of the software is achieved through static analysis[4]:

1. *Worst-Case Execution Time (WCET) Analysis* - Each basic block of the program is examined for its execution time. The longest path through the program is then found, and the worst case execution time for each process can be calculated.
2. *Scheduling Analysis* - Since a number of the processes in the system will run on a single processor, it has to be shown that they will all meet their deadlines despite interference from the other processes.

Calculating the WCET of a basic block can be done simply by adding together the execution times of the individual instructions. This gives an accurate WCET only when every single instruction takes the time given in the data book, and there are no other delays. This only occurs with legacy processors (e.g. Z80 or 68000) which have no architectural speed up features. Modern processors include speed-up features (e.g. pipelines, branch prediction units) that make

---

* This work was supported by EPSRC and BAE SYSTEMS

J. Blieberger and A. Strohmeier (Eds.): Ada-Europe 2002, LNCS 2361, pp. 88–99, 2002.

WCET analysis difficult. Despite much work on this (e.g. [8][12]) high levels of pessimism still plague the WCET analysis process.

This paper addresses the issue of pessimism reduction or removal by utilising general purpose hardware rather than CPU's for the target implementation. This change of implementation medium raises issues with the Ada language definition, which are discussed later.

1.1 FPGA Background

Field Programmable Gate Arrays (FPGAs) were first released by Xilinx in 1985[21]. An FPGA provides a grid of logic, memory blocks and connections with which a circuit can be built up (figure 1). Each logic cell can perform a number of logic functions, and also store some data in registers. The connections in the FPGA allow any logic cell to be connected to any other. These features allow complicated and large circuits to be programmed into the chip.

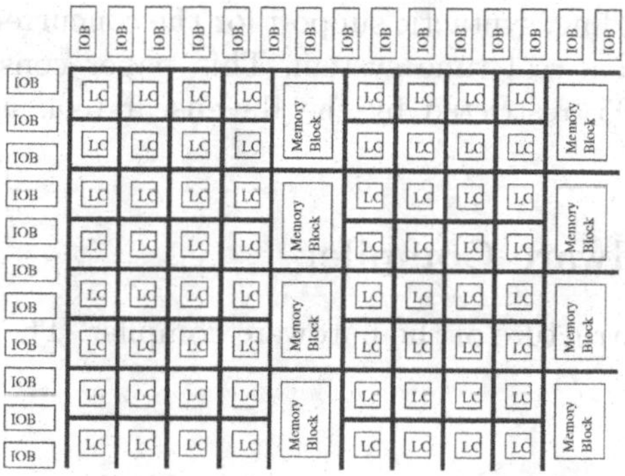

Fig. 1. FPGA structure. This shows the top left corner of an FPGA with memory blocks as well as logic cells. The programmable routing is shown as thick lines.

FPGAs can be reprogrammed in milliseconds, simply by changing their configuration bitstream. The bitstream is created by vendor tools from a high-level circuit description (e.g. VHDL).

1.2 Hardware Compilation Background

There are two forms of language available for hardware compilation:

- *Hardware Description Language (HDL)* - A typical HDL (e.g. VHDL [19], Pebble [13] and SL [9]) allows a hierarchical description of a circuit. Each block in the circuit can be described in terms of lower level blocks, and the connections between them, or a functional description of the block, possibly with other blocks used in this description.

– *High Level Language (HLL)* - A HLL allows the programmer to describe the functionality of the circuit using normal programming syntax. All translation to and arrangement of the final circuit is done by the compiler.

HDLs are unsuited to the implementation of software-based real-time systems. They have no communication constructs (though VHDL++ [6] proposes these), or timing facilities (e.g. delays and clocks) both of which are important to real-time programming languages [4]. HDLs provide coarse grained parallelism support through the circuit block structure.

There have been several implementations of HLLs for hardware compilation. Most of these are based on the C language (e.g. Handel-C [3], Transmogrifier C [7] and BRASS [5]), though Occam (Handel [16]) and Java (Xilinx Forge [21]) have been used. These languages are not suitable for real-time compilation as they do not provide the high-level communication and programming-in-the-large facilities required for real-time systems software.

Hardware compilation for real-time systems requires the support of a true real-time language by a hardware compiler. A real-time language has a number of requirements[4] including, syntactic support for the concurrency, communication and timing needs of a real time system. This paper considers the hardware compilation of Ada95, restricted by the Ravenscar (concurrent) and SPARK (sequential) subsets.

2   Ada95 Hardware Compiler

Figure 2 shows the structure of the hardware compiler. The four passes it takes are:

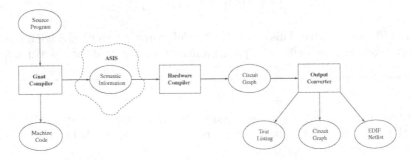

Fig. 2. Hardware compiler structure

1. *Parsing and Semantic Analysis* - The source program is compiled by the GNAT Ada compiler[1], which generates conventional code as well as the semantic information used by the Ada Semantic Interface Specification (ASIS)

---

[1] The GNAT Ada compiler is a fully validated Ada95 compiler, the public domain version is available from `ftp.cs.nyu.edu`

[2]. The latter allows access to the syntactic and semantic information produced by the existing compiler during the compilation process.

2. *Variable Analysis* - All the source code is scanned for the usage of variables. This ensures that the implementation of a variable does not interfere with its use in expressions, for example a single ported array cannot be used twice in a single expression.

3. *Circuit Graph Generation* - The program is converted to circuit form through template instantiation of the statement forms in the program. The circuit generated is an intermediate representation of a graph containing all the cells and interconnections in the final circuit.

4. *Output Generation* - The circuit graph is converted to one of three forms, either textual, graphical, or an EDIF (Electronic Design Interchange Format) netlist which can be converted to a configuration file for use on an FPGA.

A full description of the compilation process, can be found in [20].

3   Timing Analysis

This section compares the WCET analysis of the FPGA and conventional implementations. Consider the compilation of the Ada procedure given in figure 3. It is assumed, for the purpose of this evaluation, that the value of n is never more than 20, enabling the maximum number of loop iterations to be known.

```
procedure trisum (n : in integer;
                  sum : out integer) is
      -- declarations
      tri : integer;
   begin
      -- Procedure body code
      --   transforms to data and control structures
      sum := 0;
      for i in 1..n loop
         tri := 0;
         for j in 1..i loop
            tri := tri + j;
         end loop;
         sum := sum + tri;
      end loop;
   end trisum;
```

Fig. 3. Example Ada procedure. This calculates the sum of all triangular numbers up to the given parameter.

The comparison will be done across a number of timing analyses:

- *Naive* - A naive worst case analysis assumes that the worst possible timings will always happen (e.g. every memory access is a cache miss, every loop executes the maximum number of times).
- *Model* - A modelled worst case applies knowledge about the architecture to the timing analysis. This results in the effects of caches and pipelines being included in the final result.
- *Path* - Semantic analysis of the program will result in improved knowledge of loop bounds and paths through the program. Together with modelling the architecture, semantic analysis produces a great improvement in the analysed WCET.
- *Expected* - This is the average expected execution time of the longest path. This figure is analysed with a realistic view of caching and pipeline effects.

The results of these analyses are shown in table 1. The clock cycle figures for the two implementations given in table 1 cannot be compared directly, as they run at vastly differing clock speeds. Instead, the timings need to be used.

Analysis	Clock Cycles		Time (ms)	
	FPGA	CPU	FPGA	CPU
Naive	1323	341,666	0.066	0.683
Model	1323	77,766	0.066	0.155
Path	753	44,602	0.038	0.089
Expected	753	13,122	0.038	0.026

Table 1. The WCET timings of FPGA and conventional implementations of the example procedure given in figure 3. The time figures use a 20MHz clock for the FPGA and a 500MHz clock for the processor.

3.1 FPGA WCET Analysis

In the FPGA the WCET of the compiled circuit is almost exactly the same as its average case (the difference comes from certain paths in if statements taking longer than others), see table 1. The inner loop takes three clock cycles per iteration (as there are three states in the inner loop); the outer loop takes five cycles, plus the time taken for the inner loop to complete. The procedure itself will take 3 cycles, plus the time for the outer loop to complete its iterations. Given that n is never more than 20, the maximum number of cycles for the procedure to complete is 1323 cycles. The semantics of the loop can be, through path analysis [17][18], used to reduce this number to 753 cycles.

3.2   Conventional WCET Analysis

Analysing the conventional implementation can be done by adding up the times for each instruction, then modifying it to take account of the architectural speed-up features of the target processor. Using the Intel 80486 architecture as an example, the inner loop takes 58 cycles, the outer loop 45 cycles, and the code outside the loop 46 cycles. A naive assumption to make is that no instructions are pre-fetched, and that every memory access is a cache miss. Assuming a cache miss cost of 30 cycles, a WCET of 341,666 cycles is reached.

A more realistic WCET can be arrived at through modelling the effects of the pipeline and cache. The size of the code means that there would be very few instruction cache misses, but data accesses cannot be modelled as accurately. Recent work [11, 14] has shown that data cache accesses can be modelled. The number of jumps in the machine code negates the effects of the pipeline (as every jump requires the pipeline to be refilled) producing the result of 77,766 cycles. Including path analysis produces a further reduction in the WCET to 44,602.

3.3   Discussion

It can be seen that the speed up of the FPGA over a CPU implementation (for the path analysis) is around 2.4 times. This improvement is due to the much lower pessimism in the analysis of the FPGA implementation. The fact that the measured timings are in favour of the processor implementation shows that the worst case analysis of the FPGA implementation is much easier to do accurately than a conventional implementation.

In table 1, the expected execution times suggest that the conventional implementation executes approximately a third faster than the FPGA. However, the FPGA allows true concurrency. Consider two concurrent copies of the procedure in figure 3, on a conventional processor, these would have to be executed serially, taking 0.052ms, whereas on the FPGA, two copies of the circuit can be constructed and executed in parallel, still taking only 0.037ms for both processes.

4   Ada Issues

There are a number of references in the Ada language specification[1] to processor based implementations of the language. Some of these presume the attributes of a processor when defining the way the language should behave, and be implemented. This has no effect on the implementation of the sequential form of Ada, but does when the implementation specific parts of the language are used.

4.1   Representation Clauses

When trying to integrate a control program running on a processor into an application system, the program communicates with the hardware through interface logic. This logic generally has a series of registers that allow them to be controlled by the program. In order for the program to access these registers, the variables in the program need to be attached to them in some way. In Ada, this is done with representation clauses. These allow the way a variable is represented, and where it is stored, to be declared within the program.

Representation clauses that describe the way a variable is stored are easy to include in the hardware compiler. In fact, part of this is already implemented - variables are created only for the width they need to be, not to the word size of the target processor.

The problem with representation clauses is when they are used to attach variables to hardware registers. The Ada language specification requires that this be done using an address, which works well in a processor based implementation as the registers just have to appear in the memory map, but not in an FPGA implementation as these devices do not inherently have a memory map. The solution adopted is to include many small memory maps can be included in the circuit. Most hardware devices have multiple registers arranged as a small block of memory (which makes them easy to fit into a memory map). A register is linked to a pair of variables, one acting as the data bus to the device, the other the address bus, which would need to be given a fixed value. These variables are attached directly to device pins. Figure 4 shows an example of how a four register device can be connected into a program.

When connecting a variable to the system off-chip, a port has to be created first. This is a specific type, whose only purpose is to create a connection between the program and the outside world. A port will act much like an address, allowing variables to be connected to it. A new library `fpga` has been created to hold the FPGA specific extensions to the language. The naming conventions of chip packages preclude the use of ranges in the specification of the pins to be used as physically adjacent pins can have wildly different logical names.

4.2   Run-Time Issues

Priorities Priorities are mainly used to order the execution of tasks in a concurrent environment. Since the hardware implementation gives a truly parallel environment, priorities are no longer required for this purpose. This leaves the question of whether they are needed for other purposes. They can be used to regulate access to protected objects through the queueing protocols used to control the order of access, but, as noted below, this style of queueing is expensive in a hardware implementation. If some other form of queueing protocol is used, then the priorities are no longer needed in the system at all. This greatly simplifies the design process as there will be no need to assign priorities and prove that these priorities allow the set to be scheduled.

Blocking and Queueing Policies When accessing a protected object, a task will be queued or blocked if it cannot gain access immediately. When trying to access an entry, the task will be queued. If it tries to access a protected procedure or function it will be blocked. This distinction means that they need to be treated differently.

```
port_1 : fpga.port(8);
for port_1'pins use
    fpga.pins_to_port("p1", "p3", "p2", "p5", "p9", "p8", "p7", "p10");
port_2 : fpga.port(2);
for port_2'pins use fpga.pins_to_port("p21", "p25");
LCD_port : fpga.port(4);
for LCD_port'pins use fpga.pis_to_port("p45", "p65", "p47", "p57");
debug : integer range 0..15;
for debug'port use LCD_port;

    -- packed record definitions of reg1 through reg4
    -- defined as for a processor based application

for reg1'data_port use port_1;
for reg1'addr_port use fpga.address_port'(port2, 0);
for reg2'data_port use port_1;
for reg2'addr_port use fpga.address_port'(port2, 1);
for reg3'data_port use port_1;
for reg3'addr_port use fpga.address_port'(port2, 2);
for reg4'data_port use port_1;
for reg4'addr_port use fpga.address_port'(port2, 3);
```

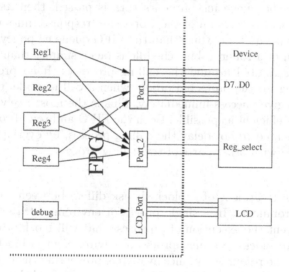

Fig. 4. Connecting a device to a program using the preferred solution. The diagram shows the registers that are created from the code given above. The device has four eight bit registers, so needs an 8-bit data bus, and a 2-bit address bus, these connections are created as an eight-bit port (port_1) and a two bit port (port_2), which are connected to the specified pins. The 'reg' variables are then connected to these ports, the data being transmitted through port_1, and the value on port_2 being set as indicated during accesses. Since the LCD has only one register, no address port is needed, so the debug variable can be connected directly to the LCD_port port.

Queueing In both single- and multiprocessor systems, a queued task is suspended until it can gain access, and other tasks can be run in the meantime. The parallel implementation closely resembles the latter of these two types. The Ada reference manual defines two queueing policies - FIFO and ICP, and allows compilers to define additional policies. ICP is a priority based system, and given that priorities can be removed from the system it is preferable that this policy is not used. FIFO (First-In, First-Out) queueing allows the process that has been waiting longest to proceed when the resource becomes available. This policy has a bounded Worst Case Response Time(WCRT) (the sum of the WCRT of each process that accesses the protected object), but has a fairly high cost in terms of the logic required to implement it. This is due to it being a priority based method with the priorities being based on time (and therefore dynamic). This requires the construction of a priority encoder, able to cope with as many tasks as need to access.

A better solution for the queueing policy is required. This new policy must not have a worse response time than FIFO, but should be smaller to implement in hardware. One policy that fits these requirements is the round-robin schedule. In this, each process gets one access in turn, if a process is not queued when its turn comes round, then it is ignored, and the next process gets its chance. If a process joins the queue just after its turn is passed, then its response time (in the worst case) is the sum of the worst case response times of all the other processes. This makes it no worse than the FIFO queueing policy. The hardware implementation of a round robin schedule is much simpler than that for FIFO, and can be distributed around the calling processes. If no process is queued on, or executing in, the protected object when a call is made, then the calling process can be given access immediately. This is the most likely case of events, so should be as efficient as possible. Both the FIFO and round-robin approaches can be implemented to not delay the calling process, by overlapping the access contention logic with other parts of the calling process.

Blocking The treatment of a blocked task differs between single and multiprocessor environments. In a single processor environment a scheduling policy is used to prevent the execution of a process that will block or could cause another process to block. In a multiprocessor environment, a blocked process can spin-lock until the resource becomes available, preventing the execution of other tasks on the same processor. If blocking occurs for extended periods, tasks can start to miss their deadlines.

Use of a scheduling policy requires that the processes are assigned a priority which can be used to schedule the access to the protected resources. By removing the need for scheduling, it had been intended to remove the need for priorities entirely, so a different solution would be preferred. If the implementation of tasks is treated as a multi-processor system with each task being placed on a single processor, then the use of spin-locks is less wasteful. This is because a spin-locking task can only delay itself, there being no other tasks trying to use the same computational resources.

As the access to a protected subprogram is no longer being controlled through priorities, there is a need to define an ordering of access for the blocked processes. For the multiprocessor environment, the order of access is undefined. It is possible, due to the properties of the hardware for a task to suffer starvation, if it is also beaten to gaining access by another task. This also raises problems when considering the WCET of a process, as it requires that all other tasks that access the Protected Object (PO) need to be considered in the calculation of the worst case access time to the PO. Using the round robin approach proposed above allows the access times to be bounded to one worst case access per task, and prevents the chance that a process can suffer starvation.

4.3 Fine-Grain Parallelism

One of the features of FPGAs is their ability to parallelise operations. Hence concurrent tasks can be implemented as parallel circuits. However, there is still a significant amount of fine-grain parallelism available within the sequential code of tasks. Potential savings can be partially realised by evaluating expressions in parallel, but there is often more parallelism available through executing statements in parallel. In general, automatic detection of all potential parallelism in application code during compilation is not possible[15]. Application code must include indication of parallel operations.

For Ada, there are a number of solutions:

- Introduce a pragma 'parallel' that indicates the statements that can be executed in parallel. This does not require a large change in the specification, and provides a means for the programmer to indicate which parts can be parallelised, and by default, those that shouldn't be. The statements immediately inside the parallel pragmas can be executed in parallel, as shown in figure 5. If the compiler cannot provide parallel execution, then the statements will be executed sequentially as normal.
- Add two pragmas 'parallel' and 'sequence'. The parallel pragma would work as before, the sequence pragma would mark those parts of the code that should not be parallelised.
- Change the syntax of the Ada language to include a 'parallel' statement (as in Occam). This provides a syntactic basis for the detection and use of parallelism, allowing it to be controlled by the language specification. This does have some problems however. Due to the explicit nature of the parallelism, the specification for most of the sequential part of the language will need to be altered in the reference manual. This is to allow for the change in static semantics regarding the access of variables. Also this solution would require that existing compilers be rewritten to cope with the added syntax and change in semantics, whereas the previous solutions are pragmas that can be ignored by existing sequential compilers.

The preferred solution is the introduction of the two pragmas 'parallel' and 'sequence'. This allows the compiler to optimise (parallelise) most of the program

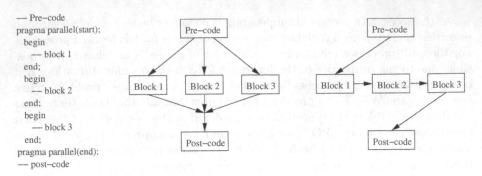

```
— Pre-code
pragma parallel(start);
  begin
    — block 1
  end;
  begin
    — block 2
  end;
  begin
    — block 3
  end;
pragma parallel(end);
— post-code
```

Fig. 5. Parallel compilation example

only ignoring those areas specifically noted by the programmer. The statements immediately within the parallel pragmas can be executed so long as the variable accesses are safe (i.e. no two parallel branches should write to the same variable), and arrays need to be treated with care. Any code outside these pragmas can be parallelised according to current parallelising compiler techniques. These pragmas will also aid the parallelising compilers targeted at processors as they state explicitly where the parallelism is at the syntactic level, rather than trying to search for it at the machine code level.

This method does not require large changes to be made to the language specification, as the restrictions within the parallel pragma is such that the statements within the parallel block can be executed correctly either in parallel or sequence. Whilst the compiler can do some checks on the correctness of the parallel sections (e.g. variable access), it is up to the programmer to write correct algorithms (as in most systems). Concurrent model checkers (e.g. the UPPAAL tool [10]) can be used to prove the correctness of the entire system, since the the parallel parts are merely fine-grained concurrency.

5   Conclusions

This paper has introduced the need for a hardware implementation of the Ada language on FPGAs in order to reduce the pessimism inherent in WCRT analysis. The benefit of this approach has been shown to be the reduction of the WCRT of a process to being less than a half of the processor based implementation.

Some of the issues that the hardware implementation raises with the Ada reference manual have been discussed, and solutions proposed to some of the problems. None of the solutions cause great changes to the Ada specification, but do provide substantial improvements in implementation efficiency for certain compilation targets.

References

[1] *Ada 95 Reference Manual*. Intermetrics, January 1995.

[2] Ada Semantic Interface Specification (ASIS). Technical Report ISO/IEC 15291, IEC, 1999.

[3] M. Bowen. *Handel-C Language Reference Manual*. Embedded Solutions Limited, 2.1 edition, 1998.

[4] A. Burns and A. Wellings. *Real Time Systems and Programming Languages*. Addison Wesley, 2nd edition, 1996.

[5] T. J. Callahan, J. R. Hauser, and J. Wawrzynek. The garp architecture and c compiler. *IEEE Computer*, 33(4):62–69, 2000.

[6] S. Franklid. Manual for VHDL++. Technical report, Dept. Information Technology, DTU Lyngby, 1999.

[7] D. Galloway. The Transmogrifier C Hardware Description Language and Compiler for FPGAs. In *FPGAs for Custom Computing Machines*, 1995.

[8] C. A. Healy, D. B. Whalley, and M. G. Harmon. Integrating the Timing Analysis of Pipelining and Instruction Caching. In *Proceedings of the 16th Symposium on Real-Time Systems*, pages 288–297. IEEE, 1995.

[9] S. Holmstrom. SL - A Structural Hardware Design Language. In *Proceedings of the 9th International Workshop on Field-Programmable Logic and Applications*, volume 1673, pages 371–376. LNCS, Springer-Verlag, 1999.

[10] H. Jensen, K. Larsen, and A. Skou. Scaling up UPPAAL - Automatic verification of real-time systems using compositionality and abstraction. In *Proceedings of Formal Techniques in Real-Time and Fault-Tolerant Systems*, volume 1926, pages 19–30. LNCS, Springer-Verlag, 2000.

[11] Y.-T. S. Li and S. Malik. *Performance Analysis of Real-Time Embedded Software*. Klewer Academic, 1999.

[12] S.-S. Lim, J. H. Han, J. Kim, and S. L. Min. A Worst Case Timing Analysis Technique for Multiple-Issue Machines. In *Proceedings of the 19th IEEE Symposium on Real-Time Systems*, pages 334–345, 1998.

[13] W. Luk and S. McKeever. Pebble: A Language for Parametrised and Reconfigurable Hardware Design. In *Proceedings of FPL '98*, volume 1482, pages 9–18. LNCS, Springer-Verlag, 1998.

[14] T. Lundqvist and P. Stenstrom. A method to improve the estimated worst-case performance of data caching. In *Proc. of the 6th Int. Con. on Real-Time Computing Systems and Applications (RTCSA'99)*, pages 255–262, December 1999.

[15] S. S. Muchnick. *Advanced Compiler Design and Implementation*. Morgan Kaufmann, 1997.

[16] I. Page and W. Luk. Compiling Occam into FPGAs. In *FPGAs*, pages 271–283. Abingdon EE&CS Books, Abingdon, UK, 1991.

[17] C. Y. Park. Predicting Program Execution Times by Analyzing Static and Dynamic Paths. *Real-Time Systems*, 5(1):31–62, 1993.

[18] P. Puschner and C. Koza. Calculating the Maximum Execution Time of Real-Time Programs. *Real-Time Systems*, 1(2):159–176, 1989.

[19] VHDL Language Reference Manual. Technical Report 1076-1993, ANSI/IEEE, 1993.

[20] M. Ward and N. C. Audsley. Hardware Compilation of Sequential Ada. In *Proceedings of CASES 2001*, pages 99–107, 2001.

[21] Xilinx product information : http://www.xilinx.com/products, 2001.

Software Development Reengineering - An Experience Report

Adrian Hoe

Lexical Integration Sdn Bhd
67 Jalan Bunga Raya
75100 Melaka, Malaysia
byhoe@greenlime.com

Abstract. Decisions regarding the disposition of an existing multilingual environments can have an enormous effect on the operations, even survival, of commercial and government organizations. Many organizations are grappling with trade-offs of older development tools and moving into more modern and efficient programming languages as advertised, while trying to leverage production capabilities and to reduce cost. In some cases, product reliability is not an important factor in decision making! Lexical is facing these difficult decisions and the clock is ticking. In an effort of searching for a programming language that fits into our development requirement, the company successfully addressed many of the hard issues facing commercial executives and managers today. This paper provides valuable insights and model for actions, through Lexical's experience, which can help making better decisions and formulate strategies in transition management. Many factors contribute to the success and survival of the company during transition, one of them is to assess learning curves of many different individuals.

1   Introduction and Overview

In the modern world, businesses and government organizations are constantly subject to drastic changes in daily operation and management. All occupations, CEOs, managers, financial planners, administrative personnel, executives, technical experts, and support staff are being constantly peppered with new technologies and different methods of running organization. Regardless of your occupation or type and size of business, you have one thing in common with everyone else: competition!

Lexical Integration Sdn Bhd is a young and dynamic software development company in Malaysia. The company is engaged in a wide variety of projects, including research and development of high-performance, application-specific software systems. The company also has a track record for delivering complex application software solutions to a broad range of businesses and governments. Lexical is no exception from the cruelty of this modern trend. As modern software systems become increasingly more complex and critical, clients are faced with ever more choices and developers are confronted with even more challenges.

J. Blieberger and A. Strohmeier (Eds.): Ada-Europe 2002, LNCS 2361, pp. 100–112, 2002.

The company must find ways to maximize profit to maintain the endless development cycles and at the same time, to assert product quality to continue its survival. Regardless of your role in a commercial business or a government organization, the insights contained in this paper can be of benefit, and help you achieve and keep a competitive advantage.

Although the project involved the reengineering of specific software for furniture industry, the experience is very likely to be applicable across many commercial and government domains. The critical necessity for migrating from older software technologies to modern software architectures crosses boundaries of virtually every application domain in the internationally competitive software marketplace.

1.1   Reengineering Multilingual Systems

Lexical was faced with maintaining a complex software system, developed in a multilingual environment, which provided important capabilities to its users. While the clients were satisfied with the system, Lexical was awarded the contract to upgrade the existing software with its increasingly expensive and difficult to maintain software written for a proprietary, "non-open" hardware platform to support a cross-platform environment. As maintainability of the code decreased, support and maintenance costs were rocketing sky-high.

Initially, the development team was directed to re-host the application, and move it to an open systems architecture. Basically, this effort involved translating the existing code from Paradox, Clipper, COBOL, FORTRAN, and Pascal into C. Although some of the resulting code functioned properly, and the application was moved to an open system architecture, the code itself was even less maintainable than the original software. As the team continued working on other modules of the application, they encountered portability issues. The re-host was immediately halted.

The development team was then directed to conduct a study on existing software systems and the next generation software systems they were going to develop and to find a solution to contain the exorbitant maintenance and support cost. Otherwise, they would lose the client. The study was to include an analysis, evaluation, and recommendations to the company as to future directions for all software development. The recommendations for the future were to ensure the continuing satisfaction of the company's clients and their user community, lower maintenance and support costs, and quality products with shorter time-to-market. The study showed the software system needed to be reengineered to provide future user needs, and the team recommended a blend of technologies and methods, including a layered, object-oriented software architecture, implemented in the Ada programming language. The resulting reengineered system produced a threefold improvement in maintainability of software. Additionally, the reengineered system has enabled new functionality to be added with minimum effort and time required at lower cost.

1.2   Maintainability Index and Metrics

The decision to reengineer the software system and the company software development environment is difficult to justify without appropriate metrics. To justify the decision, specific metrics were collected and analyzed to provide indicators of system maintainability and complexity. These metrics with independently developed polynomial equations have been used by some organizations to calculate a "maintainability index" which provides an indication of the maintainability of a software system. This maintainability index has shown the ability to help in providing sound economic justification for reengineering the software system as well as engineering of new software projects.

1.3   The Role of Software Architecture

The original version of the software system had been developed using functional decomposition methodology and typically made extensive use of proprietary platform features, operating system calls, and specific language constructs which severely hampered maintenance, reuse, and portability. These differences in the underlying software architecture had contributed significantly to the high costs of development, maintenance, and support. There would be lack of benefits to be derived from the reengineering efforts if the old software architecture was to remain.

The development team used an object-oriented layered software architecture to overcome the increasing difficulties in development and maintenance throughout the software life cycle. By using layers and object-oriented design for the application, interface, graphics, operating system, and hardware, the development team was able to deliver superb quality products and benefits to the client. The resulting new software system has not only significantly increased the return of investment for the client, but also productivity, competitiveness, and profitability of the company.

2   Project Background

ƒMRP is an integrated Manufacturing Resource Planning (MRP) for furniture industry in Malaysia. The software supports specific and complex requirements of some of the many furniture manufacturers in the country. Basically, the software helps the users in managing, planning, executing, and monitoring their daily operation. The software is also a data-mining tool to help making management decisions.

The original version of ƒMRP, referred to as V1, consists of 20 modules which were developed using various programming languages on DOS/Windows platforms. The software utilized ODBC to interface with various databases including flat-files, Paradox, .dbf, and InterBase. V1 reached its maturity in 1993 and version 2.0 or V2 was released. Like its predecessor, V2 was developed in aforesaid programming languages and ran only on Windows and NT platforms with Sybase and InterBase as the back-end database. In 1999, a completely Ada-reengineered version 3.0 or V3 was implemented and hosted on Linux. It was originally developed to target Sun Solaris but the 1997 global economy crisis had forced the client to reduce their budget. It was the layered object-oriented software architecture that enabled the development team to quickly re-target the software development to Linux with the underlying standard X11 implementation. InterBase 4 or IB4 was selected as the back-end database server for V3.

The benefits that V3 provides to its users including data-mining capabilities, real-time production monitoring, and accurate forecast are significantly critical to enable decisive actions and plans to be formulated. V3 also provides absolute inter-operability among departmental clusters that can share common data in near real-time. V1 was originally developed as stand-alone modules which were integrated along its development and, as V2, were mostly text-based. V3 takes advantage of a color graphics interface to enhance the fundamental capabilities of fMRP, with corresponding benefits to its users.

2.1   Project Evolution

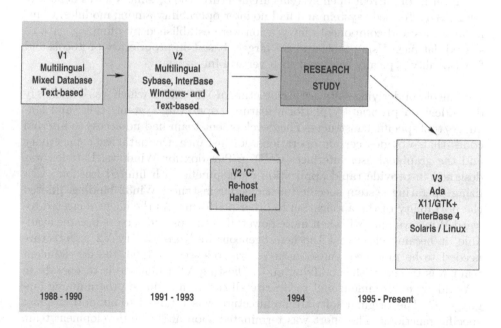

Fig. 1. Historical Overview

The original V1 capability was developed in 1988. The first module was Store Management written in Clipper to maintain stock records and to manage stock requisition and stock flow. It was originally hosted on DOS. The software was designed using a top-down functional decomposition method, with a high degree of language specific dependency. However, it was a success and the software established a track record of successful usage. The client awarded the company to develop other modules and the development began with new programmers joining the team. The development team was divided into many small teams and each team was free to use whichever programming languages or tools they deemed fit to their projects. As examples, FORTRAN was used to develop MRM (Material Requirement Management) to perform calculations of material required, in this case, the volume of rubber wood in tonnage as well as to perform conversion from one unit of measurement to another. The calculation must be precise. Otherwise it would result in insufficiency or wastage of material. V1's text-based SOM (Sales Order Management) was developed in Clipper and was reengineered to V2 using Paradox which provided a nice GUI on Windows. The original text-based PFMM (Production Flow Monitoring and Management) was developed in C and was then ported to Windows in V2. V1's text-based LGM (Logistic Management) which was developed in COBOL was then ported to Delphi (a Pascal-based RAD tool) to provide a nice GUI. Other applications were POM (Purchase Order Management), SFM (Shop Floor Management), etc.

In terms of current open systems architecture, the original V1 was definitely a legendary "closed" system and had no inter-operability among modules. Communications and components integration were established by dumping data to shared flat files. Using tools and OS largely based on proprietary protocols and functionality typically thwarted such vertical integration.

The old underlying software architecture of V1 and V2 which was extensively dependent on proprietary platform features, operating systems calls, and language/tool specific constructs. The development team had no access to internal codes that provided certain operations, for instance, the database connectivity and the graphical user interface (GUI) in Paradox for Windows. Paradox was designed to provide rapid application development with limited freedom. Utilizing operating system specific functions, for instance, Win32 binding, limited the portability of the application to other platforms. As the client migrated toward Windows and NT when more powerful desktops and servers became available, it became clear that the heterogeneous and proprietary V2 architecture needed to be modified. As soon as V2 was released in 1993, the development team was tasked with modifying and re-hosting V2 to enable it to operate in a Windows environment and to rewrite all codes in a single programming language, C. The original software architecture was retained to support product specific functions. The effort was terminated soon after the development team was confronted by portability issues when the client signaled their interest in UNIX. UNIX and Linux allow complete integration of capabilities and methodologies (based on universal, "open" technical standards and protocols) between and amongst hardware and software modules. The other problems encountered were reliability, readability, maintainability, and standardization issues. Figure 1 illustrates the historical overview of the software evolution.

Although the various software implementation were quite successful from the users' perspective, the different language and platform implementations suffered from configuration management (CM) problems. In addition to the CM challenges, the software was becoming more difficult to maintain and modify. In 1994, Lexical realized the existing implementation of V2 would not be adequate to support user needs into the future. At the same time, the clients likewise were aware that the cost of maintaining and modifying the software was becoming unacceptable, and enhancements were exacerbating the complexity of the software system. As a result of these concerns, and in anticipation of expected user requirements in the future, the clients tasked Lexical to provide a total solution, or otherwise trade-off with new software systems. The development team was instantly required to perform a research study for a single programming language that could help increase maintainability of the software and would be able to support, if not all, but most of the development requirements to ascertain the future direction of V2 and the company.

3   Research Study - The Future

The research study, code-named "Holy Grail", included four primary objectives:

1. Determine the objectives and future goals.
2. Analyze the current V2 implementations from a software engineering perspective.
3. Identify current software standards which could apply to V2 and future software projects.
4. Offer recommendations to management on how to achieve the V2 objectives.

Among the objectives and future goals identified for fMRP was the need to provide software which would be more maintainable and modifiable than the existing multilingual code. More easily maintainable code would allow the company to minimize support costs without sacrificing functionality and reliability. More easily modifiable code would enable the client to keep abreast with new user needs and their constantly evolving business rules and quickly adopt emerging technologies into the software systems. The ability to migrate the software to more powerful computer platforms, which enable the company to respond to variety of requirements and budgets, was also a sound objective.

Contemporary industry trends and standards which could apply to fMRP and future projects included a wide spectrum of technologies and tools. Undoubtedly, the need for an open systems architecture was essential and an ongoing requirement for the future. In addition, the use of modern software development methods, such as object-oriented techniques, offered substantial promise for long-term fMRP usage and support.

As the study progressed, it became clear that there were two major factors which had a direct impact on the design and structure of fMRP: the software architecture and the programming language used for implementation. The deficiencies of the original software architecture, with its reliance on hardware-specific features and operating system calls, were perpetuated in the translated C version of the code (V2). The research team concluded that a continuation of the original software architecture would effectively preclude any major improvement in the quality and maintainability of the software.

Since the study was conducted from a software engineering perspective, the role of programming language selection in support of a well-engineered software implementation was included in the evaluation of fMRP. The lack of software engineering principles in the original software prevented improvement in the software. Software engineering was seen as the application of sound engineering principles to the development of systems that were modifiable, efficient, reliable, and understandable. These principles led us to these goals, including abstraction, information hiding, encapsulation, modularity, localization, uniformity, completeness, and confirmability. It became clear that the Ada programming language offered superior support for a reengineered version of fMRP and future software projects. Ada also offered benefits in the application of an object-oriented design for fMRP. As part of their evaluation of object-oriented technologies and techniques, the research team noted the importance of applying object-oriented methods in a disciplined software engineering context, as opposed to focusing on overrated and highly abused object-oriented programming features, such as inheritance and polymorphism. From a design perspective, as well as a software engineering perspective, Ada was a superior choice for the future of fMRP application.

The reengineering effort was an investment in the future, with an expectation of leveraging off that investment to accommodate user needs in a more cost-effective and reliable manner. The research team's bottom line recommendations were as follows:

- Reengineer and redesign the system
- Use object-oriented technologies
- Use the Ada programming language

3.1   Programming Language Selection and Reengineering fMRP

The research team produced a Software Development Plan which set forth and documented the process by which fMRP would be reengineered. The Plan emphasized the use of sound software standards, such as Ada, as well as the disciplined application of software engineering principles. To support the team's recommendation of Ada as the primary programming language, they referred to Albrecht [ALB83] and Jones [JON92] which provided rough estimates of the average number of lines of code required to build one function point in various programming languages as illustrated in Figure 2. To substantiate their recommendation of Ada, they referred to Booch [BOO94a] and concluded object-oriented techniques map well to Ada. In this regard, Ada may serve as both implementation and design language:

> "Within any given computer language, sufficient tools must be provided to allow us to express problem solution. Ideally, we would like to use a language

that *allow us directly reflect our view of problem space*..... In the case where programming from the problem space into a language directly reflects our structure of the problem space, we are presented with an implementation that is understandable and therefore helpful in managing the complexity of the larger systems. Such a language must provide tools for expressing primitive objects and operations and must, in addition, be extensible, so that we can build our own abstract objects and operations. In the best case, we also need our language to enforce these abstractions.... Ada is such a language. Not only Ada is suitable as an implementation language, but *it is expressive enough to serve as a vehicle for capturing our design decisions....*"

The development team followed an iterative lifecycle approach, to ensure flexibility and fast response to changing user requirements.

Programming Language	LOC/FP (Average)
Assembly Language	300
COBOL	100
FORTRAN	100
Pascal	90
Ada	70
Object-oriented languages	30
Fourth-generation languages (4GL)	20
Code generators	15

Fig. 2. Rough estimates of the average number of LOC required to build one function point in various programming languages.[JON92]

The redesign of the software used object-oriented (OO) analysis and design techniques with an implementation in Ada. A hybrid OO methodology was used for the analysis and design, drawing from some well-known OO methodologies offered by Booch [BOO94b], Coad [COA97] and Rumbaugh [RUM91] *et al.* Basically, the development team used the best features of these and combined and adapted them to fit the requirements of ƒMRP software redesign.

The result of the object-oriented redesign of ƒMRP was a reusable layered software architecture, as shown in Figure 3. The new software architecture clearly defines the interfaces between the layers, and implement various pieces and subsystems of ƒMRP in a highly modular manner. The clear delineation between layers and between modules within layers was an explicit design goal to enable ease of maintenance and modifiability of ƒMRP code.

The reusable layered architecture had many benefits. One of the major benefits was the alleviation of risk of using a mix of software technologies and methods. While the research team had recommended the use of solid technologies, such as Ada, object-oriented design, UNIX, GTK, Motif and KDE, these technologies had typically not be combined together all in the same system to provide a seamless development environment. This underlying software architecture allowed the use of hybrid solutions consisting of a mix language, architecture, methodology, and technology for the interfacing with other commercially available products and peripherals.

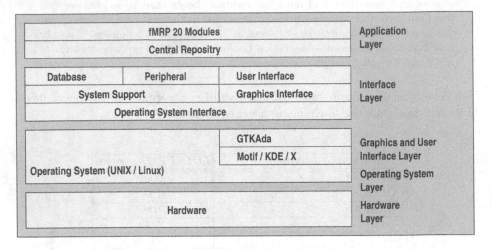

Fig. 3. New Reusable Layered Architecture

Because the team focused on a well-engineered layered software architecture, they were able to apply a wide variety of powerful technologies and methods in a disciplined and cost-effective order. Due to the successful reengineering of *f*MRP using these techniques, methods, and technologies as shown in Figure 4, the company directed the team to reengineer other software systems. These other software systems included SCM (Supply Chain Management), GTM (Government Tender Management), FAM (Fixed Assets Management), etc. All new projects would be engineered in the same manner.

Abstraction	Genericity	Hierarchy	Parameterized Class
Encapsulation	Modularity	Architecture	Concurrency
Information Hiding	Exceptions	Library Units (Package)	Process Improvement
Inheritance	Metrics	Typing	Persistence

Fig. 4. Techniques and Methods

The tasking model of Ada had attracted attention of the team as a possible benefit to multithreaded application such as PFMM (Production Flow Monitoring and Management). Original versions of PFMM were developed with 'C' and used proprietary operating system calls. This led to portability issues and difficulties for maintenance. The research team referred to Burns [BUR95]:

"Ada has language defined concurrency and concurrent activities can be identified explicitly in the code, thus it leads to more readable and maintainable programs. There are many different types of operating system, defining the concurrency in the language makes the program more portable. An embedded computer may not have any resident operating system available..."

4 Risk and Transition Management

Migration is change, and change is stressful if not managed well. Deft navigation of available options is essential, and limited viewpoints can only result in limited results. Given the availability of a wide range of programming languages, today's IT leaders must look past personally limiting viewpoints, eschew "language-loyalty" mindsets, and ensure that technical merit prevails in decision-making. If programmers or software engineers are called upon to learn new programming languages and techniques as part of the migration, this should not be problematic if the people are of good quality. Even so, training will go a long way to smoothing the transition.

The Transition Plan was designed after considering Basili and Zelkowitz's [BAS78] five important factors that influence software productivity:

1. People factors: The size and expertise of the development organization.
2. Problem factors: The complexity of the problem to be solved and the number of changes in design constraints or requirements.
3. Process factors: Analysis and design techniques that are used, languages and CASE tools available, and review techniques.
4. Product factors: Reliability and performance of the computer-based system.
5. Resource factors: Availability of CASE tools, hardware and software resources.

5 Measures of Success

5.1 The Maintainability Index

The most impressive and critical effect of the Ada reengineering effort was the impact on the measured maintainability of the code. The research study had indicated the combination of well-engineered software architectures with object-oriented analysis and design, and implementation written in Ada, would result in software that was more maintainable than code which was developed using top-down methods written in other programming languages. As shown in the chart in Figure 5, the maintainability index (MI) of fMRP was more than three times greater than the index for the equivalent software functions written in other programming languages. The information contained in Figure 6 is based on several software metrics which were collected and analyzed by both research and the development team, leading to the calculation of a "maintainability index" [OMA92] for the fielded software.

Software Baseline	MI	Software Baseline	MI	Software Baseline	MI	Software Baseline	MI
Clipper SOM V1	8.30	COBOL LGM V1	43.21	Clipper SFM	7.96	Ada FAM 2.0	74.53
Paradox SOM V2	13.77	Pascal LGM V2	39.55	Ada SFM	78.02	'C' GTM 1.0	35.11
Ada SOM V3	73.93	Ada LGM V3	77.28	'C' SCM 1.0	34.52	'C' GTM 2.0	31.75
'C' PFMM V1	38.69	FORTRAN MRM	31.85	Ada SCM 1.0	74.45	Ada GTM 1.0	71.65
'C' PFMM V2	33.44	Ada MRM	77.64	Ada SCM 2.0	75.37	Ada GTM 2.0	72.74
Ada PFMM V3	78.71	Paradox POM	15.39	Pascal FAM 4.0	40.13		
Ada PFMM V4	82.13	Ada POM	75.59	Ada FAM 1.0	73.28		

Fig. 5. Maintainability Index (MI) of various software modules of fMRP and other software systems.

$$\text{Maintainability Index} = 171 - 3.42 \times \ln(\text{aveE}) - 0.23 \times \text{aveV}(g') - 16.2 \times \ln(\text{aveLOC})$$

where aveE is average Halstead [HAL77] effort/module, aveV(g') is average extended McCabe [MCC76] [MCC89] cyclomatic complexity/module, and ave-LOC is average LOC/module.

A static analysis of various implementations in Ada and other languages was conducted using PC-Metric, a source code analysis program. The team calculated and used two widely known software metrics, which were Halstead's effort/module; and McCabe's cyclomatic complexity/module, to assess the maintainability of the fMRP family of software. Using the values from the Halstead and McCabe metrics, the team applied a set of field proven polynomial metrics to calculate the maintainability indices for each software baseline. The polynomial metrics were developed at the University of Idaho and have been field-validated by Hewlett-Packard [COL92]. Based on Hewlett-Packard's experience with software, a software package with maintainability index less than 65 is considered to be "difficult to maintain". The research team applied the maintainability index to the fMRP family of software to provide comparison and perspective and to verify that Ada together with modern software technologies had helped the company in reengineering its software development and business.

5.2   Software Complexity

A post-project study had documented increased complexity in many software baselines. The trends were reflected in the maintainability index which showed a nonlinear decrement for the 'C' version of PFMM and GTM from version 1 to 2. Both Ada versions of PFMM and GTM had indicated that maintainability had increased. The maintainability of PFMM had increased significantly due to reengineering of the software concurrency as the development teams were getting more familiar with Ada tasking.

The size of the Ada modules was much smaller than the modules written in COBOL, FORTRAN and C. The FORTRAN MRM baseline was comprised of 86,000 lines of code, with typical use of global data access and FORTRAN subroutines that is common with functionally decomposed software design. By comparison, the Ada implementation of MRM was comprised of 62,000 lines of code. In contrast, the size of the Ada modules was much bigger than the modules written in Paradox (PAL), Clipper and Pascal (Delphi). The Delphi FAM was comprised of 23,000 lines of code. By comparison, the Ada implementation of FAM was comprised of 74,000 lines of code. The reason for this difference was the Rapid Application Development (RAD) environment in which the system support modules like GUI and data access were completely transparent to developers. As in Delphi's RAD environment, an input screen can be developed without the developer writing a single line of code.

5.3   Software Reuse

The team realized a "reuse rate" of 62%, which means that 62% of Ada code modules were reused in one or more applications. This reusable Ada code was the reason for reduced software complexity and lines of code in the overall system and led to more maintainable software.

Smaller, easier to understand modules enabled the use and exploitation of the reusable layered software architecture, with explicit support for the object-oriented design employed by the development team. Reusable software modules had lowered software complexity and increased the responsiveness and quality of support, as the code was more readable and understandable.

5.4   Speed of Development

The speed of development was not taken into account in this reengineering project. This was due to the development team having to learn the Ada programming language and concurrently develop Ada codes. Both the research and development team agreed that the timeline was very dependent on different learning curves of the staff and on the availability of certain technical information in order to develop bindings to hardware peripherals and operating system software.

6   The Benefits of Ada

The benefits of Ada in terms of its explicit support for software engineering discipline and object-oriented design have been cited as major factors in the success of this reengineering project. The Ada language features provided excellent support for the implementation of layered software architecture, as well as the attainment of significant levels of code reuse. Furthermore, Ada's strong typing, parameter checking in subroutine calls, and array constraints contributed to the benefits achieved in this reengineering effort.

In addition to these powerful attributes and benefits, the clarity of Ada source code combined with the structured nature of its package specification and more descriptive names of variables, has a profound effect on software reuse and documentation. Ada software implementations are virtually "self documenting" due to the explicit representation of the functions and interfaces of the respective modules. This additional clarity of the Ada source code pays substantial rewards in the area of maintenance and modification of the software.

Having tasking construction as an intrinsic part of the language, Ada provides greater reliability. Concurrent activities can be identified explicitly in the code, resulting in additional clarity of Ada source code which is more understandable and maintainable. In general, every operating system is different and does not provide the control and timing needed by many applications. Ada tasking solves the problems by providing control and timing needed. Concurrent applications written in Ada are more portable and modifiable.

Ada is obviously an excellent programming and design language and the development team undeniably concludes that Ada has been the success factor in this reengineering effort and has helped the company to survive the brutal software lifecycles and the competitive business. The company will continue the use of Ada in all future software projects and hope that this experience report exemplifies for the interests of organizations or individuals who wish to transition to Ada.

References

[ALB83]   Albrecht, A.J., and J.E. Gaffney, "Software Function, Source Lines of Code and Development Effort Prediction: A Software Science Violation", IEEE Trans. Software Engineering, Vol. SE-9, no. 6, Nov 1983.

[JON92]   Jones, C., "Measuring Software Productivity and Quality", 1992.

[BOO94a]   Booch, G., and Bryan, D., "Software Engineering with Ada", 3rd Edition, Addison Wesley, 1994.

[BOO94b]   Booch, G., "Object-Oriented Analysis and Design With Applications", 2nd Edition, Benjamin/Cummings, 1994.

[COA97]   Coad, P., North, D., and Mayfield, M., "Object Models - Strategies, Patterns, and Applications", 2nd Edition, Prentice Hall, 1997.

[RUM91]   Rumbaugh, J., Blaha, M., Premerlani, W., Eddy, F., and Lorensen, W., "Object-Oriented Modeling and Design", Prentice Hall, 1991.

[BUR95]   Burns, A., and Wellings, A., "Concurrency in Ada", Cambridge University Press, 1995.

[BAS78]   Basili, V., and M. Zelkowitz, "Analyzing Medium Scale Software Development", Proc. 3rd International Conference of Software Engineering, IEEE, 1978.

[OMA92]   Oman, P. "Construction and Validation of Polynomials for Predicting Software Maintainability", University of Idaho, 1992.

[HAL77]   Halstead, M., "Elements of Software Science", North Holland, 1977.

[MCC76]   McCabe, T.J., "A Software Complexity Measure", IEEE Trans. Software Engineering, vol. 2, no. 6, December 1976.

[MCC89]   McCabe, T.J., and Butler, C.W., "Design Complexity Measurement and Testing", CACM, vol. 32, no. 12, December 1989.

[COL92]   Coleman, D. "1992 Software Engineering Productivity Conference Proceedings", Hewlett-Packard Company, 1992.

Development of a Control System for Teleoperated Robots Using UML and Ada95

Francisco J. Ortiz, Alejandro S. Martínez, Barbara Álvarez, Andres Iborra, and José M. Fernández

Technical University of Cartagena
Campus Muralla del Mar s/n
30202 Cartagena (Spain).
{Francisco.Ortiz, Barbara.Alvarez, AlejandroS.Martinez, Andres.Iborra, Josem.fernandez}@upct.es

Abstract. In this paper, a control system in the domain of teleoperated service robots is presented. A reference architecture - ACROSET - has been analyzed and designed following a concurrent object modeling and architectural design methodology that uses UML as describing language. The architecture of the whole system has been implemented in a blasting robot for ship hulls- GOYA –using Ada 95 and GLADE. Our previous experience in developing teleoperated service robots using Ada is also presented.

1 Introduction

The objective of this paper is to present the development process followed to obtain a control system architecture for teleoperated robots, using the Unified Modeling Language –UML [5]–, and to describe the software implementation of such an architecture on an industrial PC with Linux using Ada 95 [1].

We have experience in the development of control systems with Ada [4]. In particular, several teleoperation systems for maintenance activities in nuclear power plants have been implemented using Ada [3]. In figure 1, a scheme of a teleoperation system is shown. In general, this type of control systems consists of two units: teleoperation platform and control unit. The operator is in charge of monitoring and operating the robot according to the information provided by the teleoperation system. This system receives commands from the operator and performs the corresponding actions for executing them. For this purpose, it communicates with the robot control unit, which physically actuates on the robot to move it. The robot control unit senses the robot in order to evaluate its global state and send this information to the teleoperation system, which represents graphically to the operator the state of the robot and ensures the correctness of its behaviour. Different tools are attached to the robot for performing the maintenance operations. The tools are operated in a similar way to the robot [11].

J. Blieberger and A. Strohmeier (Eds.): Ada-Europe 2002, LNCS 2361, pp. 113–124, 2002.

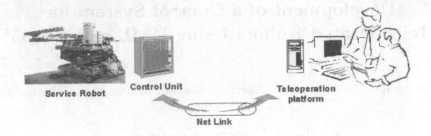

Service Robot   Control Unit   Teleoperation platform

Net Link

Fig. 1. Teleoperated service robot system scheme.

1.1 Previous Experiences

Some teleoperation systems that we have implemented using Ada are: ROSA (Remotely Operated Service Arm) [2], IRV (Inspection Retrieving Vehicle) system [12] and TRON (Teleoperated and Robotized System for Maintenance Operation in Nuclear Power Plants Vessels) system [9]. The experience of using the Ada programming language has been excellent in all the cases. A reference software architecture was obtained for the teleoperation platform [2] and the first implementation was carried out with Ada 83 for ROSA system, which is used for inspection and repairing of the tubes inside the steam generators.

In the design and development process of the mechanical system in teleoperated service robots we have to choose the appropriate actuator and sensors for each degree of freedom of the robot. The actuator and sensors system for a robot degree of freedom could be really different (e.g pneumatic actuators, hydraulic actuators, electrical engines as asynchronous or synchronous motors, etc). Because of that, the control strategies could be very different as well.

1.2 Reference Architectures

In our experience, commercial axis controller cards provide a reliable and robust solution, but restrict the choice of actuator systems to electrical engines. Because of this, a very important goal in our work is to show a reference architecture for control systems in the domain of teleoperated service robots. This architecture is not conditioned by the specific control strategy of the actuator system, the number of freedom degrees and the variety of tools that the robot manages.

A reusable reference architecture can be implemented in different hardware platforms and can be executed on many operating system. In many systems, secure and robust local control units were employed. These units were based on the use of electromechanical elements for controlling the different robots. The local control unit communicates with the remote teleoperation unit, which offers a more complex functionality to the operator. However, the functionality of the control unit can increase if more flexible platforms are used. Special real-time operating systems provide features such as kernel reliability, precise

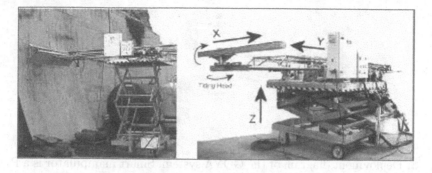

Fig. 2. GOYA system.

timers, bounded kernel preemption and other characteristics, that allow time requirements to be guaranteed. Their greatest disadvantage is that they are more expensive than other, more widely used operating systems. On the other hand, our experience shows that there are control systems without the stringent safety and time requirements that justify the use of real-time operating systems.

We now present our experience using Ada 95 for developing a new teleoperated robot: GOYA system figure 2. In this work, some features of Ada 95 for object-oriented programming have been employed such as: tagged types and related concepts such as class wide and abstract types that did not exist in Ada 83. In the next section, the GOYA system is briefly described. The design process using UML [8] is presented in section 3. Section 4 describes the actual implementation of GOYA system, focussing on the control unit using Ada 95.

2   System Description

GOYA is a teleoperated blasting system applied to hull cleaning in ship maintenance [11]. The main objective of this project is to develop a reliable and cost effective technology for hull grit blasting, capable to obtain a high quality surface preparation together with a dramatic reduction of waste and zero emissions to the environment. This technology provides a fully-automated and low-cost blasting system.

Figure 2 shows the mechanical subsystem. On the right, the robot with xyz positioning possibilities are shown. On the left, one of the initial tests on shipyards is shown. The tilting head is adapted to the surface. The subsystem consists of the following functional modules[1]:

- Elevation platform (z-axis): This mechanical part consists of a hydraulic elevation system that is raised or lowered by a hydraulic actuator.

---

[1] A more detailed description of the mechanical system is shown in [11]

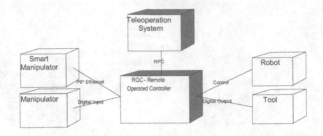

Fig. 3. Deployment diagram of the GOYA system. Smart manipulator is a PDA.

- Positioning arm (y-axis): This arm moves the tilting head relative to the surface of the ship,along the y axis. It is built starting from two mobile guided rails, each supported for a pair of skates. In their other end, the rails support a pneumatic cylinder without rod that carries the blasting tool.
- Tool positioning cart (x-axis): The tool is mounted on a sliding cart that is moved by a pneumatic cylinder without rod. This covers the x movement of the tool.
- Tool: The abrasive material is shot against the ship hull through a hose, which is opened and closed by a pneumatic system.

The control unit can work in two different ways, a teleoperated and a local mode. In the teleoperated mode, the operator monitors and operates the robot according to the information provided by the teleoperation system. This tele-operated mode is the normal manner of operation. For security purposes, the control unit can control the robot without communication with the teleoperation system through a local and electromechanical interface based on buttons, switches, indicators and displays.

3   Design Process

One of the most important issues around software architecture is the description of the system structures under consideration. It is the basis for all design activities including comprehending, communicating, analysing, trading-off, as well as for modification, maintenance, and reuse. Similar to other models, the description can be based on mathematical, textual, or graphical notations, but in order to manage the complexity of a system, a complete architecture description should be divided into multiple views. Often, each architectural view includes a set of models that describes one aspect of a system. One well-known and widely used approach to multi-viewed architectural description is the 4+1 View Model of Architecture proposed by Kruchten [10]. This model has also been adopted in the development of Unified Modeling Language (UML) [5].

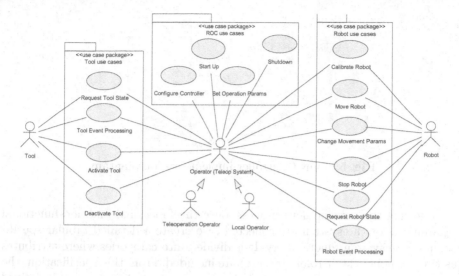

Fig. 4. General use cases of the system

UML has emerged as a standard notation for conceptual modeling using the object-oriented paradigm. Taking into account the benefits of blending object-oriented concepts with concurrency , the use of UML notation is quite helpful when designing distributed and real-time applications. The UML notation provides several diagrams [5] that allow us to represent static and dynamic properties of real systems and integrate them following the previous 4+1 architecture as we show in this section.

3.1 Concurrent Object Modeling and Architectural Design Method with UML

In order to obtain a reference architecture we have followed the COMET methodology (Concurrent Object Modeling and Architectural Design Method with UML) proposed by Gomaa in [8]. It is a design method for concurrent applications based on the USDP (Unified Software Development Process) and the spiral model of Boehm.

Starting from the system use cases, a static and dynamic design of the classes in the architecture can be derived until reaching the final implementation. Our goal is to reach a reference architecture for the design of control units in teleoperated service robot: ACROSET. In this paper, the process to obtain the reference architecture is presented. The architecture must be as complete as possible to be reused in other robots, perhaps more complex that the system presented here. In figure 3, a possible deployment diagram of the whole system is presented, with different nodes included.

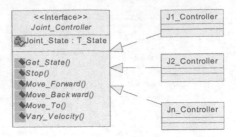

Fig. 5. Joint_Controller implementation diagram.

Following the development process, once the functional and non-functional requirements of the system are collected , we create a detailed tabular specification of the system functionality. It is divided into categories where attributes (as time response, fault tolerance, etc) are included. From this specification, the use cases of the system are extracted. A system context class diagram is derived from the use case diagram by considering the actors and which devices they utilize to interface with the system.

3.2   Discovering Classes

After the previous step, every use case is studied in order to obtain the objects that take part in it and the messages exchanged between these objects. This is the most complicated phase in the development process and it requires a considerable creative effort from the designer. Several collaboration diagrams are a consequence of this study. Once the different objects of the system are extracted from the collaboration diagrams, the classes of the system can be proposed as a generalization of objects.

One of the main objects composing the control unit is the Joint_Controller, which has to implement several methods as move_to, stop, etc. Therefore, the control architecture is based on the class Joint_Controller, defined as an interface or an abstract class. Each controller could be different, so it will be an implementation of Joint_Controller, giving the same interface to the rest of the system. There is one controller for each joint. Each of them implements its own control algorithm, which could be only software or an interface to a hardware control board. It is clear then, that if a coordinated movement is needed, there should be a coordinator of controllers (figure 6). This figure represents the class diagram of the architecture. The class Joints_Coordinator offers different basic methods of coordination between joints.

The class Tool_Controller is similar to Joint_Controller, except that it controls the tool and implements a different controller for each possible tool that could be managed by the robot. The same remark could be done for Tools_Coordinator. The process coordinator establishes the highest level in this architecture. Although the domain is teleoperated service robots, there are several processes

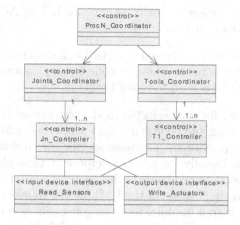

Fig. 6. Proposed architecture class diagram.

that can be performed in an autonomous manner. ProcN_Coordinator implements one of these processes. For each one of the possible autonomous processes, there should be a different Process Coordinator, changing in run time depending on the process.

3.3   Task Structuring

During the task structuring phase, the concurrent task architecture is developed. As a consequence, the system is structured into concurrent tasks and the task interfaces and interconnections are defined. To help to determine the tasks, task structuring criteria are provided by COMET to assist in mapping an object-oriented analysis model of the system to a concurrent tasking architecture. For instance, depending on the characteristics of the I/O devices (asynchronous, passive, etc), one or more tasks will be chosen to read them. That is to say, if the sampling rate of two passive devices differs we should choose two different tasks, but if it is similar, it could be simplified in one task depending on the computational necessities of the system. See section 4.2 to complete this concepts.

3.4   Implementing the Design: Code Generation

Once the static and dynamic behavior of the system has been designed, it is time to implement it depending on the better deployment in each case. As described above, all the analysis and design of the Software can be accomplished by means of a description language such as UML. We have a variety of diagrams to explain the behavior of the Software we are designing. Part of the source code of the application can be obtained from the diagrams thanks to the Code Generation AddIn that UML tools have. We use Rational Rose 2000 and in this section, some tips of the Code Generation tool will be explained. The Ada Code Generator AddIn that can be found in Rational Rose:

– Substantially reduces the elapsed time between design and execution.
– Produces uniformly-structured source code files, promoting consistent coding and commenting styles with minimal typing.

The code generated for each selected model component is a function of that component's specification and code generation properties, and the model properties. These properties provide the language specific information required to map the model onto Ada. Usually we have a component view of the system where packages of the software to produce are displayed. The first step in code generation consists of assigning classes in the UML model to every module. If a class specification assigns it to a module, the Ada generator uses this information to determine where to generate the declaration and definition for the class.

The declaration of the type representing that class is placed in the corresponding package specification, along with the other types assigned to the same package. The declarations of the subprograms associated with that class also go in the same package specification. The bodies of these subprograms are placed in the corresponding package body. Each class specification must contain the desired attributes, relationships and operations. The Ada generator uses this information to generate record components and subprograms. The Ada generator uses the specifications and code generation properties of components in the current model to produce Ada source code. For each class in a Rose model, this generator produces a corresponding Ada type. Associations, relationships, and attributes are translated to components of that type.

The implementation files are generated simply in one mouse click. These files contain one package body, with the appropriate 'with' clauses. This package body contains global declarations, skeletal subprogram, tasks and protected object bodies, and code regions. The code generator provides a complete body for some of the subprograms it generates. For other subprograms, including the user-defined ones, it only produces a skeletal body. In all cases, the generated bodies contain protected code regions. By placing each subprogram implementation within its code region, this implementation code is preserved when code is regenerated from the model. Note that Rational Rose 2000 can only generate 'skeletons' of the program; the code necessary to perform the dynamic behavior of the system has to be 'handily' programmed. In any case, if a new class is introduced, Rose can reflect the change in the model by means of reverse engineering. All generated files are placed in a hierarchy of directories that correspond to class categories and/or subsystems in the model.

4   Implementation Details Using Ada

The main components of the Goya system are the Teleoperation Platform and the Control Unit, linked by Ethernet, and finally the mechanical system of Goya robot.

1. Teleoperation Platform: The operator uses it to command the robot remotely. It has been implemented by a work station SGI with Irix 6.5.8. There are three main process running on it:

   (a) Graphical user interface, which has been developed with GtkAda and Ada95.

   (b) Kinematic control module, through GRASP, a commercial software product intended to design and simulate robots.

   (c) Teleoperation platform controller, developed with Ada 95. This controller communicates with the two processes, described above, with a communication protocol using TCP sockets. Using Ada 95 has facilitated the implementation of reading and writing tasks in different communication channels and furthermore the marshalling and unmarshalling of data types exchanged between different processes developed in C and Ada 95. To communicate with the robot control unit the distributed system annex (GLADE) [13] of Ada 95 has been employed. We have proved the benefits of using GLADE instead of developing our own protocol based on TCP sockets as we did in previous projects.

2. Control Unit, implemented with Ada 95 on an industrial PC. The Goya system is a service robot that works at low speed. Once we have determined the critical tasks, we have estimated that their response times are wide enough to allow the use of GLADE and Linux on the industrial PC. It is an operating system without real-time characteristics. Because of an economic criterion and its well-known features, Linux (Debian distribution) becomes the ideal operating system for this application. The compiler version for Ada 95 and GLADE were 3.14a from ACT. We have used digital input/output cards and encoder cards mounted on the PC. Each card has its own address space mapped into the PC memory. The manufacturer provides the card's control drivers with C functions, following the files treatment from Unix (open-read/write-close). Thanks to the Ada 95 advantages for interfacing with other languages, as C, it has been easy to export C functions by means of "pragma export". In this way, we have Ada functions to manage directly the hardware.

4.1   Control Unit Architectural Description

The reference architecture explained in section 3.2 has been implemented in Goya system. The Goya robot has three freedom degrees (xyz) and one tool. Then, four controllers are necessary, one for each freedom degree and one for the tool. In figure 5, a class diagram is shown with Jn_Controller and multiplicity 1..n; the implementation in an object diagram for this particular robot leads to: J1_Controller for the elevation platform (z-axis), J2_Controller for positioning arm (y-axis) and J3_Controller for tool positioning cart (x-axis) mounted on the titling head. We only have one tool in this robot, so the multiplicity of Tn_Controller will be 1: T1_Controller for the blasting tool. Over these joints controllers there is a coordinator object (Joints_Coordinator) that is required

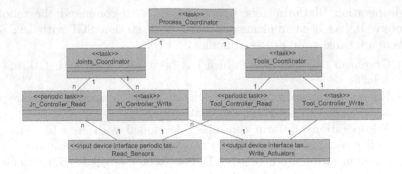

Fig. 7. Tak diagram. Different stereotypes are used.

to coordinate movements. This abstract class is implemented with the appropiate procedure Coordinate_Joints for this robot. The Tools_Coordinator is not necessary in this application because we have only one tool, but finally it is implemented to respect the architecture, offering the same interface to the rest of the application in prevention of later modifications and improvements of the robot and anticipating a possible change of tools.

The top layer is the Process_Coordinator. We have in this application an object that has implemented a state machine performing the automatic sequence for blasting a complete hull panel. The interface offered by Process_Coordinator is the same for any layer that accesses to the controllers , so every control order, not only coordinated ones, but also control orders for individual joints pass through the Process_Coordinator. The same is true for Joints_Coordinator. We have created layers with the same interface to the upper layer.

4.2   Control Unit Tasks Model

In figure 7 the task model in this application is presented. There is a task for Process_Coordinator, a task for Joints_Coordinator and two tasks for each controller (one for reading sensors state and one for writing actuators). The writing tasks are not periodic; they are suspended by means of a protected entry with a barrier.

All these tasks are needed because we are controlling different joints, often simultaneously. The operator could even give orders to any joint while another joint is moving. Coordination is needed to perform coordinated movements with different strategies of control. The robot can also implement some autonomous operations, which why the system also needs a Process_Coordinator These tasks are encapsulated in the objects shown in figure 6. A periodic task that reads sensors and a non-periodic task that writes actuators perform the interface with hardware devices. Following the task structuring criteria from Gomaa [8] we have chosen only one task for reading sensors because the updating period in I/O cards is the same. The process of writing is similar; the writing task is activated when there is an entry for next operation.

The Read-Sensors object is implemented as a protected object using one important feature in Ada 95. In this manner, all the controllers can read at the same time. The data of sensors in this protected object is updated by the Read-Sensors task. Since it is protected we can assure that the different hardware does not write the data at the same time, avoiding the danger of losing information. In this application the controllers share the I/O hardware (digital cards); in the same card we have input from platform, arm and head. We assure that every controller accesses its resorts properly with the protected object Read-Sensors.

The three tasks Jn_Controller_Read are periodical, they are continuously checking the state of the sensors, but the writing tasks are active only when there is an order of movement for the actuators. There is also another task (Write_Actuators) to write the orders to the hardware, which is activated only when there is an entry (also protected entry). In the case of sensor data and actuation, communication between tasks is performed by means of information hiding objects. As has been mentioned, protected objects pass information between the controllers and the hardware interface. Messages are used for communicating Coordinators tasks and Controllers tasks. There is no need to introduce an additional queue object because the operator orders are queued in the Teleoperation Interface system. If necessary, a buffer can be implemented in ProcN_Coordinator (figure 6). In any case, writing attempts in any protected object would be queued in a FIFO manner.

4.3   Using the Ada 95 Distributed System Annex: GLADE [13]

A goal in this reference architecture is to give the same interface to the local system and the teleoperation system. This interface is a set of procedures, to send commands, and a function to get the actual robot's state. The only difference is that the local system accesses directly to this procedures and function, meanwhile the teleoperation system accesses remotely.

We have taken advantage of using GLADE, through the remote procedure call. Due to using GLADE to communicate the Teleoperation Platform and the Control Unit, the application works in the same manner as it would be working in a single machine. Although in the present implementation we have only one processor on the Control Unit side, the use of GLADE and this interface objets allow distributing easily the application in different processors.

5   Conclusions

Although the use of Ada in general industry applications is much less widespread than other languages as C or C++, it is the language selected for the implementation of the system, due to some features that allow us to obtain an extra portability, maintainability and reliability. Some of these key issues in Ada are mechanisms for encapsulation, separate compilation and library management, exception handling or data abstraction.

Some features of Ada 95 for object-oriented programming have been employed: tagged types, related concepts such as class wide and abstract types that did not exist in Ada 83. In general, the use of Distributed System Annex of Ada is not appropriate for developing hard real-time systems, but it can be used to develop systems without stringent time and safety requirements such as GOYA. The use of GLADE and the well-interfaced structure of the proposed reference architecture allow distributing easily the application in different processors if needed. Thanks to RPC, the application works in the same manner in distributed systems as it would be working in a single machine.

UML and software development methods are indispensable to manage the complexity of big software products. The COMET methodology, used to obtain a reference architecture, and Rational Rose, with Ada 95 Code Generator, have been greatly useful to reach an implementation of a control unit in GOYA system.

References

1. Ada 95 Reference manual: Language and Standard Libraries. International Standard ANSI/ISO/IEC-8652:1995. Available from Springer-Verlag, LNCS no. 1246.
2. Alonso, A., Álvarez, B., Pastor, J.A., de la Puente, J.A., Iborra, A. Software Architecture for a Robot Teleoperation System. 4th IFAC Workshop on Algorithms and Architectures for Real-Time Control(1997).
3. Alvarez B, Iborra A, Alonso A, de la Puente, J.A, and Pastor, J.A. Developing multi-application remote systems. Nuclear Engineering International. Vol.45, No. 548, (2000).
4. Alvarez B, Iborra A, Sanchez P, Ortiz F, and Pastor, J.A. Experiences on the Product Synthesis of Mechatronic Systems using UML in a Software Architecture Framework., ITM'01 Istambul, Turkey(2001).
5. Booch G., Jacobson I., Rumbaugh J., Rumbaugh J. The Unified Modeling Language User Guide, Addison-Wesley Pub Co, New York, (1998).
6. Burns, A., Wellings, A.: Concurrency in Ada, Cambridge Univ. Press, Cambridge (1998).
7. Douglas, B.P.: Real-Time UML. Developing Efficient Objects for Embedded Systems, Addison-Wesley Object Technology Series, Reading, Massachusetts (2000).
8. Gomaa, H.: Designing Concurrent, Distributed, and Real-Time Applications with UML, Addison-Wesley Object Technology Series, Reading, Massachusetts (2000).
9. Iborra, A., Alvarez, A., Navarro, P.J., Fernández. J.M, and Pastor, J.A. Robotized System for Retrieving Fallen Objects within the Reactor Vessel of a Nuclear Power Plant (PWR). Proceedings of the 2000 IEEE Internat. Symp. Industrial Electronics. Puebla, Mexico, (2000).
10. Kruchten, F. – Architectural Blueprints – The "4+1" View Model of Software Architecture, IEEE Software, USA (1995).
11. Ortiz, F., Iborra, A., Marin, F., Álvarez, B., and Fernandez, J.M. GOYA - A teleoperated system for blasting applied to ships maintenance. 3rd International Conference on Climbing and Walking Robots, Madrid, Spain (2000).
12. Pastor, J.A, Alvarez, B., Iborra, A., Fernández, J.M. An underwater teleoperated vehicle for inspection and retrieving. First International Symposium on mobile, climbing, and walking robots. Brussels, Belgium (1998).
13. Pautet, L., Tardieu, S. GLADE user' s guide. Technical report version 3.14a. ACT.

Using a Secure Java Micro-kernel on Embedded Devices for the Reliable Execution of Dynamically Uploaded Applications

Walter Binder and Balázs Lichtl

CoCo Software Engineering GmbH
Margaretenstr. 22/9, 1040 Vienna, Austria
{w.binder | b.lichtl}@cocosoftware.com

Abstract. This paper presents the architecture of an autonomous, multi-purpose station, which executes dynamically uploaded applications. The station hardware is based on an embedded Java processor, which runs the system software and applications. The system software is built on top of a flexible, lightweight, efficient, and secure mobile object platform, which is able to receive mobile code and to execute it, while protecting the station from faulty applications. Mobile code is used for application upload, as well as for remote configuration and maintenance of the autonomous station. Applications executing on the station may be charged for their resource consumption. This paper also outlines an initial application of the autonomous station, which has been recently deployed in a pilot project.

1 Introduction

This paper gives an overview of the design and architecture of an autonomous station, which is able to securely and reliably execute dynamically uploaded applications. The autonomous station does not rely on an external power supply system, but it comprises a unit for the generation of current in order to ensure its autonomy. It is equipped with application dependent sensors and actuators, and it may be deployed in inaccessible environments. It offers its specific equipment within a specific environment to applications in a time-sharing fashion. The applications are not hard-coded in the station, but they are dynamically uploaded on demand. They are charged for their utilization of the resources provided by the autonomous station. In order to support application upload, transmission of results, and remote system maintenance, the autonomous station is connected to a public or private wireless network. The hardware of the station is based on an embedded Java processor running our system software, which is implemented in pure Java [9]. The system software is based on a lightweight, efficient, and secure mobile object platform, which is able to receive mobile code and to execute it, while protecting the autonomous station from malicious or badly programmed applications.

In the past years numerous research works have focussed on mobile object technology. This has resulted in a better understanding of the problems inherent

J. Blieberger and A. Strohmeier (Eds.): Ada-Europe 2002, LNCS 2361, pp. 125–135, 2002.
© Springer-Verlag Berlin Heidelberg 2002

to mobile objects and mobile code in general, which have to be solved in order to enable the widespread deployment of mobile code based solutions in various commercial settings, such as the embedding of a Java-based mobile object system within a proprietary hardware environment. In particular, significant research has concentrated on building secure environments for the execution of foreign, potentially malicious mobile objects, which may seriously damage the execution environment itself or other mobile objects in the system [2,3,7,8].

Actually, Java has become the de facto standard implementation language for mobile object platforms due to its network centric approach, its runtime virtual machine, and features that ease the development of mobile object systems, such as a portable code format (Java bytecode) [14], dynamic and customizable class-loading, multi-threading, built-in support for object serialization, and language safety [22]. Since the proliferation of the real-time specification for Java [6], embedded Java processors conforming with this specifications have been developed, which are able to meet certain (soft) real-time requirements.

Despite of these advantages, Java has not been designed for multi-tasking[1]. Currently, Java offers no support for isolating mobile objects from each other. The lack of a task model in Java also makes it difficult to terminate applications in order to reclaim their allocated resources. Furthermore, Java has no support for resource accounting and control, which makes it vulnerable to denial-of-service attacks and prevents the deployment of applications that shall be charged for their resource consumption. See [5] for an in-depth discussion of deficiencies of Java with respect to mobile code environments. Consequently, many recent research works have aimed at working around these shortcomings of Java related to mobile code. Different approaches have put restrictions on the programming model, used bytecode arbitration to control the execution of mobile code, and developed special runtime systems with enhanced functionalities usually found in operating systems.

In the meantime, Java-based mobile object systems are available that are secure and reliable enough to justify their deployment in commercial settings. As mobile object environments are perfectly suited for software distribution, installation, and remote maintenance, the system software of our autonomous station is based on J-SEAL2 [3], a lightweight Java-based micro-kernel, which makes Java safe for the execution of untrusted mobile code. J-SEAL2 offers a hierarchical task model allowing to isolate applications, to terminate them in a safe way, and to monitor and limit their resource consumption.

Our system software has control over a special hardware, the embedded Java processor and its peripherals (i.e., different sensors and actuators which are connected to the main station). We use a processor that natively executes Java

---

[1] In this paper the term 'task' refers to the concept of a *process* in an operating system, which allows to separate and isolate applications from each other. We are using this term (although it is overloaded with different semantics in various contexts), because it is also employed by the Java Community Process JSR 121 [13], which aims at specifying an API to isolate applications executing within the same Java runtime system.

bytecode programs, which supersedes a Java Virtual Machine (JVM) [14] implemented in software, as well as an underlying operating system layer. Therefore, the executive overhead is significantly reduced when compared to a JVM implemented in software. Moreover, because all system components and applications are implemented within a Java-based, high-level, object-oriented programming model, the reliability of the overall system is greatly improved.

This paper is structured as follows: In the following section we discuss possible applications of the autonomous station and present our requirements and design goals. In section 3 we explain how the station is managed. We focus on application upload and application communication. In section 4 we discuss possible hardware configurations and the Java runtime system executing on the station. Section 5 shows how the J-SEAL2 mobile object kernel is adapted to serve as a kind of operating system for the autonomous station. Section 6 outlines an application of the autonomous station, which has been deployed in a pilot project. The last section concludes the paper.

2 Applications and Design Goals

The autonomous station is a multi-purpose, customizable, and extensible system, which may be deployed in many different configurations. In this section we mention a few exemplary applications. Equipped with the necessary sensors and actuators, the same autonomous station may serve a series of applications at the same time.

- In a pilot project we have used autonomous stations to provide *on-demand bus stations*, where the bus only passes the station, if a customer has explicitly ordered the bus. In section 6 we present some details of this particular application.
- In the context of industrial sensing autonomous stations offer a cost-effective alternative to a system of wired sensing elements.
- The general architecture of our autonomous station is also well-suited for cheap multi-purpose satellites, as well as for spacecrafts.
- Autonomous stations may be deployed to monitor their environment. Equipped with sensors to detect toxic substances, autonomous stations can improve civil protection.
- Research institutions may use autonomous stations to collect environmental information.
- Autonomous stations can be used for traffic monitoring and for tracing.

The hardware of the autonomous station comprises a main board with CPU and memory, a wireless communication module, a power supply system that typically consists of solar cells and a rechargable battery, as well as application-specific sensors and actuators (input and output devices). Details concerning the hardware configuration of the station are presented in section 4. Depending on the concrete application, the hardware components may have to meet the following requirements:

- The autonomous station has to be built from off-the-shelf components, in order to keep the hardware costs low.
- The hardware has to be resistant against variations in temperature.
- The power supply system must be adaptable to the concrete operational area of the station. The size of the solar cells and the capacity of the rechargable battery have to be selected according to the expected insolation. On a place with low insolation a more expensive power supply system is needed.
- Because of the limited power supply, the processor has to offer competitive performance as well as reduced power consumption. Since we require a safe high-level language for application programming, the autonomous station is based on a modern Java processor, which provides a standard JVM implemented in hardware.
- Depending on the usage site, it may be necessary to protect the hardware against vandalism.

The design decision to employ a Java processor also implies that all system software, as well as the applications, have to be represented by JVM bytecode. The software may be implemented in pure Java or in any other language that can be compiled to JVM bytecode, such as Ada 95 [19]. For the system software, we have the following requirements:

- Because the station may not be easily accessible after deployment, and in order to reduce the maintenance overhead, the system is designed for remote maintenance. This means that diagnostic programs may be uploaded in order to detect the reason for a malfunction. Furthermore, new system components may be installed remotely, and existing components may be replaced with new versions without interrupting the execution of applications.
- Applications are installed and updated remotely. Applications may be terminated, freeing their allocated resources and leaving the station in a consistent state.
- Applications are charged for their resource consumption. The resources that may be charged for include power consumption, CPU and memory utilization, access to sensors and actuators, and communication.
- All system components are protected from faulty applications. Sensors and actuators cannot be directly accessed and programmed by an application, but a *device driver* (a system component) mediates access to the device.
- The autonomous station may offer its resources to multiple applications in a time-sharing fashion. Applications are isolated from each other, since they may execute on behalf of different parties.
- A *device manager* ensures that concurrent applications use multiple sensors and actuators in a consistent way.

3   Application Upload and Communication

Each autonomous station is managed and controlled by a single *supervising server* (SuSe). A SuSe may be in charge of multiple stations. The SuSe is the only communication partner of an autonomous station[2]. Clients who want to upload applications to an autonomous station or to communicate with an already uploaded application have to contact the station's SuSe, which acts as a gateway: It receives client requests from the wired network (e.g., through a TCP/IP connection) and dispatches the request to the corresponding station, which is accessible only through a wireless network[3]. Vice versa, the SuSe receives messages from an application running on a station and forwards them to the client who has deployed the application.

When a client wants to upload a new application to an autonomous station, he has to transmit the application to the station's SuSe. For this purpose, the client sends a signed message to the SuSe, including the identifier of the destination station, a Java archive (a JAR file) containing the application classes and a deployment descriptor, as well as the network location (e.g., host address, port, and protocol) where application results shall be routed to. The deployment descriptor specifies the resource requirements of the application, quality-of-service (QoS) parameters, etc.

The SuSe checks whether the requested QoS can be guaranteed. If the new application is accepted, it is assigned a unique *application identifier* (AID). The application archive is opened, the application classes are verified (and eventually modified to guarantee certain security properties, such as resource accounting and control of the application [4]), and the application is re-packaged in a special application transfer format, which may yield better compression (an important aspect regarding the low bandwidth of many wireless networks) and which can be handled by the mobile object kernel executing within the autonomous station. We are relying on compression algorithms that are especially tailored to Java class files [10] and achieve significantly better compression than commonly used methods such as ZIP. The re-packaged application is transmitted to the destination station through a wireless network. All messages originating from the application will be tagged with the AID, allowing the SuSe to dispatch them to the client.

Once installed, an application may transmit results to the client who has deployed the application. The communication module within the autonomous station tags the message with the correct AID. It is also responsible for buffering messages that cannot be transmitted immediately due to a network failure or crash of the SuSe. Based on the AID, the SuSe is able to determine the recipient. Finally, the message is delivered to the network address, which the client has

---

[2] In order to prevent the SuSe from becoming a single point of failure, the autonomous station may communicate with a set of backup SuSes, if its primary SuSe fails. The physical replication of a SuSe is crucial for applications with (soft) real-time guarantees, such as applications for civil protection, industrial sensing, or military purpose.

[3] The wireless network used to connect the autonomous station with its SuSe depends on the physical location of the station and the range of applications it shall support. For instance, in the configuration presented in section 6 the autonomous station is connected to a public GPRS (General Packet Radio Service) network [1].

provided during installation of the application. If the receiver is temporarily not available, the SuSe buffers the message.

The client may also send control messages to its application. For this purpose, he has to transmit the signed message to the SuSe, providing the destination AID, which the SuSe needs to route the message to the correct station. Within the autonomous station, the communication module dispatches the message to the corresponding application based on the AID.

4   Hardware Configuration and Java Environment

The autonomous station is an embedded system with application-specific peripherals. The core of the station is a Java processor that natively executes JVM bytecode instructions. Current Java processors offer sufficiently high performance at rather low clock rates, because there is no overhead due to a JVM implemented in software. The low clock rate helps to preserve power, which is crucial if the station has a limited power supply. The reference implementation of our autonomous station is based on a Java processor from aJile Systems[4] operating at 80MHz. All the system software and applications are implemented in pure Java; aJile provides a Java development kit including support for the Java 2 Micro Edition (J2ME), as well as special APIs to access hardware registers, serial ports, etc.

The J2ME has been designed for devices with limited resources like our autonomous station. Currently, J2ME defines two separate specification, the *Connected Device Configuration* (CDC) [12] and the *Connected, Limited Device Configuration* (CLDC) [11]. The CLDC has been designed for mobile devices with very limited computing resources, such as 120–500KB of memory. Therefore, the CLDC omits several APIs that are part of the Java 2 Standard Edition (J2SE), but not required by typical Java applications. In contrast, the CDC offers all core APIs of the J2SE, but requires considerably more memory (e.g., 2–16MB).

Our system software is based on the J-SEAL2 mobile object kernel, which is discussed in more detail in the following section. J-SEAL2 relies on several APIs of the J2SE, which are supported by the CDC, but not by the CLDC. Hence, the autonomous station has to be equipped with enough memory to use the CDC. In practice, at least 4MB of memory will be needed to run the CDC, the J-SEAL2 kernel, system services, as well as some (small) applications.

The peripherals of the autonomous station largely depend on the application context. The input and output devices must be chosen accordingly, but also the power supply system and the communication module highly depend on the environment. Typically, the power supply system consists of solar cells and a rechargable battery to ensure the autonomy of the station. However, sometimes a simpler power supply may be appropriate, ranging from an AC/DC adaptor to an uninterruptible power supply (UPS). Furthermore, in some settings mon-

---

[4] http://www.ajile.com/

itoring of the state of the power supply is needed, in order suspend low priority applications in case of a power shortage.

The requirements for the communication module are also application dependent. In some industrial environments a simple ethernet interface may be sufficient. Other settings may require a private wireless LAN, a bluetooth network, or even proprietary radio links. However, in the most common commercial setting, we assume that some kind of public wireless network will be used. Our reference implementation of the autonomous station employs a GSM module, where SMS, GSM data calls, or GPRS [1] may serve as communication bearers.

For some applications, the station may have to provide a user interface, allowing customers to interact with the station. The type of the user interface is not limited by our system; it can range from no user interface at all to a color touch-screen. The power consumption of the station and the required processing performance highly depend on the hardware peripherals in use. Some sensors are very simple to interact with, they may require only one bit digital input or output, while other devices may expose sophisticated interfaces. Thus, the system software of the station must be scalable and cause only little overhead, to support the execution of simple applications on low-cost and low-performance processors, but also of complex tasks on a station with the processing power of a workstation.

5   Adaption of the J-SEAL2 Mobile Object Kernel

The system software of the autonomous station is based on J-SEAL2[5] [3], a secure mobile object kernel. J-SEAL2 is a micro-kernel that offers a task model with strong isolation properties on top of standard Java runtime systems. It is based on the formal model of the Seal Calculus [21], which was first implemented by the JavaSeal kernel [7]. J-SEAL2 is able to securely and concurrently execute multiple Java applications in the same JVM, which are completely separated from each other. J-SEAL2 resembles the kernel of a traditional operating system, as it provides mechanisms for application isolation, efficient and mediated communication, safe termination, and resource control.

The architecture of J-SEAL2 is well suited as the basis for mobile code systems, because it offers the necessary level of host security, which is not found in current standard Java runtime systems: Executing applications and system services within separate tasks, J-SEAL2 protects the platform from malicious or badly programmed applications, as well as applications from each other. We are exploiting the advanced security mechanisms of J-SEAL2 to protect the autonomous station from faulty applications, to isolate applications from each other, and to account and control their resource consumption, which is necessary for charging. We selected J-SEAL2, because it offers several advantages with respect to our requirements:

– J-SEAL2 has been specially designed for increased host security. It provides a hierarchical task model, which allows to isolate system components (such

---

[5] http://www.jseal2.com/

as the communication module or device drivers) and applications, while they are executing within the same JVM. In the task model of J-SEAL2 a parent task acts as communication controller, access controller, and resource manager of its children. Applications that are uploaded to the autonomous station are installed as children of a trusted mediator task, which controls the execution of the applications and limits their resource consumption.

– J-SEAL2 is implemented in pure Java. In contrast to other secure mobile object platforms and Java operating systems, such as KaffeOS [2], J-SEAL2 does rely neither on a special JVM nor on native code. This is of paramount importance, as the platform has to run on a Java processor, which provides a standard JVM implemented in hardware.

– J-SEAL2 is a small and efficient micro-kernel. The kernel offers only essential primitives to implement secure and reliable system software. This is important, since the memory available on the autonomous station is limited.

– J-SEAL2 has a modular and extensible architecture. Special system services, such as device drivers, can be provided by mobile objects.

– J-SEAL2 supports resource control for physical resources (i.e., CPU and memory), for logical resources (e.g., threads), and for access to service components. For CPU and memory control, the resource consumption of the application is reified [4,20]. I.e., the application is modified to expose its resource consumption to the system. This approach enables resource control, even if the underlying Java runtime system does not support it. In our setting the application is modified for resource control by the SuSe before it is uploaded to the station. As these modifications are complex and time consuming, they should not be carried out by the station, where the resources are limited.

System components (e.g., device drivers, device manager, communication module, etc.) as well as applications execute within separate tasks. Each task may be terminated at any time, which frees its allocated resources and is guaranteed to leave the system in a consistent state[6]. Consequently, we are able to implement application upload and update, installation of new system services, and update of system services in a similar way.

6 Application of the Autonomous Station

The individual components of the autonomous station (i.e., the integrated station hardware, the J-SEAL2 kernel, the communication module, etc.) have been separately developed and deployed in the context of different academic and com-

---

[6] If the task to be terminated is executing a kernel operation, termination is delayed until completion of the kernel operation, in order to ensure the integrity of the kernel. Because kernel operations in J-SEAL2 are non-blocking and have a short and constant execution time, termination cannot be delayed arbitrarily. Details concerning task termination in J-SEAL2 are presented in [3].

mercial projects. For instance, J-SEAL2 has been used in a Swiss e-commerce project[7], providing us with valuable feedback.

Recently, we have used autonomous stations based on the architecture described in this paper to provide on-demand bus stations within a pilot project. This application is the first deployment of our autonomous station under commercial settings. The project was initiated by a bus operator in Austria, in order to avoid empty buses in the non-urban area and to improve the QoS. The customer has to press a button on the bus station to order the next bus. If there is no request by a customer, the bus will not pass the station. The on-demand bus stations are deployed in areas where the bus service is used rarely and irregularly. Consequently, the bus driver may frequently select a shorter route to save fuel and time, which also helps to compensate for delays due to traffic jams. Therefore, the overall bus punctuality (and hence the QoS) is improved.

This application involves four major components: The autonomous station allowing customers to order buses, the stations' SuSe, a server hosting an application to coordinate the routes of the buses, as well as a simple application running on cell phones to interact with the bus drivers. The server application communicates with the autonomous stations through the SuSe. In our setting the communication between the server application and the bus drivers' cell phones is managed by the SuSe as well. As the focus of this paper is the architecture of the autonomous station and its applications, details concerning the applications running on the server and on the cell phones are not covered here.

In the current version, the application executing on the autonomous station is able to serve the schedule of one bus in two directions. The configuration of the application (i.e., the bus schedule) is completely dynamic, it is communicated by the server application periodically. Therefore, the bus schedule may be changed at runtime without uploading a new version of the application. The application running on the station also logs all user actions and periodically transmits the logging data to the server. This information is important to evaluate the user behaviour and the acceptance of the on-demand bus station. Charging of the application for consumed resources is not necessary in this pilot project, because the bus operator does not allow the uploading of foreign applications.

In order to reduce the hardware costs, the user interface of the station is kept as simple as possible: It comprises two vertically grouped buttons with built-in LEDs and a 20x4 character LCD display with green background lighting. The LEDs on the buttons help to signal the possible input choices to the user. Furthermore, the station contains a beeper for acoustic feedback of user actions, as well as a motion detection sensor to activate the background lighting of the display when a potential customer approaches the station.

The communication with the SuSe is based on UDP [15] packets on top of a GPRS [1] connection. The autonomous station includes a Motorola g18 GPRS GSM embedded wireless module, which is connected to the mainboard of the station by the standard RS232 serial interface. The development of the communication software was one of the most challenging tasks in this project.

---

[7] http://anaisoft.unige.ch/

The low-level programming of the Motorola g18 is based on the standard GSM AT command interface to initialize the GSM module and to connect it to the GPRS network. After the connection has been established, the point-to-point protocol (PPP) is used [18]. Since we could not find any implementations of the PPP / IP [16] / UDP protocol stack in pure Java, we had to develop our own implementation from scratch. We have chosen UDP over TCP [17], because the implementation of the complete TCP protocol would have been much more complicated. Another important issue is the reliability and fault tolerance of the communication. The low-level communication software of the station consists of three layers:

- The lowest layer maintains the device itself; it resets the device upon a failure and initializes it when the station reboots.
- The second layer maintains the GPRS connection. It reconnects whenever the connection breaks down and signals an error of the device to the lower layer, ensuring that the device will be initialized again.
- The upper layer is a packet delivery service, which handles acknowledgement messages and the resending of packets after a timeout. To compensate for the bad reliability of current GPRS networks (no QoS supported, high and varying latency, etc.), the acknowledgement and resending of UDP packets is crucial. This layer is used by the high-level communication services of the autonomous station, which provide stream communication, encryption, compression, etc.

7   Conclusion

The contributions of our work are threefold: Firstly, we present the autonomous station, a new application of embedded Java, which relies on mobile code for program upload and remote maintenance. Secondly, we show how a mobile object platform can be adopted for the distribution and installation of applications by mobile code. We are exploiting the advanced security features of the J-SEAL2 mobile object kernel, in order to provide a reliable and secure system to host foreign applications, which are charged for their resource consumption. Finally, we present a concrete application, the on-demand bus station, which is based on the architecture of our autonomous station.

References

1. 3GPP. 3GPP Specifications Home Page. Web pages at http://www.3gpp.org/specs/specs.htm.
2. G. Back, W. Hsieh, and J. Lepreau. Processes in KaffeOS: Isolation, resource management, and sharing in Java. In *Proceedings of the Fourth Symposium on Operating Systems Design and Implementation (OSDI'2000)*, San Diego, CA, USA, Oct. 2000.

3. W. Binder. Design and implementation of the J-SEAL2 mobile agent kernel. In *The 2001 Symposium on Applications and the Internet (SAINT-2001)*, San Diego, CA, USA, Jan. 2001.

4. W. Binder, J. Hulaas, A. Villazón, and R. Vidal. Portable resource control in Java: The J-SEAL2 approach. In *ACM Conference on Object-Oriented Programming, Systems, Languages, and Applications (OOPSLA-2001)*, Tampa Bay, Florida, USA, Oct. 2001.

5. W. Binder and V. Roth. Secure mobile agent systems using Java: Where are we heading? In *Seventeenth ACM Symposium on Applied Computing (SAC-2002)*, Madrid, Spain, Mar. 2002.

6. G. Bollella, B. Brosgol, P. Dibble, S. Furr, J. Gosling, D. Hardin, and M. Turnbull. *The Real-Time Specification for Java*. Addison-Wesley, Reading, MA, USA, 2000.

7. C. Bryce and J. Vitek. The JavaSeal mobile agent kernel. In *First International Symposium on Agent Systems and Applications (ASA'99)/Third International Symposium on Mobile Agents (MA'99)*, Palm Springs, CA, USA, Oct. 1999.

8. G. Czajkowski and L. Daynes. Multitasking without compromise: A virtual machine evolution. In *ACM Conference on Object-Oriented Programming, Systems, Languages, and Applications (OOPSLA'01)*, Tampa Bay, Florida, Oct. 2001.

9. J. Gosling, B. Joy, G. L. Steele, and G. Bracha. *The Java language specification*. Java series. Addison-Wesley, Reading, MA, USA, second edition, 2000.

10. R. N. Horspool and J. Corless. Tailored compression of Java class files. *Software Practice and Experience*, 28(12):1253–1268, Oct. 1998.

11. Java Community Process. JSR-000030 J2ME Connected, Limited Device Configuration. Web pages at http://jcp.org/aboutJava/communityprocess/final/jsr030/index.html.

12. Java Community Process. JSR-000036 J2ME Connected Device Configuration. Web pages at http://jcp.org/aboutJava/communityprocess/final/jsr036/index.html.

13. Java Community Process. JSR 121 – Application Isolation API Specification. Web pages at http://jcp.org/jsr/detail/121.jsp.

14. T. Lindholm and F. Yellin. *The Java Virtual Machine Specification*. Addison-Wesley, Reading, MA, USA, second edition, 1999.

15. J. Postel. RFC 768: User Datagram Protocol, Aug. 1980.

16. J. Postel. RFC 791: Internet Protocol, Sept. 1981.

17. J. Postel. RFC 793: Transmission Control Protocol, Sept. 1981.

18. W. Simpson. RFC 1661: The point-to-point protocol (PPP), July 1994.

19. S. T. Taft. Programming the Internet in Ada 95. *Lecture Notes in Computer Science*, 1088:1–16, 1996.

20. A. Villazón and W. Binder. Portable resource reification in Java-based mobile agent systems. In *Fifth IEEE International Conference on Mobile Agents (MA-2001)*, Atlanta, Georgia, USA, Dec. 2001.

21. J. Vitek and G. Castagna. Seal: A framework for secure mobile computations. In *Internet Programming Languages*, 1999.

22. F. Yellin. Low level security in Java. In *Fourth International Conference on the World-Wide Web*, MIT, Boston, USA, Dec. 1995.

A POSIX-Ada Interface for
Application-Defined Scheduling

Mario Aldea Rivas and Michael González Harbour

Departamento de Electrónica y Computadores
Universidad de Cantabria
39005-Santander, SPAIN
{aldeam,mgh}@unican.es

Abstract: This paper presents an application program interface (API) that enables applications running on top of a POSIX operating system to use application-defined scheduling algorithms in a way compatible with the scheduling model of the Ada 95 Real-Time Systems Annex. Several application-defined schedulers, implemented as special user tasks, can coexist in the system in a predictable way. This API is currently implemented on our operating system MaRTE OS.

Keywords: Real-Time Systems, Kernel, Scheduling, Operating Systems, Ada 95, POSIX.

1   Introduction[1]

The Real-Time Annex in Ada 95 defines only one scheduling policy: FIFO_Within_Priorities. Real-time POSIX [4][6] also defines a preemptive fixed priority scheduling policy similar to it, together with two other compatible scheduling policies: a round robin within priorities policy and the sporadic server policy. These policies are accessible to Ada tasks running on a POSIX real-time operating system. Although fixed priority scheduling is an excellent choice for real-time systems, there are application requirements that cannot be fully accomplished with these policies only. It is well known that with dynamic priority scheduling policies it is possible to achieve higher utilization levels of the system resources than with fixed priority policies. In addition, there are many systems for which their dynamic nature make it necessary to have very flexible scheduling mechanisms, such as multimedia systems, in which different quality of service properties need to be traded against one another.

It could be possible to incorporate into the Ada and POSIX standards new dynamic scheduling policies to be used in addition to the existing policies. The main problem is that the variety of these policies is so great that it would be difficult to standardize on just a few. Different applications needs would require different policies. Instead, in this paper we propose defining an interface for application-defined schedulers that could be used to implement a large variety of scheduling policies. This interface is

---

[1] This work has been funded by the *Comisión Interministerial de Ciencia y Tecnología* of the Spanish Government under grants TIC99-1043-C03-03 and 1FD 1997-1799 (TAP)

J. Blieberger and A. Strohmeier (Eds.): Ada-Europe 2002, LNCS 2361, pp. 136-150, 2002.

integrated into the POSIX Ada Binding [6] and, together with its C language version, it is being submitted for consideration by the Real-Time POSIX Working Group.

The proposed interface is currently implemented in our operating system MaRTE OS (Minimal Real-Time Operating System for Embedded Applications) [2], which is a real-time kernel that follows the Minimal Real-Time POSIX.13 subset [5], providing both the C and Ada language POSIX interfaces. It allows cross-development of Ada and C real-time applications. Mixed Ada-C applications can also be developed, with a globally consistent scheduling of Ada tasks and C threads. It is directly usable as the basis for the gnat run-time system (GNARL) [9].

The paper is organized as follows: Section 2 discusses some related work on application-defined scheduling and sets the justification for our proposal. Section 3 discusses our model for application-defined scheduling. In Section 4 the Ada API is described and in Section 5 an example of its use is shown. Section 6 presents some performance metrics showing the overhead of using our implementation. Section 7 gives our conclusions and future work.

2   Related Work and Motivation

The idea of application-defined scheduling has been used in many systems. A solution is proposed in RED-Linux [11], in which a two-level scheduler is used, where the upper level is implemented as a user process that maps several quality of service parameters into a low-level attributes object to be handled by the lower level scheduler. The parameters defined are the task priorities, start and finish times, and execution time budget. With that mechanism some scheduling algorithms can be implemented but there may be others that cannot be implemented if they are based on parameters different from those included in the aforementioned attributes object. In addition, this solution does not address the implementation of protocols for shared resources that could avoid priority inversion or similar effects.

A different approach is followed in the CPU Inheritance Scheduling [7], in which the kernel only implements task blocking, unblocking and CPU donation, and the application defined schedulers are tasks which donate the CPU to other tasks. In this approach the only method used to avoid priority inversion is the priority inheritance. Although other synchronization policies could be implemented, the lack of an interface to trigger scheduling decisions by the use of mutexes makes it difficult or impossible to implement general synchronization protocols, which may be a limitation for special application-defined policies. In addition although this approach supports multiprocessor schedulers, it is not possible to have one single-threaded scheduler to schedule threads in other processors. Some multiprocessor architectures, for example using one general-purpose processor running the scheduler and an array of digital signal processors running the scheduled threads, may require that capability.

Another common solution is to implement the application scheduling algorithms as modules to be included or linked with the kernel (S.Ha.R.K [8], RT-Linux [12], Vassal [3]). With this mechanism the functions exported by the modules are invoked from the kernel at every scheduling point. This is a very efficient and general method but, as a drawback, the application scheduling algorithms can neither be isolated from each other nor from the kernel itself, so, a bug in one of them could affect the whole system.

In our approach the application scheduler is invoked at every scheduling point like with the kernel modules, so the scheduler can have complete control over its scheduled tasks. But in addition, our application scheduling algorithm is executed by a user task. This fact implies two important advantages from our point of view:

a) The system reliability can be improved by protecting the system from the actions of an erroneous application scheduler. For efficiency, our interface allows execution of the application-defined scheduler in an execution environment different than that of regular application tasks, for example inside the kernel. But alternatively, the interface allows the implementation to execute the scheduler in the environment of the application, to isolate it from the kernel. In this way, high priority tasks that are critical cannot be affected by a faulty scheduler executing at a lower priority level.

b) The application scheduling code can use standard interfaces like those defined in the POSIX standard. In some systems part of these interfaces might not be accessible for invocation from inside the kernel.

We have designed our interface so that several application-defined schedulers can be defined, and so that they have a behaviour compatible with other existing scheduling policies in POSIX, both on single processor and multiprocessor platforms. In addition, the interface needs to take into account the implementation of application-defined synchronization protocols.

One of the design criteria for our Ada interface has been to avoid requiring changes to existing run-time systems or to the compilers. This is important to make it easier to implement the interface and thus increase the chances that it is widely used.

The dynamic scheduling mechanism proposed for Real-Time CORBA 2.0 [10] represents an object-oriented interface to application-defined schedulers, but it does not attempt to define how that interface communicates with the operating system. The interface presented in this paper is the OS low-level interface, and thus an RT CORBA implementation could use it to support the proposed dynamic scheduling interface.

In summary, the motivation for this work is to provide developers of applications running on top of standard operating systems (POSIX) with a flexible scheduling mechanism, handling both task scheduling and synchronization, that enables them to schedule dynamic applications that would not meet their requirements using the more rigid fixed-priority scheduling provided in those operating systems. This mechanism allows isolation of the kernel from misbehaved application schedulers. In addition, we wish to provide this mechanism both for applications developed in C or Ada.

3   Model for Application-Defined Scheduling

Fig. 1 shows the proposed approach for application-defined scheduling. Each application scheduler is a special kind of task, that is responsible of scheduling a set of tasks that have been attached to it. This leads to two classes of tasks in this context:

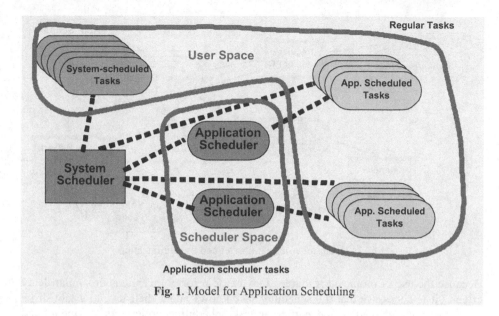

Fig. 1. Model for Application Scheduling

- *Application scheduler tasks*: special tasks used to run application schedulers.
- *Regular tasks*: regular application tasks

The application schedulers can run in the context of the kernel or in the context of the application. This allows implementations in which application tasks are not trusted, and therefore their schedulers run in the context of the application, as well as implementations for trusted application schedulers, which can run more efficiently inside the kernel. Because of this duality we will model the scheduler tasks as if they run in a separate context, which we call the scheduler space. The main implication of this separate space is that for portability purposes the application schedulers cannot directly share information with the kernel, nor with regular tasks, except by using the POSIX shared memory objects, which is the mechanism for sharing memory among entities with different address spaces.

According to the way a task is scheduled, we can categorize the tasks as:

- *System-scheduled tasks*: these tasks are scheduled directly by the run-time system and/or the operating system, without intervention of a scheduler task.
- *Application-scheduled tasks*: these tasks are also scheduled by the run-time system and/or the operating system, but before they can be scheduled, they need to be activated by their application-defined scheduler.

Although an application scheduler task can itself be application scheduled, implementations should not be required to support this feature, because usually these tasks will be system scheduled.

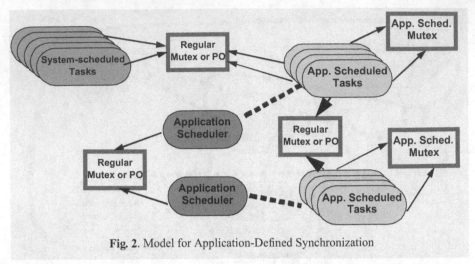

Fig. 2. Model for Application-Defined Synchronization

Because the use of protected resources may cause priority inversions or similar delay effects, it is necessary that the scheduler task knows about their use, to establish its own protocols adapted to the particular task scheduling policy. As we mentioned above, one of the goals of our interface is that it does not require changes to existing Ada run-time systems, and this means that we cannot change the priority ceiling locking defined in Ada's Real-Time Annex for protected objects. For this reason, we have designed our scheduling interface around the POSIX mutexes, which are accessible through the POSIX Ada Bindings. The application can still use protected objects if the `Ceiling_Locking` policy is acceptable for the chosen scheduling policy, and also for synchronization between system- and application-scheduled tasks. Fig. 2 shows the basic model of these scheduling interfaces, in which two kinds of mutexes will be considered:

- *System-scheduled mutexes.* Those created with the current POSIX protocols: `No_Priority_Inheritance`, `Highest_Ceiling_Priority` (immediate priority ceiling), or `Highest_Blocked_Task` (basic priority inheritance). They can be used to access resource shared between application schedulers, between sets of application-scheduled threads attached to different schedulers, or even between an application scheduler and its scheduled threads (in this case the mutex and its protected state must be placed in a POSIX shared memory object).

- *Application-scheduled mutexes*: Those created with the protocol `Appsched_Protocol`. The behaviour of the protocol itself is defined by the application scheduler.

3.1. Relations with Other Tasks

Each task in the system, whether application- or system-scheduled, has a system priority:

- For system-scheduled tasks, the system priority is the priority assigned using `pragma Priority` or the subprogram `Ada.Dynamic_Priorities`.

Set_Priority, possibly modified by the inheritance of other priorities through the use of mutexes or protected objects.

- For application-scheduled tasks, the system priority is lower than or equal to the system priority of their scheduler task. The system priority of an application-scheduled task may change because of the inheritance of other system priorities through the use of mutexes or protected objects. In that case, its scheduler also inherits the same system priority (but this priority is not inherited by the rest of the tasks scheduled by that scheduler). In addition to the system priority, application-scheduled tasks have *application scheduling parameters* that are used to schedule that task contending with the other tasks attached to the same application scheduler. The system priority always takes precedence over any application scheduling parameters. Therefore, application-scheduled tasks and their scheduler take precedence over tasks with lower system priority, and they are always preempted by tasks with higher system priority that become ready. The scheduler always takes precedence over its scheduled tasks.

If application-scheduled tasks coexist at the same priority level with other system-scheduled tasks, then the Real-Time Annex scheduling rules apply as if the application-scheduled tasks were scheduled under the FIFO_Within_Priorities policy; so a task runs until completion, until blocked, or until preempted, whatever happens earlier. Of course, in that case the interactions between the different policies may be difficult to analyse, and thus the normal use will be to have the scheduler task and its scheduled tasks running at an exclusive range of system priorities.

In the presence of priority inheritance, the scheduler inherits the same priorities as its scheduled tasks, to prevent priority inversions from occurring. This means that high priority tasks that share resources with lower system-priority application tasks must take into account the scheduler overhead when accounting for their blocking times.

3.2. Relations Between the Scheduler and Its Attached Tasks

When an application-defined task is attached to its application scheduler, the latter has to either accept it or reject it, based upon the current state and the scheduling attributes of the candidate task. Rejection of a task causes POSIX_Error to be raised during the attachment process.

Each application-defined scheduler may activate many application-scheduled tasks to run concurrently. The scheduler may also block previously activated tasks. Among themselves, concurrently scheduled tasks are activated like FIFO_Within_Priorities tasks. As mentioned previously, the scheduler always takes precedence over its scheduled tasks.

For an application-scheduled task to become ready it is necessary that its scheduler activates it. When the application task executes one of the following actions or experiences one of the following situations, a scheduling event is generated for the scheduler, unless the scheduling event to be generated is being filtered out (discarded).

- when a task requests attachment to the scheduler
- when a task blocks or gets ready
- when a task changes its scheduling parameters
- when a task invokes the *yield* operation (i.e., `delay 0.0` operation)
- when a task explicitly invokes the scheduler
- when a task inherits or uninherits a priority, due to the use of a system mutex or a protected object
- when a task does any operation on a application-scheduled mutex.

The application scheduler is a special task whose code is usually a loop where it waits for a scheduling event to be notified to it by the system, and then determines the next application task or tasks to be activated.

Although the scheduler can activate many tasks at once, it is a single task and therefore its actions are all sequential. For multiprocessor systems this may seem to be a limitation, but for these systems several schedulers could be running simultaneously on different processors, cooperating with each other by synchronizing through regular mutexes and condition variables, or protected objects. For single processor systems the sequential nature of the scheduler should be no problem.

4   Interface

The interface offered to the programmer is divided into three packages:

- `POSIX_Application_Scheduling`: a completely new package where the main part of the interface is defined. This package defines the scheduling events and actions and also operations to manage scheduler and scheduled tasks.
- `POSIX_Mutexes`: This is an existing package in the POSIX Ada Bindings, to which we have added the interface for management of application-scheduled mutexes.
- `POSIX_Timers`: This is also an existing package in the POSIX Ada Bindings, to which we have added the CPU-Time clocks. This functionality is not yet included in the POSIX Ada binding but it has already been standardized in the C family of POSIX standards [4]. It is very interesting for implementing scheduling algorithms based on the execution time consumed by the tasks, such as the sporadic server, round robin, and others.

The main elements of the interface are in package `POSIX_Application_-Scheduling`, and they are described in detail in the following subsections.

4.1. Interfaces for the Scheduler Tasks

4.1.1. Scheduling Events

The interface describes an abstract data type for the scheduling events that the system may report to a scheduler task. The system stores the scheduling events in a FIFO queue until processed by the scheduler. The information included in these events is:

the event code; the identifier of the task that caused the event; and additional information associated with the event, and dependent on it; it can be an inherited (or uninherited) system priority, information related to an accepted signal, a pointer to an application-scheduled mutex, or application-specific information.

The specific events that may be notified to a scheduler task are shown in Table 1:

Table 1: Scheduling Events (cont.)

Event Code	Description	Additional information
NEW_TASK	A new task has requested attachment to the scheduler	none
TERMINATE_TASK	A task has been terminated	none
READY	A task has become unblocked by the system	none
BLOCK	A task has blocked	none
YIELD	A task yields the CPU (due to a delay 0.0)	none
SIGNAL	A signal belonging to the requested set has been accepted by the scheduler task.	Signal-related information
CHANGE_SCHED_PARAM	A task has changed its scheduling parameters	none
EXPLICIT_CALL	A task has explicitly invoked the scheduler	Application message
TIMEOUT	A timeout has expired	none
PRIORITY_INHERIT	A task has inherited a new system priority due to the use of system mutexes or protected objects	Inherited system priority
PRIORITY_UNINHERIT	A task has finished the inheritance of a system priority	Uninherited system priority
INIT_MUTEX	A task has requested initialization of an application-scheduled mutex	Pointer to the mutex
DESTROY_MUTEX	A task has destroyed an application-scheduled mutex	Pointer to the mutex
LOCK_MUTEX	A task has invoked a "lock" operation on an available application- scheduled mutex	Pointer to the mutex
TRY_LOCK_MUTEX	A task has invoked a "try lock" operation on an available application- scheduled mutex	Pointer to the mutex
UNLOCK_MUTEX	A task has released the lock of an application-scheduled mutex	Pointer to the mutex
BLOCK_AT_MUTEX	A task has blocked at an application-scheduled mutex	Pointer to the mutex
CHANGE_MUTEX_-SCHED_PARAM	A task has changed the scheduling parameters of an application-scheduled mutex	Pointer to the mutex

There are some Ada-specific events that might have been useful to a scheduler, but that are not available because the underlying POSIX standard does not know about them. For example, a task becoming completed, or a task blocked waiting for a child to elaborate. In the schedulers that we have built, these situations can be handled through the usual BLOCK event. If more accurate handling of these events is desired, cooperation from the application developer would be required, by establishing additional communication between the scheduled thread and its scheduler, via Invoke_Scheduler (see section 4.2) and/or by accessing shared data structures.

4.1.2. Executing Scheduling Actions

Another important abstract data type is the interface for storing a list of scheduling actions. This list will be prepared by the scheduler task and reported to the system via a call to one of the Execute_Actions operations. The possible actions that can be added to one of these lists are the following:

- Accept or reject a task that has requested attachment to this scheduler
- Activate or suspend an application scheduled task
- Accept or reject initialization of an application-scheduled mutex
- Grant the lock of an application-scheduled mutex

The main operations of our interface are the Execute_Actions family of procedures, which allow the application scheduler to execute a list of scheduling actions and then wait for the next scheduling event to be reported by the system. If desired, a timeout can be set as an additional return condition which will occur when there is no scheduling event available but the timeout expires. The system time measured immediately before the procedure returns can be requested if it is relevant for the algorithm.

The Execute_Actions procedures can also be programmed to return when a POSIX signal is generated for the task. This possibility eases the use of POSIX timers, including CPU-time timers, as sources of scheduling events for our scheduler tasks. Use of CPU-time timers allows the scheduler to impose limits on the execution time that a particular task may spend. The specification of the Execute_Actions procedures is:

```
procedure Execute_Actions
   (Sched_Actions : in  Scheduling_Actions;
    Set           : in  POSIX_Signals.Signal_Set;
    Event         : out Scheduling_Event;
    Current_Time  : out POSIX.Timespec);

procedure Execute_Actions_With_Timeout
   (Sched_Actions : in  Scheduling_Actions;
    Set           : in  POSIX_Signals.Signal_Set;
    Event         : out Scheduling_Event;
    Timeout       : in  POSIX.Timespec;
    Current_Time  : out POSIX.Timespec);
```

Other overloaded versions of these procedures with less parameters are available for the cases in which the application is not interested in obtaining the current time, or is not interested in waiting for a signal to be received.

4.1.3. Other Interfaces

The `Become_An_Application_Scheduler` procedure allows a regular task to become an application scheduler:

```
procedure Become_An_Application_Scheduler;
```

The ideal interface for this purpose would be a pragma that would enable the task to be created as an application scheduler from the beginning, but that would imply a modification to the compiler.

After the task has become an application scheduler it can set its attributes through different operations in the interface. The attributes are the kind of timeout that is supported (relative or absolute), the clock used to determine when the timeout expires, and the event mask that allows scheduling events to be discarded by the system, and thus are not reported to the application scheduler. A subset of the scheduler attributes interface is shown below:

```
procedure Set_Clock (Clock : in POSIX_Timers.Clock_Id);
procedure Set_Flags (Flags : in Scheduler_Flags);
type Event_Mask is private;
procedure Set_Event_Mask (Mask : in Event_Mask);
```

4.2. Interfaces for the Application-Scheduled Tasks

The `Change_Task_Policy_To_App_Sched` procedure allows a regular task to set its scheduling policy to application-scheduled, attaching itself to a particular scheduler. The scheduling parameters associated with the task can be set via the `Change_Task_Policy` procedure of the generic package `Application_Defined_Policy`. In this package the generic parameter is the scheduling `Parameters` type, which of course must be defined by the application.

```
procedure Change_Task_Policy_To_App_Sched
    (Scheduler : in Ada.Task_Identification.Task_Id);

generic
    type Parameters is private;
package Application_Defined_Policy is
    procedure Change_Task_Policy
        (Scheduler : in Ada.Task_Identification.Task_Id;
         Param     : in Parameters);
    procedure Get_Parameters
        (T     : in  Ada.Task_Identification.Task_Id;
         Param : out Parameters);
end Application_Defined_Policy;
```

The `Invoke_Scheduler` procedure allows a scheduled task to explicitly invoke its scheduler. A generic version of this procedure is also offered for the case in which the scheduled task needs to send a message with information to its scheduler. The type of this message is the generic parameter.

```
procedure Invoke_Scheduler;

generic
   type Message is private;
package Explicit_Scheduler_Invocation is
   procedure Invoke (Msg : in Message);
   function Get_Message (Event : in Scheduling_Event)
               return Message;
end Explicit_Scheduler_Invocation;
```

An interface for handling task-specific data has been added. At first we had planned using the task-specific data interface defined in package Ada.Task_Parameters defined in Ada 95 Annex C, but we found out that this package did not allow us handling tasks that had terminated, and it is usually an important part of the application scheduler to do cleanup operations after a task terminates. For this reason we have defined our own generic package for task-specific data that may be shared between the scheduler and its scheduled tasks.

5   Example of an Application-Defined Policy: EDF

5.1. Basic EDF

The following example shows the pseudocode of a set of periodic tasks scheduled under an application-defined Earliest Deadline First (EDF) scheduling policy. In first place we define a data type for the scheduling parameters, and we instantiate the generic package Application_Defined_Policy using this type:

```
type EDF_Parameters is record
   Deadline, Period : POSIX.Timespec;
end record;

package EDF_Policy is new
   Application_Defined_Policy(EDF_Parameters);
```

The scheduler can be in one of the three following states: Idle, when there are no tasks registered to be scheduled; Waiting, when there are tasks registered but none active; and Running, when there are one or more active tasks:

```
type EDF_State is (Idle, Waiting, Running);
```

The EDF scheduler has a list of tasks that are registered for being scheduled under it. Each of these tasks can be active, blocked, or timed (when it has finished its current execution and is waiting for its next period):

```
type Scheduled_Task_State is (Active, Blocked, Timed);
```

The scheduler uses the following operations:

- The Schedule_Next procedure uses the current time and the list of registered tasks to update the list, calculate the current state, the next task to be executed, and the earliest start time of the set of active tasks (not including the next one to run).

- The `Add_To_List_Of_Tasks` procedure adds a new task to the list of scheduled tasks.

- The `Eliminate_From_List_of_tasks` procedure eliminates a terminated task from the list of scheduled tasks.

- The `Make_Active` procedure changes the state of a task in the list to `Active`.

- The `Make_Blocked` procedure changes the state of a task in the list to `Blocked`.

- The `Make_Timed` procedure changes the state of a task in the list to `Timed`.

The pseudocode of the scheduler is the following:

```
task body EDF_Scheduler is
    Sch_State : EDF_State;
    Current_Task : Task_Id;
    Now, Earliest_Start : POSIX.Timespec;
    Event : Scheduling_Event;
    Sched_Actions : Scheduling_Actions;
begin
    Become_An_Application_Scheduler;
    Set_Clock(Clock_Realtime);
    Set_Flags(Absolute_Timeout);
    Now:=Get_Time(Clock_Realtime);
    loop
        Schedule_Next(Sch_State, Current_Task,
                        Earliest_Start, Now);
        case Sch_State is
            when Idle ->
                Execute_Actions(Null_Sched_Actions, Event, Now);
            when Waiting =>
                Execute_Actions_with_Timeout
                        (Null_Sched_Actions, Event,
                        Earliest_Start,Now);
            when Running =>
                Add_Activate(Sched_Actions,Current_Task)
                Execute_Actions_with_Timeout
                        (Sched_Actions, Event,
                        Earliest_Start,Now);
        end case;

        -- process scheduling events
        case Get_Event_Code(Event) is
            when New_Task =>
                Add_To_List_of_Tasks (Get_Task(Event),now);
            when Terminate_Task =>
                Eliminate_From_List_of_Tasks (Get_Task(Event));
            when Ready =>
                Make_Active(Get_Task(Event));
            when Block =>
                Make_Blocked(Get_Task(Event));
            when Explicit_Call =>
                Make_Timed(Get_Task(Event));
```

```
      when Timeout => null;
      when Others => null;
   end case;
 end loop;
end EDF_Scheduler;
```

Finally, the pseudocode of one of the application-scheduled tasks is the following:

```
task body Periodic_Task is
   Param : EDF_Parameters:=(Deadline,Period);
begin
   EDF_Policy.Change_Task_Policy
         (Task_Id_of(EDF_Scheduler),Param);
   loop
      -- do useful work
      Invoke_Scheduler; -- task will wait until the next period
   end loop;
end Periodic_Task;
```

5.2. Constant Bandwidth Server

Extending the EDF scheduler to support other compatible scheduling algorithms is easy. As a proof of concepts we have implemented the Constant Bandwidth Server (CBS) [1], which efficiently schedules soft real-time aperiodic tasks while guaranteeing the response times of hard real-time activities. Adding the CBS to the EDF scheduler implies extending the scheduling parameters type with an additional *budget* field that limits the execution time of the task during its server period, and using a CPU-time timer to enforce that budget. The set of events processed by the scheduler needs to be increased to support the signal generated by the expiration of that timer, as well as another signal used by the system to activate a CBS aperiodic task. The performance of this implementation is described in the following section.

6   Performance Metrics

Table 2 shows some performance metrics on the use of different application-defined scheduling policies, measured on a 1.1GHz Pentium III. We can see that the context switch between two tasks for a simple scheduler like a round-robin within priorities is even less than with a regular `delay until` statement with no application-defined scheduling (due to the overhead of the Ada run-time system). For a more complex scheduling algorithm like the CBS, the context switch time is only slightly higher. The result is efficient enough to be able to run high frequency tasks that are scheduled by application defined policies. For example, the scheduling overhead associated with a 1KHz task, assuming two context switches per execution, is only 1.2% for the CBS.

Table 2: Performance on a 1.1GHz Pentium III

Scheduling Algorithm	Context switch (μs)	Overhead for a 1KHz task
Regular Ada delay until statement	5	1%
Round robin within priorities	4.5	0.9%
CBS	6	1.2%

7   Conclusions and Further Work

We have defined a new API for application-defined scheduling. There are two versions of the API, one in C and the other one in Ada. Both are designed in the context of a POSIX operating system. The main design requirements have been to have a compatible behaviour with other existing POSIX fixed priority scheduling policy, to be able to isolate the scheduler from the kernel and from other application schedulers, to be able to run both on single processor and multiprocessor systems, and to be able to describe application-defined synchronization protocols.

The proposed API has been implemented in MaRTE OS, which is a free software implementation of the POSIX minimal real-time operating system, intended for small embedded systems. It is written in Ada but provides both the POSIX Ada and the C interfaces. Using this implementation we have programmed and tested several scheduling policies, such as a priority-based round robin scheduler, EDF, and more complex dynamic scheduling policies. We have also tested some application-defined synchronization protocols, such as the full Priority Ceiling Protocol. Preliminary performance data show a nice level of efficiency.

The main limitations of our proposed interface from the point of view of an Ada application are:

- We cannot use protected objects for application-defined synchronization protocols. We can only use POSIX mutexes for this purpose.

- The scheduler task cannot be created as a scheduler task from the beginning; it has to be created dynamically. In addition, its scheduled tasks must be created with one of the POSIX fixed-priority scheduling policies, and then switched to become application scheduled tasks.

The reason for these limitations has been our desire to keep the implementation simple and not require changing the run-time system nor the compiler. In the future, it would be interesting to make these changes so that we could use protected objects for application-defined synchronization, and pragmas for setting the scheduler task and the scheduled tasks properties from the beginning.

MaRTE OS, including the application-defined scheduling services defined in this paper can be found at: http://marte.unican.es

References

[1]   L. Abeni and G. Buttazzo. "Integrating Multimedia Applications in Hard Real-Time Systems". *Proceedings of the IEEE Real-Time Systems Symposium*, Madrid, Spain, December 1998

[2]   M. Aldea and M. González. "MaRTE OS: An Ada Kernel for Real-Time Embedded Applications". Proceedings of the International Conference on Reliable Software Technologies, Ada-Europe-2001, Leuven, Belgium, *Lecture Notes in Computer Science, LNCS 2043*, May, 2001.

[3]   G.M. Candea and M.B. Jones, "Vassal: Loadable Scheduler Support for Multi-Policy Scheduling". *Proceedings of the Second USENIX Windows NT Symposium*, Seattle, Washington, August 1998.

[4]   IEEE Std 1003.1-2001. *Information Technology -Portable Operating System Interface (POSIX)*. Institute of Electrical and electronic Engineers.

[5]   IEEE Std. 1003.13-1998. *Information Technology -Standardized Application Environment Profile- POSIX Realtime Application Support (AEP)*. The Institute of Electrical and Electronics Engineers.

[6]   IEEE Std 1003.5b-1996, *Information Technology—POSIX Ada Language Interfaces— Part 1: Binding for System Application Program Interface (API)—Amendment 1: Realtime Extensions*. The Institute of Electrical and Engineering Electronics.

[7]   B. Ford and S. Susarla, "CPU Inheritance Scheduling". *Proceedings of OSDI*, October 1996.

[8]   P. Gai, L. Abeni, M. Giorgi, G. Buttazzo, "A New Kernel Approach for Modular Real-Time Systems Development", *IEEE Proceedings of the 13th Euromicro Conference on Real-Time Systems*, Delft, The Netherlands, June 2001.

[9]   E.W. Giering and T.P. Baker (1994). The GNU Ada Runtime Library (GNARL): Design and Implementation. *Wadas'94 Proceedings*.

[10] OMG. *Real-Time CORBA 2.0: Dynamic Scheduling*, Joint Final Submission. OMG Document orbos/2001-06-09, June 2001.

[11] Y.C. Wang and K.J. Lin, "Implementing a general real-time scheduling framework in the red-linux real-time kernel". *Proceedings of IEEE Real-Time Systems Symposium*, Phoenix, December 1999.

[12] V. Yodaiken, "An RT-Linux Manifesto". *Proceedings of the 5th Linux Expo*, Raleigh, North Carolina, USA, May 1999.

Closing the Loop: The Influence of Code Analysis on Design

Peter Amey

Praxis Critical Systems, 20, Manvers St., Bath BA1 1PX, UK
peter.amey@praxis-cs.co.uk

Abstract. Static code analysis originally concerned the extraction from source code of various properties of a program. Although this kind of reverse engineering approach can uncover errors that are hard to detect in other ways, it is not a very efficient use of resources because of its retrospective nature and the late error detection that results. The SPARK language and its associated Examiner tool took a different approach which emphasises error *prevention* ("correctness by construction") rather than error *detection*. Recent work with SPARK has shown that very early application of static analysis can have a beneficial influence on software architectures and designs. The paper describes the use of SPARK to produce designs with demonstrably low coupling and high cohesion.

1 Introduction

Software development lifecycles usually make a clear distinction between *development* activities and *verification* activities. The classic V model is a good example. The distinction made some sense when verification was largely synonymous with testing since, clearly, you cannot dynamically test something until you have produced it. Unfortunately, the same thinking has affected the way that static analysis tools have been developed and deployed. There is now compelling evidence that the use of analysis tools *throughout development*, especially prior to compilation, can bring significant economic and technical benefits [1,2]. Some of this arises straightforwardly from earlier error detection but more subtle effects involving the influence of analysis on design appear to be equally, or perhaps even more, significant. The paper explores these effects and the important benefits that can accrue.

2 Static Analysis - An Historical Overview

The early development of static analysis tools, which resulted in MALPAS [3] and SPADE [4] in the UK, was largely concerned with the reverse engineering of existing source code; this can be termed *retrospective analysis*. The reasons for this were straightforward: certification authorities and major consumers of software such as the UK Ministry of Defence, were being offered complex, software-intensive systems which came with very little evidence for their suitability and

J. Blieberger and A. Strohmeier (Eds.): Ada-Europe 2002, LNCS 2361, pp. 151–162, 2002.

safety for deployment. These agencies either had to accept the vendors' assurances that the system was satisfactory or find some way of exploring and understanding the system for themselves. In this environment retrospective static analysis tools offered one of the very few ways forward. The view that analysis is something that should take place near the end of the project lifecycle prevails to this day and has been reinforced by some more recent analysis tool developments. For example ASIS-based tools perform their analyses on information supplied by the compiler; clearly the code must be compilable before the analysis can begin. Similarly, analysis based on techniques such as abstract interpretation requires a complete, linkable closure of the program to be effective; again this is only available late in the project lifecycle.

3   The Disadvantages of Retrospective Analysis

Postponing static analysis to late in the development process has both technical and economic drawbacks. Technically it tends to have only a very limited impact on the quality of the finished product. By definition it cannot influence the way the code has been designed and constructed so its role is limited to the uncovering of errors in the supposedly finished product. Even here the benefit is diminished because of the reluctance to change code which is perceived as being "finished". Significant deficiencies, uncovered by analysis, may be allowed to remain in delivered code because the cost of correction and re-testing is considered too high. These deficiencies remain and may pose a risk to future development and maintenance activities. This reluctance to change code, despite errors being exposed by analysis, was a significant conclusion of a static analysis experience report presented at SIGAda 2000 [5]; it is an inevitable consequence of retrospective analysis approaches.

4   Correctness by Construction

In the UK, the developers of the SPADE toolset learned from its initial deployment that the real issues involved were associated with design rather than just with analysis. Well written programs were straightforward to analyse whereas badly written ones defied the most powerful techniques available. Therefore the need was not for ever more powerful analysis techniques but rather support for *constructing* correct programs. This reasoning led to SPARK [6,7,8] and its support tool, the SPARK Examiner. A key design feature of the SPARK language is the use of annotations to strengthen package and subprogram specifications to the point where analyses could be performed without needing access to their implementations; this allows analysis of incomplete programs. The ability to analyse program fragments allows static analysis to be deployed very early in the development process, prior to compilation, which leads to significant benefits. Some of this is very straightforward: errors detected by static analysis performed at the engineer's terminal as he writes code are corrected immediately. They never make it to configuration control, don't have to be found by

testing and don't generate any re-work. The economics of this are very powerful; see for example the Lockheed C130J mission computer project where error
densities were reduced by an order of magnitude while, at the same time, costs
were reduced by three quarters [1,2].

More subtly, the use of analysis as an integral part of the development process
alters the way in which engineers approach the writing of code. They quickly get
used to the kinds of constructs that the SPARK Examiner complains about and
avoid using them. They tend to write simpler, more prosaic code which is more
often correct and also turns out to be easier to understand, test and maintain.
These effects are most pronounced where the process involves formal verification
or code proof: the style of coding soon changes to make the code easier to prove;
see for example [9].

More recently, Praxis Critical Systems has begun to see ways of gaining even
more leverage from the use of static analysis; this goes beyond error detection
and low-level code style issues and has an impact on program architectural design itself. The approach makes use of properties measured by static analysis
directly to drive design decisions. The result is significant improvements in certain important design properties.

5   SPARK Annotations

SPARK's annotations are special comments introduced by the prefix "#". They
have significance to the SPARK Examiner although they are, of course, ignored
by an Ada compiler. The purpose of annotations is to strengthen the specification
of packages and subprograms. A full description of the system of annotations
can be found in [6,7,8]. For the purpose of analysing design qualities the key
annotations are: *own variables*, *global annotations* and *dependency relations*.

An *own variable annotation* indicates that a package contains persistent data
or "state". For example:

```
package P
--# own State;
is
...
end P;
```

tells us that package P contains some persistent data that we have chosen to call
State. The own variable State can be an abstraction of the actual variables
(known in SPARK as *refinement constituents*) making up the package's state.

A *global annotation* indicates the direct or indirect use of data external to a
subprogram and the direction of data flows involved. For example:

```
procedure K (X : in Integer);
--# global in out P.State;
```

tells us that the execution of procedure K causes the own variable State in package P to be both referenced and updated.

Finally, *a dependency relation* indicates the information flow dependencies of a subprogram, i.e. which *imported* variables are used to obtain the final values of each *exported* variable. For example:

```
procedure K (X : in Integer);
--# global in out P.State;
--# derives P.State from P.State, X;
```

tells that the final value of P.State after execution of K is some function of its intitial value and of the parameter X. Other annotations can provide a more precise relationship between imports and exports for proof purposes but these are beyond the scope of this paper.

A less significant annotation, *inherit*, governs inter-package visibility. For the purposes of this paper it can be considered to be the transitive closure of a package's with clauses; *inherit* shows direct and indirect package use whereas *with* shows only direct use.

SPARK annotations provide a strong indication of the degree of coupling between objects. A data item declared inside a subprogram does not appear in its annotations at all (even if it is of some complex abstract type declared in another package); a parameter appears only in the derives annotation; and data manipulated globally appears in both the global and derives annotation.

6   Desirable Design Properties

Well designed programs have a number of heavily interconnected properties that are described below. A good design will strike a balance between these various characteristics and extremes should be treated with suspicion. For example a design which placed the entire program in a single procedure might score well on encapsulation but would be very poor when measured for cohesion!

Encapsulation Encapsulation is the clear separation of specification from implementation; this is sometimes described as a "contract model" of programming. It is an important principle that users of an object should not be concerned with its internal behaviour. Were this not the case then loose coupling could not be achieved. The principle of encapsulation applies not only to data and operations but even to type declarations: for example, a limited private type provides more encapsulation than a full Ada type declaration.

Abstraction Abstraction is a necessary component of encapsulation. Abstraction allows us to strip away (ignore) certain levels of detail when taking an external view of an object; the detail is hidden by being encapsulated in the object. The term "information hiding" is frequently used in this context. This term is somewhat inappropriate for critical systems about which reasoning is important: information, by definition, *informs*. We cannot reason in the absence of information; however, we can ensure that our reasoning takes place at an appropriate level of abstraction, which we achieve by hiding *detail*. Hiding unnecessary detail allows us to focus on the *essential* properties of an object. The essential properties are those which support encapsulation by allowing use of an object without the need to be concerned with its implementation.

Loose coupling Coupling is a measure of the connections between objects. Highly coupled objects interact in ways that make their separate modification difficult. Undesirable, high levels of coupling arise when abstractions are poor and encapsulation inadequate. Software components can be strongly or weakly coupled. The OOD literature is not entirely consistent as to which forms of coupling are weak and which are strong and therefore less desirable. SPARK provides a simple and clear distinction: the appearance of a package name only as a prefix in an *inherits* annotation represents weak coupling (use of a service) but its appearance in a *global* or *derives* annotation indicates strong coupling (sharing of data).

Cohesion Whereas coupling is measured *between* objects, cohesion is a property *of* an object. Cohesion is a measure of focus or singleness of purpose. For example, a car has both door handles and pistons but we would not expect to find both represented by a single software object. If they were, we would not have high cohesion and modifying the software to support a 2-door rather than 4-door model (or to replace a Straight-4 with a Vee-8 engine) would involve changing rather unexpected parts of the design. There is a clear distinction between the isolation provided by highly-cohesive objects and the need to arrange such objects in hierarchies as described below.

Hierarchy Here we recognise that in the real-world objects exhibit hierarchy. Certain objects are contained inside others and cannot be reached directly. When we approach a car we can grasp a door handle but not a piston: the latter is inside the engine object which is itself inside the car. Many OOD methods are prone to producing unduly flat networks of objects (that would make door handles and pistons of equal prominence) which can easily encourage extra, undesirable, coupling between objects.

7   The Influence of Analysis on Design

To produce a "good" design, we seek to optimise the properties described above. This is where life gets difficult: we can all agree that loose coupling is desirable but how do we measure it and achieve it? Here the analysis performed by tools such as the SPARK Examiner is a direct help. For example, the Examiner performs *information flow analysis* [10] and this is a direct and sensitive measure of coupling between program units. High coupling manifests itself as large SPARK flow annotations (global and derives annotations) and loose coupling by small ones. We can seek to manipulate the design so that the annotations are in their smallest and most manageable form. This results in loose coupling and is consistent with the observation that well written programs are easy to analyse.

Information flows, and coupling, are a consequence of where "state"—persistent data—is located in the program's design. Values of state variables have to be calculated and set using information from other parts of the system and current values of state have to be conveyed from their location to the places which need those values; these are information flows. Information flows lead to couplings between components. Again the language rules of SPARK and the analysis performed by the Examiner come to our aid: own variable annotations describe the presence of state variables even though they are concealed according to the rules of Ada; this makes it possible to reason about them. There are also rules which govern the permitted refinements of abstract state variables on to their concrete constituents.

8   Information Flow Driven Design

The information obtained from analysis makes it possible to steer designs in the direction of highest cohesion and loosest coupling by constantly seeking to minimise information flow. There must, of course, be some information flow or the program would do nothing, but what we are seeking is to limit the flow to that essential to perform the desired task and not allow it to be dominated by extraneous flows between objects that a better design would eliminate. The control that allows information flow to be minimised is the location and choice of abstraction of system state. We can steer the program design in the required direction in two ways. The first is to make use of knowledge of how the analysis works to predict the kinds of designs that will work best and incorporate this knowledge into a set of design heuristics. The second is to carry out static analysis of the emerging system early (and often) and to be ready to refactor the design as soon as undesirable information flows—and hence coupling—start to emerge. This information flow driven design method is outlined below; a fuller description can be found in [11]. An approach that meets these goals has the following steps:

1. Identification of the system boundary, inputs and outputs.
   (a) Identify the boundary of the *system* for which the software is intended.
   (b) Identify the *physical* inputs and outputs of the system.
2. Identification of the SPARK software boundary within the overall system boundary.
   (a) Select a *software* boundary within the overall system boundary; this defines the parts of the system that will be statically analysed.
   (b) Define boundary packages to give controlled interfaces across the software boundary and translate physical entities into problem domain terms. These packages, to use the terminology of Parnas and Madey [12], translate *monitored variables* into *input data items* and *output data items* into *controlled variables*.
3. Identification and localization of system state.
   (a) Identify the essential state of the system; what *must* be stored?

(b) Decide in what terms we wish the SPARK information flow annotation of the main program to be expressed. Any state located outside the main program will appear in its annotations, any local to it will not. We seek here an annotation that describes the desired behaviour of the system in terms of its problem domain rather than simply a description of a particular software solution. See [13] for examples of annotations as a *system* rather than *software* description.

(c) Using these considerations, assess where state should be located and whether it should be implemented as abstract state machine packages or instances of abstract data types.

(d) Identify any natural state hierarchies and use refinement to model them.

(e) Test to see if the resulting provisional design is a loop-free partial ordering of packages and produces a logical and minimal flow of information. Backtrack as necessary.

4. Handling initialization of state.

(a) Consider how state will be initialized. Does this affect the location choices made?

(b) Examine and flow analyse the system framework.

5. Implementing the internal behaviour of components.

(a) Implement the chosen variable packages and type packages using top-down refinement with constant cross-checking against the design using the Examiner.

(b) Repeat these design steps for any identified subsystems.

9   Case Study - A Cycle Computer

The case study can be found in full in [11]. For the purposes of this paper we simply show the result of following the process decribed in Section 8 and the annotations of the main, entry-point subprogram that results. The consequences of *not* achieving the optimum design, as revealed by the size and form of the SPARK annotations, can then be shown.

9.1   Requirements

The cycle computer consists of a display/control unit to mount on the handlebars of a bicycle and a sensor that detects each complete revolution of the front wheel. The display unit shows the current instantaneous speed on a primary display and has a secondary display showing one of: *total distance, distance since last reset, average speed* and *time since last reset*. The display/control unit has two buttons: the first *clears* the time, average speed and trip values; and the second switches between the various secondary display *modes*. Unfortunately, but typically of many software projects, the hardware has already been designed: see Figure 1.

There is a clock that provides a regular tick (but not time of day) and the sensor, a reed relay operated by a magnet on the bicycle wheel, provides a pulse each time the wheel completes a revolution.

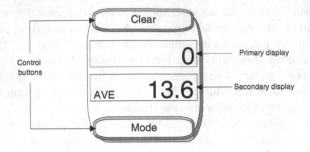

Fig. 1. Cycle Computer Hardware

9.2   Outline Design

Following the design process described in Section 8 we identify boundary packages for:

1. The clock.
2. The sequence of timed pulses received from the wheel sensor (pulse_queue).
3. A boundary abstraction encompassing both the display screens.
4. A boundary abstraction encompassing both the buttons.

Some state data needs to be stored for the controller to perform its function.

1. To calculate instantaneous speed we need (for smoothing purposes) a rolling average, over a short period, of values from the pulse queue.
2. For average speed we need to calculate an average of values from the pulse queue but over the entire period since the clear button was last pressed.
3. To display total distance travelled we need a count of the total number of pulses received since the system was first activated.
4. For trip distance we need a count of the total number of pulses since the last reset.
5. For the elapsed time or stopwatch function we need to record the clock tick value at the last reset.
6. Finally, all calculated values depend on the wheel size which must be stored in a suitable location. For simplicity the routines that would be needed for the user to be able to program the wheel size into the device have been excluded.

Items 1 to 4 are items of abstract state best considered internal to the controller; they should be implemented as instances of abstract data types.

Item 5 is a simple integer-typed value best implemented as a discrete Ada variable local to the main program.

The final item, wheel size, offers more interesting design choices. It could be implemented as a scalar local variable in the main program; however, since all displayed speeds depend on its value it is better to consider it to be external to the controller. We therefore store it in an abstract state machine package; this package also provides a suitable location for the operations to set a new wheel size value.

State initialization does not appear to present any problems; that in boundary packages is implicitly initialized by the environment and that declared local to the main program can be initialized during the first stages of program execution. Again, the wheel size requires some consideration. It is almost certainly best to regard the wheel size state as being initialized because we want to make it an import to the main program (to show that it affects the displayed speed). This suggests the need to set up a default wheel size during elaboration of the variable package which will be used unless a different size is programmed by the user. It is now fairly simple to produce and analyse a package specification skeleton of the entire system. The main program annotation (excluding facilities for programming the wheel size) should be of the form:

```
--# global in       Clock.State,
--#                  Pulse_Queue.State,
--#                  Buttons.State,
--#                  Wheel.Size;
--#        out  Display.State;
--# derives Display.State
--#             from Clock.State,
--#                  Pulse_Queue.State,
--#                  Buttons.State,
--#                  Wheel.Size;
```

These annotations are expressed in terms of the problem domain (e.g. the state of the display) and represent the minimum information flows required to provide the desired behaviour. Completion of the system requires only the implementation of the various type packages and variables.

10   Refactoring of Designs After Analysis

It is instructive to observe the result of making different design decisions from those outlined above.

10.1   Missed Abstractions

If we fail to observe that the two displays and the two buttonss are tightly interconnected and therefore neglect to place an abstraction around them then their individual states would become visible in the SPARK annotations of the main program. Instead of reasoning about the abstract Display.State we have the more detailed PrimaryDisplay.State and SecondaryDisplay.State (and similarly for two buttons). The changes affect the main program annotations thus (changes from the optimal annotations are shown in italics):

```
--# global in      Clock.State,
--#                Pulse_Queue.State,
--#                ClearButton.State,
--#                ModeButton.State,
--#                Wheel.Size;
--#            out PrimaryDisplay.State,
--#                SecondaryDisplay.State;
--# derives PrimaryDisplay.State
--#          from Clock.State,
--#               Pulse_Queue.State,
--#               Wheel.Size &
--#     SecondaryDisplay.State
--#          from Clock.State,
--#               Pulse_Queue.State,
--#               ClearButton.State,
--#               ModeButton.State,
--#               Wheel.Size;
```

This annotation is longer and more complex than the original and reveals the close coupling between, for example, the displays. Most things which affect the primary display also affect the secondary display; this is consistent with our understanding of the system. If, for example, the bicycle goes faster the higher speed shows on the primary display but the average speed will also change and this affects the secondary display. The only difference between the two dependencies is that the clear and mode buttons affect only the secondary display; this is useful information when considering the display packages themselves but can be considered unnecessary detail at the main program level. Examination of the flow relations directly prompts us to provide abstractions for the displays and buttons to the overall benefit of the design.

10.2   Badly Positioned State

Badly handled OOD approaches often lead to proliferation of objects to handle particular events or parts of the system behaviour. We could, for example, introduce a "pulse count handler" to replace our original design choice of storing pulse counts locally within the main program. The handler package would take the form of an abstract state machine that tracked each wheel pulse received and could provide trip and overall distance information. Because this object is external to the main controller its state becomes visible in the main program annotations which will change as follows:

```
--# global in      Clock.State,
--#                Pulse_Queue.State,
--#                Buttons.State,
--#                Wheel.Size;
--#            out Display.State;
```

```
--#            in out Pulse_Handler.State;
--# derives Display.State
--#               from Clock.State,
--#                    Pulse_Queue.State,
--#                    Pulse_Handler.State,
--#                    Buttons.State,
--#                    Wheel.Size &
--#          Pulse_Handler.State
--#               from Pulse_Handler.State,
--#                    Pulse_Queue.State,
--#                    Buttons.State;
```

This is significantly less clear than the original. We can probably accept that the display is affected by the Pulse_Handler but we also have to deal with an entirely new clause in the flow relation showing that the Pulse_Handler depends on itself and the Pulse_Queue (but not, for example, the clock). Furthermore, the new items in the annotation are not in problem domain terms; Pulse_Handler is an internal design artefact not part of the external system we are building. Again consideration of information flow, revealed by static analysis, prompts us to regard pulse count handling as an internal rather than an external property of the system and thus improve our design.

Note that both of the poor design choices in Section 10 can be detected and corrected *before* the packages concerned are implemented; we are analysing only emerging design constructs.

11   Conclusions

Project risk and project cost are both increased if processes for error detection are weighted towards the back end of the project life cycle; this is equally true for static analysis and dynamic testing. Static analysis, in contrast with dynamic testing, can be carried out early in the project lifecycle provided that the language and tools used permit analysis of incomplete programs. Early analysis has a straightforward benefit because errors found early are easy and cheap to correct; however, there is a more subtle benefit from early analysis concerned with program design. Static analysis, as performed by the SPARK Examiner, measures properties of the program, such as information flow, which are powerful indicators of design quality. High levels of information flow indicate excessive coupling or poor state abstractions and are revealed by large or complex SPARK annotations. We can therefore conceive static analysis as being much more than a verification activity: it is actually a powerful design aid. The benefits of this are enormous: good design features such as loose coupling provide benefit throughout all remaining lifecycle stages. The code is easier to analyse and test; easier to understand; and easier to modify.

Praxis Critical Systems have recently delivered two systems whose designs were influenced by early analysis aimed at minimising information flow and we have had feedback from another SPARK user who has taken the same approach. All three of these projects have shown the benefits to be both practical and valuable.

References

1. Croxford, Martin and Sutton, James. *Breaking through the V&V Bottleneck.* Lecture Notes in Computer Science Volume 1031, 1996.
2. Sutton, James. *Cost-Effective Approaches to Satisfy Safety-critical Regulatory Requirements.* Workshop Session, SIGAda 2000.
3. B.D. Bramson. *Malvern's Program Analysers.* RSRE Research Review 1984.
4. Bernard Carré. *Program Analysis and Verification* in *High Integrity Software.* Chris Sennett (Ed). Pitman. ISBN 0-273-03158-9.
5. C. Daniel Cooper. *Ada Code Analysis: Technology, Experience, and Issues.* Proceedings SIGAda 2000.
6. Finnie, Gavin et al. *SPARK - The SPADE Ada Kernel.* Edition 3.3, 1997, Praxis Critical Systems[1].
7. Finnie, Gavin et al. *SPARK 95 - The SPADE Ada 95 Kernel.* 1999, Praxis Critical Systems[1].
8. Barnes, John. *High Integrity Ada - the SPARK Approach.* Addison Wesley Longman, ISBN 0-201-17517-7.
9. King, Hammond, Chapman and Pryor. *Is Proof More Cost-Effective than Testing?.* IEEE Transaction on Software Engineering, Vol. 26, No. 8, August 2000, pp. 675–686.
10. Bergeretti and Carré. *Information-flow and data-flow analysis of while-programs.* ACM Transactions on Programming Languages and Systems, 1985[1], pp. 37–61.
11. Amey, Peter. *The INFORMED Design Method for SPARK.* Praxis Critical Systems 1999, 2001[1].
12. D.L. Parnas and J. Madey. *Functional Documentation for Computer Systems,* in *Science of Computer Programming.* October 1995. pp. 41–61.
13. Amey, Peter. *A Language for Systems not Just Software.* Proceedings, SIGAda 2001[2].

---

[1] Praxis Critical Systems documents are available on request from sparkinfo@praxis-cs.co.uk
[2] Also downloadable from www.sparkada.com

High-Integrity Systems Development for Integrated Modular Avionics Using VxWorks and GNAT

Paul Parkinson [1], Franco Gasperoni [2]

[1] Wind River, Unit 5 & 6 Ashted Lock Way, Birmingham, B7 4AZ, United Kingdom
Paul.Parkinson@windriver.com

[2] ACT Europe, 8 Rue de Milan, 75009 Paris, France
gasperon@act-europe.fr

Abstract. This paper presents recent trends in avionics systems development from bespoke systems through to COTS and emerging Integrated Modular Avionics architectures. The advances in Ada and RTOS technologies are explained and the impact of requirements for RTCA/DO-178B and EUROCAE/ED-12B certification and achievements are presented in the context of the GNAT and VxWorks technologies.

1 Introduction

Many avionics systems have successfully been implemented in Ada on bespoke hardware platforms, and have usually performed a dedicated function with limited interaction with narrowly defined external interfaces to external subsystems. However, in recent years, the need has evolved for new applications with ever-increasing levels of functionality, requiring interaction with many external systems, which has had a negative impact on development timescales. This has conflicted with market forces which have exerted pressure for shorter development cycles to bring new systems to market faster. In addition, avionics programmes have been under pressure to reduce life cycle costs, and as bespoke systems have been regarded as the largest single contributory cost factor, alternatives have been sought.

One of the trends which has emerged as a result is the adoption of COTS (commercial off the shelf), but not just in the sense of commercial grade components recommended by the US Department of Defense, but in terms of system-level boards and importantly, COTS software.

Programme offices have learned that significant cost savings can be made where an already available COTS board can be used to perform a function for which a proprietary system would have previously been developed. The risk to the programme is reduced in terms of development timescales and engineering development costs.

However, lessons have been learned from the mistakes made during early COTS adoption, as some of these actually increased programme risk, rather than reducing it

J. Blieberger and A. Strohmeier (Eds.): Ada-Europe 2002, LNCS 2361, pp. 163-178, 2002.
© Springer-Verlag Berlin Heidelberg 2002

as intended. These pitfalls included the use of single-source supplier, closed proprietary interfaces, and dependencies on hardware architectures which would become obsolete during an in-service lifetime exceeding thirty years.

One of the trends which has emerged as a result is Integrated Modular Avionics (IMA), which has placed demands on software systems, including Ada implementations and Real-Time Operating Systems (RTOS). These systems have placed new demands on the certification efforts required for deployment. These interesting issues are discussed in the following sections.

1.1 The Development of High-Integrity Systems

Standards for safety-critical systems have tracked advances in avionics development, and there is now a range of standards which apply to hardware and/or software, covering civil and/or military programmes, and may apply to a single country or a group of nations. These standards also vary in the approaches which they take towards ensuring safety-criticality. The US standard RTCA/DO-178B [1], and its European equivalent EUROCAE ED-12B, place a strong emphasis on testing to demonstrate absence of errors. The UK defence software standard Def Stan 00-55 [2], instead promotes proof of correctness in the design, rather than absence of errors. Despite the differences in the philosophies, recent research work has shown that there is some correlation between these standards [3], and they all place stringent requirements on avionics applications which need to be certified.

The DO-178B/ED-12B standard defines five levels of safety-criticality, ranging from Level E at the least critical, to Level A at the most critical, as shown in table 1 below:

Table 1. DO-178B/ED-12B Safety Criticality Levels

Failure Condition	Software Level	Outcome
Catastrophic	Level A	Death or injury
Hazardous / Severe - Major	Level B	Injury
Major	Level C	Unsafe workload
Minor	Level D	Increased workload
No Effect	Level E	None

The implications for certification are significant, as there is a significant increase in certification effort required as the safety critical level is increased. This applies to software specification, design, implementation and testing phases. DO-178B defines 28 objectives for Level D, rising to 57 for Level C, through to 66 for Level A, which requires significantly more rigour than the lower levels.

Table 2. DO-178B/ED-12B Testing Requirements

Software Level	Testing Requirements Examples
Level A	MCDC Coverage
Level B	Decision Coverage
Level C	Statement Coverage

The top three safety levels are of particular interest to Ada developers, as they require development tool support to perform code coverage. This is usually performed via instrumentation of the source code with trace points prior to compilation by the Ada compiler; then during program execution, a log is generated which can be analyzed to determine the behaviour of the program. Level C specifies Statement Coverage, which requires every statement in the program to have been invoked at least once. Level B specifies Decision Coverage, which requires every point of entry and exit in the program has been invoked at least once and every decision in the program has taken on all possible outcomes at least once. Finally, Level A requires Modified Condition / Decision Condition (MCDC) testing which is explained below. This increases the number of test permutations immensely, and also places additional burdens on the development tool and systems under test.

MCDC Illustration. The complexity of MCDC testing is illustrated by the following code fragment:

```
if A=0 and then B<2 and then C>5 then P; end if;
```

This contains three variables, three conditions and four MCDC cases (as shown in Table 3). For DO-178B Level B certification, two test cases which result in both the execution and non-execution of statement P are required, whereas for Level A certification, all four possible test cases need to be generated.

Table 3. MCDC Test Cases

A=0	B<2	C>5	P
T	T	T	T
F	?	?	F
T	F	?	F
T	T	F	F

The DO-178B standard is used to certify a complete system implementation and not just individual components of a system, therefore certification evidence must be produced for all software components used within that system. So for COTS, this means that certification evidence will be required for the Ada application, the Ada runtime system and the RTOS beneath it – these are addressed in the following subsections.

1.1.1 Ada Application & Runtime Certification

Ada applications rely on an Ada runtime system to provide services such as tasking or exceptions in their deployed environment. While the size and complexity of the runtime system is usually not an issue in commercial applications, in safety-critical systems it is, since the certification of the Ada runtime system can in itself prove to be a considerable task.

To deal with this issue, the approaches that have emerged in the past ten to fifteen years restrict the Ada features that can be used in safety-critical applications. The resulting benefit is a simplification of the underlying Ada runtime. Unfortunately, every Ada vendor has come up with its set of Ada restrictions.

Ada 95 with its safety and security annex, the follow-on work done by the Annex H Rapporteur Group [4] as well as the work on the Ravenscar Profile [5, 6, 7] have brought some clarity in this domain. We are hopeful that Ada 0X will contain at least one standardized high-integrity profile. This will enhance portability in the realm of safety-critical applications. A side effect of this will be the extension of the ACATS test suite. As a result, Ada users would have a number of conformant implementations to choose from.

1.1.2 RTOS Certification and VxWorks/Cert

A number of avionics applications which have been certified for deployment have used proprietary in-house RTOS implementations, generally consisting of a kernel with task scheduler some resource management capabilities. The development, maintenance and certification of such kernels may have been manageable on past programmes, but it difficult to envisage how this approach can be viable for future programmes. This is because today's more complex systems, with multiprocessor configurations and many communications interfaces demand more sophisticated functionality from an RTOS. For programmes developing and maintaining an in-house proprietary RTOS, this places a significant additional burden on the programme's developers.

Another approach which has been adopted in a number of safety critical avionics programmes, is to take a commercial RTOS and to certify it as part of the system certification activities.   Honeywell Aerospace adopted this approach in the development of the Global Star 2100 Flight Management System, which runs on VxWorks®, and was certified to DO-17B Level C [8].

However, the next logical step, was for a commercial RTOS vendor to provide an off-the-shelf product with DO-178B certification evidence which could be used in the development of safety critical systems. This is an appropriate approach because the FAA has produced guidelines in N8110.RSC [9], which outline how "reusable software components" (RSC), including an RTOS, can be certified to DO-178B as part of a system. The net result is that the off-the-shelf component can be reused in many programmes, without the need to redevelop certification evidence for the RTOS kernel each time, provided that it is not changed. The approach taken by Wind River to provide these reusable software components in detail in a later section.

1.2 The Route to COTS

Avionics programmes have sought to achieve portability and interoperability for hardware platforms in the drive towards COTS. The Ada programming language has helped towards this end by enabling software abstraction from both the processor and system architectures.

However, many Ada applications have run on top of a dedicated Ada runtime and kernel which has been not only specific to a processor architecture, but also to an Ada technology supplier. This has means that when some programmes migrate architectures, for example when transitioning from Motorola 68k to PowerPC, may unexpectedly face problems relating to vendor lock-in due to a proprietary Ada kernel implementation. Programmes have also sought to avoid vendor lock-in when selecting an Ada compiler technology. The Ada '95 programming language standard [10], and associated compiler technology verification tests go a long way to providing evidence of intrinsic compatibility between compiler technologies, far more so that for C/C++ counterparts. However, close examination of the Ada compiler technology is also required to determine its openness, and whether the programme using a specific vendor's compiler will become locked into that technology, or will be able to migrate to another technology at a future date.

1.3 The Emergence of Integrated Modular Avionics

In addition to the drive towards COTS to reduce life cycle costs, avionics programmes have also needed to consider the performance requirements of new avionics applications, which have increased dramatically. In order to address these needs, a new model has been developed, *Integrated Modular Avionics* (IMA), which has the following high-level objectives:

- **Common processing subsystems.** These should allow multiple applications to share and reuse the same computing resources. This facilitates a reduction in the number of deployed subsystems which are not fully utilised and provides a more efficient use of system resources which leaves space for future expansion.

- **Software abstraction.** This should isolate the application not only from the underlying bus architecture but also from the underlying hardware architecture. This enables portability of applications between different platforms and also allows the introduction of new hardware to replace obsolete architectures.

IMA seeks to achieve these objectives through the implementation of a layered software model, with an RTOS and architecture-specific software providing an isolation layer above the hardware, and above this portable applications reside.

IMA is likely to become pervasive in avionics in the next few years, as number of high-profile industry research programmes including ASAAC [11] and the EU-funded Project Victoria are developing software architectures for IMA which will impact on the future developments of software technology from commercial vendors, and may also have input into relevant avionics software standards.

1.3.1 Support for Emerging IMA Architectures

The Avionics Computing Resource Minimal Operational Performance Specification [12] defines two important concepts which are widely used in IMA, these are Spatial Partitioning and Temporal Partitioning.

Spatial Partitioning. This defines the isolation requirements for multiple applications running concurrently on the same processing platform. The applications should not be able to interfere with each other, and is usually achieved through the use of different virtual memory contexts, enforced by a processor's memory management unit (MMU). These contexts are referred to as *Partitions* in the ARINC-653 Specification [13], and contain an application with its own heap for dynamic memory allocation, and a stack for the application's tasks. Applications running in an IMA partition must not be able to deprive each other of shared application resources or those that are provided by the RTOS kernel. These requirements will have an impact on the design and implementation of the Ada runtime system and the underlying RTOS kernel.

Temporal Partitioning. This defines the isolation requirements for multiple applications running concurrently on the same processing platform. This ensures that one application may not utilise the processor for longer than intended to the detriment of the other applications. The ARINC-653 Specification defines a model where an application may be allocated a timeslot of a defined width, and other applications may be allocated timeslots of similar of differing durations. The ARINC scheduler then enforces the processor utilization, by forcing a context switch to a new application at the end of each timeslot.

2 VxWorks/Cert and VxWorks AE653/Cert

In 1999, Wind River set out to develop a VxWorks product which could be certified to DO-178B Level A, and also to define a certification product roadmap to address the needs of safety critical programmes in the near future. The development of the resulting VxWorks/Cert product has already been used on a number of programmes and is described in the next subsection; VxWorks technology advances to assist the development of IMA applications are also described in the subsequent subsection.

2.1 Development of VxWorks/Cert

In order to produce a version of VxWorks suitable for high integrity systems, close scrutiny of the FAA guidelines and other up and coming standards was required, including the RTCA SC-255 Requirements Specification for Avionics Computer Resource (ACR) [12] and other standards, such as ARINC-653. Then a multiple pass analysis of the whole of the source code base for VxWorks 5.4 and PowerPC architecture-specific code was undertaken. The end result was a certifiable subset of the VxWorks 5.4 API [14]; functionality that had been excluded was that which could compromise predictability or lead to memory fragmentation.

Restrictions of interest to Ada developers are that C++ runtime support was removed, and restrictions on dynamic memory allocation were introduced. This only allowed dynamic memory allocation to occur at system initialization time, which allowed the execution of Ada elaboration code, or C applications to create data structures from the heap. After a call has been to the kernel API memNoMoreAllocators() to indicate that system initialization has completed, the VxWorks kernel prevents further dynamic memory allocation and dynamic creation and deletion of tasks, irrespective of whether they are VxWorks tasks or Ada tasks.

The development of high integrity applications with VxWorks/Cert can be undertaken using an enhanced version of the Tornado™ integrated development environment, which is closely integrated with ACT's GNAT Pro for Tornado development tools. This subject was recently discussed by one of the authors in an industry journal [15].

In order to develop the certification evidence for VxWorks/Cert, a number of qualified CASE tools were employed. These were used in conjunction with automatic test harnesses which generated and collated MCDC test results. These results have been analyzed and audited, and in the rare cases full coverage results are not generated, a manual justification for the proof of correctness of behaviour has been developed. Such cases include entry and exit from an interrupt service routine (ISR), which cannot be tracked by CASE tools in some circumstances (e.g. during kernel start-up). The complete VxWorks/Cert certification evidence has been developed by Verocel in a hyperlinked format, navigable in an HTML browser. This not only greatly assists the certification audit process, by providing fast and accurate cross-referencing capability between different levels of specification, design documentation, source code and test results, but can also be extended, enabling programmes to add certification evidence for their Ada applications.

2.2 Development of VxWorks AE653/Cert

In order to fulfill the needs of IMA development programmes, Wind River has added spatial partitioning and temporal partitioning to VxWorks technology.

2.2.1 Spatial Partioning

VxWorks AE implements spatial partitioning through *Protection Domains*, which are analogous to ARINC-653 partitions. Protection domains are flexible containers into which application tasks, objects and resources can be placed. Each protection domain employs its own stack and heap locally, which guarantees resource availability, as they cannot be usurped by applications running in other protection domains. Protection domains provide protection against errant memory accesses from applications running in other protection domains, implemented using an MMU virtual memory context. The implementation of protection domains is described in more detail in the *High Availability for Embedded Systems* white paper [16].

The certifiable version of VxWorks AE, *VxWorks AE653,* also guarantees kernel resource availability by binding a separate instance of the VxWorks kernel to each application protection domain, and providing a message passing backplane between protection domains. This implementation contrasts with monolithic kernel implementations where an errant application can deprive other applications of kernel resources. The use of separate kernel instances also means that separate Ada runtimes can be used within each application protection domain.

2.2.2 Temporal Partioning

The task scheduling models used in avionics systems are interesting. In recent years, there has been a trend in many embedded and real-time systems to migrate from the traditional time-slicing model towards pre-emptive priority-based scheduling schemes, as these provide predictable and deterministic behaviour. These schemes have been successfully used in conjunction with Ada-based applications in major avionics programmes, such as GENESYS [17].

However, because IMA systems can support multiple applications running on the same processor, and for this a time-based partitioning scheme is required. The ARINC-653 Specification defines a temporal partitioning scheduling model which guarantees time slots to partitions, and within these partitions applications tasks can be scheduled using other scheduling policies. VxWorks AE653 implements ARINC-653 partition scheduling via a protection domain scheduler, this provides guaranteed time slots to applications within each protection domain, and uses priority-based preemptive scheduling for tasks within the domain.

3 GNAT Pro High Integrity Edition

GNAT Pro High-Integrity Edition (GNAT Pro HIE in the remainder of this document) is intended to increase safety as well as reduce the certification cost of applications that need to meet safety-critical certification standards such as RTCA/DO-178B or EUROCAE ED-12B.

In addition to providing two high-integrity Ada profiles, GNAT Pro HIE contains a number of features especially useful for safety critical programming. The following sections will describe each of these elements.

3.1 GNAT Pro HIE Certification Benefits

An important benefit of GNAT Pro HIE when it comes to user code certification is the ease in which object code can be traced to the original source [18].

A compiler option allows display of the low-level generated code in Ada source form. This acts as an intermediate form between the original source code and the generated object code, thus supporting traceability requirements. This intermediate presentation can be used as a reference point for verifying that the object code matches the source code. This expanded low-level generated code can also be used as a reference point for run-time debugging. As an example, consider the following code:

```
procedure Try is
   X : array (1 .. 100) of Integer := (1, 2, others => 3);
begin
   null;
end;
```

Using a special switch you can display (or save to a file) the low-level Ada source code that is internally created by the compiler and from which the final object code is generated. For the above the source code is:

```
procedure try is
   x : array (1 .. 100) of integer;
   x (1) := 1;
   x (2) := 2;
   I5b : integer := 2;
   while I5b <  100 loop
      I5b := integer'succ(I5b);
      x (I5b) := 3;
   end loop;
begin
   null;
   return;
end try;
```

Thus, instead of having to go from high-level Ada source directly to assembly and object code, GNAT Pro HIE allows programmers to introduce the low-level Ada code step when mapping source to object code. Because the low-level Ada code used is very simple, this code maps straightforwardly to the generated assembly and object code. Furthermore, this low-level Ada code is mostly target independent.

As a result, the benefits of this approach are:

- The code certification process is less costly since the semantic gap between each step (Ada to low-level Ada to assembly to object code) is reduced

- The code certification process can be speeded up as it can be done in 3 parallel steps by 3 separate teams (Step 1: Ada to low-level Ada; Step 2: low-level Ada to assembly; Step 3: Assembly to object code)
- Because low-level Ada is mostly target independent, part of the certification work can be reused.

3.2 GNAT Pro HIE Programming Benefits

GNAT Pro HIE contains a number of features especially useful for safety-critical programming:

- The GNAT Pro HIE compiler has a special switch to generate Ada representation clauses about the choice of data representations.
- The compiler produces an extensive set of warning messages to diagnose situations that are likely to be errors, even though they do not correspond to illegalities in Ada Reference Manual terms: Missing returns from functions, inner variable hiding an outer variable with the same name, infinite recursion, uninitialized variables, unused variables, unnecessary with clauses, etc.
- The compiler performs various style checks that can be used to enforce rigorous coding standards, easing the verification process by ensuring that the source is formatted in a uniform manner.
- Annex H of the Ada 95 Reference Manual [10] is fully implemented, and all implementation-dependent characteristics of the GNAT implementation are defined in the GNAT Reference Manual [19], further supporting the goal of reviewable object code.

3.3 GNAT Pro HIE Profiles

GNAT Pro HIE offers the choice of two profiles. Both profiles restrict the Ada constructs that a profile-compliant application can employ. In either case, if an application uses a construct not allowed by the profile, compilation will fail. Furthermore, the binder will check that all units in the applications are compiled using the same profile. The two GNAT Pro HIE profiles are:

- **No-Runtime profile** (no Ada tasking). This profile guarantees that no Ada runtime library is used in conforming applications. With this profile only the application source code will appear in the final executable and needs to be certified. This profile is derived from the GNORT technology described in [18].

- **Ravenscar profile** (Ravenscar Ada 95 tasking [5, 6, 7]). This profile complements the previous one by providing a simple Ada runtime implementing the Ravenscar tasking subset. In this case the Ada runtime is designed to expedite the certification process for an application that needs to use concurrency. In certain situations it may be simpler and less expensive to certify a concurrent program built on the Ravenscar Profile than to certify a sequential program with no runtime library (and where the concurrency needs to be simulated in application code).

The programmer chooses the profile by using a compilation switch that specifies whether she wants No-Runtime, Ravenscar, or the full Ada 95 runtime.

Both profiles are upwardly compatible with the SPARK Ada profile defined by Praxis Critical Systems [20]. In this case, upwardly compatible means that GNAT Pro HIE can compile any SPARK Ada compliant program. Furthermore, when using the "No-Runtime" profile, the user is guaranteed that the final SPARK Ada application will contain only code written by the user.

The implementation of the Ravenscar profile relies on VxWorks/Cert. It is remarkable to consider that Ravenscar Ada 95 tasking can be implemented on top of the VxWorks/Cert API with only 200 source lines of simple Ada code for the runtime and 60 source lines of Ada for the libraries. This is because the VxWorks/Cert kernel provides all the necessary synchronization and scheduling primitives to do a straightforward implementation of Ravenscar. The number of VxWorks/Cert primitives used to implement Ravenscar is around 10. These primitives include creating tasks, setting their priority plus mutex operations.

When using the No-Runtime profile in conjunction with VxWorks/Cert it is possible to make direct calls to VxWorks/Cert to create tasks, synchronize them using the VxWorks mutex primitives, etc. As a matter of fact GNAT Pro HIE, regardless of the profile, comes with a complete Ada binding to the 400 routines in the VxWorks/Cert API.

Note that all Integrated Modular Avionics issues dealing with spatial and temporal partitioning are taken care of transparently by VxWorks AE653. Furthermore, for each VxWorks AE653 protection domain the programmer can select a different GNAT Pro HIE profile.

3.4 GNAT Pro HIE Ada Restrictions

Although restricted in terms of dynamic Ada semantics, both profiles fully support static Ada constructs such as generics and child units. The use of tagged types (at library level) and other Object-Oriented Programming features is also allowed, although the general use of dynamic dispatching may be prohibited at the application level through pragma `Restrictions`. Generally speaking pragma `Restrictions`, as defined in Ada 95 Annex H, can be used to further constrain the Ada features that a programmer can use in the safety-critical application being developed.

The features excluded from the GNAT Pro HIE profiles are as follows:

- Exception handlers (see the section "Exceptions in GNAT Pro HIE" below)
- Packed arrays with a component size other than 1, 2, 4, 8, 16 or 24 bits

- The exponentiation operator
- 64-bit integer (the type Long_Long_Integer) or fixed-point types
- Boolean operations on packed arrays (individual elements may be accessed)
- Equality and comparison operations on arrays
- The attributes External_Tag, Image, Value, Body_Version, Version, Width, and Mantissa
- Controlled types
- The attributes Address, Access, Unchecked_Access, Unrestricted_Access when applied to a non library-level subprogram
- Non library-level tagged types
- Annex E features (Distributed Systems)

In addition the No-Runtime profile excludes all the tasking constructs while the Ravenscar profile only allows Ravenscar Ada 95 tasking as defined in [5].

Explicit withs of library units are permitted. However, in an environment where the code needs to be certified, the programmer takes responsibility for ensuring that the referenced library units meet the certification requirements.

3.5 Exceptions in GNAT Pro HIE

Exception handlers are forbidden in GNAT Pro HIE, so exceptions can never be handled. However, exceptions can be raised explicitly with a raise statement (which are allowed in GNAT Pro HIE) or, if run time checking is enabled, then it is possible for the predefined exceptions such as Constraint_Error to be raised implicitly.

The result of such a raise is to call procedure __gnat_last_chance_handler, which must be provided by the programmer at the application level. This procedure should gracefully terminate the program in a fail-safe mode. To suppress all runtime error checking and disallow raise statements one can use the No_Exceptions restriction of Annex H.

3.6 Allocators in GNAT Pro HIE

Dynamic memory allocation and deallocation is permitted in GNAT Pro HIE. Use of these features will generate calls to routines __gnat_malloc and __gnat_free that must be provided by the programmer at the application level. To prohibit the use of allocators or unchecked deallocation, programmers can use the No_Local_Allocators, No_Allocators, No_Implicit_Heap_Allocations, No_Unchecked_Deallocation restrictions defined in Annex H. These restrictions can be enforced at the application level. For instance No_Local_Allocators prohibits the use of allocators except at the library level. Such allocators can be called once at elaboration time, but cannot be called during execution of the program.

3.7 Array and Record Assignments in GNAT Pro HIE

Array and record assignments are permitted in GNAT Pro HIE. Depending on the target processor these constructs can generate calls to the C library functions memcpy() or bcopy(). A certifiable version of these routines is provided in VxWorks/Cert.

3.8 Functions Returning Unconstrained Objects

GNAT Pro HIE allows functions returning unconstrained objects (e.g. unconstrained arrays). To implement this capability the compiler uses a secondary stack mechanism requiring runtime support. A sample implementation comes with GNAT Pro HIE. However, since no certification material is provided for this sample implementation, it is the programmer's responsibility to certify it. To disable this capability GNAT Pro HIE provides a No_Secondary_Stack Restrictions pragma.

3.9 Controlling Elaboration with GNAT Pro HIE

One of the objectionable issues in a certification context is the fact that the Ada compiler generates elaboration code without the programmer being aware that such code is being generated. The elaboration code must be generated to meet Ada semantic requirements, and it is always safe to do so. However, the elaboration code needs to be certified and this increases certification costs (why was this elaboration code implicitly generated by the compiler, what Ada requirement does it meet, what test cases do we need to devise for the elaboration code, etc.)

GNAT Pro HIE provides a Restrictions pragma No_Elaboration_Code, that allows programmers to know when elaboration code would be generated by the compiler. When the pragma Restrictions No_Elaborations_Code is specified in a compilation unit, the GNAT Pro HIE compiler stops with an error every time it needs to generate elaboration code. It is up to the programmer to rewrite the code so that no elaboration code is generated. As an example consider the following:

```
package List is
   type Elmt;
   type Temperature is range 0.0 ... 1_000.0;
   type Elmt_Ptr is access all Elmt;
   type Elmt is record
      T     : Temperature;
      Next : Elmt_Ptr;
   end record;
end List;

pragma Restrictions (No_Elaboration_Code);
with List;
procedure Client is
   The_List : List.Elmt;
begin
   null;
end Client;
```

When compiling unit Client the compiler will stop with the error

```
client.adb:4:04: violation of restriction "No_Elaboration_Code"
at line 1
```

To understand why GNAT needs to generate elaboration code for object The_List, remember that Ada requires that all pointers be null initialized. To see the elaboration code that would be generated the user can remove the No_Elaboration_Code restriction and use the -gnatG switch to view the low-level version of the Ada code generated by GNAT. In this case you get

```
package list is
   type list__elmt;
   type list__temperature is new float range 0.0E0 ..
(16384000.0*2**(-14));
   type list__elmt_ptr is access all list__elmt;
   type list__elmt is record
      t : list__temperature;
      next : list__elmt_ptr;
   end record;
   freeze list__elmt [
     procedure list___init_proc (_init : in out list__elmt) is
     begin
        _init.next := null;
        return;
     end list___init_proc;
   ]
end list;

with list; use list;
procedure client is
   the_list : list.list__elmt;
   list___init_proc (the_list);
begin
   null;
   return;
end client;
```

The reason why elaboration code is generated inside procedure Client is because the pointer inside The_List object must be initialized to null. To avoid elaboration code the programmer can add an explicit initialization as shown below:

```
pragma Restrictions (No_Elaboration_Code);
with List; use List;
procedure Client is
   The_List : List.Elmt := (0.0, null);
begin
   null;
end Client;
```

By making the initialization explicit, rather than sweeping it under the compiler's rug, initialization becomes part of the requirements mapping and application design. In a certification context it may be preferable to certify code that you write explicitly rather than code that gets generated for you implicitly by a compiler.

3.10 Controlling Implicit Loops and Conditionals with GNAT Pro HIE

Certain complex constructs in Ada result in GNAT generating code that contains implicit conditionals, or implicit for loops. For example, slice assignments result in both kinds of generated code.

In some certification protocols, conditionals and loops require special treatment. For example, in the case of a conditional, it may be necessary to ensure that the test suite contains cases that branch in both directions for a given conditional. A question arises as to whether implicit conditionals and loops generated by the compiler are subject to the same verification requirements.

GNAT Pro HIE provides two additional restriction identifiers that address this issue by controlling the presence of implicit conditionals and loops:

```
pragma Restrictions (No_Implicit_Conditionals);
pragma Restrictions (No_Implicit_Loops);
```

These are partition-wide restrictions that ensure that the generated code respectively contains no conditionals and no loops. This is achieved in one of two ways. Either the compiler generates alternative code to avoid the implicit construct (possibly at some sacrifice of efficiency) or, if it cannot find an equivalent code sequence, it rejects the program and flags the offending construct. In the latter situation, the programmer will need to revise the source program to avoid the implicit conditional or loop.

4 Summary and Conclusions

The avionics industry has witnessed a major shift towards COTS in recent years. Ada and RTOS suppliers have needed to enhance their technologies in order to assist this migration process.

This paper has outlined how Wind River and ACT have enhanced VxWorks and GNAT to meet the specific needs of the aerospace and defence market, and has demonstrated how COTS software technology can be used to build high integrity systems for safety critical applications.

References

1. RTCA, "DO-178B - Software Considerations in Airborne Systems and Equipment Certification", URL http://www.rtca.org
2. UK Ministry of Defence, "Requirements for Safety Related Software in Defence Equipment", Def Stan 00-55.
3. Dr. C. H. Pygott, "A Comparison of Avionics Standards", DERA/CIS3/TR990319/1.0, British Crown Copyright 2000.

4. "Guidance for Use of Ada in High Integrity Systems", ISO/IEC TR 15942.
5. Ted Baker and Tullio Vardanega, "Session Summary: Tasking Profiles", Ada Letters September-October 1997, Vol. XVII, Number 5, pages 5-7.
6. A. Burns and B. Dobbing, "The Ravenscar Tasking Profile for High Integrity Real-Time Programs", pp. 1-6 in Proceedings of ACM SigAda Annual Conference, ACM Press, Washington DC, U.S.A. (8-12 November 1998).
7. Alan Burns, "Guide for the use of the Ada Ravenscar Profile in high integrity systems – the work of the HRG", Ada User Journal, Vol. 22, Number 3, September 2001, pp182-187.
8. Wind River Datasheet, "Honeywell customer success story", http://www.windriver.com.
9. FAA Draft Notice N8110.RSC.
10. S. Tucker Taft et al.: Ada 95 Reference Manual - Language and Standard Libraries. International Standard ISO/IEC 8652:1995(E), Springer, LNCS 1246, ISBN 3-540-63144-5
11. J. Kemp, A. Wake, W. Williams, "The Development of the ASAAC Software Architecture", ERA Avionics Show 2000.
12. RTCA SC-255 "Requirements Specification for Avionics Computer Resource (ACR)", http://www.rtca.org.
13. ARINC-653 Specification, http://www.arinc.org.
14. "VxWorks/Cert Subset Definition and Rationale v1.2a", Wind River Systems.
15. Paul Parkinson, " Hochverfügbar – Komplexe langlebige System mit Ada und VxWorks Entwickeln" (Developing High-Integrity Systems with VxWorks and Ada), pp 36-39, Electronik Praxis, 2 Oktober 2001.
16. "High Availability for Embedded Systems" white paper, Wind River Systems. http://www.windriver.com.
17. "GENESYS – An Application of OO Technology to Aircraft Display Systems", Neil Davidson, BAE Avionics Ltd. Symposium on Reliable Object Oriented Programming, IEE, 24th October 2001
18. Roderick Chapman and Robert Dewar, "Re-engineering a Safety-Critical Application Using SPARK 95 and GNORT", Reliable Software Technologies, Ada-Europe'99, LNCS 1622, pp 40-51.
19. "GNAT Reference Manual", http://www.gnat.com.
20. John Barnes, "High Integrity Ada: The SPARK Approach", Addison Wesley, 1997

How to Use GNAT to Efficiently Preprocess New Ada Sentences*

Javier Miranda, Francisco Guerra, Ernestina Martel, José Martín, and
Alexis González

Applied Microelectronics Research Institute
University of Las Palmas de Gran Canaria. Canary Islands, Spain.
{jmiranda, fguerra}@iuma.ulpgc.es

Abstract. In this paper we propose a technique to add a preprocessing
phase to the GNAT front-end. This technique reduces time required to
implement a high quality preprocessor and it facilitates the use of the
GNAT front-end to experiment with Ada extensions. We briefly introduce the GNAT architecture, we describe our proposed technique and
we present our proposed modifications to the GNAT sources to support
it.

Keywords: Compilers, preprocessing, Ada, GNAT.

1 Introduction

One simple way to experiment with language extensions is to write a preprocessor. In the general case (a language extension fully embedded into an existing
language), this task is not trivial; we need to implement the scanner, parser and
probably most of the semantics of the language. Although several well known
tools facilitate this task (i.e. lex[1] and yacc[2], or aflex[3] and ayacc[4] in the
Ada context), we still have to add all the tables and routines which handle all
the required semantic information. This is time consuming and error prone.

The preprocessor is basically re-implementing the scanner, parser and probably most of the semantics analysis already implemented inside a real compiler.
Therefore, the best way to implement the preprocessor is to reuse the front-end
of an existing compiler. If we reuse the front-end and we do not modify its general behaviour we have an additional and important advantage: we can upgrade
our preprocessor as soon as a new version of the compiler is available. Therefore, all the upgrades made to the compiler are automatically inherited by our
preprocessor.

GNAT (GNU NYU Ada Translator), is a front-end and runtime system for
Ada 95[5]. It is distributed under the GNU Free Software Licence and, therefore,
all the compiler sources are available. In a previous paper[6] we describe how to

---

* *This work has been partially funded by the Spanish Research Council (CICYT), contract number TIC2001–1586–C03–03.*

J. Blieberger and A. Strohmeier (Eds.): Ada-Europe 2002, LNCS 2361, pp. 179–192, 2002.

modify the GNAT scanner and parser to support new pragmas, attributes and sentences. In this paper we present a technique which allows to modify the GNAT front-end to efficiently implement preprocessors. The main advantages of this technique are: 1) it does not modify the current behaviour of the front-end components, 2) it reduces the time required to develop the preprocessor (all the routines which make the work of the scanner, parser and semantic analyser are reused), and 3) it reduces the compilation time of the Ada extension (it is not necessary to add a new pass on the sources to preprocess the code).

This paper is structured in two parts. In the first part (section 2) we present our proposed technique. In the second part (section 3) we make a detailed description of the technique by means of an example. We finalise with some conclusions and references to related work.

2 Part 1: General Description of the Technique

The GNAT front-end comprises five phases, which communicate by means of a rather compact Abstract Syntax Tree (AST): lexical analysis phase, syntax analysis phase, semantic analysis phase, expansion phase (tree transformations that generate a tree closely equivalent to C), and finally the GIGI phase (transformation of the tree into a GCC tree). See Figure 1.

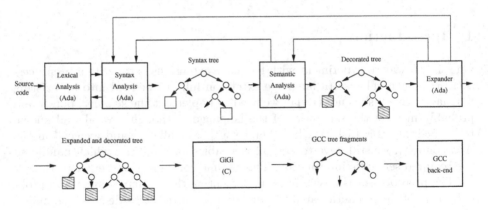

Fig. 1. Front-end phases

Given an Ada extension A', our goal is to add a new phase to the GNAT front-end (the preprocessing phase) where the analysis of A' nodes and their corresponding expansion into Ada 95 nodes is done (see Figure 2). After this phase, we feed the semantic analyser with the resulting AST (which is now only composed of Ada 95 nodes).

The preprocessing phase requires to semantically traverse the whole AST to analyse both A' and Ada 95 nodes (because in the general case the context of A' sentences can be provided by Ada 95 sentences or vice-versa). In the GNAT

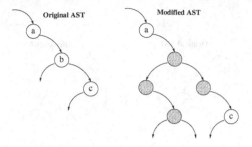

Fig. 2. preprocessing Phase

Although it is possible to embed the preprocessing phase into the GNAT phase of semantics analysis and expansion, we strongly recommend to keep it separate. The reasons are: 1) In the general case, the expansion of an A' node can require the reanalysis of its corresponding subtree, and it is simpler to handle an AST composed of source nodes (nodes generated by the parser) than an AST composed of nodes automatically generated by the GNAT expander, and 2) the isolation facilitates the verification of the expansion (we can easily display the resulting tree after the expansion of the A' nodes).

architecture this introduces a minor problem. When the AST is semantically analysed, all its entities are decorated. Although it is possible to undo this work, in the GNAT 3.13p distribution this is not trivial.

Our proposed solution consists of the creation of a copy of the AST: the *Mirror AST*. All the nodes of the Mirror AST have an additional field which references its original node (see Figure 3).

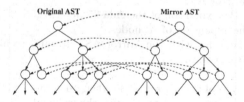

Fig. 3. The Mirror AST

In a first stage of the preprocessing phase we traverse the Mirror AST to analyse all its A' and Ada 95 nodes, and to expand all the A' nodes into subtrees composed of Ada 95 nodes which provide the functionality of the A' node. This expansion is done in the original AST by means of the additional field (see Figure 4). In a second stage the original AST (which is now composed of Ada 95 nodes) is analysed and expanded in the GNAT usual way.

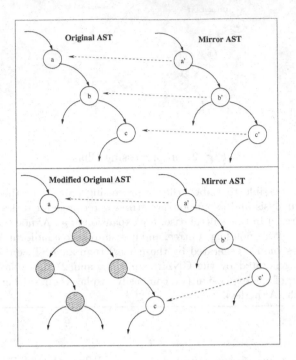

Fig. 4. preprocessing Phase

Summary of The Preprocessing Phase

1. **First Stage**
   (a) Build the Mirror AST.
   (b) Deactivate the expansion of the Ada 95 nodes.
   (c) Activate the expansion of A' nodes.
   (d) Call the semantics with the Mirror AST to analyse all its nodes and to expand the A' nodes.

   During the analysis of the Mirror AST, when an A' node is found, the reference to the original node is used to modify the original AST. Each A' node is replaced in the original AST by a subtree composed of Ada 95 nodes which can also call several added Run-Time subprograms.

2. **Second Stage**
   (a) Re-activate the AST expansion of the Ada 95 nodes.
   (b) Call the semantics again with the modified original AST. Now the original tree is only composed of Ada 95 nodes. Therefore, GNAT expands this AST into the GIGI source tree.

3 Part 2: Detailed Description of the Technique

In this section we will see the proposed modifications of the GNAT front-end sources to support the proposed methodology. We assume that the GNAT scanner and parser have been previously modified to support the syntax of the new sentences ([6] can be used as a brief reference guide). First we will see how to add a new switch to the GNAT front-end to activate the preprocessor and to display the result of the preprocessing. Then we look at the high level packages which implement the preprocessing, and finally we see the proposed modifications to the low level package *Atree* to build the Mirror AST.

3.1 Adding New Switches

We need to separate the Ada language from our proposed Ada extension. Therefore it is interesting to activate the new GNAT preprocessing mode by means of a new switch. However, we do not want to be affected by the GNAT switches. We propose to open a new switches space. Therefore, all the switches associated to our preprocessor have the + prefix. We propose two switches:

-gnat+P Activates the preprocessing mode.

-gnat+g Generates the source code from the modified original AST. This switch allows to see the result of the preprocessing phase[1].

In order to achieve this goal we must modify two GNAT front-end files: *opt.ads* and *switch.adb*.

– **opt.ads** In this file we add two boolean variables to remember if the preprocessor switches have been activated or not.

```
package Opt is
  ...
  Preprocess_Code          : Boolean := False;
  Display_Preprocessed_AST : Boolean := False;
  ...
end Opt;
```

– **switch.adb** In this file we modify the GNAT switches scanner: 1) we open the new switches space, and 2) we analyse them and update the corresponding Boolean variable. We propose to reuse the GNAT subprograms which print the contents of an AST to display the preprocessed AST. Therefore we also activate the corresponding debug option by means of *Set_Debug_Flag*.

```
with Opt;
package body Switch is
  ...
    procedure Scan_Switches (Switch_Chars : String) is
```

---

[1] The functionality of this new switch is very similar to the current functionality of the -gnatdg GNAT switch. That is the reason for the election of the 'g' letter.

```
           ...
           procedure Scan_Extended_Switches is              -- (2)
              -- Switches activated with -gnat+
           begin
              if Program /= Compiler then
                 raise Bad_Switch;
              end if;
              if C = 'P' then
                 Ptr := Ptr + 1;
                 Opt.Preprocess_Code := True;
              elsif C = 'g' then
                 Ptr := Ptr + 1;
                 Set_Debug_Flag ('g');
                 Opt.Display_Preprocessed_AST := True;
              else
                 raise Bad_Switch;
              end if;
           end Extended_Switches;

        begin
           ...
           -- Loop to scan through switches given in switch string
           while Ptr <= Max loop
              C := Switch_Chars (Ptr);
              if C = '+' then                               -- (1)
                 Ptr := Ptr + 1;
                 C := Switch_Chars (Ptr);
                 Scan_Extended_Switches;
              elsif ...
                 -- GNAT switches
                 ...
              end if;
           end loop;
           ...
        end Scan_Switches;
     end Switch;
```

3.2   Activating the Preprocessor

To activate the preprocessor we must modify the Ada package *Sem* which controls the semantic analysis and the expansion phase. We must also provide the new subprograms which analyse the new sentences and the new subprograms which expand these sentences into the equivalent Ada 95 sentences.

All the GNAT subprograms responsible for the semantic analysis can be found in the packages named *Sem_ChXX*, where the number XX indicates the chapter of the Ada 95 Reference Manual associated to these sentences (see Figure 5). Similarly, all the GNAT subprograms responsible for the expansion can be found in packages named *Exp_ChXX*. In order to separate the preprocessor code from the rest of the GNAT sources we propose to add the new subprograms responsible for the preprocessor semantic analysis and expansion on the packages *Sem_Prep* and *Exp_Prep* respectively.

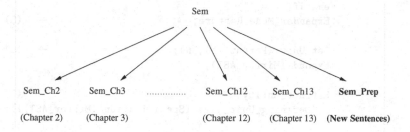

Fig. 5. Semantic Packages

Let's assume that the new sentences to be preprocessed can only be found in the context of the Ada main subprogram. Let's see the proposed modifications to *sem.adb* and proposed contents for the *Sem_Prep* and *Exp_Prep* packages.

- **sem.adb.** This package has a subprogram named *Analyze* used to traverse the AST. Depending on the node kind it calls the corresponding subprogram which analyses the node. After this analysis it calls the expander. When the expander is deactivated this second call has no effect (just returns !). In the following fragment you will see one possible modification of it which can be used to build, analyse and expand the new compilation unit and sentences. (Most of this code could be placed in a separate package. It has been left here to facilitate the understanding of the technique).

```
with Sem_Prep; use Sem_Prep;   -- Semantic analysis of the new
                                  sentences.
with Exp_Prep; use Exp_Prep;   -- Expansion of the new sentences.
with Opt;      use Opt;
...
package body Sem is

  procedure Analyze (N : Node_Id) is
    Mirror_AST : Node_Id;
  begin
    ...
    case Nkind (N) is
      when N_Subprogram_Body =>
        if Current_Sem_Unit = Main_Unit
          and then Preprocess_Code
        then
          Mirror_AST := Mirror.Copy_Separate_Tree (N);  -- (1)
          Set_Unit    (Parent (N), Mirror_AST);         -- (2)
          Set_Parent  (Mirror_AST, Parent (N));
```

```
                Expander_Mode_Save_And_Set (False);          --  (3)
                Analyze_Subprogram_Body (Mirror_AST);        --  (4)
                if Errors_Detected /= 0 then
                   return;
                end if;
                Expander_Mode_Restore;                       --  (5)

                Set_Unit (Parent (N), N);                    --  (6)
                Expand (Mirror_AST);

                Extract_Entity                               --  (7)
                   (Defining_Unit_Name (Specification (Mirror_AST)));

                if Display_Preprocessed_AST then             --  (8)
                   Operating_Mode := Check_Semantics;
                   return;
                end if;
             end if;
             Analyze_Subprogram_Body (N);                    --  (9)

          when N_New_Sentence =>
             Analyze_New_Sentence (N);               --  (11)
             Expand_New_Sentence (N);                --  (12)

          when ... =>
             ...
       end case;
       ...
       Expand (N);                                          --  (10)
       ...
    end Analyze;
    ...
 end Sem;
```

When we analyse the main subprogram body and the switch to activate the
preprocessing is on, we do the following: 1) Build the Mirror AST 2) Link
the root of the Mirror AST with the parent of the original AST 3) Deactivate
the expander (to avoid the expansion of the Ada 95 nodes) 4) Analyse the
subprogram in the Mirror AST 5) Reactivate the expander 6) Link again
the original AST with its parent node 7) Extract the entity associated to
the specification of the mirrored subprogram body from the current scope
(otherwise, when we reanalyse the original AST, GNAT will detect a duplicated subprogram) 8) If the switch to display the code generated by the
preprocessor is on, we deactivate the code generation and return to display
it 9) Otherwise, analyse the modified original AST and finally 10) Expand
the equivalent subtree.

During the analysis of the subprogram (step 4), when we find the new sentences we do the following: 11) Analyse its node and 12) Expand the node
into the equivalent subtree composed of Ada 95 nodes (note that, instead of

calling the GNAT *Expand()* subprogram, we directly call the corresponding subprogram *Expand_New_Sentence()*. The reason is that we have previously deactivated this subprogram on the step 3).

– **sem_prep.adb** In the subprogram which implements the semantic analysis of the new sentences we simply do our work in the GNAT usual way.

```
package body Sem_Prep is
   ...
   procedure Analyze_New_Sentence (N : Node_Id) is
   begin
      ...
   end Analyze_New_Sentence;

end Sem_Prep;
```

– **exp_prep.adb** In the subprogram which implements the expansion of the new sentences we do also do our work in the GNAT usual way. The only difference is that before returning we must replace the original node (in the original AST) by the the root of the new subtree.

```
package body Exp_Prep is
   ...
   procedure Expand_New_Sentence (N : Node_Id) is
      New_Subtree_Root : Node_Id;
      ...
   begin
      --  Build the equivalent Ada95 subtree.
      ...
      Nmake (New_Subtree_Root, ... );
      --  Replace the subtree in the original AST
      Rewrite
        (Old_Node => Mirror.Original_Node (N),
         New_Node => New_Subtree_Root);
   end Expand_New_Sentence;

end Exp_Prep;
```

3.3 Building the Mirror AST

The GNAT package **atree.adb** contains the low level routines which handle the AST nodes. In order to build the Mirror AST we tried to reuse some of its subprograms. We found two good candidates: *Copy_Separate_Tree* and *Original_Node*. However, their code must be adapted to our new requirement (each node of the Mirror AST must have an additional field which references its original). Instead of modifying these subprograms we decided to isolate our code in a local package named *Mirror*.

```
package Atree is
   ...
   package Mirror is
      function Copy_Separate_Tree (Source : Node_Id) return Node_Id;
      function Original_Node (Node : Node_Id) return Node_Id;
      --  Original node associated to a mirrored node.
      pragma Inline (Original_Node);
   end Mirror;
end Atree;
```

All the GNAT AST nodes are generated in a single dynamically resizeable table. Therefore, when we create the Mirror AST, all its nodes are also stored in this table (see Figure 6). Similarly to the GNAT version of the *Copy_Separate_Tree* and *Original_Node* subprograms, we have not added the additional field to the GNAT nodes structure. We have implemented the new field by means of a separated table (see Figure 6). The reason is to do not disturb the current efficiency of the power of 2 for the node size. The information stored in the Nth element of this separated table corresponds to the element N of the nodes table. Therefore, only the positions associated to the mirrored nodes have valid information in this table (the first positions are not used).

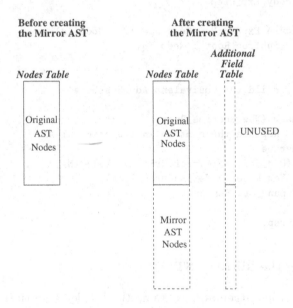

Fig. 6. Node Tables

In the next fragment of code you see the differences of our subprograms with respect to the original GNAT version.

```
package body Atree is
   ...
   package body Mirror is
      package Additional_Field is new Table.Table        -- (1)
         (...
          Table_Name             => "Additional_Field");

      function Original_Node (Node : Node_Id) return Node_Id is
      begin
         return Additional_Field.Table (Node);             -- (2)
      end Original_Node;

      function Copy_Separate_Tree (Source : Node_Id) return Node_Id is
         ...
         function Copy_Entity (E : Entity_Id) return Entity_Id is
         begin
            ...
            Preserve_Comes_From_Source (New_Ent, E);       -- (3)
            return New_Ent;
         end Copy_Entity;
         function Copy_List (List : List_Id) ...
         function Possible_Copy (Field : Union_Id) ...
      begin
         if Source <= Empty_Or_Error then
            return Source;
         elsif Has_Extension (Source) then
            return Copy_Entity (Source);
         else
            Nodes.Increment_Last;
            New_Id := Nodes.Last;
            --  Copy the node
            ...
            --  Store the reference to the original node.
            Additional_Field.Set_Last (New_Id);            -- (4)
            Additional_Field.Table (New_Id) := Source;

            --  Recursively copy descendents
            ...
         end if;
      end Copy_Separate_Tree;
   end Mirror;
end Atree;
```

The main differences are:

1. We use a new table to store the additional field.
2. When the additional field is requested we return the information stored in this new table.
3. When an entity is copied we remember if it was directly generated by the parser.

4. When a node is copied we update the size of the *Additional Field* table and we store the reference to the original node in the *Additional Field* table.

4 Discussion

The basic idea is to add another phase (the preprocessing phase) which allows the programmer to define the source transformations "as if" they were simple text transformations (first "replace X by ABC"; second "replace Y by DEF", etc.). Obviously the programmer can optimise the work by doing several transformations in the same stage (first "replace X by ABC, Y by DEF"; second ...). This work is done by replacing a node by a subtree that provides the desired functionality. During the preprocessing phase the original AST has no semantic information. This information is stored in the mirror AST because, in the general case, it is necessary to know the context of the new sentences to make its transformation. Therefore, the new nodes added to the original AST must not have semantic information (thus simplifying our work) and they can only be linked with nodes in the original AST. By following this methodology we can call the GNAT semantic analysed after the preprocessing phase with the modified original AST. This AST can be now analysed and processed as if it was the original AST (the compiler can not differentiate it from the AST created by the parser).

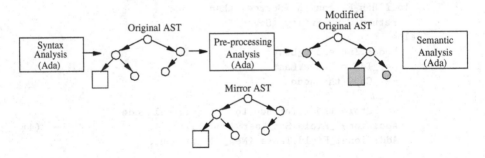

Fig. 7. The preprocessing phase

Although the transformations can also be implemented inside the GNAT expander, the main advantages of adding this new phase are:

1. It simplifies the work, because the preprocessor programmer knows that his/her transformations do not interfere with the transformations done by the GNAT expander (which has not been still activated). His/her work only depends on the original AST and his/her AST transformations. Additionally the programmer does not need to handle many internal details of the front-end (for example, implicit labels do not need to be handled because they will be handled later by the compiler).

2. It simplifies the debugging. The modified original AST can be displayed. This allows to the preprocessor programmer to see if the preprocessor is doing well its work. The current GNAT implementation only allows the programmer to see the original AST or the resulting AST after the expansion phase. Therefore, as the expander recursively re-expand the new nodes when necessary the programmer can not see the result of the transformations.
3. It simplifies the maintenance. The preprocessor does not depend on the concrete transformations done by the front-end and, therefore, it is compatible with the new versions of the front-end.
4. It reduces the minimum sources set that the programmer needs to handle. The programmer does not need to handle neither the GNAT semantic analyser (94.000 lines) nor the expander (59.000 lines length).
5. It enhances the error notification. It is simple to modify the gnat package "errout" to add a prefix to all the error messages generated during the preprocessing phase. For example:

```
432:12: (Preprocessing) Bad identifier.
```

This aspect is not only important for the user. It is also important for the preprocessor programmer because during the preprocessing phase the Mirror AST is also semantically analysed. Therefore the preprocessor programmer needs to differentiate the error messages generated when traversing the mirror AST from the error messages generated when traversing the modified original AST.

Although the proposed technique is not "indispensable" we think it can be useful for Ada working groups which have to experiment with Ada extensions in a fair time. These teams are not interested in all the implementation details of the GNAT front-end. They just want to use the minimum sources set required to verify their proposals.

5   Conclusions

We have proposed a technique which reduces the time required to implement a high quality preprocessor and it facilitates the use of the GNAT front-end to experiment with Ada extensions. The proposed technique adds a preprocessing phase to the GNAT front-end and has the following advantages:

1. It does not modify the current behaviour of the GNAT front-end.
2. It reduces the time required to develop the preprocessor because all the GNAT routines which make the work of the scanner, parser and semantic analyser are reused.
3. It reduces the compilation time of the Ada extension because it is not necessary to add a new pass on the sources to preprocess the code.
4. It facilitates the verification of the expansion (it is easy to display the resulting tree after the preprocessing phase).

The technique consists on the creation of a Mirror AST (a duplicate of the GNAT Abstract Syntax Tree whose nodes have an additional field with the reference of its original node). In the preprocessing phase this Mirror AST is traversed and the nodes associated to new sentences and analysed and replaced in the original AST by a subtree composed of Ada95 nodes which provide its functionality.

This technique has been used to implement Drago[8,9], an Ada extension which facilitates the programming of fault-tolerant and cooperative applications by means of coordinated groups of distributed processes. However the proposed technique can be easily applied to experiment with other Ada extensions. In this way GNAT can be used as an excellent platform to experiment with new proposals for future revisions of the Ada language.

6   Acknowledgement

We wish to thank professor E. Schonberg for his valuable comments, that have improved the final version of this paper.

References

1. Lesk, M.E. *Lex - a lexical analyzer generator*, AT&T Bell Laboratories. Number 39, May, 1975.
2. Johnson, S.C. *Yacc - yet another compiler compiler*, AT&T Bell Laboratories, Number 32, May, 1975.
3. Self, J. *Aflex - An Ada Lexical Analyzer Generator v1.1*, Department of Information and Computer Science. University of California, Irvine, UCI-90-18, May, 1990.
4. Taback D., Tolani D. and Schmalz R., AYacc v1.0. Department of Information and Computer Science. University of California, Irvine, UCI-88-16, May, 1988.
5. Intermetrics, Inc. 1995. *Ada 95 Language Reference Manual*. Intermetrics, Inc., Cambridge, Mass. (January).
6. Miranda J., Guerra F. Martin J. and Gonzalez A. *How to Modify the GNAT Frontend to Experiment with Ada Extensions*. Reliable Software Technologies. Ada-Europe'99. 1999. pp.226–237.
7. Comar, C., Gasperoni, F., and Schoberg, E. *The GNAT Project: A GNU-Ada9X Compiler*. Technical report. New York University. 1994.
8. Miranda, J., Álvarez, A., Guerra, F. and Arévalo, S. *Drago: A Language for Programming Fault-Tolerant and Cooperative Distributed Applications*. Reference Manual. *http://www.iuma.ulpgc.es/users/gsd/*
9. Miranda, J., Álvarez, A., Guerra, F. and Arévalo, S. *Programming Replicated Systems in Drago*. International Journal of Computer Systems: Science and Enginnering 15 (1), January, 2000.

Exposing Uninitialized Variables: Strengthening and Extending Run-Time Checks in Ada

Robert Dewar[1], Olivier Hainque[2], Dirk Craeynest[3], and Philippe Waroquiers[3]

[1] Ada Core Technologies
Fifth Avenue, 73, NY 10003 New York, United States of America
dewar@gnat.com
[2] ACT Europe
Rue de Milan, 8, 75009 Paris, France
hainque@act-europe.fr
[3] Eurocontrol/CFMU, Development Division
Rue de la Fusée, 96, B-1130 Brussels, Belgium
{dirk.craeynest,philippe.waroquiers}@eurocontrol.int

Abstract. Since its inception, a main objective of the Ada language has been to assist in the development of large and robust applications. In addition to that, the language also provides support for building safety-critical applications, e.g. by facilitating validation and verification of such programs. The latest revision of the language has brought some additional improvements in the safety area, such as the Normalize_Scalars pragma, which ensures an automatic initialization of the non-explicitly initialized scalars. This paper presents Initialize_Scalars, an enrichment of the Normalize_Scalars concept, and an extended mode to verify at run-time the validity of scalars, both designed for easy use in existing large applications. Their implementation in GNAT Pro (the GNU Ada 95 compiler) is discussed. The practical results obtained on a large Air Traffic Flow Management application are presented.

1 Introduction

One common cause of bugs that are difficult to find is the use of uninitialized variables. They often lead to unpredictable behaviour of programs, showing up only under special circumstances not necessarily encountered during testing. As an example, one release of the Eurocontrol CFMU[1] Air Traffic Flow Management application [1] had such a bug in compatibility code used to reload the binary data produced by the previous release. When a new field is introduced, the old binary data must be read and a default value must be given for this new field, resulting in code similar to the following:

---

[1] Eurocontrol is the European organization for the safety of air navigation. CFMU is the Central Flow Management Unit within this organization, in charge of the European flight plan processing and air traffic flow management.

J. Blieberger and A. Strohmeier (Eds.): Ada-Europe 2002, LNCS 2361, pp. 193–204, 2002.

```
if Reading_Current_Version then
   Boolean'Read (Stream, A_Flight.New_Field);
else
   A_Flight.New_Field := True;
end if;
```

This sequence was wrongly coded as follows, leading to an uninitialized New_Field for all the flights computed with the previous release and re-read with the new version:

```
if Reading_Current_Version then
   Boolean'Read (Stream, A_Flight.New_Field);
end if;
```

This bug was not detected during operational evaluation of the new release despite the extensive testing (including multiple binary data migration rehearsals). It was nonetheless triggered during the real migration, resulting in some temporary inaccuracy in the computation of the air traffic control load. The effect was limited to one elapsed day, since the new flights were computed by the new version of the software that correctly initializes this New_Field.

To avoid occurrences of similar bugs in other cases, CFMU deemed it necessary to investigate the practical ways of detecting uninitialized variables in this large application under constant evolution. The main objective was to improve the robustness of the application, preferably by using automated tools and techniques. A major constraint was the performance requirements of the system.

At the beginning of this investigation, Ada Core Technologies and CFMU discussed possible approaches. These discussions resulted in the specification and implementation in the GNAT compiler of features that help to detect uninitialized variables with additional run-time checks.

2   Detecting Uninitialized Variable Usage

Various techniques and methods are already available to track down uninitialized variables. This can be done either at "code level" (before running, using code analysis techniques) or at run-time (by insertion of code whose only purpose is to detect such usage).

2.1   Static Detection of Uninitialized Variables

Formal Validation Techniques: One well-known way to avoid using uninitialized variables is to avoid writing code that creates them. However, such approaches (e.g., formal validation techniques like SPARK [2]) are difficult to apply on large-scale applications like Eurocontrol's, which by their nature make extensive use of various features (e.g. tasking, exceptions, recursion, dynamic memory, usage of COTS products, and so forth). It is even less practical if this approach has to be applied on a large already existing code base (1.5 million Ada source lines for the CFMU application).

Compiler Warnings: In some cases, classical compiler principles can be used to produce warnings about dubious code (e.g. usage of a variable before it is initialized). Typically, the GNAT compiler emits such warnings in various cases, through front and back ends circuits that trace possible static flow paths. All such warnings were corrected in the CFMU application when it was converted from Ada83 to Ada95 [3].

However, the problem of statically detecting all and only the error cases can be shown to be equivalent to the halting problem, and thus has no general solution. In particular, array elements are not easily tracked, and no set of warnings can catch all the cases without generating an excessive number of false positive warnings.

2.2   Detecting Uninitialized Variables at Run Time

Purify-like Solutions: Purify is a well-known tool that helps to detect uninitialized variable usage, amongst other nice features and capabilities. It inserts checks in the compiled object code, which means that having the source code is not necessary. In addition, by maintaining a "shadow" memory to track initializations, Purify can detect invalid uses without requiring invalid bit patterns.

However, this approach has some limitations. The technology is very advanced but complex and does sometimes introduce difficulties, e.g. when transforming COTS libraries. Also, the instrumentation is highly dependent on which compiler is used and in which environment. For example, the following code:

```
main ()
{
  int i;
   i = i + 1;
}
```

could not be handled properly by Purify version 5.2 and 5.3 beta on HP-UX 11 when compiled with aCC (even an instrumented correct program gave a memory fault). When compiled with cc, the transformed code correctly detected the invalid usage of variable i. When compiled with the gcc C compiler provided with GNAT 3.15w, Purify correctly detected the invalid usage of i. On Windows NT with Microsoft Visual VC++ 6.0, the misuse of i was not detected by Purify (but the instrumented code was not giving a segmentation violation).

The above problems probably originate from the fact that Purify works at object code level. This is both a strength (no need for the source) but also a weakness, since it seems difficult to insert in the object code the additional assembly instructions that will detect an access to uninitialized memory.

Purify is also a "all or nothing" tool that cannot be applied selectively: it searches for all problems it can search in all object files and libraries. The resulting instrumented code is significantly larger and slower than the original code (3 to 5 times slower, taking about 40% more memory [4]), which often precludes the usage of 'Purified' applications in an operational context.

In the past, Purify was successfully used in CFMU to detect memory leaks inside Ada code compiled with GNAT. However, it did not detect the usage of uninitialized scalars that were later detected using the Initialize_Scalars GNAT enhancements.

Normalize_Scalars: After initial discussions between ACT and Eurocontrol, one of the suggestions was to use the Normalize_Scalars feature of Ada95 to detect this bug at run-time or to at least obtain a predictable behaviour of the application. However, this pragma was designed for the purpose of eliminating non-determinacy from safety-critical programs, which is why it appears in Annex H of [5]. This is a somewhat different goal from detecting uninitialized variables, and consequently Normalize_Scalars has limitations that make its use difficult for large applications.

Application wide consistency - Normalize_Scalars is a configuration pragma that implies that the full partition is compiled with this pragma, including the Ada run time. This problem can of course be solved by having the compiler vendor supply a pre-compiled run-time for use with Normalize_Scalars. In the case of GNAT, this solution is even simpler as the run-time code is available and can be recompiled easily. In case the application is integrating COTS products for which sources are not available, special arrangements must be made with each of the COTS providers so that a Normalize_Scalars version is provided. In any case, the requirement for partition-wide consistency is quite inconvenient, and precludes the use of Normalize_Scalars for testing small parts of a large application.

Invalid values only if possible - The Normalize_Scalars specification ensures that if possible, an invalid value (out of range) is used to initialize otherwise uninitialized scalar objects. Of course, if the full bit range is covered by the values of the scalars, then there is no invalid value. In this case, Normalize_Scalars ensures a predictable behaviour by initializing to a "normal" value but cannot detect the usage of this "normal" value.

Manual coding to detect invalid values - The Ada95 language revision added features to check the validity of a bit pattern (cf. Ada Reference Manual [5], RM H.1.1.) In conjunction with Normalize_Scalars, it is thus possible to detect errors with code such as:

```
if A_Flight.A_Field'Valid then
   .... -- this field can be used
else
   .... -- error handling
end if;
```

In practice, this kind of manual technique cannot be applied on a large scale application, essentially because of the existing code base size, so an automatic validity check would be more useful.

As the use of uninitialized variables in Ada 95 should not "by itself lead to erroneous or unpredictable execution" ([5], RM 13.9.1-11), a compiler is free, and sometimes required, to insert "hidden" code checking the validity of scalar values. In practice, such constructs as case statements or array assignments may require checks avoiding wild jumps or memory corruption, but most other operations can simply proceed with invalid data, possibly leading to invalid results.

If we want to maximize the chance of discovering usage of uninitialized variables during testing, then it is desirable to increase the amount of checking done at run-time. In case there is no invalid value for the type bit range, an alternative solution has to be found to detect access to uninitialized data.

3 GNAT Enhancements: Initialize_Scalars Pragma and New Checking Levels

To overcome the limitations of Normalize_Scalars, CFMU and ACT undertook to specify and implement an alternative approach to Normalize_Scalars, resulting in an enhancement contract to develop:

- a new pragma Initialize_Scalars,
- a way to choose the initial values of otherwise uninitialized scalars,
- compiler support for fine grained additional validity checking levels.

3.1 The Pragma Initialize_Scalars

The pragma Initialize_Scalars ensures, as does the Normalize_Scalars, an initialization of otherwise uninitialized scalars. However, the constraint that the pragma must be used for the whole partition has been removed. This means that it can be used in a much wider scope than Normalize_Scalars, whose primary target was embedded safety-critical applications that rarely use COTS libraries. It also makes it convenient to use for a small part of a large application, and avoids the requirement of recompiling the run-time library. (Cf. GNAT Reference Manual [6]).

3.2 Choice of Initial Value

The standard requires Normalize_Scalars to initialize to an invalid value if possible and requires the documentation of cases in which no invalid value can be generated. In order to be able to detect more usage of uninitialized variable, the initial value used by Initialize_Scalars can be chosen at bind time from among the following options:

- all bits 0,
- all bits 1,
- invalid value if possible (corresponding to Normalize_Scalars behaviour),
- a specified bit pattern.

Running the application or the application tests using different settings can detect more bugs. Any difference of behaviour between runs using different initial values are indications of the use of uninitialized values. Of course, this technique does not guarantee to find all bugs, but increases the chances of discovering them if the test coverage is wide enough. Furthermore, it is of particular value in the case where no invalid values exist, since the variation in behavior can indicate uninitialized values, even if all values are valid.

3.3 Additional Validity Checking

In GNAT version 3.13, only the RM mandated validity checkings were supported. They could be turned off, but there was no facility for forcing additional checks. In version 3.14, the notion of optional validity checks was added, and a switch with several levels was introduced as follows:

- gnatV0 → no checking,
- gnatV1 → RM checking,
- gnatV2 → check all assignment right hand sides.

The provision for checking assignment right hand sides was done precisely to improve validity checking in connection with the use of Normalize_Scalars. However, this turned out to miss many cases so an initial enhancement was provided that added two additional levels:

- gnatV3 → check all tests,
- gnatV4 → check all expressions.

Experimentation against Eurocontrol's applications showed that intermediate levels were needed. In particular, it was found that checking all "in out" parameters caused difficulties, due to coding that was indeed incorrect with regard to validity checking, but that was in practice harmless in normal operation. Therefore, control over validity checking was eventually improved to allow specification of exactly which situations result in additional checks. Furthermore, a pragma Validity_Checks was introduced to allow control to be specified at the source level, and to be varied within a single unit. The possible settings in the final implementation of -gnatV (cf. GNAT User's Guide [7]) are as follows:

- gnatVa/n → turn on/off all validity checks (including RM),
- gnatVc/C → turn on/off checks for copies,
- gnatVd/D → turn on/off RM checks (on by default),
- gnatVf/F → turn on/off checks for floating-point,
- gnatVi/I → turn on/off checks for "in" params,
- gnatVm/M → turn on/off checks for "in out" params,
- gnatVo/O → turn on/off checks for operators,
- gnatVr/R → turn on/off checks for returns,
- gnatVs/S → turn on/off checks for subscripts,
- gnatVt/T → turn on/off checks for tests.

With the relevant checking mode on, the usage of an invalid value is detected and reported by raising a Constraint_Error exception.

3.4   Implementation in GNAT of Initialize_Scalars and gnatV

There were three considerations to the implementation of these new facilities in GNAT.

First, in order to ensure that Initialize_Scalars can be used on a selective basis, all possible cases of a client being compiled with or without the pragma, and the packages it uses being compiled with or without the pragma, must work. This involved the generation of some additional dummy initialization routines, which in practice are nearly always inlined, resulting in no additional run-time overhead.

Second, to allow the specification of invalid values at bind time, the code generated for Initialize_Scalars differs from that generated for Normalize_Scalars in that the values used to initialize otherwise uninitialized data are always copied from fixed memory locations, instead of being supplied as compile-time known constants as was done for Normalize_Scalars. This is slightly less efficient, but allows the memory locations to be modified at bind time. Indeed it would be possible to modify them at run time (e.g. by the use of an environment variable), and that is a planned future enhancement.

Finally, the insertion of additional validity checks required some care, because the compiler and its various optimization algorithms are quick to eliminate the additional checks on the grounds that they are obviously not required if the data is valid. Of course the whole point is that such checks are required because the data may be invalid, and the optimization procedures had to be modified to avoid the removal of needed tests. The actual validity checking was easily implemented, since the compiler already had mechanisms for the 'Valid attribute.

4   Application to Eurocontrol and Obtained Results

4.1   Bugs Discovered

GNAT has only reported real errors (uninitialized scalar usage). In other words, the Initialize_Scalars and gnatV checks have caused constraint errors only for uninitialized variables (no false positives). Not all the reported bugs had functional impacts, however, as the following example illustrates. GNAT reported a bug in code similar to:

```
Found : boolean;
Data  : A_Record_With_A_Status;

Find_A_Record (For_Key, Found, Data);

if Found and Data.Status = Not_Interesting then
  Found := False;
end if;
....
```

The procedure `Find_A_Record` sets `Found` to true if it finds a record corresponding to `For_Key`. If a record is found, `Data` is initialized otherwise it is not initialized. Some of the found records are however not interesting and must be filtered out. The above code is technically incorrect (an uninitialized `Status` is accessed in case `Found` is false) but this has no functional impact. One possible easy correction is to replace the "and" by an "and then". Other corrections are of course possible (i.e. change the code in order to obtain a more elegant structure based on a cleaner specification of `Find_A_Record`).

When Initialize-Scalars was started to be used, the large majority of bugs were detected by the additional run-time checks on enumerated and boolean values. Most of these bugs are usually quite straightforward to correct once they are detected. Without Initialize-Scalars, they are however sometimes very tricky to detect. As an example, a bug was detected in a procedure that was waiting for an X protocol event to be received (up to a certain deadline). When the deadline was reached before asking X if an event occurred, the variable telling if an X event was pending was left uninitialized. This was then potentially leading to a call to X to handle the event even when the deadline was expired.

Float validation checking (gnatVf) has also detected quite a number of bugs in some numeric algorithms with unusual data (e.g. flight plans that do not respect the aircraft maximum performances). A lot of these bugs have been discovered by injecting massive amount of data. When floats are left uninitialized, conventional testing does not always reveal such bugs, as the massive results have to be analyzed in detail with respect to numerical correctness.

Finally, Initialize-Scalars and validation checking are not only discovering functional bugs. They also helped to detect efficiency bugs. E.g., a bug was discovered in a procedure that has to search in a list of (key, value) the value for a certain key. This was implemented on a generic list package providing a passive iterator. The boolean variable used to exit the iterator was left uninitialized. This had no functional effect as the return value was initialized properly even when the key was not found. When the key was found, however, potentially all the rest of the list was still traversed for no reason.

4.2   Incorrect Programming Idiom with "in out" Parameters

The following wrong programming idiom has lead to the need of fine grain control over validity checks resulting in the gnatV switch described previously.

```
procedure Read_Or_Write
   (Read_Mode : Boolean; A_Scalar : in out Natural) is
begin
   if Read_Mode then
      A_Scalar := ....; -- read from somewhere
   else
      Write (A_Scalar); -- write somewhere
   end if;
end Read_Or_Write;
```

```
N : Natural;
....
Read_Or_Write (Read_Mode => True, A_Scalar => N);
N := N + 2;
Read_Or_Write (Read_Mode => False, A_Scalar => N);
```

The idea is to write 'low level' symmetrical read/write procedures that can either read or write elementary types. Read/Write functions for composite types can then be programmed without needing to check if the operation to execute is the read or the write operation as this is delegated to the low level elementary type procedures. This is in fact a 'manual' implementation of the 'Read/'Write attributes of Ada95, designed and programmed at a time Ada83 was used at CFMU.

This idea looks attractive at first sight as it avoids programming and maintaining read and write procedure independently. When the compiler inserts a validity check for scalars parameters, then the above code is raising a constraint error whenever Read_Mode is True and A_Scalar is not initialized. We first started to correct this design error by splitting the code in separate read and write procedures for scalars. However, a lot of generics were expecting this kind of symmetrical procedures as generic parameter. As the same generics were instantiated with scalars or composite types, this kind of correction had a snowball effect, obliging to rework all the Read_Or_Write procedures.

A discussion was held with ACT, which resulted in a much finer control over what validity checks to insert. The case above was solved by having switches to specifically enable/disable the validation for in and in/out parameters. We are now disabling the validation for in/out parameters. This does not mean however that a real bug would not be discovered, only that it would be discovered not at the point of the wrong call but rather at the point where the called procedure would wrongly use the uninitialized scalar. In other words, when -gnatVM is used, a call to Read_Or_Write with N uninitialized does not raise constraint error, but a constraint error is raised inside Read_Or_Write when the Write procedure is called.

4.3   Performance Impact

The performance impact of tools influences how and when they can be used. The factors to be looked at are build time (compile, bind and link), the executable size and the run-time performance. Table 1 summarizes the impact of various combinations of GNAT switches on a representative CFMU test program. The 'mode' column identifies switch combinations with a set of values amongst:

- 0 → no optimization,
- 2 → optimization (gcc -O2 + back-end inlining),
- i → Initialize_Scalars pragma,
- v → gnatVaM (all validation checks, except for in out parameters),
- r → reference manual checking (i.e. gnatVd) + integer overflow check,
- n → all validity checks off (including reference manual checkings).

Table 1. Performance impact of various switch combinations.

mode	current use	build time	executable size	run time
0r		100	100	100
0iv	development	118	107	160
2n		190	68	69
2r	operational	197	69	70
2iv		252	72	91

The numbers are relative to the 0r mode, which was the default development setup before the introduction of Initialize_Scalars. The impact of Initialize_Scalars and gnatVaM on the three factors is reasonable enough for daily usage by developers. The run-time penalty is however considered too costly for operational usage due to the high performance requirements of the CFMU application. Currently, the choice is to use the reference manual checks, which avoids the most horrible consequences of uninitialized scalars (erroneous execution) for a very small run-time penalty.

4.4 Running with Different Initial Values

CFMU intends to run the application test suite with different values to initialize the scalars. Typically, we will run the automatic regression tests with scalars bit patterns initialized to all 0 and all 1 (in addition to the currently used 'invalid values' initialization). This should help detect the uninitialized variables for which no invalid values can be generated (when the full bit pattern of the type is needed to represent all values).

Waiting for a future enhancement of the compiler, changing the default initial value implies to rebind the executable. As a temporary solution, CFMU has developed code to override the initial values at startup time, using a shell environment variable.

5   Conclusions

5.1   Usage During Development

With Initialize_Scalars and gnatV, a significant number of latent (and in some cases potentially serious) bugs were discovered in the large CFMU application. For all these cases, once the bug was discovered with the help of Initialize_Scalars, it was straightforward to pin-point the error in the code logic and ensure a correct initialization by modifying the logic or providing a required initial value. Detection of uninitialized variable usage is now done earlier in the development in an efficient and pragmatic manner. Based on this experience, we recommended the use of Initialize_Scalars and gnatVa as a default development mode when writing new code or enhancing existing code.

The GNAT compiler provides fine grain control over validity code insertion. This makes it possible to use Initialize_Scalars and validity checking on large existing applications that sometimes cannot be fully adapted to all the validity checkings provided.

5.2 Operational Test Usage

The Initialize_Scalars and additional checking level of GNAT has a limited impact on the code size, code performance and compile time. This impact is reasonable enough so that CFMU has transitioned to using Initialize_Scalars and gnatV checking as the default development mode. CFMU also intends to install for the first few weeks of operational evaluation the version compiled with Initialize_Scalars and gnatVaM. This is possible because the performance degradation in both memory and CPU usage is acceptable for limited capacity evaluation purposes.

Due to the very high performance requirements of the CFMU application, after a few weeks of operational test of this "checking version", the application compiled with optimization (i.e. with Ada RM checks and GNAT optimization switches on, but without Initialize_Scalars) will be installed. This optimized version, after a few more months of operational evaluation, will go operational.

5.3 Impact of Usage of Initialize_Scalars on How to Program

There is a trend in programming guidelines to "force" initializing everything at declaration resulting in code like:

```
B : Natural := 0;

if .... then
  B := 5;
else
  B := 8;
end if;
```

The difficulty with such an approach is that the initial value is meaningless. If this value is used accidentally, the results are potentially just as wrong as the use of an uninitialized value, and furthermore, the explicit initialization precludes the approach we have described in this paper, and thus may introduce bugs that are much harder to find and fix. The automatic initialization under control of the compiler using Initialize_Scalars is a far preferable approach.

We therefore recommend that when a scalar is declared, the programmer should avoid initializing it if the code is supposed to set the value on all paths. It is better to let Initialize_Scalars + gnatVa detect the bug in the code logic rather than trying to deal with meaningless initial values. Even for safety-critical programs, we can first compile with Initialize_Scalars + gnatVa + invalid values and then, if needed, field the code with Initialize_Scalars + all zero values (if it is the case that zero values give the code a better chance of avoiding seriously improper behavior).

References

[1] Waroquiers, P.; *Ada Tasking and Dynamic Memory: To Use or Not To Use, That's a Question!*, Proceedings of International Conference on Reliable Software Technologies - Ada Europe 1996, Montreux, Switzerland, June 10–14, 1996, Alfred Strohmeier (Ed.), Lecture Notes in Computer Science, vol. 1088, Springer-Verlag, 1996, pp.460–470.

[2] Barnes, J.; *High Integrity Ada; The Spark Approach*, Addison Wesley, 1997.

[3] Waroquiers, P., Van Vlierberghe, S., Craeynest, D., Hately, A., and Duvinage, E.; *Migrating Large Applications from Ada83 to Ada95*, Proceedings of International Conference on Reliable Software Technologies - Ada Europe 2001, Leuven, Belgium, May 14–18, 2001, Dirk Craeynest, Alfred Strohmeier (Eds.), Lecture Notes in Computer Science, vol. 2043, Springer-Verlag, 2001, pp.380–391.

[4] *Purify on-line Unix manual*, Rational Software Corporation, June 2000.

[5] Taft, S.T., Duff, R.A., Brukardt, R.L. and Plödereder, E.; *Consolidated Ada Reference Manual. Language and Standard Libraries*, ISO/IEC 8652:1995(E) with COR.1:2000, Lecture Notes in Computer Science, vol. 2219, Springer-Verlag, 2001.

[6] *GNAT Reference Manual - The GNU Ada95 Compiler*, Version 3.15a, Ada Core Technologies, 30 January 2002.

[7] *GNAT User's Guide for Unix Platforms*, Version 3.15a, Ada Core Technologies, 30 January 2002.

Adding Design by Contract to the Ada Language

Ehud Lamm

The Open University of Israel, Max Rowe Educational Center, P.O.B 39328
Ramat-Aviv, Tel-Aviv 61392, Israel
mslamm@mscc.huji.ac.il

Abstract. Annotating software components with contracts, which are
then enforced by the programming language, and the methodology of Design by Contract, can help increase software reliability. Contracts are of
special importance for component based design. We study how contracts
can be integrated with existing Ada features, in particular Ada support
for inheritance. Recently published results about inheritance and contracts prove to be of special importance for integrating contracts into
Ada.

1 Design by Contract

Design by contract (DbC) is a software engineering methodology that formalizes
the intuitive notion that the relations between software components are based
on contractual obligations. Contracts try to help answering such questions as
how well can you trust a component, and who is to blame when a component
misbehaves, the client who may have misused the component or the component
itself.

The most thorough implementation of the DbC approach can be found in the
Eiffel programming language, and is explained in detail by [15]. As implemented
in Eiffel, class methods define *pre-conditions* and *post-conditions* which are the
requirements and promises of the methods (respectively).[1]

A contract carries mutual obligations and benefits. The client should only call
a contractor routine when the routine's pre-condition is respected. The routine
ensures that after completion its post-condition is respected.

Ada is most often marketed as the programming language of choice for software engineering, especially where reliability important. Indeed, among general
purpose imperative programming languages Ada has a unique feature set for
dealing with the difficulties software engineering. Alas, Ada does not fully support the design by contract approach, though some Ada features, notably generic
units, impose contractual obligations. Design by contract is one of the widely
discussed and accepted concepts in software engineering [1, 2, 3, 6, 8, 10, 11, 16]
and while the exact approach for integrating design by contract into programming languages is widely debated, many advantages can be reaped even from

---

[1] Eiffel also allows the programmer to specify class invariants. Invariants will not be
discussed in this paper.

J. Blieberger and A. Strohmeier (Eds.): Ada-Europe 2002, LNCS 2361, pp. 205–218, 2002.

rudimentary implementations. An important advantage is the standardization of the contract notation, which will ease communicating specifications, and reduce specification errors that are the result of lack of expertise in using specific tools. It also eases run time contract checking, which is important when contracts cannot be verified statically, and is of major importance when dealing with separately compiled code, and off the shelf components.

1.1   DbC and Components

Subtle software errors can result from faulty interaction between software components. This is even true for well designed and tested components.

DbC offers help with the component integration problem, by specifying component obligations and enabling their automatic enforcement. This helps, most importantly, with the problem of assigning blame [4].

Assigning Blame. It is highly important, when an error occurs, to be able to identify the faulty component. Pre-condition failures are obviously the responsibility of the calling routine, where as post-condition failures are the responsibility of the called routine itself. The situation becomes more subtle with the introduction of more advanced language features such as inheritance and genericity. With these it is possible to have problems stemming from the connection between two components, which are themselves faultless. A correct contract mechanism will identify the code connecting the components (e.g., the generic instantiation) as the code causing the problem.

1.2   Kinds of Contracts

[1] defines four levels of contracts between components: syntactic (interfaces and types in the programming language), behavioral (pre- and post- conditions), synchronization (e.g., mutual exclusion between operations) and quality of service (e.g., average response time of a distributed service). They progress from static non-negotiable properties, to the specification of dynamic properties that may be subject to run time negotiation.

In this paper we will focus on behavioral contracts, supplementing Ada's strong syntactic contracts which are enforced by the type system, visibility rules, generic programming facilities etc.[2] Behavioral contracts enable the programmer to specify properties that are hard or impossible to specify statically using the type system. It is preferable, when possible, to use compile time enforceable specifications, like generic parameter specifications.

Behavioral contracts will be used to capture important aspects of behavior. Examples:

– Properties of arguments, that cannot be expressed conveniently using the type system (e.g., Stack not Empty, before Pop operation).

---

[2] Notice, however, that Ada's concurrency features, especially protected objects, provide some of the expressiveness needed for synchronization contracts.

- Relations between arguments or between the object's operations (e.g, for Is_Empty() to be TRUE, Length() must return 0).

1.3 Approaches to Checking for Contract Violations

Pre-condition checks are done before a routine begins execution; post-condition checks are done before control returns to the caller.

The obvious solution to the performance impact of run time contract checking is to suppress contract tests after the program is verified and tested, the same approach used to reduce the overhead of subtype constraint checking in Ada. One important disadvantage is that this makes production code less safe, and thus is ultimately based on testing and manual verification.

Contract violations that can be proven at compile time can be seen as compilation errors, though are more likely – since the deduction ability will not be specified by the language – to be treated as compile time warnings.

Contract violations during run time are handled by raising exceptions.

Taxonomy of Contract Checking Tools. We propose the following division of labor between contract checking tools.

1. Code for contract checks at run time will be produced by the compiler, unless otherwise suppressed (by a Pragma or using the compiler's own optimizer proving capabilities).
2. Compilers will be encouraged to optimize contract checks, using static analysis. Information on checks optimized away, must be clearly provided using Pragma Reviewable.
3. Supporting tools, such as static debuggers and theorem provers, would assist analyzing programs instrumented with contracts. When applicable such tools may provide check suppressing pragmas for the compiler. It is assumed that advanced, interactive, theorem proving will remain at this level for time to come. Notice that this type of tools may require special training in logic, that most programmers do not possess.

2 Suggested Design

Contracts, by their very nature, should be part of the specification of interfaces [3, 5]. However, since Ada lacks an orthogonal concept of interfaces [12], we propose to try and engineer the solution to provide contractual obligations in as straightforward a manner on the variety of interface declarations in Ada.

While it is possible to treat contracts as first-class, and attach them to various interfaces [7, 8], this approach is deemed too complicated. It seems more practical to attach pre- and post- conditions to the various routine definitions, while contract semantics depend on the kind of interface being defined (e.g., tagged type or generic formal parameters).

2.1   Specifying Contracts

Contracts will be expressed as boolean expressions supplemented with the old keyword and the ability to reference functions return values from their post-condition. It will be possible to attach pre- and post- conditions to procedures, functions and entries.

Contracts will not provide complete behavioral specifications, but rather establish properties that are of special interest. Contracts that require more than simple boolean expressions can often be implemented manually using boolean functions.

Following Eiffel, post-conditions may reference old values of expressions. The value of the expression old exp in a post-condition, at execution time on routine exit, is the value of exp evaluated on entry to the routine.

Allowing old expressions to reference arbitrary data (e.g., heap data, via pointers) is problematic. The old values of expressions are evaluated just before normal execution of the routine begins. The values are assigned to temporary variables. Assignment is done according to the normal Ada rules. Local entities defined inside the routine are not available.

This has several repercussions. Unless the expression is of a Controlled type, and assignment was redefined, the assignment only produces a shallow copy of the expression. On the other hand, if the type is Controlled, a complete data structure may be copied, this will harm efficiency and may even raise Storage_Error.

These issues, as well as the problem with contracts with side effects, are illustrated by the following example.

```
package Queues is
   type Queue is limited private;
   -- ...
   procedure Deq(Q:in out Queue; X:out Integer);
      -- pre:  not(Is_Empty(Q))
      -- post: ???
   function Length(Q:Queue) return Natural;
   function Is_Empty(Q:Queue) return Boolean;
private
   type Node;
   type Queue_Data is access Node;
   type Queue is
      record
         D   :Queue_Data;
      end record;
end;
```

Suppose the programmer wants the post-condition of Deq to specify that after the call the queue length is decremented. The programmer could specify this property in several ways:

```
Length(Q)= old Length(Q) - 1
Length(Q)= Length(old Q) - 1
```

The first expression will require recording of a Natural value (`Length(Q)`), where as the second approach requires copying Q. The second expression may not work correctly depending on how Q is changed inside `Deq` (e.g., if the head of the list is freed, `Length` will access deallocated memory). Had `Queue` (or `Queue_Data`) been defined to be a Controlled type, the second expression may have meant copying the entire linked list, in which case it would have been essential to provide a `Finalize` operation to free the memory allocated to the temporary. This kind of reasoning ultimately depends on the implementation details of the `Queue` data type and the `Deq` operation, and thus it is reasonable to leave it to the programmer.

Notice a third possible implementation of the post-condition, made possible by adding a field storing the current length to the `Queue` record. Though the most efficient, this formulation causes the post-condition to be specified in the body of the package since the components of `Queue` are not visible in the public part of the package specification (this issue is explained in detail below). Since the property being specified is of great importance to users of `Deq`, one would prefer using the expression `Length(Q)= old Length(Q)-1`, which allows the post-condition to be visible to clients.

Had the programmer decided on manually copying the linked list structure for use in the post-condition, using a `Clone` function, it would have been his responsibility to ensure that the memory is released, in order to avoid the memory leak. The post-condition `Length(Q)=Length(old Clone(Q))-1` is not enough. How can the memory allocated by `Clone(Q)` be released? The obvious solution is to delegate the contract check and memory reclamation to a separate boolean function, thus allowing us to sequence the required operations (checking the contract, and releasing memory).

```
procedure Deq(Q:in out Queue; X:out Integer);
-- post: Check_Length_And_Release(old Clone(Q), Length(Q)+1);

function Check_Length_And_Release(Q:Queue;Required_Length:Natural)
  return Boolean;
      -- 1) Res:=Length(Q)=Required_Length
      -- 2) Free(Q.D)
      -- 3) return Res
```

Following the Ada approach on side effects from functions, contract side effects are deemed the responsibility of the programmer. Methodologically, contracts should not have side effects since contract checking may be suppressed when compiling programs.

2.2   New Syntax

Pre- and post- conditions in routine and entry specifications may be marked using new keywords such as **precondition** and **postcondition**, or following the Eiffel syntax: **require** and **ensure**. It is clumsy but possible to use existing keywords: **use when** can specify pre-conditions, and **at exit** can be used to specify post-conditions. Other options are **use with** for pre-conditions, and **return with** or **at end** for post-conditions. Adding the keyword **old** seems better than trying to reuse existing keywords.

Example:

```
procedure Deq(Q:in out Queue; X:out Integer)
 use when not(Is_Empty(Q))
 at exit Length(Q)= old Length(Q)-1;
```

Inside the post-condition of a function, the function name will refer to the current return value from the function.

2.3   Run Time Contract Violations

A run time contract violation raises an exception. The package **Standard** will include two new exceptions: **precondition_error** and **postcondition_error**.

Inheritance hierarchy errors (see the discussion of inheritance below) and generic instantiation errors, identified during pre-condition or post-condition evaluation, will raise the relevant exception; the exception information, in this case, will inform the maintainer of the code that a compositional error was identified, and will point to the code that is at fault.[3] This approach is based on the premise that hierarchy errors cannot (and should not) be fixed at run time, so the distinction between them and other contract violations is of little importance for exception handling code.

Postcondition_error behaves as if it is raised just after the routine completes. The routine itself can *not* provide an exception handler to handle violations of its own post-condition. Obviously, a routine can check its post-condition manually. Such checks should not be common practice, as reliable coding would catch errors as they occur, instead of realizing just before the routine exits that it didn't operate correctly.

An advantage of this approach is that the contract violation exceptions can be raised from wrapper routines that check the pre-condition, invoke the routine, and upon its return verify the post-condition.

3   Contracts and Ada Language Features

We will now focus our attention on specific Ada features of interest, and study the contractual relations they impose, concentrating on the problem of assigning blame. We follow the general approach of [3, 4].

---

[3] It is probably advisable to standardize the encoding of this information. Using standard Ada exception facilities the information has to be encoded using strings.

Private Types and Information Hiding. Following the Eiffel design [15], clients should be able to verify pre-conditions, if they choose to do so. Consequently pre-conditions on routines exported from packages must be specified in the specification file, and only reference visible entities. Post-conditions, which are the responsibility of the routine itself, may ensure properties that are invisible to clients.

Post-conditions that need to reference hidden entities will be specified in the private part of the spec or completed in the body of the package. Naturally, the programmer will have to code the entire contract, repeating the information visible in the spec (as is usual in Ada). The hidden part of the post-condition is, of course, and-ed to the visible post-condition (i.e., the hidden part cannot serve as an escape clause in the contract).

Exceptions. When a routine terminates abnormally by raising an exception, re-raising an exception or by not handling an exception, it is not required to ensure that its post-condition holds. If the routine terminates normally, after handling exceptions, it must ensure that its post-condition holds.

This approach is more compatible with Ada's exception handling mechanism than is the Eiffel approach [15]. It also provides for greater flexibility. This design is similar to the one used by jContractor [10].

Subprogram Generic Parameters. Consider the following example.

```
generic
   with function Sqrt(X:Float) return Float;
   -- pre: X>=0
procedure Print_Quad_Solutions(A,B,C:Float);

procedure Print_Quad_Solutions(A,B,C:Float) is
   Discr:float:=B**2-4.0*A*C;
   X1,X2:float;
begin
   X1:=(-B+Sqrt(Discr))/(2.0*A);
   put(Float'Image(X1));
   -- ...
end;
```

Print_Quad_Solutions is parameterized with a Sqrt function, in order to support various algorithms for calculating square roots.

Sqrt is not supposed to work on negative numbers. If it is passed a negative number, it will fail, and Print_Quad_Solutions is to be blamed. However, if Sqrt requires a stronger pre-condition like $X > 0$, and it is passed 0, Print_Quad_Solutions is not to be blamed for the fault – since the routine cannot be aware of arbitrary conditions imposed by its generic parameters.

Print_Quad_Solutions should acknowledge that it will ensure that $X >= 0$ in its spec, thus proclaiming to work with Sqrt routines that require this condition or a weaker one.

If Print_Quad_Solutions fails to establish the condition it promised (i.e., $X >= 0$) then it is to be blamed when Sqrt's pre-condition is not met. If, however, this condition is met, while the pre-condition of the actual Sqrt is not met, the blame must rest with the programmer instantiating Print_Quad_Solutions.

In order to implement this design, formal subprogram parameter specifications must be allowed to include contracts. The parameter routines themselves are passed accompanied with their contracts.

Before invoking the subprogram, two preconditions must be checked. If the pre-condition defined by the generic unit is not met, the generic unit is to blame. If this condition is met, the actual pre-condition of the subprogram is checked. If it does not evaluate to true, the instantiation is to be blamed for the fault. From an implementation point of view, the pre-condition of the actual can be passed as another, hidden, subprogram parameter (a boolean function).

Formally, the formal routine's pre-condition must **imply** the pre-condition of the actual and the actual's post-condition must imply the formal's post-condition.

Notice that in the Print_Quad_Solutions example, it was possible to specify the contract using a subtype Positive_Float. This would have been a better solution, since it eliminates the possibility of an instantiation problem being identified at run time. The contract based solution is, however, more general (e.g., suppose we needed to check that an integer is even). Methodologically, properties that can be specified using the type system should not be specified using explicit contracts.

Inheritance. [16] realized that pre-conditions must be weakened, and post-conditions strengthened down an inheritance hierarchy. Essentially, to satisfy the Liskov-Wing substitution principle, and be a behavioral subtype [13, 14], a derived class must require less and promise more.

More formally, if B is derived from A, then for each primitive operation P (of A and B), $pre(P_A) \Rightarrow pre(P_B)$ and $post(P_B) \Rightarrow post(P_A)$. Notice, that checking these implication at run time is trivial, since $p \Rightarrow q \equiv \neg p \vee q$, and all the required information can easily be computed when it is needed.

[16] ensures this relation between contracts using what Meyer terms *a low-tech solution*. Essentially, a programmer of a derived type can only specify conditions to be or-ed with the original pre-condition, or and-ed with the original post-condition. The Eiffel language implements this strategy using the **require else** and **ensure then** syntactic forms.

The problem with this approach is that it can hide mistakes in programmer supplied contracts [4]. A canonical example (translated into Ada):

```
type A is tagged null record;
procedure p(T:A;i:integer);
-- pre: i>0
```

```
type B is new A with  null record;
procedure p(T:B;i:integer);
-- pre: i>10
```

Extending A with B is a mistake, because B's pre-condition is stronger than A's pre-condition, thus violating the substitutability principle. The cause of this error may have been a logical error, or it may have been a simple typo. Tools that simply combine pre-conditions with a disjunction will come up with the synthesized pre-condition for P_B: $(i > 0) \lor (i > 10)$. Invoking B's P with 5 will not raise a pre-condition violation, since the synthesized pre-condition is true.

Keep in mind that not only do we want to be able to catch the pre-condition violation, we want to be able to conclude that the mistake is the responsibility of the programmer creating the A-B inheritance hierarchy, and not the responsibility of the programmer invoking P. This is because P may have been invoked as a result of a dispatching call, from the inside of an A'class routine. The programmer writing the A'class routine is only aware of the pre-condition specified by A.

As [4] concludes, there are three types of contract errors: pre-condition violations, post-condition violations, and **hierarchy errors**. As we have shown, the same kind of problem can arise from the use of subprograms generic parameters, so the last type of error may be termed more generally composition errors. We now show how to implement checking for hierarchy errors.

Class-wide Programming. Class-wide types enable the programmer to write interface oriented code. All types in the hierarchy support the common interface of the class-wide type. We use class-wide types to show the subtleties of interface based contract checking.[4]

The following example is based on examples in [3, 5].

```
type Counter is abstract tagged null record;
function Get_Value(C:Counter) return Integer is abstract;
procedure Inc(C: in out Counter) is abstract;
procedure Dec(C: in out Counter) is abstract;

type PCounter is abstract new Counter with null record;
procedure Dec(C: in out PCounter) is abstract;
-- pre: Get_Value(C)>0

type Pc is new PCounter with record
    Val:Integer:=0;
end record;
function Get_Value(C:Pc) return Integer;
```

---

[4] Special care must be taken in the presence of features like **interface** definitions, as proposed by Ada Issue 251 (AI-251), which allow a type to support multiple interfaces.

```
procedure Inc(C: in out Pc);
procedure Dec(C: in out Pc);

type Any_Counter is access all Counter'class;

-- Main routine
procedure Main is
   C:Any_Counter:=Counter_Factory(...);
begin
   Dec(C);
end;
```

The inheritance hierarchy is malformed because of the pre-condition PCount-er imposes on Dec.

Suppose Counter_Factory() returns an object of the type Pc. Main should not be blamed for the pre-condition violation in the call to Dec, since it is only responsible for the contract of the Any_Counter interface, which is the contract of the type Counter itself. Put more strongly, it is trivial to add another level of indirection, thus creating a separately compiled client, with a type containing Any_Counter which during run time is initialized with a reference to a Pc object. This client, obviously, cannot be blamed for the hierarchy error.[5]

To ensure the correct assignment of blame, contract checking should include two stages. First, the Any_Counter pre-condition is checked. If it doesn't hold, a pre-condition violation is triggered and Main is to be blamed. Only if this pre-condition holds (as is the case here), the specific object C.all is to checked.

Checking the object depends on the run time tag of the object (C'tag), and involves checking the inheritance hierarchy above C'tag, ensuring the proper implication relation holds between derived types. In this case the check will show that the relation between Counter and PCounter is improper, and a hierarchy error will be signaled.

It is important to realize that the first contract checking stage depends on the static type of C, while hierarchy checking depends on the run time tag. An implementation can replace the call to the primitive operation itself with a call to a wrapper routine, with the same signature, but which is specific to the static type (in the example this would be Counter). This routine will implicitly know its place in the hierarchy (the routine is primitive for the same type as in the original call). This wrapper routine starts by checking the pre-condition determined by the static type, and then invokes the hierarchy checking which is determined by the current object tag. In the example the routine will be Counter_Dec(C) which will dispatch to Counter_Dec(Pc) when Counter_Factory creates a Pc object.

Notice that the contract check can *not* be done inside Dec(Pc) since the first check depends on the view the client has (in the example above Counter didn't have its own contract), and not on the contract of the object itself.

---

[5] Notice that PCounter may have been added to the hierarchy well after Main was written.

Post-condition processing follows basically the same logic. A formal definition (cast in Java) can be found in [3].[6]

Implementation Inheritance. Inheritance can be used to reuse an implementation, without wanting to create a behavioral subtype. The contractual relationships we require will find such inheritance hierarchies to be malformed.

It is possible to augment the language with syntax that will be used to mark uses of inheritance that should not be checked for substitutability. A better approach is to use contract checking to enforce the paradigmatic use of inheritance.

Non IS-A uses of inheritance can be replaced by composition. Another solution is for the programmer to use private inheritance.

```
with Lists;
package Queues is
    type Queue is limited private;
    -- declare Queue operations
private
    type Queue is new Lists.List with null record;
end;
```

A client using the Queues package is bound only to the explicit requirements of the exported Queue operations. The inheritance relationship between Queue and List is not checked since the routine invoked when a Queue operation is executed does not contain hierarchy checking code, since the visible type Queue is not tagged.

Inside the package body the Queue operations may be implemented by explicitly converting the parameter to the type List, and invoking its primitive operations. These calls will check the inheritance hierarchy above List as, indeed, should be the case. If List or any of its ancestors are the result of private inheritance, the same logic applies and the relevant hierarchy checks will be skipped.

Derived Types as Generic Parameters. Generic formal parameters of a derived type are used in Ada to support mixin inheritance [9, Sect. 4.6.2], which creates contractual obligations. Consider:

```
generic
    type Super is new A with private;
package Mix is
    type C is new Super with private;
    -- ...
end;

package Mix_Instance is new Mix(Super=>B);
```

---

[6] The cited paper uses garbage collected heap allocated objects, which in the Ada solution can be made stack allocated.

If by instantiating Mix it is possible to create a type C which is not a behavioral subtype of A, than the package Mix is to be blamed for the inheritance hierarchy error. Alternatively, the generic actual parameter B may not be a valid behavioral subtype of A. This is clearly the responsibility of the code defining the type B by inheriting from A. However, in both of these cases A and B may be temporary types created only to be mixed further, in which case the improper inheritance relations may be justified.

C may fail to be a behavioral subtype of B. This may indicate an instantiation error, since the package Mix is only aware of the contract of A, and cannot guaranty the correct relation with an arbitrary type Super.

The issues surrounding mixin inheritance via generic units in the presence of contracts demand further study.

Tasks and Protected Objects. Behavioral contracts on task entries and protected object entries and routines, are not meant to serve as synchronization contracts. In particular, they are not meant to replace entry barriers (when clauses).

Pre-conditions will be evaluated when the call is selected. This allows pre-conditions to access protected data. This is essential in order to allow normal behavioral contracts to be specified for protected forms of ordinary abstract data types.

Post-conditions will, of course, be evaluated before the entry or protected operation completes.

Separate Compilation and Backward Compatibility. Contract checking code is implemented using wrapper routines. As explained above, the wrapper routine invoked by client code is determined by the interface to which the programmer programs. This approach is consistent with separate compilation. The wrapper routines that will be generated can be determined from the information available from the specifications of separately compiled units.

The addition of design by contract facilities to the languages should not break legacy code. Thus, routines that do not have explicit pre- and post- conditions behave as though their contracts are always satisfied.

In order to support the calling of routines that have contracts, from code that was compiled before the introduction of contracts into the language, the compiler output should include the original entry point of each routine, so that the routine can be invoked directly, not just via the wrapper routines. If the code for this entry point invokes the contract checking wrappers for routines that it invokes, it is possible that upstream contractual exceptions will be raised, even though the original caller is not contract-aware. This approach is legitimate since contract violations should not occur, unless the system is indeed faulty.

If this result is unacceptable, the compiler should produce two routines (or entry points) from each routine: one that is invoked via the contract checking wrapper, and that invokes the contract checking wrappers for all the routines that it calls, and another that does not invoke any form of contract checking.

When code written in the contract enhanced language calls routines compiled with the old language, no contract checking wrapper routines should be invoked. This can easily be done if the compiler knows that the routine does not have a contract. To deduce this information package specification files are not enough, since post-conditions may be specified in package bodies. If this information cannot be supplied to the compiler (e.g., via a Pragma) recompiling the previous code is unavoidable.

4   Other Ada Features

The Ada standard defines several foreign language interface packages. Should contracts be applicable to routines imported from foreign languages? There several possible solutions to this question. (1) Contracts on imported routines may be banned. This is the obvious solution, but will result in lowering abstraction level. This problem can be solved by the programmer, who could wrap imported routines inside Ada routines that would supply contracts. (2) Imported routine definitions may include contracts. This is a elegant solution, but may complicate implementations. (3) Intra-language contract propagation may be considered, when interface packages are designed for languages supporting DbC. This approach is of great interest, since it relates to component based design. It is not discussed here, and is left for future research.

Should Ada provide *synchronization contracts*? It turns out that many synchronization contracts can be expressed using Ada's protected object mechanism. A simple example is handling contract violations by waiting for the contract to be fulfilled. This type of handling, applicable only to concurrent systems, can be implemented using guarded entries.

The distributed systems annex (Annex E) of the Ada standard specifies a language based approach to distributed computing (e.g., remote procedure calls). Distributed programming raises interesting contractual problems, many of them related to quality of service issues. The run time model of enforcing behavioral contracts, based on raising exceptions, can work with distributed partitions, according LRM E.4 (15).

To assist the design and implementation of supporting tools, it should be possible to extract contracts using ASIS queries.

5   Conclusions

Contracts may help software quality and reliability. We proposed an approach for adding design by contract facilities to the Ada programming language. The proposal requires quite a major change to the language.

The solution we propose concentrates on run time contract checking, and uses a contract notation based on simple boolean expressions (i.e., we do not propose using temporal logic and model checking). Thus, tools like SPARK and tools based on abstract interpretation will remain important tools for high integrity software verification.

Even if our proposal is rejected, due to its impact, the study of combining advanced Ada features and contracts is of interest for future language design.

References

[1] Antoine Beugnard, Jean-Marc Jézéquel, Noël Plouzeau, and Damien Watkins. Making components contract aware. In *IEEE Software*, pages 38–45, june 1999.

[2] Andrew Duncan and Urs Hölze. Adding contracts to Java with handshake. Technical Report TRCS98-32, The University of California at Santa Barbara, December 1998.

[3] Robert Bruce Findler and Matthias Felleisen. Contract soundness for object-oriented languages. In *Object-Oriented Programming, Systems, Languages, and Applications*, 2001.

[4] Robert Bruce Findler, Mario Latendresse, and Matthias Felleisen. Behavioral contracts and behavioral subtyping. In *Foundations of Software Engineering*, 2001.

[5] Robert Bruce Findler, Mario Latendresse, and Matthias Felleisen. Object-oriented programming languages need well-founded contracts. Technical Report TR01-372, Rice University, 2001.

[6] Benedict Gomes, David Stoutamire, Boris Vaysman, and Holger Klawitter. *A Language Manual for Sather 1.1*, August 1996.

[7] Richard Helm, Ian M. Holland, and Dipayan Gangopadhyay. Contracts: Specifing behaviorial compositions in object-oriented systems. In *Object-Oriented Programming, Systems, Languages, and Applications*, pages 169–180, 1990.

[8] Ian M. Holland. Specifying reusable components using contracts. In *European Conference on Object-Oriented Programming*, pages 287–308, 1992.

[9] Intermetrics, Inc., Cambridge, Massachusetts. Ada 95 rationale, 1995.

[10] Murat Karaorman, Urs Hölzle, and John Bruno. jContractor: A reflective Java library to support design by contract. In *Proceedings of Meta-Level Architectures and Reflection*, volume 1616 of *Lecture Notes in Computer Science*, July 1999.

[11] Reto Kramer. iContract — the Java design by contract tool. In *Technology of Object-Oriented Languages and Systems*, 1998.

[12] Ehud Lamm. Component libraries and language features. In Dirk Craeynest and Alfred Strohmeier, editors, *Reliable Software Technologies – Ada-Europe 2001*, volume 2043 of *Lecture Notes in Computer Science*, pages 215–228. Springer-Verlag, May 2001.

[13] Barbara H. Liskov and Jeannette M. Wing. A behavioral notion of subtyping. *ACM Transactions on Programming Languages and Systems*, November 1994.

[14] Barbara H. Liskov and Jeannette M. Wing. Behavioral subtyping using invariants and constraints. Technical Report CMU CS-99-156, School of Computer Science, Carnegie Mellon University, July 1999.

[15] Bertrand Meyer. *Eiffel: The Language*. Prentice Hall, 1992.

[16] Bertrand Meyer. *Object-Oriented Software Construction*. Prentice Hall, 2 edition, 1997.

Static Dependency Analysis for Concurrent Ada 95 Programs*

Zhenqiang Chen[1], Baowen Xu[1,2,*], Jianjun Zhao[3], and Hongji Yang[4]

[1] Department of Computer Science & Engineering, Southeast University, 210096, China
[2] State Key Laboratory of Software Engineering, Wuhan University, 430072, China
[3] Dept. of Computer Science & Engineering, Fukuoka Institute of Technology Japan
[4] Department of Computer Science, De Montfort University, England

Abstract. Program dependency analysis is an analysis technique to identify and determine various program dependencies in program source codes. It is an important approach for testing, understanding, maintaining and transforming programs. But, there are still many difficulties to be solved when carrying out dependency analysis for concurrent programs because the execution of statements is nondeterministic. In this paper, we propose a novel approach to analyze dependencies for concurrent Ada 95 programs. Two graphs: concurrent program flow graph and concurrent program dependency graph are developed to represent concurrent Ada programs and analyze dependency relations. The paper also presents a dependency analysis algorithm, which can obtain more precise information than most previous methods we know.

1 Introduction

Ada 95 [12] is a concurrent and object-oriented programming language designed to support the construction of long-lived, highly reliable software systems. The execution of an Ada program consists of the execution of one or more tasks. Each task represents a separate thread of control that proceeds independently. Because the execution of a concurrent program is nondeterministic, it is difficult to analyze and understand an Ada 95 program. Most approaches and tools [10, 21] for sequential programs are not applicable to concurrent programs, because they do not cope with the nondeterministic execution of statements. Thus, the development of techniques and tools to support analyzing concurrent Ada 95 software is urgently needed.

Dependency analysis is an analysis technique to identify and determine various program dependencies in program source codes [5, 17]. It has been widely used in software engineering activities, such as program understanding, testing, debugging,

---

* This work was supported in part by the National Natural Science Foundation of China (NSFC) (60073012), National Science Foundation of Jiangsu, China (BK2001004), Opening Foundation of State Key Laboratory of Software Engineering in Wuhan University, Foundation of State Key Laboratory for Novel Software Technology in Nanjing University, Visiting Scholar Foundation of Key Lab. in University, SEU–NARI Foundation.
* Correspondence to: Baowen Xu, Department of Computer Science and Engineering, Southeast University, Nanjing 210096, China.   E-mail: bwxu@seu.edu.cn

J. Blieberger and A. Strohmeier (Eds.): Ada-Europe 2002, LNCS 2361, pp. 219–230, 2002.
© Springer-Verlag Berlin Heidelberg 2002

and maintenance [5, 8, 10, 11, 17, 18]. It provides a solution for analyzing concurrent programs. But, there are still many problems to be solved, because the execution process of concurrent programs is nondeterministic.

In our previous work, we have developed several methods for analyzing dependencies in recursive [20], Object-Oriented [3, 19], and concurrent programs [2, 23]. This paper focuses our attention on approaches to analyzing dependencies for concurrent Ada 95 programs to obtain more precise dependency information efficiently.

The rest of this paper is organized as follows. Section 2 presents some related work and outlines our approach. Section 3 introduces the representations for concurrent Ada 95 programs. Section 4 discusses all kinds of dependencies and the dependency analysis algorithm. Conclusion remarks are given in Section 5.

2 Related Work

There have been many dependency analysis methods proposed in literatures, among which some are concerned with concurrent programs. However, most of them are unfit for statically, precisely analyzing dependencies of concurrent Ada 95 programs.

Cheng proposes a representation for parallel and distributed programs [5, 6]. His program dependency nets (PDN) contains edges for data and control dependency, selection, synchronization and communication dependency edges. The dependency analysis algorithm is based on graph reachability problem in PDN. But the semantics of synchronization and communication dependencies are not fully considered and the result is not precise because they do not take into account that dependencies between concurrently executed statements are not transitive.

In [22, 23], Zhao proposes a static dependency analysis algorithm for concurrent Java programs based on multi-thread dependency graph (MDG). The MDG consists of a collection of TDGs (thread dependency graph) each represents a single thread. And the interactions of threads are modeled by synchronization and communication edges. His dependency analysis algorithm is also a graph reachability problem and the intransitivity is not considered. Thus, the result is not precise.

To get more precise dependence information, Krinke [15] introduces an algorithm for analyzing concurrent threads without synchronization. In this algorithm, the interface dependency is introduced to represent the communication dependency, which is not transitive. But by careful classification and different algorithm, the result is more precise. However, synchronization is widely used in concurrent programs and sometimes it is necessary, Krinke's algorithm can't be widely used in practice.

In the method introduced by Goswami [9], concurrency program dependency graph is used to represent concurrent processes in Unix environment. The algorithm is still a graph reachability problem and the intransitivity problem is not solved.

In addition to these static methods, there are several dynamic analysis algorithms [13, 14]. The dependencies in dynamic methods only catch the dependencies on a given input along some execution paths. They cannot be applied to static analysis.

In the following sections, we will propose our dependency analysis approach for concurrent Ada 95 programs. In this method, the concurrent control flow graph extends the general control flow graph to represent concurrent programs. All kinds of dependencies are presented in a concurrent program dependency graph. By a special algorithm, which is not a simple graph reachability problem, we can obtain more precise information.

The main benefits of our method are listed as follows. First, concurrent Ada 95 programs can be represented in a simple way without losing useful information by concurrent control flow graph. This is the base of our dependency analysis. Second, the concurrent dependency graph is constructed based on the concurrent control flow graph as a whole. In concurrent environment, some dependencies obtained from separate analysis might not hold when as a whole (see Sect. 4.2). Third, our dependency analysis algorithm based on set operations can obtain more precise information than the graph reachability based methods.

3 Representing Concurrent Programs

Ada 95 provides a complete facility for supporting concurrent programming. In this section, we will discuss how to represent concurrent Ada 95 program in a simple and precise way without losing useful information. We will introduce how to represent a common way to represent a sequential program first.

Definition 1: A control flow graph (CFG) [8, 10, 11, 15] is a direct graph CFG= $<S_S, S_E, s_I, s_F>$, where S_S are statements or predicate expressions. S_E is an edge set. For two nodes s_1 and s_2, if s_2 might be executed just after the execution of s_1, edge $<s_1, s_2> \in S_E$. s_I and s_F represent the start and the end of the program respectively.

If $<s_1, s_2> \in S_E$, s_1 is a direct predecessor of s_2 and s_2 is a direct successor of s_1, denoted by PRE(s_1, s_2). In a CFG, if there exists a path from s_1 to s_2, s_2 is a successor of s_1, denoted by PRE* (s_1, s_2). If s_1 on every path from s_1 to s_2, s_1 is a dominator of s_2, denoted by DOM(s_1, s_2).

3.1 Representing a Single Task

In Ada [12], a task represents a separate thread of control that proceeds independently and concurrently between the points where it interacts with other tasks. Thus a task can be represented by a CFG. But the control flows among concurrently executed tasks are not independent, because of inter-task synchronization and communications. It is not enough to represent concurrent programs only by CFG. The synchronization and concurrency must be represented explicitly.

3.2 Representing Concurrency

When a task object is activated, its body starts to be executed. The CFG of the task body is connected to the master's CFG by concurrency edges according to the rules of the activation and termination of task [7, 12]. Fig. 1 shows a connection of concurrent tasks shown by the program segment.

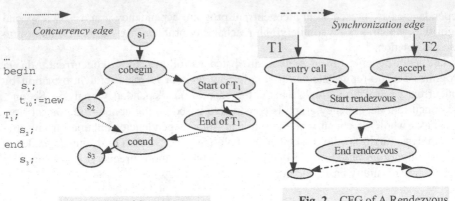

Fig. 1. CFG of Concurrency   **Fig. 2.** CFG of A Rendezvous

3.3 Representing Rendezvous

In Ada [12], rendezvous is a kind of synchronization in nature. It occurs when a task calls another's entry. For each accept statement, add a pair of nodes, which represent the start and end of this rendezvous, and encapsulate the accept statement sequence. Fig. 2 shows the connection of one rendezvous. The edge from the entry call statement to its direct successor is removed from the CFG of the task. If more than one task calls the entry of another, edges are added from each entry call statement to all the start rendezvous nodes of the possible accept statements.

3.4 Representing Select_statements

In Ada 95 [12], select_statements are used for nondeterministic message passing. There are four forms of select_statement: *select accept, timed entry call, conditional entry call* and *asynchronous transfer of control*(ATC). All kinds of select_statements are represented as branch statements according to their semantics. For ATC, we add additional control flows from each statement of abortable_part to the trigger- ing_statement, because we cannot make sure whether the entry call can be selected immediately or how long it will wait in static analysis.

3.5 Concurrent Control Flow Graph

In the CFG of a sequential program, if statement s_2 may be immediately executed after s_1, edge $<s_1, s_2>$ will belong to S_E. If applying this definition to concurrent programs, the CFG will be too complex to analyze and understand, because the order of execu- tions of statements are unpredicted, and it is difficult to decide whether a statement may be executed after another. At the same time, the control flows among concur- rently executed tasks are not independent, because of inter-task synchronization and communications. It is not enough to represent a concurrent program only by a CFG. Thus we introduce *concurrent control flow graph* to represent concurrent tasks.

Definition 2: A concurrent control flow graph (CCFG) of a program P consists of a collection of CFGs each representing a single task. And synchronization edges (see Sect. 3.2) and concurrency edges (see Sect. 3.3) which model inter-task interactions are appended, at the same time the edges from the entry call statements to its direct successors (see Sect. 3.2) are removed according to the inter-task synchronization.

In [1], Blieberger and et al have proposed a representation —— tasking control flow graph (TCFG) for concurrent Ada programs, which is constructed according to the semantics of synchronization and concurrency similar with our CCFG. However, there are three main differences from our CCFG: 1) There may be several (at least one) "end nodes" of a rendezvous in TCFG, and there has one and only one "start and end node" for each rendezvous in CCFG. 2) Our representation for ATC is more rational when analyzing dependencies. 3) There is additional information introduced to detecting deadlock in TCFG.

4 Analyzing Dependencies for Concurrent Programs

In the following sections, we use the following stipulations: for a variable V used at a statement s, if its value is not changed, we say that V is "referred" at s, otherwise V is "defined" at s. The variable set referred at s is denoted by $S_{REF}(s)$. The variable set defined at s is denoted by $S_{DEF}(s)$.

Generally, there are two types of dependencies: *control* and *data dependency*. Informally, for two statements s_1 and s_2 of a subprogram P, s_2 is control dependent on s_1 iff whether or not s_2 can be executed depends on execution of s_1, denoted by $CD(s_1, s_2)$. If a variable v defined at s_1 is used at s_2 and there is a path from s_1 to s_2 on which v is not redefined, then s_2 is data dependent on s_1, denoted by $DD(s_1, s_2)$.

4.1 Definitions

In sequential programs, shared variables (global variables) are treated as *in/out* parameters of the subprogram [11]. Inter-procedural dependencies are computed by parameters passing, we needn't go deep into the subprograms. But in concurrent programs, the codes of different tasks may be overlapped during their executions. They will influence each other by read or write shared variables. Data dependency cannot be presented precisely only by parameters. Therefore we introduce another concept to represent inter-task data dependency.

Definition 3: Let s_1 and s_2 be statements from different tasks, if the variable V defined in s_1 may be directly referred in s_2 during their execution, then s_2 is directly inter-task data dependent on s_1, denoted by $TDD(s_1, s_2)$.

The rendezvous between tasks may influence the execution of programs. In a certain environment and execution some rendezvous might never be triggered or could not complete. In these situations the tasks related to the rendezvous would be suspended and could not be scheduled any more until it is **abort**ed by another task. Therefore if in a task there is a rendezvous statement (entry or accept) on the path from the start of the task to a statement s, whether s can be executed or not, will depend on the execution of the rendezvous statement. In this paper, this kind of control dependency is called *synchronal dependency*. There are two kinds of synchronal dependency: intra-task synchronal dependency and inter-task synchronal dependency.

Definition 4: Let s_1 and s_2 be two statements of a same task, if s_1 is a rendezvous statement and DOM (s_1, s_2) is TRUE, then s_2 intra-task synchronally depends on s_1, denoted by $SD(s_1, s_2)$.

When there are at least two tasks to complete one rendezvous, and one task sends the entry call and the other can execute the corresponding accept statement, the two statements in a rendezvous will depend on each other, defined as Definition 5.

Definition 5: Let s_1 and s_2 be statements from different tasks, where one is a entry call statement and the other is the corresponding accept statement, and the rendezvous can be triggered, s_1 inter-task synchronally depends on s_2, denoted by $TSD(s_1, s_2)$.

Definition 6: A concurrent program dependency graph (CPDG) of a program P is a direct graph $G = <S_S, S_E>$, where S_S is the same node set in the CCFG of P; S_E is the edge set, edge $<s_m, s_n> \in S_E$, iff $CD(s_n, s_m) \vee DD(s_n, s_m) \vee TDD(s_n, s_m) \vee SD(s_n, s_m) \vee TSD(s_n, s_m)$.

In order to describe indirect dependencies between statements, we introduce possible executed paths and dependency sequence.

Definition 7: For a statement sequence $S_s = <s_1, s_2, ..., s_k>$ where $s_i \in S_S$ $(i = 1, 2, ..., k)$, if after the execution of $s_i (i = 1, 2, ..., k-1)$, subsequence $<s_{i+1}, s_k>$ might be executed, S_s is a possible executed path.

Definition 8: For a statement sequence $S_s = <s_k, s_{k-1}, ..., s_1>$ where $s_i \in S_S$ $(i = 1, 2, ..., k)$, if for all s_i $(i = 1, 2, ..., k-1)$ $DEP(s_{i+1}, s_i)$ is TRUE (DEP $\in$ {CD, DD, TDD, SD, TSD}), then S_s is a dependency sequence beginning with s_1.

4.2 Properties and Related Theorems

In our previous work [18], we have proved that in a sequential program, if $DEP^*(s_1, s_2)$ (indirect data or control dependency), $PRE^*(s_1, s_2)$ is TRUE. If we reverse it, we have corollary1.

Corollary 1: Let s_1 and s_2 be statements from the same task, then
$$\neg PRE^*(s_1, s_2) \Rightarrow \neg DEP^*(s_1, s_2).$$

To obtain inter-task data dependency, a predicate $CON(s_i, s_j)$ is often introduced. Let s_i and s_j be two statements of different tasks, $CON(s_i, s_j)$ is TRUE iff s_i and s_j might be executed concurrently. From the definition of the inter-task data dependency and predicate $CON(s_i, s_j)$, we have lemma 1.

Lemma 1: Let s_1 and s_2 be statements from different tasks and V be a variable, then
$$CON(s_1, s_2) \wedge \exists V (V \in S_{DEF}(s_1) \cap S_{REF}(s_2)) \Rightarrow TDD(s_1, s_2).$$

Proof: CON (s_1, s_2) is TRUE means s_1 and s_2 might be executed concurrently, in a schedule, s_2 might be executed just after the execution of s_1. If there is a variable V where $V \in S_{DEF}(s_1) \cap S_{REF}(s_2)$), s_2 might refer the V defined at s_1, i.e. TDD (s_1, s_2). ∎

Although a task can be treated as a sequential program, the data dependency cannot be analyzed independently and dependency analysis must base on the CCFG as a whole. For the example shown in Fig.3, if task T1 is analyzed independently, statement 4 depends on 1. But if the program is taken as a whole, 4 will never refer the variable B defined at 1, because 7 is a dominator from 1 to 4, the definition of B at 1 is overloaded at 7 due to the synchronization between T1 and T2.

Property 1: Dependencies in concurrent programs are not transitive.

To our knowledge, there are two types of factors, leading to this intransitivity:

(1) The dependence is propagated to several different control flows of the same task. But a task can have one and only one control flow in any execution. Thus there could not exist dependencies between different control flows. In the CFG of a task, it is represented as that dependence is transited to a node, which is not a predecessor. For the example shown in Fig. 3, according to definition of inter-task data dependence, statement 5 depends on 8, 8 depends on 4, but 5 will never depend on 4.

```
--T1                      --T2                      --T3
...                       ...                       ...
B:= 1;  --1               accept Entry1             T2.Entry1;
T2.Entry1;--2                    --6                      --9
if...then --3             do                        B:=3;  --10
  A:=B+C;--4                B:=2;  --7               ...
else                      end;
  D:=E+1;--5              E:=A+C;--8
end if;                   ...
```

Fig.3. Ada program segment

(2) Due to the resource competition, synchronization and some other reasons, the following cases might occur: In any execution, there are several tasks that compete for a resource. But only one of them can obtain this resource and consume it, which leads to mutex among these program segments, i.e. only one of these segments can be executed in any execution. For the example, task T1 and T3 compete the Entry1 of T2. If T1 can trigger this rendezvous, T3 will never trigger it; vice versa. Thus, statement 4 and 10 will never occur in a same execution and 4 does not depend on 10.

From all the definitions, we have Lemma 2.

Lemma 2: If a dependency sequence $<s_k, s_{k-1}, ..., s_1>$ is a possible executed path, s_1 depends on s_k, i.e. dependency on an executed path is transitive.

Proof: According to the definition of a possible executed path, statement sequence $s_k, s_{k-1}, ..., s_1$ is a possible schedule sequence. The execution of s_k might influence s_{k-1}, and this influence is handed on by $s_{k-1}, s_{k-2}, ...$ to s_1, i.e. s_k might influence the execution of s_1, thus s_1 depends on s_k. ∎

In order to get more precise dependency information, we should go on analyzing the nodes that can reach to s, and removing nodes that actually cannot reach to s.

Thus, a predicate MUTEX(s_1, s_2) is introduced where s_1 and s_2 are statements from different tasks. MUTEX(s_1, s_2) is TRUE if s_1 and s_2 might execute exclusively, i.e. if s_1 and s_2 has not been executed, and after the execution of s_2, s_1 will never be executed and vice versa. From this predicate and the definition of TDD, we have:

Lemma 3: Let s_1 and s_2 be statements from different tasks,
$$\text{MUTEX}(s_1, s_2) \Rightarrow \neg \text{TDD}(s_1, s_2) \wedge \neg \text{TDD}(s_2, s_1)$$

Proof: According to the definitions of MUTEX(s_1, s_2) and TDD(s_1, s_2), whether s_2 might be executed after the execution of s_1 is the necessary condition for TDD(s_1, s_2). That MUTEX(s_1, s_2) is TRUE represents that s_2 has not be executed, and after the execution of s_1, s_2 will never be executed, s_2 cannot use variables defined by s_1 and s_1 can not use variables defined by s_2.

The dependency on a possible executed path is transitive, but it cannot be directly used to analyze dependencies because the path on a CCFG is not immediate a possible executed path. From the CPDG of a program P, we can get all the dependency sequences beginning with s, but the dependency on a dependency sequence is not transitive. Thus, we introduce a theorem that ensures a dependency sequence restricted by certain conditions is a possible executed path. Before it, we introduce four sets with each node s_i of a dependency sequence $<s_k, s_{k-1}, ..., s_1>$: $S_{MUTEX}(s_i)$, $S_{NOT\text{-}PRE}(s_i)$, $S_{IN}(s_i)$ and $S_{OUT}(s_i)$. Where

$S_{MUTEX}(s_i) = \{ s_j \mid \text{MUTEX}(s_i, s_j) \}$
$S_{NOT\text{-}PRE}(s_i) = \{ s_j \mid \neg \text{PRE}^*(s_j, s_i), \text{where } s_i \text{ and } s_j \text{ are statements from one task..} \}$
$S_{IN}(s_i) = S_{OUT}(s_{i-1})$ $(i = 2, 3, ..., k)$ where $S_{IN}(s_1) = \varnothing$.
$S_{OUT}(s_i) = S_{MUTEX}(s_i) \cup S_{NOT\text{-}PRE}(s_i) \cup S_{IN}(s_i)$.

$S_{NOT\text{-}PRE}$ is introduced to resolve the first type of factors, which lead to intransitivity. S_{MUTEX} is introduced to resolve the second type of factors.

Theorem 1: Let $S_s = <s_k, s_{k-1}, ..., s_1>$ be a dependency sequence, if $s_i \notin S_{out}(s_{i-1})$ ($i = 2, ..., k$), then s_1 depends on s_k, denoted by TDEP*(s_k, s_1).

Proof: From Lemma 2, if dependency sequence S_s is a possible executed path, TDEP*(s_k, s_1) is TRUE. Thus, the main task is to prove that S_s is a possible executed path under the condition.

From the computation of $S_{OUT}(s_i)$, we know that $S_{OUT}(s_i) \supseteq S_{OUT}(s_{i-1}) \supseteq \cdots \supseteq S_{OUT}(s_1)$. If $s_i \notin S_{out}(s_{i-1})$, $s_i \notin S_{out}(s_{i-2})$, ..., $s_i \notin S_{out}(s_1)$. s_i is a predecessor of s_{i-1}, ...s_1. Thus, after the execution of s_i, $<s_{i-1}, ..., s_1>$ might be executed. S_s is a possible executed path.

This theorem is the base of our dependency analysis algorithm. It implies that no further analysis is needed on the sequence when the current statement does not satisfy the condition of Theorem 1.

4.3 Constructing CPDG

A statement, which can never be executed, will never influence other statements. Such statements should be removed from the CCFG to get more precise information. For the entry call statement and the corresponding accept statement, s_1 and s_2, whether

CON(s_1, s_2) is TRUE is the precondition of the triggered rendezvous [16] and some rendezvous might never be finished [4]. The untriggered and unfinished rendezvous edges are removed from the CCFG before constructing the CPDG.

All the statement pairs that make CON hold can be obtain by the MHP algorithms shown [4, 16]. And it is easy to obtain statement pairs that fit PRE*(s_i, s_j) by scanning the source program once. For a statement pair (s_1, s_2), if $\neg$CON(s_1, s_2) $\wedge \neg$ PRE*(s_1, s_2) $\wedge \neg$ PRE*(s_2, s_1), MUTEX(s_1, s_2) is TRUE.

According to the definitions and lemmas above, program P's CPDG can be constructed in three steps.

- Step1, we repeatedly remove rendezvous edges that cannot be triggered and nodes that cannot be reached from the start node of the P's CCFG.
- Step2, we take the CCFG refined by step1 as the sequential program's CFG and construct an intermediate program dependency graph, PDG1, in a common way [11].
- Finally, the responding edges are added to PDG1 using above definitions and lemmas. The result graph is the CPDG of P.

After the CPDG of a program P was constructed, all the dependency sequences can be obtained easily by traversing the CPDG.

4.4 Dependency Analysis Algorithm

Dependency analysis on the PDG of a sequential program is a simple graph reachability problem, because control and data dependencies are transitive [11, 18]. But in concurrent programs, dependencies are not transitive. The methods for sequential programs cannot be applied to concurrent environments directly. New approaches must be developed to obtain more precise information.

According to Theorem 1, the node set $S_{DEP}(s)$ that s depends on is {s_i | TDEP*(s_i, s)}. In fact the number of the dependency sequences begin with a node might be exponential. It costs too much time to compute dependency set along each sequence. Our dependency analysis algorithm shown in Fig. 4 is a conservative algorithm. The result is a superset of the ideal set. In this algorithm, the $S_{IN}(s)$ of a node s is an intersection of all its direct predecessor's S_{OUT}. This might reduce the set $S_{IN}(s)$. Furthermore, the algorithm used to compute the statement pairs that make CON hold is conservative. They include statement pairs that cannot be executed concurrently. According to the method to compute TDD, there are spurious dependencies in the CPDG. Therefore, our algorithm enlarges the set $S_{DEP}(s)$. But the algorithm to obtain ideal set is a NP program. Thus, we take a conservative algorithm to make it practice.

4.5 Complexity Analysis

Given a statement and the CPDG of program P, the dependency algorithm will eventually terminate. Because the information that can appear in the S_{OUT} sets of all nodes are definite and the S_{OUT} sets of all nodes decrease monotonically.

Let our algorithm be applied to program with n statements. The worst case time bound for computing dependency set for every node in the CPDG is O (n^4).

```
Input:  the CPDG of P, a node s on CPDG.
Output: S_DEP, the dependency set of s
Initialization: W={s}, S_DEP ={s}
1.   Let S = S_MUTEX(s) ∪ S_NOT-PRE(s); delete all nodes in S_OUT(s)
     from the CPDG, and the corresponding edges; Let S_OUT(s)
     =∅;Let the S_OUT and S_IN of other nodes include all nodes
     in CPDG;
     repeat
2.      Remove an element s_m from W;
        examine all reaching edges;
3.      for an edges e = <s_m, s_n> do
4.          S_IN(s_n)= S_IN(s_n) ∩ S_OUT(s_m);
5.          S =(S_MUTEX(s_n)∪S_NOT-PRE(s_n)∪S_IN(s_n))∩ S_OUT(s_n);
6.          if S ≠ S_OUT(s_n)∧ s_n ∉ S_in(s_n) then
7.              W = W ∪ { s_n};
8.              S_OUT(s_n)=S;
9.              S_DEP = S_DEP ∪ { s_n};
            end if;
        end for;
     until  W = ∅;
```

Fig. 4. Dependency analysis algorithm

It is easy to get CCFG and statement pairs that fit PRE*(s_i, s_j) by scanning the source program once. According to the MHP algorithm in [16], we can get all pairs of statements that may happen in parallel in time O (n^3). By the definition of TDD (s_i,s_j), in step2 to build CPDG, some inter-task data dependency and all general data dependency can be gotten in time $O(n^2)$ and in step3 by lemma 1 the other inter-tasks can be gotten in time $O(n^2)$. By passing the CCFG once we can get all control dependencies. Therefore in time O (n^3) we can get a CPDG.

In Fig. 4 from lines 6 and 8 we know that the S_{out} sets of all nodes decrease monotonically, line 6 states a node just enters the next repetition only when the S_{out} of the node changes. So the time of a node's repetition is no more than n, all the repeating times are no more then n^2. In Fig. 4, every line can be finished in O (n) and each node s_m has no more than n successors. Every repeat can be finished in O (n^2). Therefore the whole time cost is O (n^2)* O (n^2) = O (n^4).

4.6 Parameter Passing

In the system dependency graph (SDG) [11] of a sequential program, the interprocedural dependency can be represented by the dependencies between formal and actual parameters. This is just because the static dependency graph of a given subprogram is unchanged no matter where it is called. But this is not the case in a concurrent environment, because global variables accessed in a procedure might interact with those in a task, which can be executed concurrently with the procedure. Therefore, we distinguish parameter passing in following cases.

- The calls to the operations of protected objects are treated as those in sequential programs [11], and protected elements work as parameters of the operations.
- If a subprogram does not access global variables, and it does not include entry call statements, it's parameters are passed as those in a SDG, otherwise the subprogram is imbedded in the caller.
- If the actual parameters of a task entry call do not access global variables, parameters are passed as those in a sequential program, otherwise we add an identified entry to every entry call with actual parameters accessing shared variables.

5 Conclusion

Dependency analysis is an important method to analyze source codes. It has been widely used in many fields, such as program testing, understanding, maintenance, optimizing. In this paper, we propose a new method to analyzing dependencies for concurrent Ada 95 programs. Two models: concurrent control flow graph (CCFG) and concurrent program dependency graph (CPDG) are developed to cope with the concurrency of Ada tasks. The CCFG consists of a collection of control flow graphs each representing a single task, and concurrency edges and synchronization edges are added to represent task interactions. Our CPDG is obtained from the CCFG as a whole. This is different from the previous methods that connect the separate program dependency graphs by synchronization and communication dependency edges.

The paper also presents an efficient dependency analysis algorithm. Its result is more precise than the methods based on graph reachability algorithms [5, 9, 23], although our approach is a conservative algorithm, because the inter-task data dependency is not transitive. We have implemented our algorithm in our "Ada Reverse Engineering and Software Maintenance Supporting System ARMS" (appraised in Dec.30, 2000), in which it works as a part of program slicing and ripple analysis. The experiment result shows that in most of our applications the time cost is linear with the line number of the source codes. And we also find that the more synchronization among tasks, the less efficiency and accuracy.

Although our algorithm can obtain more precise slices than most previous static methods we know, due to the limitation of static analysis, the entry families are not distinguished, and the wait time is not considered in our approach and the algorithm itself may be improved to get more precise information.

References

1. Blieberger, J., Burgstaller, B., Scholz, B.: Symbolic Data Flow Analysis for Detecting Deadlocks in Ada Tasking Programs, in: Proceedings of Ada-Europe'2000, Potsdam, Germany, 2000, 225-237
2. Chen, Z., Xu, B.: Slicing Concurrent Java Programs. ACM SIGPLAN Notices, 2001, 36(4): 41-47.
3. Chen, Z., Xu, B., Yang, H.: Slicing Tagged Objects in Ada 95. in: Proceedings of AdaEurope 2001, LNCS, Springer-Verlag, 2001, 2043: 100-112.

4. Chen, Z., Xu, B., Yang, H.: Detecting Dead Statements for Concurrent Programs. in: Proceedings of SCAM 2001, IEEE CS Press. 65-72
5. Cheng, J.: Dependency Analysis of Parallel and Distributed Programs and Its Applications. International Conference on Advances in Parallel and Distributed Computing, IEEE CS Press, Shanghai, (1997) 370-377
6. Cheng, J.: Task Dependence Nets for Concurrent Systems with Ada 95 and Its Applications, ACM TRI-Ada International Conference, (1997) 67-78
7. Dillon, L.K.: Task Dependence and Termination in Ada. ACM Transactions on Software Engineering and Methodology, 1997, 6(1): 80-110
8. Ferrante, J., et al: The Program Dependence Graph and Its Use in Optimization. ACM Transactions on Programming Languages and Systems, 1987, 9(3): 319-349
9. Goswami, D., Mall, R., Chatterjee P.: Static Slicing in Unix Process Environment. Software -- Practice and Experience, 2000,30(1): 17-36
10. Harrold, M.J., et al: Efficient Construction of Program Dependence Graphs. ACM International Symposium on Software Testing and Analysis, (1993) 160-170
11. Horwitz S., Reps T., Binkley D.: Inter-procedural Slicing using Dependence Graphs. ACM Transactions on Programming Languages and Systems, 1990, 12(1): 26-60
12. ISO/IEC 8652:1995(E): Ada Reference Manual-Language and Standard Libraries.
13. Kamkar, M., Krajina, P.: Dynamic Slicing of Distributed Programs. International Conference on Software Maintenance, Nice, France, (1995) 222-229
14. Korel, B., Ferguson, R.: Dynamic Slicing of Distributed Programs. Applied Mathematics and Computer Science Journal, 1992, 2(2): 199-215
15. Krinke, J.: Static Slicing of Threaded Programs. ACM SIGPLAN Notices, 1998, 33(7): 35-42
16. Naumovich, G., Avrunin, G.S.: A Conservative Data Flow Algorithm for Detecting all Pairs of Statements That May Happen in Parallel. Proceedings of the 6th International Symposium on the Foundations of Software Engineering, (1998) 24-34
17. Podgurski, A., Clarke, L.A.: Formal Model of Program Dependencies and its Implications for Software Testing, Debugging and Maintenance. IEEE Transactions on software Engineering, 1990, 16(9): 965-979
18. Xu, B.: Reverse Program Flow Dependency Analysis and Applications. Chinese Journal of Computers, 1993, 16(5): 385-392
19. Xu, B., Chen, Z., Zhou, X.: Slicing Object-Oriented Ada95 Programs Based on Dependence Analysis. Journal of Software, 2001,12(Suppl.): 208-213
20. Xu, B., Zhang, T., Chen, Z.: Dependence Analysis of Recursive Subprograms and Its Applications. Chinese Journal of Computers, 2001, 24(11): 1178-1184.
21. Yang, H., Xu, B.: Design and Implementation of A PSS/ADA Program Slicing System. Chinese J. Computer Research and Development, 1997, 34(3): 217 – 222
22. Zhao, J.: Slicing Concurrent Java Programs. 7th IEEE International Workshop on Program Comprehension, (1999) 126-133
23. Zhao, J.: Multithreaded Dependence Graphs for Concurrent Java Programs. International Symposium on Software Engineering for Parallel and Distributed Systems, (1999) 13-23

DataFAN: A Practical Approach to Data Flow Analysis for Ada 95

Krzysztof Czarnecki[1], Michael Himsolt[1], Ernst Richter[1], Falk Vieweg[1], and
Alfred Rosskopf[2]

[1] DaimlerChrysler Research and Technology, Ulm, Germany
`forename.surname@daimlerchrysler.com`
[2] European Aeronautics Defence and Space Company (EADS), Military Aircraft,
München, Germany
`alfred.rosskopf@m.eads.net`

Abstract. Safety- and mission-critical software requires developing high-quality, reliable code. Static analysis tools have been proposed to assist developers in the early detection of critical errors and achieving a better code quality. In this paper, we present a set of practical requirements for the industrial use of such tools and report on the development of DataFAN, a data-flow analysis tool satisfying these requirements.
Keywords: static analysis, language tools, ASIS, quality assurance, verification, safety critical, mission critical, SPARK

1 Introduction

As a language promoting the development of high-quality code, Ada is the language of choice on a large number of safety- and mission-critical projects in the aerospace industry, particularly in Europe and the US. As shown in [Käl00], Ada avoids many of the usual programming traps of C-based languages such as those involving implicit conversions or the incorrect use of the break statement. However, that paper also concluded that one of the most severe errors that remain uncaught by an Ada compiler are uninitialized variables. Static analysis tools have been proposed to address this and related problems (e.g., [FO76] or SPARK [Bar97]). Unfortunately, our previous project experience at EADS Military Aircraft showed that the available tools fail to satisfy a number of criteria in order to be widely adopted in practice (see [Ros96]). As a result, we started the DataFAN project, a joint effort between DaimlerChrysler Research and Technology and EADS Military Aircraft to identify the practical requirements on static analysis tools, evaluate tools on the market, and develop a new tool satisfying the requirements. This paper reports on the results of this project.

The paper is organized as follows. Section 2 gives a brief overview of static analysis approaches and their application in the context of Ada. We present our requirements for a practical approach to static analysis for detecting critical errors and improving code quality in Section 3. In Section 4, we evaluate the different approaches to static analysis based on our requirements. Section 5

J. Blieberger and A. Strohmeier (Eds.): Ada-Europe 2002, LNCS 2361, pp. 231–244, 2002.

reports on the development of DataFAN, a tool to satisfy these requirements. Section 6 compares DataFAN with other tools on the market. Section 7 reports on the current status of our project, and Section 8 concludes the paper. Related work will be discussed throughout the paper where appropriate.

2   Static Analysis of Ada Programs

Static analysis is a term used for any method that analyzes the properties of a program without executing it. In this paper we only consider automatic static analysis as opposed to manual one such as source code inspection by humans. Important applications of static analysis include [Ros96]:

1. collecting information on program structures and dependencies;
2. collecting source code metrics;
3. checking adherence to programming standards and guidelines; and
4. checking for problems with code quality and correctness.

Examples of industrial strength Ada tools in the first category are Understand for Ada [UA] and Ada Cross-Referencer [ACR01]. An example for the tool category two and three is AdaSTAT [AS].

In this paper, we focus on category 4, which relates to program verification. Examples of the kinds of errors that static analysis can detect are variables that are read before being initialized, out of bounds access to arrays, integer overflow, division by zero, and dereferencing pointers that contain no data. Additionally, static analysis may detect code anomalies such as variables that are not used, ineffective assignments, and unreachable code.

The importance of static analysis for the purposes of verification has been particularly advocated in the area of safety-critical software. Several standards contain explicit requirements for static analysis of safety critical software, e.g. [MoD91, MoD97, DO92]. Furthermore, the ISO technical report [HRG] by the Safety and Security Rapporteur Group (HRG) provides guidance on the use of different Ada language features in safety-critical systems and the applicability of different static analysis techniques. Finally, the *Safety and Security* Annex H of the Ada 95 Reference Manual [ARM, Sect. H.3.1] requires an implementation to "provide control- and data-flow information, both within each compilation unit and across the compilation units of the partition." Unfortunately, such information is not produced by current compilation systems and must be obtained through additional tools.

The value of static analysis is not limited to safety-critical software, whose failure may lead to loss of life or physical injury. It is also useful for verifying less critical software, particularly mission-critical software, whose failure may cause other problems such as significant economic losses. We decided to explicitly address the latter case in the DataFAN project, too, which meant that the tool and approach should be applicable at a low cost. Finally, it is important noting that, since static analysis cannot find all errors, it needs to be applied together with dynamic analysis, i.e., testing. Recent research on combining data flow analysis with runtime information also points into this direction (see e.g., [MS01, Ram96]).

3 Requirements for a Practical Approach to Static Analysis for Ada Programs

From the experience of one of the authors on projects in the aerospace area at EADS Military Aircraft, a practical static analysis tool must allow for a *lightweight* introduction (i.e., with a minimal effort) and must also require only a minimal effort for its repeated use on a project (see [Ros96]). Otherwise, it is not likely to be adopted by a project. This is mainly due to the fact that static analysis tools are usually perceived to be *luxury* tools, as opposed to the indispensable, *bread-and-butter* tools such as a compiler and a debugger. Consequently, we postulate the following requirements for a practical static analysis tool:

1. No special prerequisites: The tool should work on any Ada83 or Ada95 program, i.e., should not require the use of some language subset or any annotations (particularly if they can be inferred from the source) or addition specifications. Furthermore, it should work on sources developed for different compilers[1] and be available on different platforms.
2. Reasonable analysis time: The analysis time for a realistic application in the size of 50 KLOCS should be in the range of minutes, but not hours.
3. Useful information only: The tool should provide useful information only; in particular, users are not interested in sifting trough false positives (i.c., cases where the tool reports that an error may occur, while this is not the case). Users should be able to select which checks to perform and to control the verbosity level.
4. Simple use: Users should not be required to learn any complicated theories in order to be able to use the tool. The concepts and the interface should be intuitive.
5. Precise location of errors: The tool should give the user precise locations of the detected errors and help him in determining their cause.

Let us make a few remarks about requirement 1. The purpose of this requirement is to allow for an easy introduction of the tool to a project. Several different subsets of the full Ada language for developing safety-critical systems have been proposed (e.g., SPARK [Bar97] or Penelope [Gus90]). Because different safety-critical projects may choose to use different subsets, and because we also want to be able to check mission-critical software that may be less restrictive about using the full set of Ada languages features, a practical static analysis tool should

---

[1] Although Ada is a highly portable language, there are some source features that may vary across different compilers. For example, different compilers may provide some compiler-specific pragmas, or have some special requirements about the file structure of a program (e.g., one compilation unit per file).

accept any valid Ada program. In case that a project chooses to use a specific Ada subset, this can be checked by a separate tool, i.e., a conformance checker (such as AdaSTAT [AS]). Of course, static analysis is not capable to completely analyze every construct in an arbitrary Ada program and certain constructs may be more expensive to analyze than others (see [HRG] for a detailed analysis of what constructs allow for which analysis). Therefore, a tool accepting arbitrary Ada programs will only analyze these parts of the program that it is capable of analyzing and ignore the rest.

4   Practical Applicability of Different Static Analysis Techniques

Let us take a look at the different static analysis techniques that can be used for finding errors in Ada programs [HRG]:

1. Control flow analysis locates poorly structured control flow, such as syntactically unreachable code.
2. Data flow analysis can detect paths in a program that would read a variable that has not been set a value (i.e., *uninitialized variables*[2]); it can also detect anomalies such as multiple writes without intervening reads.
3. Information flow analysis identifies how execution of a unit of code creates dependencies between the inputs and outputs. These dependencies can be verified against the dependencies in a specification.
4. Symbolic execution allows verifying properties of a program by algebraic manipulation of the source text without requiring a formal specification. In addition to checking for uninitialized variables, it allows *range checking* (i.e., overflow analysis, rounding errors, range checking, and array bounds checking).
5. Formal code verification is the process of proving that the code of a program is correct with respect to the formal specification of its requirements.

Control flow is an inexpensive analysis, but it is only of limited value for Ada programs. If the goto statement is not used, and some restrictions are made on the placement of exit and return statements, Ada code becomes inherently well structured. Data flow can detect uninitialized variables, which makes it valuable. It is significantly more expensive than control flow analysis, but it still can be performed in a reasonable time. Information flow analysis requires additional annotations to check the code against, which violates our requirement 1. Symbolic execution can more reliably detect uninitialized variables than data flow analysis and can also detect other classes of errors through range checking. Unfortunately, this is a very expensive analysis (cf. Section 6). Finally, formal code verification requires a formal specification, which is against our requirement 1. It also requires nontrivial skills from the user, which violates requirement 4.

The DataFAN project focuses on data flow analysis because it is a valuable analysis that can still be performed in a reasonable time.

---

[2] Also known as *undefined variables*.

5   DataFAN Overview

DataFAN is a data flow analysis tool for Ada 95 that was designed to satisfy the requirements from Section 3. The main components of DataFAN are shown in 1. The first step is to generate flow graphs consisting of basic blocks (see [ASU86]) containing variable declarations, accesses to variables, and subprogram calls. The current implementation uses ASIS for gnat [RS+96] to access the abstract syntax trees (ASTs) of the program to be analyzed. The analysis kernel performs the data flow analysis on the flow graphs and passes a list of errors and anomalies to the report generator. The report generator prints error and anomaly lists in a format similar to a compiler, so that any of the popular programming editors (e.g., emacs or TextPad) can be used to jump to the source location of an error or anomaly. Additionally, the report generator may produce program listings with embedded error and anomaly reports (e.g., see Figures 2, 3, 4, and 5). The current implementation has a command-line interface providing options to control the kind of errors and anomalies to be reported and the verbosity level of the reports.

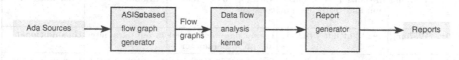

Fig. 1. Main Components of DataFAN

The errors and anomalies detected by DataFAN are summarized in Table 5. The class of the error or anomaly is characterized by its access pattern, where D stands for *declare*, DI for *declare and initialize at declaration*, IO for *in-out parameter*, W for *write*, and R for *read*. The problems are further classified into errors and warnings (a warning corresponds to an anomaly), and into unconditional and conditional problems. An *unconditional* problem is such that if its location is executed during the execution of the entire program at least once, the problem is guaranteed to occur. A *conditional* problem is such that if its location is executed during the execution of the entire program, the problem may or may not occur. In general, an unconditional problem always requires some fixing or clean up in the code, but a conditional one may just be a false alarm. Fig. 2 and Fig. 3 give an example of an unconditional and a conditional DR error.

Note: The terms *unconditional* and *conditional* are also used in the SPARK Examiner reference manual [SM, p. 40], where an unconditional error is defined as one that "applies to all paths through a program (and consequently to all its possible executions)," and a conditional error is "one that applies to some but not all program paths." These definitions are inconsistent with what SPARK Examiner reports. For example, a read access to an uninitialized variable in a conditional branch of an if statement would be classified according to the definition in the SPARK Examiner reference manual as conditional. However, it is unconditional according to our definition (in the previous paragraph), and both DataFAN and SPARK Examiner report it as unconditional. Except for cases such as the one described in the note on loop unrolling in Section 5, our definition of conditionality and the SPARK Examiner reports seem to be consistent.

Table 1. Problems detected by DataFAN

Class	Type	Description	Problem indication	Applies to	Conditionality
DR	Error	Read but not written before	Uninitialized variable	Variable or out parameter	Unconditional or Conditional
OD	Error	Not written	Unset out parameter	Out parameter	Unconditional or Conditional
D	Warning	Not accessed	Unused variable	Variable	Unconditional or Conditional
				In or in-out parameter	Unconditional
DW	Warning	Written but not read	Unused variable	Variable	Unconditional or Conditional
WW	Warning	Written again before read	Previous write ineffective	Variable, out or in-out parameter	Unconditional or Conditional
DIR	Warning	Initialized at declaration and read, but not written	Variable used like a constant	Variable	Unconditional
IOR	Warning	Read but not written	In-out parameter used like an in parameter	In-out parameter	Unconditional
IOW	Warning	Written but not read before	In-out parameter used like an out parameter	In-out parameter	Unconditional

All problems except DR and WW represent a global property of a variable or parameter and thus are reported at their declaration (e.g., see Fig. 4). DR and WW problems are reported at the location of the access causing the problem (i.e., the read in DR, and the second write in WW). These accesses can be either *direct* or *indirect*. A direct access is at the location where a variable is accessed explicitly such as being the right- or left-hand side of an assignment. An indirect access is at the call site of a subprogram whose body directly or indirectly accesses this variable.

In the case of a DR error, if the declaration of the variable and the read access are within the same subprogram, then we have a *direct* (i.e., intraprocedural) DR error and DataFAN will report it at the location of the direct read access. If the declaration and the read access are located in two different subprograms, the error will be reported at the indirect access located in the subprogram where the variable was declared, and we have an *indirect* (i.e., interprocedural) DR error[3]. The DR errors in Fig. 2 and Fig. 3 were direct. Fig. 5 demonstrates an indirect DR error. Please note that, in the case of an indirect DR error, the

---

[3] DataFAN inlines all elaboration calls to package units and the main procedure into the environment task [ARM]. This way, an access to an uninitialized package variable in the main procedure is reported as a direct DR error in the main procedure, rather than an indirect DR error at the main procedure call in the environment task.

```
1: procedure Uncond_Direct_DR is
2:   X : Integer;
3:   Y : Integer;
4:
5: begin
6:     X := Y;
              ^
```

```
uncond_direct_dr.adb:6:10: Unconditional data flow error (Direct DR):
Read access to variable 'Y' which has never been written before.
Problem: The variable 'Y' is read in an undefined state.
uncond_direct_dr.adb:3:3: Declaration of variable 'Y'
```

```
7: end Uncond_Direct_DR;
```

Fig. 2. Example of an unconditional direct DR error

```
1: procedure Cond_Direct_DR(Condition : Boolean) is
2:   X : Integer;
3:   Y : Integer;
4:
5: begin
6:       if Condition then
7:             Y := 1;
8:       end if;
9:       X := Y;
              ^
```

```
cond_direct_dr.adb:9:10: Conditional data flow error (Direct DR):
Read access to variable 'Y' which potentially has not been written before.
Problem: The variable 'Y' is read in a potentially undefined state.
cond_direct_dr.adb:7:9: Last write access to variable 'Y'
cond_direct_dr.adb:3:3: Declaration of variable 'Y'
```

```
10: end Cond_Direct_DR;
```

Fig. 3. Example of a conditional direct DR error

```
1: procedure Uncond_DW is
2:   X : Integer;
     ^
```

```
uncond_dw.adb:2:3: Unconditional data flow warning (DW):
The variable 'X' is written but never read.
Problem: The variable 'X' and write accesses to it are superfluous.
```

```
3:
4: begin
5:   X := 1;
6: end Uncond_DW;
```

Fig. 4. Example of an unconditional DW warning

```
1: procedure Uncond_Indirect_DR is
2:    X : Integer;
3:    Y : Integer;
4:
5:    procedure Indirect_Access is
6:    begin
7:       X := Y;
8:    end Indirect_Access;
9:
10: begin
11:    Indirect_Access;
       ^
```

uncond_indirect_dr.adb:11:3: Unconditional data flow error (Indirect DR):
Indirect read access to variable 'Y' which has never been written before.
Problem: The variable 'Y' is indirectly read in an undefined state.
uncond_indirect_dr.adb:7:10: Read access to variable 'Y'
before first write access.
uncond_indirect_dr.adb:3:3: Declaration of variable 'Y'

```
12: end Uncond_Indirect_DR;
```

Fig. 5. Example of an unconditional indirect DR error

actual direct accesses incurred by the subprogram call that lead to the error are also listed. This way, the user will be able to more easily find the cause of the error. The difference between a direct and an indirect WW warning is similar, except that we consider the relative location of the consecutive writes rather than the declaration and the read.

In general, a problem report consists of a problem description, problem indication, and in the case of a DR or WW problem, possibly of an additional *access list*, and the location where the involved variable is declared. Access lists help the user to determine the exact cause of a problem. For example, in the case of indirect problems, the access list contains the actual accesses incurred by the subprogram call corresponding to the indirect access (see Fig. 2). Another example is the reporting of write accesses that cause a DR error to be conditional rather than unconditional (see Fig. 3)[4].

DataFAN performs an *interprocedural* data flow analysis using an *iterative fixpoint algorithm* (see [NNH99]) that analyzes variable access patterns for problems (with some similarity to the pattern based approach descibed in [FO76]). The algorithm is *call-site insensitive*, meaning that the effect of every subprogram is computed independently of its call sites. A call-site insensitive algorithm is less expensive than a call-site sensitive one and it also avoids the problems of

---

(The latter does not have a corresponding program text in the sources, which would confuse the user.)

[4] The examples shown so far only demonstrate access lists with one element, but, of course, access lists may have more than one element.

the latter in the context of recursive calls. If DataFAN used a call-site sensitive algorithm, it would report all indirect problems at the location of a direct access, but they would have to be qualified by call paths. However, because DataFAN reports an indirect access together with the actual direct accesses that caused it, a call-site insensitive algorithm is sufficient to precisely locate the cause of an error or anomaly.

Another special property of our algorithm is computing whether a problem is a conditional or unconditional one. The main difficulty is determining conditionality in loops. As an example, consider a for loop that in its body first reads an uninitialized variable and then writes it. The read will lead to a DR error in the first iteration of the loop, but not in the following ones. As a result, a straight-forward iterative fixpoint algorithm would not be able to infer that this DR error is an uncoditional one because it cannot distinguish between the first iteration and the remaining ones. In order to properly detect the conditionality, it is necessary to extend the data flow analysis with information for determining if a given access is located more than once on a given set of execution paths with a certain access pattern. The details of this algorithm are beyond the scope of this paper and will be published elsewhere.

Note: Loop unrolling [Bar97, p. 218] is not sufficient to solve the problem outlined in the previous paragraph. For example, consider a loop containing an if statement whose then branch initializes a yet uninitialized variable in the first iteration, whereas the else branch reads it. In fact, SPARK Examiner, when presented with such a program, will report an unconditional case of an uninitialized variable at the read access in the else branch, although it should clearly report at most a conditional one. Using a data-flow-based approach rather than loop unrolling, DataFAN will report a conditional DR in this case.

DataFAN accepts an option specifying the severity level of the problems to be reported. Level 1 includes unconditional errors, level 2 adds unconditional warnings, level 3 adds conditional errors, and level 4 adds conditional warnings. The default level is 1. Typically, users will be interested in level 1 or 2. This is because there is usually a large number of conditional problems reported that are just false alarms, as shown in Table 2. The table shows the number of problems per kind that DataFAN reported for a set of 8 software packages of different sizes (all but one downloaded from the Internet). The number of unconditional problems reported for JEC (part of a jet engine control software) is 121 (mainly due to variables that are initialized by another program through shared memory), whereas the number of conditional problems is 4071. Most of the conditional ones are false alarms, implying that only a higher level of criticality would justify the high effort required to manually check them.

The class of problems that DataFAN can locate precisely is still significant. For example, running DataFAN on the archetypal embedded control program that was described and used to test SPARK Examiner in [Ros96] will provide the user with one expected precise identification of the uninitialized variable embodied in the program.

Table 2. Analysis results for 8 software packages (u. = unconditional, c. = conditional)

Name	KLOC[a]	analysis time[b]	all problems	all u.	u. errors	u. DR	u. OD	u. warnings	u. D	u. DW	u. DIR	u. IOR	u. IOW	u. WW	all c.	c. errors	c. warnings
nlp	0.6	0.9s	33	6	0	0	0	6	1	3	0	0	0	2	27	0	27
isbn	0.6	2.2s	12	0	0	0	0	0	0	0	0	0	0	0	12	2	10
tetris	1	1.7s	5	0	0	0	0	0	0	0	0	0	0	0	5	0	5
sha	1.5	2.3s	34	12	0	0	0	12	0	2	0	0	0	10	22	2	20
pgm	1.6	6.3s	19	5	0	0	0	5	0	1	3	0	0	1	14	4	10
unzipada	2.8	13.2s	379	85	0	0	0	85	12	46	1	0	2	24	294	9	285
p2ada	3.5	11.1s	106	4	0	0	0	4	2	0	1	0	0	1	102	17	85
JEC	58	17m	5206	1135	121	121	0	1014	7	132	176	0	2	697	4071	646	3425

[a] KLOC = thousand lines of code (lines containing comments only were not counted).
[b] Analysis time on Pentium III, 450 MHZ, 256 MB RAM, and Windows 2000 SP2.

6   Comparison with Other Tools

In this section, we will compare DataFAN to other similar tools that are commercially available. The commercial tools performing data flow analysis or symbolic execution for Ada that we are aware of are listed in Table 3.

Table 3. Commercial tools performing data flow analysis or symbolic execution for Ada

	SPARK95 Examiner	Ada Analyzer	Verifier
Version	5.01/08.00	SOLARIS.3.0.2A	1.3, Ada 83
Vendor	Praxis Critical Systems	Little Tree Consulting	Polyspace
Analysis	interprocedural data flow analysis[a]	intraprocedural data flow analysis[b]	symbolic execution
Availability	Subset of Ada Windows and Unix	Ada 83 and Ada 95 Apex on Unix	Ada 83 Unix

[a] Examiner also performs information flow analysis and formal code verification, but these are not considered in this paper.
[b] Ada Analyzer also performs standards-conformance checking, structural analyzes such as generating call trees and with- dependency hierarchies, and metrics calculation. These are not considered here.

Table 4 compares DataFAN and the three tools from Table 3 according to the criteria from Section 3 and also the language coverage, number of kinds of problems detected, and completeness and precision. The results are discussed in the remainder of this section.

Table 4. Comparison of tools

Criterion	DataFAN	Examiner	Ada Analyzer	Verifier
No special prerequisites	+	-	+	+/-
Reasonable analysis time	+	+	+	-
Useful information only	+	-	+	+
Simple use	+	-	+/-	+/-
Precise location of problems	+	-	-	+
Language coverage	+	-	+	++
Kinds of problems detected	+	+	-	++
Precision level	+	+	+	++

No special prerequisites. DataFAN and Ada Analyzer have no special requirements on the analyzed programs and accept any Ada 83 or 95 program as input.
Verifier currently only accepts Ada 83. programs[5] Examiner fails to satisfy the
no special prerequisites criterion. First, even for the purpose of data-flow analysis, global data in the input program needs to be annotated with *own* and *global*
annotations. Furthermore, Examiner accepts only a severely restricted subset of
Ada. As a result, only programs that were originally developed in this subset
can be analyzed (see [Ros96]).

Reasonable analysis time. DataFAN, Ada Analyzer, and Examiner perform data
flow analysis. In general, data flow analysis can be performed in reasonable
time, particularly in the case (as it is for all these tools), if access types are not
analyzed. For example, DataFAN completes analysis of a 50 KLOC program in
less than half an hour (see Table 2)[6]. Verifier carries out symbolic execution (such
as interval and polyhedron analysis), which is much more precise than data flow
analysis, but is significantly slower. A further problem is the fact that an error
in the analyzed source such as an uninitialized variable may cause the tool to
stop because it may make further symbolic evaluation pointless. Unfortunately,
embedded software often contains variables that are only read, but seemingly
never written. This is because the variables may be set by some other program
through shared memory. This was the case for our 58 KLOC test software JEC.
On a Pentium III 700 MHz machine with 512 MB RAM running Linux, Verifier
needed 7 to 10 hours of analysis to get to the next such variable, which then
had to be annotated with the pragma *volatile*, in order to tell Verifier that the
variable is initialized by some other program. Unfortunately, after repeating the

---

[5] DataFAN and PolySpace Verifier both use the gnat compiler as their front-end.
Ada Analyzer is part of the Rational Apex environment. As a result, DataFAN and
Verifier can only analyze programs that are compilable by gnat, and Ada Analyzer
requires the input program to be compilable by the Apex compiler.

[6] We were only able to use Ada Analyzer on a older Sun Sparc machine running Solaris,
on which it was much slower than DataFAN on a Pentium III running Windows 2000,
but we cannot compare both times because of the different hardware. We were not
able to test SPARK Examiner on larger codes because we had no access to larger
programs written in the SPARK language.

analysis for 9 times, the Verifier evaluation period ended before we were able to complete the analysis for the entire source. This problem might have not occurred if Verifier had been used regularly throughout the development time of the software. Depending on the criticality level, the more precise analysis of Verifier may outweigh the long analysis times.

Useful information only. DataFAN allows the user to decide which kinds of problems should be reported using the severity level option. Examiner reports all errors and warnings at once and the user cannot control it. Verifier allows filtering using a GUI. Ada Analyzer has a separate command for detecting uninitialized variables and for detecting multiple writes before read.

Simple use. DataFAN can be simply run on a program without any complex parameter settings or code preparation and it issues succinct and intuitive problem reports. Examiner requires understanding the SPARK annotations and language subset constraints. Verifier requires some understanding of the different analysis levels and parameter settings, but it performs the most powerful analysis. It provides a GUI interface for browsing in the analysis results, but the navigation is has some rough edges. AdaAnalyzer is tightly coupled with the Apex environment and requires some knowledge of it.

Precise location of problems. DataFAN, Examiner, and Verifier report the location of a faulty variable access. Ada Analyzer only specifies the name of the involved variable, but it generates Boolean condition expressions for erroneous paths. In the case of an indirect error, DataFAN reports the location of the call causing the problem and also the actual faulty accesses executed by making the call (i.e., the access lists, see Fig. 5). Examiner only reports the location of the call. Verifier marks the call and the accesses as erroneous, but it does not report the causal connection between them. Ada Analyzer cannot detect indirect problems. DataFAN and Examiner can generate listings with embedded error reports.

Language coverage. Examiner covers and accepts the SPARK subset only. The remaining tools accept all Ada programs, but analyze parts that they are capable of analyzing. None can analyze access types, exceptions, or object-oriented Ada 95 features. Verifier can analyze arrays component-wise and provides some support for analyzing tasking structures. Ada Analyzer performs only intraprocedural analysis.

Kind of problems detected. Examiner detects similar problems as DataFAN. Ada Analyzer detects DR, WW, and D problems (but only direct ones). Verifier detects uninitialized variables, but also division by 0, out-of-bound array access, integer or float overflow and underflow, arithmetic exceptions, and illegal type conversions.

Precision level. Data flow analysis is much less precise than symbolic execution. In particular, data flow analysis does not interpret the value of expressions and it looks for possible errors in a purely structural way. As a result, some errors that Verifier determines as unconditional will be recognized by DataFAN, Ada Analyzer, and Examiner as conditional. According to PolySpace, on average about 20% or less of operations (e.g., variable accesses) that Verifier checks cannot be proven by it to be either errors or false alarms and need to be checked manually. The higher precision of Verifier comes at the cost of longer analysis times.

7   Current Status and Future Work

DataFAN is still under development. As of writing, DataFAN can analyze subprograms (including gotos and recursive subprograms), packages, stubs, generics, and renaming. The implementation of the analysis of scalar and record variables is completed, and the implementation of the analysis of arrays is currently underway.

Language features that are currently not covered include access types, exceptions, tasking, and object-oriented features of Ada 95. After completing arrays, we plan to develop a concept for performing data flow analysis in the the presence of Ravenscar-profile-conformant tasking [BDR98].

8   Conclusions

Static program analysis tools have been proposed as a way to detect runtime errors in a program without running it a long time ago (e.g., see [FO76, Ost81]). Unfortunately, despite the undisputed value of such tools for the early detection of critical errors and for achieving a better code quality, only relatively few industrial projects is actually using them. In this paper, we have proposed a set of requirements for the practical use of such tools. In particular, we believe that one of the most important issues is minimizing the effort associated with adopting and using such a tool on a project. We report on the development of DataFAN, a data-flow analysis tool for Ada that is designed to satisfy these requirements. We also compare it to other tools available on the market. Our conjecture is that a tool based on data flow analysis has the potential to satisfy our set of requirements in most cases and the results of our work so far are encouraging. Emerging tools based on symbolic execution (such as PolySpace Verifier) provide better precision levels and can also detect additional classes of errors. Unfortunately, the long analysis times of symbolic execution can probably be only afforded on projects with the highest level of criticality. Advances in the symbolic execution technology may change this situation in the future, however.

References

[ACR01]   DaimlerChrysler Research. Ada Cross-Referencer. In Proceedings ACM SIGAda Annual International Conference (SIGAda2001), 2001, p. 131

[ARM]   Ada Reference Manual (Information technology - Programming languages
          - Ada), International Standard ISO/IEC 8652:1995(E)
[AS]   AdaSTAT, a static analysis tool for Ada95, DCS IP LLC Corporation,
          http://www.adastat.com
[ASU86]   A.V. Aho, R. Sethi, J.D. Ullman. *Compilers: Principles, Techniques, and
          Tools.* Addison-Wesley, Reading, Massachusetts, USA, 1986
[Bar97]   J. Barnes. *High Integrity Ada: The SPARK Approach.* Addison-Wesley,
          Harlow, England, 1997
[BDR98]   A. Burns , B. Dobbing and G. Romanski. The Ravenscar Tasking Profile
          for High Integrity Real-Time Programs. In *Ada-Europe 98*, LNCS 1411,
          Springer-Verlag Berlin Heidelberg, 1998, pp. 263-275
[DO92]   Software Considerations in Airborne Systems and Equipment Certifica-
          tion. Issued in the USA by the Requirements and Technical Concepts for
          Aviation (document RTCA SC167/DO-178B) and in Europe by the Eu-
          ropean Organization for Civil Aviation Electronics (EUROCAE document
          ED-12B), December 1992
[FO76]   L. D. Fosdik and L. J. Osterweil. Data Flow Analysis in Software Reliabil-
          ity. In *ACM Computing Surveys*, Vol. 8, No. 3, September 1976
[Gus90]   D. Guspari et al. Formal Verification of Ada Programs. In *IEEE Transac-
          tions on Software Engineering*, Vol. 16, Sept. 1990
[HRG]   Programming Languages - Guide for the Use of the Ada Program-
          ming Language in High Integrity Systems. ISO/IEC technical report
          15942, final draft, ISO/IEC JTC1 /SC 22/WG 9 N 359r, July 1, 1999,
          http://wwwold.dkuug.dk/JTC1/SC22/WG9/ documents.htm
[Käl00]   B. Källberg. Is An Ada Lint Necessary? In *Ada-Europe 2000*, LNCS vol.
          1845, Springer-Verlag, 2000, pp. 29-40
[MS01]   E. Mehofer and B. Scholz. A Novel Probabilistic Data-Flow Framework. In
          International Conference on Compiler Construction (CC), 2001
[MoD91]   Requirements for the Procurement of Safety Critical Software in Defence
          Equipment. Interim Defence Standard 00-55, UK Ministry of Defence, 1991
[MoD97]   Defence Standard 00-55, 'Requirements for Safety Related Software in De-
          fence Equipment', Ministry of Defence, (Part1: Requirements; Part2: Guid-
          ance). August 1997
[NNH99]   F. Nielson, H.R. Nielson, and C. Hankin. *Principles of Program Analysis.*
          Springer-Verlag, Berlin, Germany, 1999
[Ost81]   L. J. Osterweil. Using Data Flow Tools in Software Engineering. In *Program
          Flow Analysis: Theory and Applications*, S.S. Muchnick and N.D. Jones
          (Eds.), Prentice-Hall Software Series, 1981
[Ram96]   G. Ramalingam. Data Flow Frequencey Analysis. In *Proceedings of the
          ACM SIGPLAN'96 Conference on Programming Language Design and Im-
          plementation*, 1996, pp. 267-277.
[Ros96]   A. Rosskopf. Use of Static Analysis Tool for Safety-Critical Ada Appli-
          cations - A Critical Assessment. In *Ada-Europe'96*, LNCS 1088, Springer-
          Verlag, 1996, pp. 183-197
[RS+96]   S. Rybin, A. Strohmeier, A. Kuchumov, and V. Fofanov. ASIS for GNAT:
          From the Prototype to the Full Implementation. In *Ada-Europe'96*, LNCS
          1088, Springer-Verlag, 1996, pp. 298-311
[SM]   SPARK Examiner. User Manual - Release 2.5 [Demo version], Praxis Crit-
          ical Systems, March 1997 EXM/UM/2.5
[UA]   Understand for Ada, Scientific Toolworks, Inc., http://www.scitools.com/

Prioritization of Test Cases in MUMCUT Test Sets: An Empirical Study*

Yuen T. Yu[1] and Man F. Lau[2]**

[1] Department of Computer Science,
City University of Hong Kong,
Kowloon Tong, Hong Kong
csytyu@cityu.edu.hk
[2] School of Information Technology,
Swinburne University of Technology,
Hawthorn, VIC 3122, Australia
edmonds@it.swin.edu.au

Abstract. Software developers often have to test a program with a large number of test cases to reveal faults in the program. Some of these test cases may detect faults, and some may not. This leads to an important question on how to arrange the test cases to be executed so that more faults can be detected earlier. With a higher rate of fault detection at the early stage of testing, software developers can then spend more time on fixing the faults. This paper studies several ways of prioritizing test cases in a MUMCUT test set, which guarantees to detect certain types of faults in a Boolean specification written in irredundant disjunctive normal form. Our results suggest a certain ordering that reveals more faults earlier in the testing phases.

Keywords: Empirical study, software testing, specification-based testing, test case prioritization

1   Introduction

Software faults are the results of human errors during software development. Software testing aims at detecting faults by executing the program under test with pre-selected test cases and comparing the actual output with the expected output from the specification. Most of the software testing techniques address the problem of how to generate "good" test cases, that is, test cases that have high chances of revealing software faults. The collection of all the test cases used is known as a test set.

---

* The work described in this paper was supported in part by a grant from City University of Hong Kong (project no. 7100131), and in part by a grant from the Research Grants Council of the Hong Kong Special Administrative Region, China (project no. CityU 1083/00E).
** Corresponding author.

J. Blieberger and A. Strohmeier (Eds.): Ada-Europe 2002, LNCS 2361, pp. 245–256, 2002.

Specification-based testing derives test cases from the specification rather than the actual implementation. One of the advantages is that test cases can be derived early in the development, which in turn allows software developers to reveal, locate and fix the software faults earlier. This leads to the delivery of better quality product. Among different approaches in the specification-based testing, the fault-based approach of test case generation aims at finding test cases that detect certain types of faults. Therefore, if such a fault is indeed present in the software, the test cases will detect them. Although there are similar approaches in hardware testing, the main focuses are different. For example, the focus in hardware testing is mainly on manufacturing flaws whereas the focus in software testing is on human errors [11,17].

Many researchers have argued for the specification of software requirements based on the formal theory of logic and mathematics. Such specifications are generally referred to as formal specifications. One of the advantages of formal specification technique is that the meaning of the resulting specification is precise, and hence, helps to better understand the software requirements as well as better test case generation from the specification. Typical formal specification techniques include VDM [9], Z [1,15], algebraic semantics [2] and Boolean expressions [12].

Another advantage of using formal specification techniques is that it opens up the possibility of automatically checking for inconsistencies among the requirements. This is possible for formal techniques even as simple as Boolean expressions. For instance, Levenson *et al.* [12] have proposed to express the software specification of an aircraft collision avoidance system, TCAS II, in Boolean expressions, and they have reported success in detecting inconsistencies among the different requirements in the specification.

Specifications written in Boolean expressions are referred to as *Boolean specifications*. Recent researches [3,5,7,16,17] have suggested various fault-based strategies that derive test cases from Boolean specifications. Various types of faults have been considered. These types of faults will be discussed in Section 2.2. Empirical results [4,17] indicate that the proposed test case generation methodologies are quite effective in detecting these types of faults.

The MUMCUT strategy [4,5] is a fault-based testing strategy that generates test cases from Boolean specifications. It guarantees to detect seven types of faults in Boolean expressions in irredundant disjunctive normal form [3,5]. Moreover, it has been proved [3] that the size of a MUMCUT test set is polynomial in the number of terms and the number of variables of the Boolean expression. A MUMCUT test set is a set of test cases that satisfy the MUMCUT strategy.

If the fault-detecting capability of the test cases in a test set is not uniform, execution of test cases in different orders may yield different results. We are interested in prioritizing the test cases so that more faults are revealed as early as possible, thereby achieving better quality of the software.

Recently, there have been several empirical studies on test case prioritization, such as in [6,14]. In these studies, the test sets are derived according to code coverage criteria, such as the total branch coverage criteria. The effectiveness of different execution orders of the same test set is measured by the *weighted average of the percentage of faults detected* (APFD) over the entire test set. This paper studies the rate of fault detection for different ways of prioritizing the test cases in a MUMCUT test set using the APFD measure. Our results suggest that a certain ordering of the test cases in the MUMCUT test set achieves a higher APFD value, which we shall explain in detail in Section 5.

The organization of this paper is as follows. Section 2 provides an overview of the MUMCUT strategy. Section 3 describes different ways to prioritize the test cases in the MUMCUT test sets. Section 4 presents the design of the experiment and Section 5 discusses the experimental results. Section 6 concludes the paper and suggests further work.

2 Preliminaries

2.1 Notation and Terminology

We first introduce the notation and terminology used in this paper. We use ".", "+" and "‾" to denote the Boolean operators AND, OR and NOT, respectively. Moreover, we will omit the "." symbol whenever it is clear from the context. The truth values "TRUE" and "FALSE" are denoted by 1 and 0, respectively. We use $\mathbb{B}$ to denote the set of all truth values, that is $\mathbb{B} = \{0, 1\}$. The n-dimensional Boolean space is denoted by $\mathbb{B}^n$. In a Boolean expression, a variable may occur as a *positive* literal or a *negative* literal. For example, for the same variable a in the Boolean expression $ab + \bar{a}c$, a and $\bar{a}$ are positive literal and negative literal, respectively.

A Boolean expression is in *disjunctive normal form* if it can be expressed as a sum of products. For example, the Boolean expression $ab + a\bar{b}c + abc$ is in disjunctive normal form. A Boolean expression in disjunctive normal form is said to be *irredundant* [8,13] (or, *irreducible* [17]) if (1) none of its terms may be omitted from the expression; and (2) none of its literals may be omitted from any term in the expression. For example, the expression $ab + ac$ is irredundant whereas $ab + a\bar{b}c + abc$ is not because the latter expression is equivalent to the former. A Boolean expression in disjunctive normal form can be easily transformed into irredundant disjunctive normal form [13].

Consider the situation that S is a Boolean expression in disjunctive normal form with m terms and n variables. In general, S can be expressed as

$$S = p_1 + \ldots + p_m \tag{1}$$

where p_i ($i = 1, \ldots, m$) denotes the i-th term of S. Moreover, let $p_i = x_1^i \cdots x_{k_i}^i$ where k_i is the number of literals in p_i, and x_j^i ($j = 1, \ldots, k_i$) denotes the j-th literal in p_i. Note that, x_j^i may be a positive or a negative literal. For example, if $S = ab + \bar{a}c$, then $p_1 = ab$ ($x_1^1 = a, x_2^1 = b$) and $p_2 = \bar{a}c$ ($x_1^2 = \bar{a}, x_2^2 = c$). We use $p_{i,\bar{j}} = x_1^i \cdots \bar{x}_j^i \cdots x_{k_i}^i$ ($j = 1, \ldots, k_i$) to denote the term obtained from p_i by negating its j-th literal x_j^i.

A *test case* for testing the Boolean expression S is an element (or a point) in the n-dimensional Boolean space $\mathbb{B}^n$. A test case is a *unique true point* of the i-th term p_i in S if p_i evaluates to 1 and, for all $j \neq i$, p_j evaluates to 0. The set of all unique true points of p_i in S is denoted by $\mathrm{UTP}_i(S)$. A test case is a *near false point* for the j-th literal x_j^i of p_i in S if $p_{i,\bar{j}}$ evaluates to 1 and S evaluates to 0. The set of all near false points for x_j^i of p_i in S is denoted by $\mathrm{NFP}_{i,\bar{j}}(S)$.

2.2   Types of Faults

We now describe the types of faults related to the Boolean expression that may occur during implementation due to human errors. The Boolean expression S is assumed to be in irredundant disjunctive normal form. This paper considers only single faults, which may be further classified into seven types of faults as follows.

1. *Expression Negation Fault* (ENF):- The Boolean expression is implemented as its negation. In this case, the implementation is equivalent to $\bar{S}$.
2. *Literal Negation Fault* (LNF):- A literal in a term in the Boolean expression is replaced by its negation. For example, the specification $abc + de$ is implemented as $ab\bar{c} + de$.
3. *Term Omission Fault* (TOF):- A term in the Boolean expression is omitted. For example, the specification $ab + cd + ef$ is implemented as $ab + cd$.
4. *Literal Omission Fault* (LOF):- A literal in a term of the Boolean expression is omitted. For example, the specification $abcd + def$ is implemented as $abc + def$.
5. *Operator Reference Fault* (ORF):- The AND operator ($\cdot$) in the Boolean expression is replaced by the OR ($+$) operator and vice versa. For example, the specification $abc + de$ may be incorrectly implemented as $ab + c + de$ or $abcde$.
6. *Literal Insertion Fault* (LIF):- A literal is inserted into a term of the Boolean expression. For example, the specification $ab\bar{c}+de$ is implemented as $ab\bar{c}d+de$ or $ab\bar{c}\bar{d} + de$.
   For LIF, we do not consider the insertion of the following literals in the expression:
   (a) a literal that is already present in the term, because the resulting implementation is equivalent to the original expression; and
   (b) the negation of a literal that is already present in the term, because the result is effectively the same as that due to TOF with that particular term omitted.
   For example, inserting $\bar{a}$, $\bar{b}$, or c in the first term of $ab\bar{c} + de$ will produce an expression equivalent to de, which is the same as that due to TOF with the first term omitted.
   It should be noted that the insertion of a literal in an expression does not necessarily cause an error. For example, when the literal b is inserted in the first term of $a + \bar{b}$, the resulting implementation $ab + \bar{b}$ is equivalent to the original specification.

Table 1. Examples on various types of faults

Original expression, $S = ab + cd$

Type of faults	Implementation
ENF	$I = \overline{ab + cd}$
LNF	$I = \bar{a}b + cd$
TOF	$I = cd$
LOF	$I = b + cd$
ORF	$I = a + b + cd$
LIF	$I = abc + cd$
LRF	$I = cb + cd$

7. *Literal Reference Fault* (LRF):- A literal in a particular term of the Boolean expression is replaced by another literal. For example, the specification $ab\bar{c} + de$ is implemented as $abd + de$ (in which $\bar{c}$ has been replaced by d) or $ab\bar{d} + de$ (in which $\bar{c}$ has been replaced by $\bar{d}$).

For LRF, we do not consider the replacement of a literal by

(a) its negation, because the result is effectively the same as that due to LNF;

(b) another literal that is already present in the original expression, because the result is effectively the same as that due to LOF; or

(c) the negation of another literal that is already present in that term, because the result is effectively the same as that due to TOF.

It should be noted that the replacement of a literal by another literal does not necessarily cause an error. For example, when the literal b in the first term of $bc + \bar{a}b + a\bar{b} + \bar{c}d$ is replaced by the literal a, the resulting implementation $ac + \bar{a}b + a\bar{b} + \bar{c}d$ is equivalent to the original specification.

Table 1 gives a summary of these seven types of faults using $S = ab + cd$ as the original expression.

2.3   The MUMCUT Testing Strategy

Chen and Lau [3] have proposed three different strategies, namely, the MUTP, MNFP and CUTPNFP strategies, to select test cases that guarantee the detection of the seven types of faults discussed in Section 2.2.

For the MUTP (Multiple Unique True Point) strategy, test cases have to be selected from the set $\text{UTP}_i(S)$ $(i = 1, \ldots, m)$ so that every possible truth value of the literal not appearing in p_i is covered. The collection of test cases from all $\text{UTP}_i(S)$ $(i = 1, \ldots, m)$ is referred to as a MUTP test set.

For the MNFP (Multiple Near False Point) strategy, test cases have to be selected from the set $\text{NFP}_{i,\bar{j}}(S)$ $(i = 1, \ldots, m, j = 1, \ldots, k_i)$ so that every possible truth value of the literal not appearing in p_i is covered. The collection of test cases from all $\mathrm{NFP}_{i,\bar{j}}(S)$ $(i = 1, \ldots, m, j = 1, \ldots, k_i)$ is referred to as a MNFP test set.

For the CUTPNFP (Corresponding Unique True Point and Near False Point) strategy, a unique true point $\boldsymbol{u}$ is selected from $\mathrm{UTP}_i(S)$ $(i = 1, \ldots, m)$ and a near false point $\boldsymbol{n}$ is selected from $\mathrm{NFP}_{i,\bar{j}}(S)$ $(i = 1, \ldots, m, j = 1, \ldots, k_i)$ such that $\boldsymbol{u}$ and $\boldsymbol{n}$ differ only in the corresponding truth value of the literal x_j^i in p_i. The collection of the unique true point and near false point pairs from all UTP_i and $\mathrm{NFP}_{i,\bar{j}}(S)$ pairs $(i = 1, \ldots, m, j = 1, \ldots, k_i)$ is referred to as a CUTPNFP test set.

The MUTP, MNFP, and CUTPNFP strategies combined together form the MUMCUT strategy. A MUMCUT test set is a set of test cases satisfying all of the MUTP, MNFP and CUTPNFP strategies. It has been proved in [3] that the MUTP strategy can detect ENF, LNF, TOF and LIF, and the MNFP strategy can detect ENF, LNF, and LOF. Neither the MUTP nor the MNFP strategy can detect the ORF. However, when the three strategies are used in combination, all the types of faults mentioned in Section 2.2 can be detected [3].

3   Prioritization of Test Cases

The goal of test case prioritization is to find a way of scheduling the test cases in a test set in order to optimize certain objectives, typically to maximize the rate of fault detection [14]. Previously there have been some empirical studies [6,14] on the prioritization of test sets that are constructed according to code coverage criteria, such as the branch coverage criteria. These studies use the *weighted average of the percentage of faults detected* (APFD) to measure the rate of fault detection of a test set. The APFD value of a test set varies between 0 and 100, inclusively, in such a way that a higher APFD value means better rate of fault detection.

Consider a test set $\{t_1, t_2, t_3, t_4, t_5\}$ such that the test cases in the set together detects 10 faults in a program. Table 2 shows the faults detected by each test case in the test set. Figure 1 shows the relationship between the cumulative percentage of faults detected by scheduling the test cases in the order $\langle t_1, t_2, \ldots, t_5 \rangle$. The area under the curve (that is, the area of the shaded region) represents the weighted average percentage of fault detected (APFD) over the entire test set when the test cases are executed in that particular order. For the particular order $\langle t_1, t_2, \ldots, t_5 \rangle$, the APFD value is 62%. This rate of fault detection can be improved by executing the test cases in the orders $\langle t_5, t_4, t_3, t_2, t_1 \rangle$ and $\langle t_5, t_3, t_4, t_1, t_2 \rangle$, with the corresponding APFD values of 72% and 78%, respectively. Since the APFD measure used in previous experimental studies is a good indicator of the rate of fault detection, it is also used in this study.

This paper studies the problem of prioritizing the test cases in MUMCUT test sets. Previous studies on test case prioritization, such as [6,14], consider only code coverage test sets. Our work here differs from theirs in three ways. First, code

Table 2. Test cases and the faults detected

Test case	Fault									
	1	2	3	4	5	6	7	8	9	10
t_1	x	x	x	x						
t_2	x				x	x	x			
t_3	x	x			x		x			
t_4			x	x						x
t_5				x		x		x	x	x

coverage test sets do not generally guarantee the detection of any specific types of faults, whereas MUMCUT test sets guarantee to detect all the types of faults discussed in Section 2.2. Second, code coverage test sets are often "incomplete" since 100% code coverage is rarely achievable in practice. In contrast, there are practical algorithms to generate complete MUMCUT test sets. Third, code coverage test sets require the availability of the source code whereas MUMCUT test sets can be derived solely from the Boolean specifications.

The MUMCUT test set is composed of test cases that satisfy the MUTP strategy, the MNFP strategy and the CUTPNFP strategy, respectively. Each strategy can detect different types of faults. The CUTPNFP strategy [3] is targeted at the detection of LRF. Based on the study of fault class analysis in [11], LRF belongs to a fault class that is stronger than LNF and ENF. That is, if a test case can detect LRF, the same test case can also detect the corresponding LNF and ENF. Thus, it makes sense to execute the test cases that satisfy the CUTPNFP strategy first. Among the rest of the faults, intuitively LOF is more difficult to detect than TOF. Since test cases that satisfy the MNFP strategy can detect LOF, they should be selected as the next group of test cases for execution. Finally, the rest of the test cases, that is, those satsifying the MUTP strategy, are executed to detect any remaining faults. We referred to this ordering as the *CNU* order, that is, CUTPNFP then MNFP then MUTP.

In an earlier exploratory study [18], the CNU order has been compared with the random order, in which test cases are executed at random, and the serial order, in which test cases are executed in the order of their values. The objective of that study is to explore whether there will be significant differences in the rate of fault detection among different orders of execution. The results show that the mean APFD values of the CNU order is significantly higher than that of the random or serial order, indicating that the CNU order detects more faults significantly faster. Moreover, the CNU order produces a much smaller standard deviation of the APFD values across different Boolean specifications when compared to the random or serial order. This means that the performance

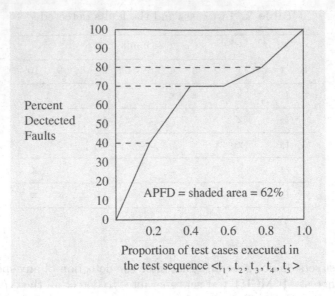

Fig. 1. The weighted average percentage of fault detected (APFD)

of the CNU order is more consistent. The study has clearly demonstrated that better fault-detecting performance can be consistently achieved by scheduling test cases in the MUMCUT test set in the CNU order. This motivates the present more detailed study, which attempts to find out whether the CNU order is indeed the best among the various possible orders of prioritizing the test cases in the MUMCUT test set. We will compare the results of executing the test cases in the MUMCUT test set in all possible arrangements on the three different groups of test cases for the CUTPNFP strategy, MNFP strategy, and MUTP strategy. These arrangements are the CNU order, *CUN* order, *NCU* order, *NUC* order, *UCN* order and *UNC* order.

4   The Experimental Setting

In this paper, we use a set of Boolean specifications, previously published in [17], which originates from the specifications of the TCAS II, an aircraft traffic collison avoidance system. This set of specifications has been used in [10,17] to evaluate the fault-detecting capabilities of the test sets generated by various methods. It has also been used in [4,17] to evaluate the size of the test sets generated for testing Boolean specifications. As in those previous studies, these specifications are first transformed into Boolean expressions in irredundant disjunctive normal form. A collection of MUMCUT test sets is then generated using the method described in [4].

For each Boolean expression in irredundant disjunctive normal form, all possible implementations with a single fault of the seven types mentioned in

Section 2.2 are created. All implementations that are equivalent to the original specifications are identified and removed. Test cases in each MUMCUT test set are then executed according to different orders: CNU, CUN, NCU, NUC, UCN and UNC. The number of incorrect implementations detected by each test case is recorded and used to compute the corresponding values of APFD.

For those specifications whose number of possible MUMCUT test sets does not exceed 1000, all the MUMCUT test sets are generated. When a specification has more than 1000 possible MUMCUT test sets, a random sample of 1000 MUMCUT test sets is generated. We compute the value of APFD for each generated MUMCUT test set. For each specification, the mean of the APFD values for all the generated MUMCUT test sets is computed. Figure 2 shows the boxplot[1] of these APFD values of all Boolean specifications against different execution orders.

5   Results and Observations

As explained in Section 3, a MUMCUT test set consists of 3 different groups of test cases that satisfy, respectively, the MUTP, MNFP and CUTPNFP strategies. For the sake of simplicity, we will use *U-group* to refer to the group of test cases that satisfies the MUTP strategy, *N-group* to refer to the group of test cases that satisfies the MNFP strategy, and *C-group* to refer to the group of test cases that satisfies the CUTPNFP strategy.

Interestingly, there are three different observations from Figure 2 that all lead to the suggestion that the UCN order is the best among the six different orders of execution under study:

1. Among the six different execution orders, the UCN order has the highest mean APFD value. Note that the boxplot of UCN is almost entirely above all other boxplots, except the one for UNC. Moreover, the UCN boxplot is higher than the UNC boxplot by about half the height of the latter.
2. The 6 different execution orders can be divided into 3 pairs. The first pair is the "U--" pair (that is, UCN and UNC), in which test cases in the U-group are executed first. The second pair is the "C--" pair, in which test cases in the C-group are executed first. The third pair is the "N--" pair, in which test cases in the N-group are executed first. The APFD values of the "U--" pair are the greatest among all the APFD values. The APFD values of the "C--" pair are greater than those in the "N--" pair. This suggests that test cases from the U-group should be executed first, followed by those from the C-group and then the N-group. Such an execution order is precisely the UCN order.

---

[1] A boxplot is a graphical representation of the summary of a data set in 5 numbers, namely, the minimum value, lower quartile, median, upper quartile, and the maximum value. The height of the box indicates the span of the central 50% of the values in the data set between the lower quartile and the upper quartile.

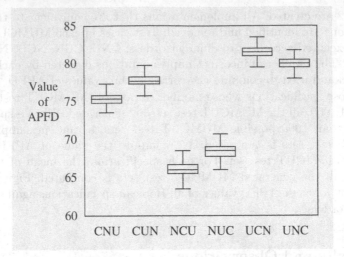

Fig. 2. A boxplot of APFD (The overall performance of various execution orders)

3. Consider the APFD values within each pair. Within the "U--" pair, the APFD values for the UCN order is greater than that for the UNC order. This again suggests that the C-group is better in fault detection rate than the N-group (given that both orders begin with the execution of the U-group of test cases). Similarly, considering the APFD values within the 'N--" pair suggests that the U-group is better than the C-group, and considering the APFD values within the "C--" pair suggests that the U-group is better than the N-group. This also suggests that U-group is better than the C-group, which in turn is better than the N-group, that is, the UCN order is the best.

Based on the above observations from three different perspectives, it is suggested that if the test cases of a MUMCUT test set are executed in the UCN order, more software faults can be detected earlier when compared to other orderings in this study. Finally, as indicated from Figure 2, the interquartile ranges (as represented by the height of the box in the boxplot) of the UCN order is very small, the UCN order also gives a consistent rate of fault detection.

6   Conclusion and Future Work

Previous empirical studies [6,14] have demonstrated that by scheduling test cases in different execution orders, software faults can be revealed in a higher rate. In this paper, we perform a further empirical study on prioritizing the test cases in a MUMCUT test set.

It is known [3] that the MUMCUT strategy guarantees to detect all the types of faults discussed in Section 2.2. Based on a set of previously published Boolean specifications, this study experiments with the six different orders of executing the test cases in a MUMCUT test set by comparing the values of the APFD (the weighted average percentage fault detected).

Our results demonstrate that, for the set of Boolean specifications under study, if the test cases are executed in UCN order, more software faults can be detected earlier. In other words, to detect more software faults faster, software testers should execute test cases that satsify the MUTP strategy first, followed by those that satisfy the CUTPNFP strategy, and finally by the test cases that satisfy the MNFP strategy. This is quite surprising because the fault class analysis proposed by Kuhn [11] suggests that high APFD values can be achieved if test cases for the CUTPNFP strategy in a MUMCUT test set are executed first. However, our results show that they are not as good as the test cases for the MUTP strategy.

Although our results suggest that the test cases in a MUMCUT test set should be scheduled in UCN order to achieve a higher rate of fault detection, the underlying reasons are not yet clear. As such, it may be too early to draw the conclusion that the UCN order is necessarily the best. We plan to conduct further experiments for a more comprehensive study. Moreover, the experimental results apparently suggest that there may be some implicit relationships among the types of faults. This should lead to further work on the fundamental nature of these faults and the test cases.

Acknowledgement

The authors are grateful to Emily Wong who helped to perform the experiment described in this paper.

References

1. N. Amla and P. Ammann. Using Z specifications in category-partition testing. In *Systems Integrity, Software Safety, and Process Security: Building the Right System Right: Proceedings of the 7th Annual IEEE Conference on Computer Assurance (COMPASS'92)*, pages 3–10, 1992.
2. H. Y. Chen, T. H. Tse, F. T. Chan, and T. Y. Chen. In black and white: an integrated approach to class level testing of object-oriented programs. *ACM Transactions on Software Engineering and Methodology*, 7(3):250–295, 1998.
3. T. Y. Chen and M. F. Lau. Test case selection strategies based on boolean specifications. *Software Testing, Verification and Reliability*, 11(3):165–180, 2001.
4. T. Y. Chen, M. F. Lau, and Y. T. Yu. An empirical evaluation of the MUMCUT strategy for testing Boolean specifications. In *Proceedings of the 3rd Annual IASTED International Conference on Software Engineering and Applications (SEA'99)*, pages 262–268, 1999.
5. T. Y. Chen, M. F. Lau, and Y. T. Yu. MUMCUT: A fault-based strategy for testing Boolean specifications. In *Proceedings of Asia-Pacific Software Engineering Conference (APSEC'99)*, pages 606–613, 1999.

6. S. Elbaum, A. G. Malishevsky, and G. Rothermel. Prioritizing test cases for regression testing. In *Proceedings of International Symposium on Software Testing and Analysis (ISSTA'00)*, pages 102–112, 2000.

7. K. A. Foster. Sensitive test data for logic expressions. *ACM SIGSOFT Software Engineering Notes*, 9(2):120–125, 1984.

8. D. D. Givone. *Introduction to Switching Circuit Theory*. McGraw-Hill, 1970.

9. C. B. Jones. *Systematic Software Development using VDM*. Prentice-Hall, second edition, 1989.

10. N. Kobayashi, T. Tsuchiya and T. Kikuno. Non-specification-based approaches to logic testing for software. *Information and Software Technology*, 44(2):113-121, 2002.

11. D. R. Kuhn. Fault classes and error detection capability of specification-based testing. *ACM Transactions on Software Engineering and Methodology*, 8(4):411–424, 1999.

12. N. G. Leveson, M. P. E. Heimdahl, H. Hildreth, and J. D. Reese. Requirements specification for process-control systems. *IEEE Transactions on Software Engineering*, 20(9):684–707, 1994.

13. W. V. Quine. The problem of simplifying truth functions. *American Mathematical Monthly*, 59:521–531, 1952.

14. G. Rothermel, R. H. Untch, C. Chu, and M. J. Harrold. Test case prioritization: An empirical study. In *Proceedings of the International Conference on Software Maintenance*, pages 1–10, 1999.

15. H. Singh, M. Conrad, and S. Sadeghipour. Test case design based on Z and the classification-tree method. In *Proceedings of the First IEEE International Conference on Formal Engineering Methods*, pages 81–90, 1997.

16. K. C. Tai. Theory of fault-based predicate testing for computer programs. *IEEE Transactions on Software Engineering*, 22(8):552–562, 1996.

17. E. J. Weyuker, T. Goradia, and A. Singh. Automatically generating test data from a boolean specification. *IEEE Transactions on Software Engineering*, 20(5):353–363, 1994.

18. Y. T. Yu and M. F. Lau. A study of prioritizing test cases in MUMCUT test sets. In *Proceedings of the IASTED International Conference on Applied Informatics – Symposium 3: Software*, pages 466–471, 2001.

About the Difficulties of Building a Pretty-Printer for Ada

Sergey Rybin[1], Alfred Strohmeier[2]

[1] Scientific Research Computer Center, Moscow State University
Vorob'evi Gori, Moscow 119899, Russia
rybin@possum.srcc.msu.su
[2] Swiss Federal Institute of Technology in Lausanne (EPFL), Software Engineering Lab
CH-1015 Lausanne EPFL, Switzerland
alfred.strohmeier@epfl.ch

Abstract. The paper discusses possible approaches for developing an Ada pretty-printer. The main problems of pretty-printing are outlined and analysed. Possible architectures for a pretty-printer are presented and compared. The strengths and weaknesses of the ASIS technology as a basis for developing a pretty-printer are discussed. Users' requirements for the next revision of the ASIS standard are derived from this discussion.

Keywords. Ada, ASIS, Pretty-Printer.

1 Introduction

Beautifying source code by means of a pretty-printer may be a well-deserved compensation after hours of coding and debugging efforts. However, there are more important reasons to reformatting source code, e.g. maintenance of code developed by a programmer not sticking to any style at all or by several programmers following different styles. Performing the task without tool assistance is cumbersome at the best, but also error-prone. As a consequence, the need for pretty-printers has been recognised for a long time.

At a first look, the problem pretty-printing problem seems to be well-defined, and since the need for it is well established and recognised, one could hope that high quality pretty-printers should by readily available. This is not the case for Ada, and we suspect that the same holds for many other programming languages.

The purpose of this paper is to outline some of the difficulties related to pretty-printing Ada source code [3], to explain the problems encountered when building a pretty-printer on top of ASIS, and to discuss some alternative solutions.

The experiences gained in different pretty-printer projects form the background for stating some users' requirements for the next revision of the ASIS standard.

2 Difficulties of Pretty-Printing

2.1 Variety of Needs

The first problem stems from defining the meaning of the attribute "pretty". Clearly there are as many opinions and therefore needs as there are individuals and organiza-

J. Blieberger and A. Strohmeier (Eds.): Ada-Europe 2002, LNCS 2361, pp. 257-268, 2002.

tions. Even if an official style guide, like [1], is followed, there is still a lot of space for variations. To be useful, a pretty-printer should therefore be able to deal with many different coding styles. As a consequence, the pretty-printer has to accommodate a large number of parameters. As an example, gnatpp, the prototype pretty-printer of the GNAT Ada compilation tool set [5] has 24 parameters for defining the output layout and this number will certainly increase in future releases.

Clearly, some parameter combinations are better than others, and some of them don't even make sense. As a consequence, a sophisticated user interface is needed to deal with a large number of parameters.

A natural way to generate easily pretty-printer parameters is to derive them from existing Ada source code, considered to be well formatted by the user. This task can be solved by a source scanner that collects layout information, such as indentation level, identifier and keyword casing, maximum line length, typical splitting of complex syntax elements such as record definitions, "if" and "case" statements, etc. Such a tool can be easily implemented on top of ASIS. The main problem with such a style analyser is that the "well-formatted" source might not follow uniform rules and that there might be "outliners". Rather than collecting facts, the tool would therefore gather statistics about different aspects and then make decisions and guesses based on some reasonable criteria. For example, if 90% of all the keywords are in lowercase, then this might be the correct setting for the pretty-printer parameter. On the other side, if the longest line in the source contains 300 characters (perhaps the result of some accidental removal of line breaks), but the average line length is 50 characters, some more sophisticated statistical analysis based on robust techniques might be needed, or the style analyser might just defer the decision to the user.

2.2 Knowledge about the Meaning of Constructs

When formatting manually source code, the programmer often uses information about the meaning of constructs. S/he might do so when inserting line breaks within a long expression, or when cutting a long list of actual parameters into pieces. Other examples are grouping of very short statements on a single line. Clearly, no pretty-printer can reproduce this kind of application semantics-based formatting.

2.3 Stability of Pretty-Printing

Clearly, it is very desirable that pretty-printing be idem potent, i.e. when applied twice (with the same parameters) the result should remain the same. A step further would be to be able to mix the result of a pretty-printer with hand-made corrections and not to loose the latter ones when submitting the code again to the pretty-printer.

2.4 Comments

Comments pose a special problem for at least two reasons.

Firstly, a comment can start almost everywhere, and since it will complete only at the end of the line, the "interrupted" construct has to resume on the next line, and consistent formatting can be quite difficult.

Secondly, comments do not have any syntactic structure that could be used for their formatting. It is even impossible to know if a comment relates to the source code that precedes or follows it. These kinds of problems can be solved by tagging or marking comment lines, stating e.g. that a comment relates to what precedes, that it is the start of a new paragraph, that it should not be touched upon at all, e.g. because it contains a semi-graphical picture, etc.

It might be worth to expand a little bit on this second point. Even though comments are not part of the semantics of the program as defined by the language, they are an important part of the code documentation. In addition, they are often used as a mechanism by ancillary tools, such as pre-processors, version control systems, etc. One consequence is that a line containing only a comment should never be appended behind a language construct to become a so-called end-of-line comment.

For any strategy of comment processing there is a number of situations where its performance is poor. Even if we decide to keep comments unchanged (this seems to be the simplest solution for a pretty-printer), there will be conflicts with other formatting rules, and side-effects resulting from formatting proper source code:

- What should we do with comment lines that exceed the maximum line length limitation?
- Should we indent comment lines together with the code lines?
- What about comments vertically aligned with source code?

The following trivial example illustrates the last two problems:

```
begin
   Variable := Value;
   --                ^^^^^ this value means something
```

Suppose that the indentation level is set to five (that is, the assignment statement should be moved three positions to the right). It does not matter whether or not we decide to indent comments, the original intent of the comment to "underline" by "^^^^^" the right-hand side of the assignment statement will be broken anyway.

We think that only a simple set of formatting rules should be defined for formatting comments, as a kind of compromise between two goals: to have the resulting code look pretty and to minimise unwanted negative effects on comment contents. We propose the following basic rules:

- Comment lines should be indented in the same way as code lines (otherwise the result source will never look really pretty);
- Only the contents of free-style text paragraphs are reformatted. We consider a sequence of comment lines to form a single paragraph written in free-style if it contains mainly "words", and if the words are mostly separated by blank spaces. For such paragraphs, the pretty-printer moves words between comment lines, like a typical word processor.

2.5 Line Length

The line length, be it the maximum length imposed by the compiler, or the length chosen by the programmer, has a big impact on formatting.

When the line length is shortened, the pretty-printer will have to spread over several lines expressions and lists that previously held on a single line. In that case, one has to decide where to break the expression, and also how much to indent on the next line.

On the other side, when the line length is increased, the pretty-printer can join related lines into a single line, e.g. lines belonging to the same expression. However, by doing so, the pretty-printer might destroy a layout that the programmer wanted preserved.

Finally, it is quite possible to have to deal with a situation somewhere between the two previous ones: an expression holds on fewer lines than the original formatting, but occupies nevertheless more than one line.

2.6 Length of Language Constructs

In Ada, there is no limitation on the complexity of language constructs, and therefore on their number of characters: expressions and subprogram calls hundreds of characters long are not uncommon. The pretty-printer therefore needs to perform large look-ahead, either by multi-pass pretty-printing or by simulating such a multi-pass by recursion.

2.7 Vertical Alignment of Constructs

Vertical alignment is another challenge. In order to improve readability of source code, it may be useful to align vertically the delimiters of repeated constructs:

- The colon and assignment delimiters in declaration sequences and formal parts;
- The assignment delimiter in a sequence of assignment statements;
- The arrow delimiter in named parameter, component or discriminant associations.

It might also be nice to align vertically end-of-line comments on the starting double dashes.

It is not trivial to define formally the conditions where vertical alignment is desirable, and to implement it. In all cases, look ahead has to be performed beyond the needs of usual syntax analysis.

3 Suitability of ASIS for Implementing a Pretty-Printer

Any reasonable code layout is based on the syntax structure of the code. Therefore, any pretty-printer needs some kind of parser or some other way to get the syntax structure of the code. In addition, some semantics information is also needed, e.g. to convert identifiers following a specific upper/lower case schema.

In case of Ada, ASIS comes immediately to one's mind when thinking about a portable solution for a pretty-printer. Indeed, for many years pretty-printers and code reformatting tools have been claimed to be typical and effective applications of the ASIS technology, although we still do not have any high-quality ASIS-based pretty-printer.

As a reminder of the purpose of ASIS, we quote its standard [2]: "The Ada Semantic Interface Specification (ASIS) is an interface between an Ada environment (as defined by ISO/IEC 8652:1995) and any tool requiring information from it. An Ada environment includes valuable semantic and syntactic information. ASIS is an open and published callable interface which gives CASE tool and application developers access to this information." We might also recall that there is an implementation of ASIS for the GNAT Ada compiler, called ASIS-for-GNAT [6][7][8], and that it is available as a part of the public version of the GNAT Ada technology [5].

One limitation resulting form the previous statement is that ASIS can process only legal Ada compilation units. Therefore, it can not be used for helping a programmer type-setting a not yet finished or not yet error-free piece of code, as usual in programming environments, and as achieved e.g. by Ada-aware EMACS.

We restrict therefore our consideration to pretty-printing error-free compilation units, as usual for pretty-printers. In that case, the ASIS structural queries indeed provide the full syntax information of the code to reformat. In addition, the ASIS semantic query called Corresponding_Name_Definition provides for each identifier occurrence the corresponding defining name. It is therefore possible to use the same upper/lower case letters for an identifier everywhere by referring to its declaration.

On the overall, ASIS seems to fulfil our needs, with the noticeable exception of comments. For formatting comments, ASIS is in fact of little help.

ASIS structural queries return information about the abstract syntax structure of the code. In other words, they return only non-terminal syntax elements. For simple names and literals, ASIS returns their text images, and classification queries allow computing all the other terminals (except for the use of upper/lower case letter in keywords). However, comments are completely ignored.

Happily, ASIS provides means for getting the images (as character strings) of syntax elements as well as the images of the code lines in the original source. Such text images contain comments exactly in the right positions. Unfortunately, and that is a real problem, it is impossible to get back from the inside of the image to the syntax structure of the original code.

As a consequence, a pretty-printer based on ASIS not only has to traverse the syntax tree of the code to be reformatted, but it also has to step sequentially through all its lexical elements in order to find the exact positions of comment lines and end-of-line comments. The first traversal is provided in ASIS by the generic Traverse_Element procedure, whereas the second one has to be implemented manually from scratch. The main problem is to synchronise so to speak these two traversals to make sure that comments are attached at the right place in the abstract syntax tree.

As a first conclusion, we can say that ASIS has serious limitations when used as a basis for a pretty-printer. These limitations stem from the fact that ASIS focuses on the abstract syntax, and does not provide any means for linking the abstract syntax objects with the concrete sequences of lexical elements representing these objects in the source. As the analysis of the pretty-printer problem has shown, providing a link from a syntax element to its unstructured text image is not enough.

After discussing possible pretty-printer architectures, we will come back to this problem and provide some suggestions for extending ASIS' functionality that could be taken into account during the next revision of the ASIS standard.

4 Possible Pretty-Printer Architectures

We will now discuss and compare possible approaches to the design and implementation of ASIS-based pretty-printing tools. For all these approaches, we have some practical development or design experience.

4.1 Generating the Source Code from the Abstract Syntax Tree

Generating the source from the abstract syntax tree is probably the first idea that comes to mind when developing a pretty-printer on top of ASIS. The idea is straightforward: from the source to format we go to the corresponding ASIS Compilation Unit, we traverse the syntax structure of this ASIS Compilation Unit and we print out the text reconstructed from this structure. On the way, we use general knowledge about the Ada syntax, the ASIS element classification schema together with structural queries to reconstruct the keywords and delimiters, and the string images of names and literals as provided by ASIS. In this approach, the layout of the original source is completely ignored. The resulting layout is solely based on the syntax structure of the code and the formatting rules implemented in the tool, and specified by parameters.

The program Display_Source, included in the ASIS-for-GNAT distribution as an example for the use of ASIS, is based on this approach. Display_Source is a very basic pretty-printer: it does not have any parameters, i.e. the formatting rules are "hard-wired", and comments are simply ignored, i.e. not passed on to the output. As an advantage, Display_Source is compact in size.

4.2 Set of Specialized Formatting Tools

As another possible solution for the Pretty-Printer problem, we may consider a set of tools each performing a simple formatting task. For example, one tool may standardise the use of upper/lower cases in identifiers, another the presentation of keywords, another may add or remove white spaces according to formatting rules for separators, yet another may set and remove line breaks according to the desired maximal line length, etc. Finally, additional tools could translate textual source code to HTML, Postscript, or some other format. Some tools of this kind were developed at EPFL [4].

The advantage of this approach is the simplicity of the design and implementation of each of these tiny tools compared with a full-fledged pretty-printer. E.g. it is trivial to remove and to add white spaces if we do not have to care about a maximum line length.

One disadvantage of the approach is that it might not be easy to combine the small tools, each with its own parameters, in order to achieve some overall global effect. Also there might be performance problems, as we will see in the next section.

4.3 Multi-pass Pretty-Printer as a Combination of Specialized Tools

Let's suppose we have readily available all the tools described in the previous subsection. We can easily get a complete solution for the pretty-printer problem just by encapsulating all these tools in a driver. This driver would have to process the full set of formatting parameters, translate them into parameters for the specific tools and then call these tools in the right order, perhaps repeatedly. In this call sequence, each tool will take as an input the output of the previously called tool, like in a Unix pipe.

Unfortunately, this approach suffers a heavy performance penalty. Indeed, each specific tool that is ASIS-based needs to compile its input source. The resulting pretty-printer will therefore have to compile not only the original source, but also all its intermediate transformations.

4.4 One-pass Pretty-Printer

In compiler technology, the pros and cons for and against one-pass versus multi-pass approaches have been the subject of debate for a long time, and a pretty-printer can in some way be considered a compiler. One-pass approaches result in better performance, but the implementation is more sophisticated, and hence functionality must sometimes be limited to the essential. On the contrary, multi-pass solutions are usually slower (because there is some overlapping in the tasks performed by the different passes), but separate passes are much simpler than the single pass of a one-pass approach. The approach is also more flexible, because a pass can be changed (almost) in isolation, or an additional pass can be added. In order to alleviate somewhat the performance penalty, and especially in order to avoid parsing several times the same textual source code, multi-pass approaches usually use some internal representation of the source program.

We chose the one-pass approach for the GNAT pretty-printer. The internal structure is somewhat hybrid since we use both the original source code and its abstract syntax tree. These two data structures are traversed in parallel and a token of the output source is generated almost immediately after traversing the corresponding token in the argument source.

Traversing of the abstract syntax tree is implemented by using the traversal engine provided by ASIS, i.e. the generic Traverse_Element procedure. To traverse the input source as a sequence of lexical elements, we use the queries of Asis.Text to get line by line the input source and to convert each abstract ASIS line into its text image. At any given time, we process the text image of only one line, which is placed in an internal line buffer. Synchronisation of traversing the abstract syntax tree, traversing the input sequence of lexical elements and generating the output code is based on the following rules:

- when printing a lexical element, the pointer to the current position in the internal line buffer is moved ahead accordingly, skipping all white spaces;
- after printing a lexical element, a check is made if the next lexical element is an end-of-line comment, and if it is, this end-of-line comment is printed out;
- when the current position pointer reaches the end of the current line, the next line is read in the buffer automatically and a check is made if this line is a comment line. Empty lines are skipped; comment lines are printed and then skipped.

The main control flow is determined by traversing the abstract syntax tree. For each syntax element being visited, the corresponding specific pre- and post-operations, provided by the pretty-printer application code, define the details of traversing the original source and generating the output for this particular element. When traversing a piece of the original source, we use a priori knowledge about its syntax structure to detect which keyword, what kind of element, what kind of delimiter should be expected, and when. For example, for A_Procedure_Body element, in the pre-operation we expect the keyword **procedure**, we write the corresponding character string to the output source (starting on a new line and using the settings for keyword casing), and then we look for the next Ada lexical element in the line buffer. If we have an end-of-line comment or a comment or empty lines, we deal with them as stated above and this is all for the pre-operation defined for a procedure body. Then we enter its structure in the abstract syntax tree and recursively perform similar actions for its components, i.e. the components of a procedure body. When we come back to this procedure body element in the corresponding post-operation, we are expecting the keyword **end** in the line buffer, and we have to write this keyword to the output source and then to append the procedure name, followed by a semi-colon.

We use a very simple criterion for deciding if a construct can be placed on one line: we take the text image of the construct and try to normalise it by adding or removing white spaces according to the formatting rules. This approach allows to stick to a given line length limitation, but at the time being, we are not able to nicely format on several lines large expressions or long nested subprogram calls.

4.5 Multi-pass Pretty-Printer Based on a Specialized Internal Representation of the Source Code

We also considered an approach based on a specialized internal representation of the code to be formatted. The idea was to create a full syntax tree containing all the elements of the concrete syntax, i.e. all the keywords, delimiters and comments that exist in the original source. Then this tree could be decorated by layout information, that is, line breaks and sequences of white spaces would be attached to the nodes of the tree. Finally, the resulting pretty output would be generated from this tree.

To build such a full tree, we need to traverse both the syntax structure and the sequence of lexical elements of the original source, quite similar to what was described in the previous subsection; it might be a little simpler, since we do not have to take care of generating the output. To decorate the tree by layout information, we may use an approach based on small specialized tools, like described in 4.2, but with the important difference that they all work on an internal representation, and therefore do not suffer the same performance penalty. Finally, the output would be generated from the decorated full tree.

The drawback of this approach lies in the hard work needed to define and finally implement such a full syntax tree. We think this effort is excessive, especially because both the GNAT compiler and ASIS already use an abstract syntax tree with references to the linear text representation of the program, and that they offer therefore an alternative approach as explained in 4.4.

5   Presentation of the Capabilities of the Pretty-Printer for GNAT

The ASIS-based pretty-printer **gnatpp** should become part of the core GNAT Ada technology and distribution in a near future. At the time of writing this paper, we are performing tests on its first release.

The design and implementation of **gnatpp** are based on the approach described above in subsection 4.4. It can process only legal Ada sources. The choice of available formatting parameters and their default values are based on the style checks performed by the GNAT compiler and the style rules imposed on the source components of this compiler.

Except for comments and empty lines, **gnatpp** does not take into account the layout of the input source and it recreates the output source from scratch. As a result, the only separators in the output source are space characters and platform-specific line breaks; form feeds and tabulation characters can occur only inside comments if the input version contains such characters. **gnatpp** does not destroy so-called "paragraphs" – that is, sequences of constructs such as declarations or statements separated by empty lines, but it reduces any sequence of more then one empty line to exactly one empty line. At the time being, we do not support various options for placing spaces around tokens; we just use the style shown in the examples of the Ada Reference Manual [3], also adopted by the GNAT style rules.

In its first version, **gnatpp** provides at least the following basic formatting facilities:

- Setting a maximum line length; this limit should never be exceeded in the output source. If a construct is too long to be placed on a single line, it is split;
- Setting identifier and keyword casing;
- Setting indentation level;
- Alignment for parts of variable declarations, assignment statements, component associations in aggregates, parameter associations in subprogram calls; alignment is bounded by paragraphs, that is, it is performed independently for any declaration, statement or association sequence bounded by empty lines;
- Adding optional names after the terminating end of bodies;
- Adding the loop name to an exit statement;
- For some constructs, it is possible to choose between different variants of their layout. For example, for record definitions two layouts are available:

```
type Rec is record
      C : Component_Type;
      ...
end record;
-- or:
type Rec is
      record
         C : Component_Type;
         ...
      end record;
```

- For comments, a rather conservative approach based on the principles stated in 2.4 is used: it is possible to choose the way of indenting comment lines, to ask for "word processing" inside a comment paragraph, and to get rid of tabulations and form feeds by replacing them with spaces and line breaks.

As a sequence of Ada lexical elements, the source code output by the current version of **gnatpp** is completely equvalent to the input source. For the next version, we are thinking about adding some semantically-transparent transformations, such as replacing simple use-visible names by the corresponding fully extended names, or by replacing the **others** choice in case statements and record variants with the corresponding sets of explicit choices.

6 Requirements for the Next ASIS Revision

In this section, we would like to summarise part of the experience gathered during the pretty-printer project described above by proposing user needs to be dealt with during the next revision of the ASIS standard. We think that similar requirements might be shared by other projects where the ASIS-based tool has to deal not only with syntax and with semantics of the Ada code to be analysed, but also with its physical layout; we have especially in mind source code transformation and program documentation tools. We have to admit we are not yet ready to provide any detailed technical suggestions for satisfying these needs by changes to ASIS.

6.1 Adding Comments to ASIS Elements

As already said, the very primitive support provided in the current ASIS standard for comments was one of the main sources of our design and implementation problems. In Ada, we may have comments before, after, or inside a compilation unit (or between compilation units, depending on how the notion of a compilation environment is implemented). To simplify, we will explain our ideas for the case when a comment is part of a program unit. The point then is that any comment may occur inside, before or after some ASIS Elements representing Ada syntax constructs.

Suppose we extend the ASIS Element abstraction by adding a new Element kind, named A_Comment. This change would affect all the ASIS structural queries that return Element lists; queries returning a single Element would not be affected. For all queries returning Element lists, we would add a Boolean flag indicating if comments before the first element, between elements of the list, or after the last element should also be returned. Consider e.g.:

```
procedure Foo is
begin
   I := J;
   -- comment1
   Bar (X);
   -- comment2
end Foo;
```

In this example, the Body_Statements query with the Include_Comments flag set should return four elements: An_Assignment_Statement, A_Comment (for comment1), A_Procedure_Call_Statement, and A_Comment (for comment2). Like other elements, the A_Comment element kind would provide the Enclosing_Element query, and the queries from Asis.Text, i.e. Element_Span and Element_Image.

Of course, there are some non-trivial design issues related to the A_Comment Element kind. For example, how to get a comment if it is located between **is** and **begin** keywords? How to get comments that are part of an assignment statement (there is no Element list in that case)? Should we make a difference between end-of-line comments and comment lines?

Also, ASIS-based applications not interested in dealing with comments will have to deal with a more complex interface, due to the proposed additions, without any counterpart. A compromise might possibly be achieved by a new ASIS Special Needs Annex for comment processing.

6.2 Adding a Token Abstraction to Asis.Text

Asis.Text provides the queries needed for dealing with the textual representation of the Ada source. In the current ASIS standard, queries defined in this package return the coordinates of a given Element, and for an Element one can get its text image. The package also defines the abstraction of a line in the source code, and for a line it is also possible to get its text image. Unfortunately the returned images are just character strings. We suggest to add as an abstraction a token, similar to the notion of a lexical element defined in the Ada standard [3]. The corresponding operation could be:

- get the image of an ASIS Element and of ASIS Line as a list of tokens;
- for any token: get the innermost ASIS elements the token belongs to, get the span and the text image.

It might be possible to get further along the ideas of the subsections 6.1 and 6.2 and require from ASIS proper access to any lexical element, otherwise said, any token of an Ada compilation units. Our suggestion is just one possible approach. Another approach would be to add the abstraction of a token not at the level of the Asis.Text package, but at the very top level of ASIS abstractions, alongside the Element abstraction, and to define a mapping between Elements and tokens.

6.3 Improving the ASIS Element List Abstraction or Adding an Alternative Traversal Mechanism

The generic procedure Traverse_Element provides a very powerful and flexible means for traversing the syntax structure of Ada code, but it is the only traversal engine provided by ASIS. In some cases it is too powerful, that is, either too complicated or too expensive or both.

Traverse_Element implements a recursive top-down traversal. However, for many applications, we need, given some Element, to go forward and backward through the list of Elements it belongs to. E.g. for a declaration, we need to go through the corresponding declaration sequence, for a parameter association, through the list of actual parameters and so on. In the pretty-printer, this need appears when we have to look ahead in order to determine layout characteristics. Of course, this kind of travelling through a list can be achieved with Traverse_Element, but the result is a recursive traversal inside another one, controlled by appropriate parameters to limit the general recursive traversal to a simple list traversal. In addition, for each recursive traversal, Traverse_Element must be instantiated with actual generic state, pre- and post-operation parameters. The resulting code is complicated, non-effective and hard to debug. Also, with Traverse_Element, the list can only be traversed from left to right, whereas the reverse order might sometimes be convenient for Element lists.

Given all these reasons, we think it would be appropriate for ASIS to provide facilities for traversing simple linked lists. They can be implemented for the ASIS Element list abstraction provided under the condition that the following queries be defined for ASIS Elements:

- test detecting if an Element belongs to some Element list,
- query returning the Element list containing the given Element,
- for an Element being a part of an Element list, queries returning the previous and next Elements in the list.

Of course, all these possibilities can be implemented as ASIS secondary queries, but only with poor performance. We suspect that the internal data structures of the compiler used as a basis for implementing Element have the needed links in ready-to-use form, so the direct implementation of the functionality as primary ASIS queries would be much more effective.

7 Conclusion

Pretty-printing is widely considered a simple problem, and therefore often proposed as a student project. We tried to show that the user requirements of a pretty-printer are in fact quite complex, and its implementation for a modern programming language, like Ada, very demanding. Even a powerful infrastructure for building programming tools, as is the case for ASIS, does not completely solve the problem. It might be worth to take into account some of the difficulties we encountered to make the revised version of ASIS an even better tool.

References

[1]   Christine Ausnit-Hood, Kent A. Johnson, Robert G. Pettit, Steven B. Opdahl (Eds.); Ada 95 Quality and Style; Lecture Notes in Computer Science, vol 1344; Springer-Verlag, 1997; ISBN 3-540-63823-7.

[2]   Ada Semantic Interface Specification (ASIS); International Standard ISO/IEC 15291 1999 (E).

[3]   S. Tucker Taft, Robert A. Duff (Eds.); Ada 95 Reference Manual: Language and Standard Libraries, International Standard ISO/IEC 8652:1995(E); Lecture Notes in Computer Science, vol. 1246; Springer-Verlag, 1997; ISBN 3-540-63144-5.

[4]   http://lglwww.epfl.ch/ada/formatter.html (EPFL's work on pretty-printing, including a text-to-HTML translator)

[5]   ftp://cs.nyu.edu/pub/gnat

[6]   Sergey Rybin, Alfred Strohmeier, Eugene Zueff; ASIS for GNAT: Goals, Problems and Implementation Strategy; Proceedings of Ada-Europe'95, Toussaint (Ed.), LNCS (Lecture Notes in Computer Science) 1031, Springer, Frankfurt, Germany, October 2-6 1995, pp. 139-151.

[7]   Sergey Rybin, Alfred Strohmeier, Alexei Kuchumov, Vasiliy Fofanov; ASIS for GNAT: From the Prototype to the Full Implementation; Reliable Software Technologies - Ada-Europe'96: Proceedings, Alfred Strohmeier (Ed.), LNCS (Lecture Notes in Computer Science), vol. 1088, Springer, Ada-Europe International Conference on Reliable Software Technologies, Montreux, Switzerland, June 10-14, 1996, pp. 298-311.

[8]   Sergey Rybin, Alfred Strohmeier, Vasiliy Fofanov, Alexei Kuchumov; ASIS-for-GNAT: A Report of Practical Experiences - Reliable Software Technologies - Ada-Europe'2000 Proceedings, Hubert B. Keller, Erhard Ploedereder (Eds), LNCS (Lecture Notes in Computer Science), vol. 1845, Springer-Verlag, 5th Ada-Europe International Conference, Potsdam, Germany, June 26-30, 2000, pp. 125-137.

A Tailorable Distributed Programming Environment*

Ernestina Martel, Francisco Guerra, and Javier Miranda

Applied Microelectronics Research Institute
University of Las Palmas de Gran Canaria
Spain
{emartel,fguerra,jmiranda}@iuma.ulpgc.es

Abstract. In this paper we propose the architecture of a generic fault-tolerant graphical environment, and a tool to customise it for a concrete environment. This graphical *Environment for Programming Distributed Applications* (EPDA) is tailorable and includes support for deployment and dynamic reconfiguration of distributed applications. Its minimum functionality comes from the development of an Environment for Programming Ada Distributed Applications which has been adapted to Glade and to the Group_IO communication library. It can be installed as robust to guarantee the continuity of its service in presence of node failures.

Keywords: Distributed Configuration, Ada, Glade, Group_IO

1 Background

Development and evolution of distributed applications are facilitated by separating the system structure from the functional description of individual component behaviour. This approach, referred to as *configuration programming* [1], separates the distributed application programmmig from its configuration. The *distributed application programming* defines the behaviour of the distributed application by means of a programming language and the adequate communication mechanisms. The *distributed application configuration* describes the structure of the distributed application in terms of software components and their interconnections, and specifies the allocation of its components to machines. Such configuration can be made by hand ([2], [3], [4]), which is tedious and error-prone. The use of configuration languages ([5], [6], [7]) and associated environments for describing, constructing and managing distributed applications is particularly appropriated. Such environments can be graphical [8] and sometimes without an associated configuration language [9].

One of the challenges in the provision of distributed applications is the accommodation of *evolutionary changes* [10]. This may involve modifications or

* *This work has been partially funded by the Spanish Research Council (CICYT), contract number TIC2001–1586–C03–03*

J. Blieberger and A. Strohmeier (Eds.): Ada-Europe 2002, LNCS 2361, pp. 269–281, 2002.

extensions to the application which must be programmed to support them (for instance, if we need to incorporate a replica to a running group, the new replica may need the group state and the group must have the necessary functionality for it). Such changes recover the system from failures, increase availability or migrate application code at runtime; in short to let distributed applications evolve to include new functionality or new technology. Furthermore, many application domains require the system to accommodate changes dynamically, without stopping or disturbing the operation of those parts of the system unaffected by the change. Evolutionary changes are currently supported by the configuration languages Durra [5], Darwin [6] and Glade [11], the working environment LuaSpace [12], and ZCL framework [13]. The CORBA tool for high availability Pirahna [14], provides mechanisms which let CORBA distributed applications evolve in order to increase their availability, restart failure objects and upgrade software components. By contrast, the Ada Reference Manual [15] does not provide specific features for evolutionary changes. However, when a a running server with state is stopped and then restarted somewhere else, the programmer can use Shared_Passive packages, provided for the Distributed System Annex of the Ada RM, in order to preserve the state of the running server.

This paper presents a graphical *Environment for Programming Distributed Applications* (EPDA) which facilitates the construction, configuration, execution, monitoring and evolution of distributed applications. The EPDA provides support for deployment and dynamic reconfiguration of distributed applications by means of the client/server model. EPDA is itself fault-tolerant, which is needed for monitoring and reshaping fault-tolerant distributed applications. Moreover, in this paper we have focused on the customisation of the EPDA to a concrete distributed application platform. For that, we have designed a tool called EPDA-Modeller, which customises a generic EPDA to different distributed application platforms.

This paper is structured as follows. In section 2 we introduce how to specify the structure of a distributed application. In section 3 the functionality of the EPDA is presented. The section 4 presents how EPDA functionality is provided through its *Graphical User Interface* (GUI). In section 5, we propose a client/server architecture for EPDA. In section 6, the tool for EPDA modelling is presented. In section 7 an usage example of both EPDA and EPDA-Modeller is presented. Finally, we present some conclusions and the current work.

2   Structure of a Distributed Application

Descriptions of constituent software components and their interconnections in a distributed application provide a clear form to specify the structure of a distributed application. The description of a component can be expressed in terms of their properties. A distributed application can be considered as a hierarchic structure of components. The components at the bottom are the basic distribution units or *single components*, whereas components in other layers are *composite components*, a collection of single or other composite components.

Let us analyse the structure of applications built by means of two well-known paradigms: the group and RPC paradigms. The former has been analysed with Group_IO [4] and the latter has been built with GLADE ([7], [11]).

The main components of a *distributed application built with Group_IO* are *applications* and *agents*. Each distributed application is composed by at least one agent, which is the name given to the basic unit of distribution and execution. Some agent collection can behave as a *group* [16]. If an application has groups, it must be formed by at least one agent.

Each Group_IO constituent component has its own properties. Some component properties are: application name, the location where the agent binaries are and where they will be executed, the mark for the critical agents in the system (those which must be restarted if they fail), the minimum number of replicas for a replicated group which are necessary to provide its service, etc.

The relationship rules which must follow the components of distributed applications built with Group_IO are: an application must have at least an agent and optionally some application agents may form a group; if there is a group, this is formed at least by one agent. Moreover, an agent can be part of several groups. UML notation has been used to represent relationship rules between constituent components in Figure 1, which also shows some component properties.

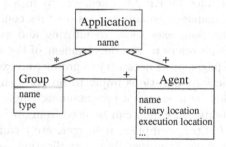

Fig. 1. UML notation for Group_IO

The main components of a *distributed application built with Glade* are: *applications*, *partitions* and *Ada library units*. An application is formed by partitions, which is the basic distribution unit. A partition is a collection of Ada library units. The bi-directional connection between two partitions describe a *channel*. Therefore, Glade applications are formed by partitions, Ada library units and optionally channels.

Glade application properties include its name, the start method, the name of the main procedure, the boot server location, the task pool parameters, the location of the binary and where it must be launched, the control version and the registration filter. Partition properties are: its name, the name of its main procedure, the location of the binary and where it must be launched, the termination and reconnection policies and a filter name (if it is needed). Channel properties include the name of its partitions and a filter name (if it is needed).

Relationship rules between constituent components along with some component properties are presented in Figure 2 by means of UML notation.

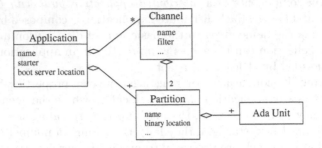

Fig. 2. UML notation for Glade

3   EPDA Functionality

The functionality provided by EPDA is achieved by means of the following distributed application management operations over its constituent components: construction, configuration, execution, monitoring and evolution. Distributed application *construction* refers to the development of the software entities and the correct setting of parameters necessary to produce an executable image of the application. Construction operations imply to program the components of the distributed application by means of a programming language and the adequate communication mechanisms, which can be used from an EPDA. The necessary programming tools (editor, compiler, debugger, etc.) can be called from the EPDA or alternatively once the distributed application components have been built through other external tools, the EPDA can be used for the remaining management operations (configuration, execution, monitoring and evolutionary operations). Distributed application *configuration* deals with the description of software components by means of their properties, the definition of their mutual interactions and the use of system resources according to the application's requirements (e.g. placement of components on the nodes of a distributed network). Configuration operations include adding a new component to the application, removing, updating, checking an existing one or testing whether a node has the resource requirements necessary to execute a component. Such operations take place before the execution of the application. Distributed application *execution* operations include to run its constituent components or finalise them. Distributed application *monitoring* allows to consult component properties before the execution (static monitoring) and the state of the application during its execution (dynamic monitoring): components which need restarting, members which have been added to a running group, etc. Distributed application *evolution* involves changes in constituent components at runtime. Some evolutionary operations imply to restart a failed object, to increase the availability of services, to migrate components, etc.

In order to facilitate configuration and evolutionary operations, we introduce the concept of *logical node*. The main distribution unit in a distributed application runs on a logical node. Each logical node is assigned to one physical node of the distributed system. The distinction between logical and physical nodes allow us to have two views of our distributed system: logical and physical view. Independently of our real distributed system, the logical view enables us to define multiple logical nodes where the application will be executed, whereas the physical nodes of the distributed system along with their related logical nodes are specified in the physical view. This separation between the physical and logical view facilitates the placement of distributed applications to different distributed system configurations where they are executed. That is, it has been achieved a certain independence between distributed applications and the hardware where they are executed. For example, we can build a distributed application in a centralised hardware with a single processor. We can execute the distributed application in a centralised manner by assigning the logical nodes of the application to the same physical node (with a single processor) at configuration time. In this way the debugging of the application is simplified. Once the non-distributed execution of the application is complete and debugged, the change to a distributed execution is immediate: it is only necessary to alter the bindings between logical and physical nodes and to restart the application.

EPDA goes through the following states as management operations over distributed applications are completed: idle, building and running (see Figure 3). These states are used by an EPDA to distinguish allowed operations. That is, construction and configuration operations are allowed in idle and building states. Distributed applications are in building state when construction or configuration operations are being performed. Execution operations are allowed in both idle and running states. Distributed applications pass to running state after the run operation is issued and to idle state after the finalise operation over a running component is issued. Monitoring operations can take place in any state. Evolutionary operations are enabled when distributed applications are running.

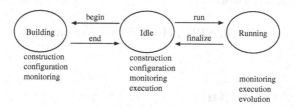

Fig. 3. EPDA states

4   EPDA GUI

The EPDA provides its functionality through a GUI, which has been structured
in two sections: the application and node sections. Every section has a menu bar
where the necessary operations for application or node management has been
located. The *application section* has two parts: the left part is used for describing
the structure of distributed applications. The UML notation has been replaced
by a tree structure which has been considered more user friendly. The right part
is used for editing the component properties. Once the confirmation button is
clicked, the application description (components, properties and relationships)
is accepted. The GUI prevents the user from violating the relationship rules for
the components of a distributed application described in section 2. Figure 4-a
shows the application section of the GUI for distributed applications built with
Group_IO. The *node section* allows to define the logical and physical nodes and
the association between them. The left part of the node section is used for node
names and the association between logical and physical nodes, while the right
part is used for node properties. Once the confirmation button is clicked, the
node description is accepted. The GUI prevents the user from assigning a logical
node to more than one physical node. In the Figure 4-b the node section of the
GUI for distributed applications built with Group_IO is shown.

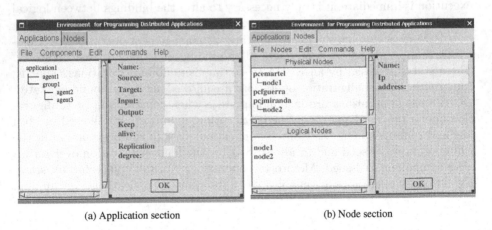

(a) Application section   (b) Node section

Fig. 4. EPDA client GUI for Group_IO

5   EPDA Architecture

We propose an EPDA architecture based on the client/server model (see Figure
5). The client by means of the GUI, issues requests to the server, which is responsible of the construction, configuration, execution, monitoring and adaptation of
distributed applications. The client provides the structure of a distributed application to the server, which stores it in its database. Specifically, a database has

been selected to keep the information of every component in the server's disk for several reasons: it provides an easy way to query and update the configuration information; besides, if the database design is adequate, it avoids the duplicity and redundancy of data, so it reduces the necessary disk space.

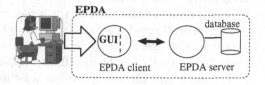

Fig. 5. Client/Server EPDA

The user executes the operations over distributed applications through the GUI provided by the client. The EPDA server executes the operations, which are received from the EPDA client, according to the state of these applications. Besides, as several users from different locations can request operations to the server, some data concurrency control is needed. For that, the reader/writer approach is used: any operation which implies a change on the application structure blocks any following operation on the same component; however, several operations to query are concurrently executed.

5.1   EPDA Client

The EPDA client is composed by two parts: the GUI and the protocols to communicate with the EPDA server.

Any application or node description which is accepted through the GUI is sent to the EPDA server, which stores in its database. The configuration, execution, monitoring and evolutionary operations over a selected component are also sent to the server which performs them and sends the result back to the client. For instance, in order to edit a component (static monitoring), the user selects such component and communicates its intention to the server, which sends the component properties back to the client. The EPDA client shows those properties in the right part of the application section. If the user updates them, the changes are sent to the server, which updates its database. The communication protocol Group_IO has been selected in order to communicate both client and server.

5.2   EPDA Server

The server keeps the state and structure of distributed applications in its database. In order to prevent the server from being a single point of failure, the server is implemented as a replicated group. Each replica is implemented by means of deterministic code which keeps a local copy of the database [17]. We use Group_IO to ensure that all the replicas receive exactly the same sequence of requests in the same order in an uniform way. Moreover, according to the state machine model [18] all the replicas execute the same sequence of actions and achieve the same state. Therefore, the distributed application management on the server side is always available in a continuous way: if one replica fails, the remaining alive replicas provide the service.

In this approach, when a request is received by the server group, all the replicas perform similar code and go through the same sequence of states, and in the same order. In that way, when an execution operation is sent to the server, every replica does the corresponding work over the distributed application. That is, if the server group has N replicas and the run operation is issued, the application is started N times. To avoid this problem, the requests from the EPDA server group to others services (remote execution, timing, etc.) must execute only one time. This is possible by means of group-to-process communication (also called N-to-1 communication) provided by Group_IO: the messages which are sent by the N replicas are filtered so that only a single copy of each replicated message is actually issued. In this approach the replicated server delegates the execution operations to a single process outside the group.

In order to prevent the process outside the group from being a single point of failure, there are several processes, each one located on a physical node of the distributed system. Let us call each one of these processes *EPDA proxy*. This proxy is responsible for the execution operations of any component on its physical node. For instance, the distributed system in Figure 6 is formed by four physical nodes, there must be four proxies, one for every machine (the user must have installed them when the EPDA is installed). Thus, *P1* is the EPDA proxy in charge of any execution operation in the machine called *my_pc*, *P2* manages execution operations in *your_pc* and so on. In Figure 6, the group server re-sends an execution operation to the proxy *P3*, by means of N-to-1 communication, in order to execute a component in *her_pc*. Such proxy executes the component and returns the result back to the group of EPDA replicas by means of a process-to-group communication (1-to-N communication).

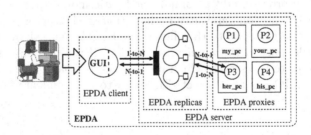

Fig. 6. Robust EPDA

Therefore, the client sends any request to the group of EPDA replicas by means of a process-to-group communication (see in Figure 6 as 1-to-N). The replicas of EPDA server re-send any execution operation to the corresponding proxy along with the necessary information for it by means of group-to-process communication (N-to-1). Once the operation has been performed, this proxy notifies the operation state to the server (1-to-N communication). Finally, the group of EPDA replicas notifies the result of the operation to the client by means of group-to-process communication (N-to-1). In this approach, every replica of the EPDA server knows the state of the execution operations which has been performed by the EPDA proxy[1].

Although the proxy allows the group of replicas to behave as a single process, sometimes the replicas can cooperate to build efficient solutions for distributed system management. That is, each replica can execute a piece of an operation and sends the results to the others (when necessary). For example, if a component must be started in all or some nodes where the EPDA replicas are running and we allow each replica to execute the component, the group-to-process communication is not necessary. This solution is also suitable for operations that involve a external service (remote execution, timing, etc.).

In summary, in our solution external services are provided by a proxy. However, when the service must be executed in all or some of the nodes where the EPDA server replicas are running this work can be done by the involved EPDA replicas. The communication between replicas and proxies is provided by Group_IO.

6   EPDA-Modeller: A Support for Customising an EPDA

In the previous sections we have proposed an EPDA architecture which is suitable for two different paradigms: RPC and group communication. These paradigms have been analysed by means of Glade and Group_IO platforms. We have seen that some parts of these EPDAs are common to these paradigms. For example, Glade has partitions and Group_IO has agents but with their own properties. Moreover, relationships between distributed components can be represented by a tree. Additionally, proxies are required in order to perform execution operations of distributed application's components. We call *EPDA-core* to all this set of common EPDA elements.

We aim to design a tool to customise the EPDA-core for a concrete distributed programming platform. We call such tool EPDA-Modeller (see Figure 7). The allowed component types, their properties and interconnections are specific features necessary to customise an EPDA-core. Although the EPDA-core may provide default management operations, they can also be customised or some new operations can be added. For example, execution operation is common to all the platforms, but its behaviour may differ from one to another (in the

---

[1] Although some functionalities of this proxy are similar to the PVM daemon (*pvmd*) [19], they are different in the sense the proxy has no knowledge about the state of other proxies in the distributed system as such information is kept in the replica's database.

RPC paradigm we only launch a single component, and in the group paradigm we need to launch all the group members).

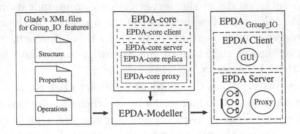

Fig. 7. EPDA-Modeller Tool

Just like the previously described EPDA architecture, the EPDA-core follows the client/server model. The *EPDA-core client* is composed by a GUI similar to the EPDA client GUI, except for the specific features, and the basic code to communicate with the server. The EPDA-core client GUI includes both application and node sections along with their menu bars. Both sections have the corresponding areas to place the instances of tree structure (GUI's left area) and component properties (GUI's right area) of the specific distributed application platform. EPDA-core client GUI's menu bar includes common management operations like construction, configuration and monitoring operations (evolutionary operations are not present in all distributed application platforms). The customised EPDA client GUI allows: to create instances of only the allowed component types, to fulfil the right component properties, to establish component interconnections without violating the relationship rules, and to perform the allowed management operations.

On the server side, the *EPDA-core server* contains the basic code to provide communication between the server and both clients and proxies: on the one hand, the EPDA-core replica contains the basic code to provide the communication between the group of EPDA replicas and both clients and proxies; on the other hand, the EPDA-core proxy contains the basic code to provide the communication between the proxy and the group of EPDA replicas. The EPDA-Modeller uses the application structure and the properties of its components, provided by the user, to create the tailor-made database with its associated API (*Application Programming Interface*). As for the execution operations, the user provides the specific proxy code necessary for every operation along with the parameters necessary to build the specific replica functionality. The customisation of both replica and proxy code is achieved by the EPDA-Modeller from the information provided by the user (structure, properties and operations) along with the EPDA-core server (EPDA-core replica and EPDA-core proxy). For that, the EPDA-Modeller builds the specific replica and proxy code from the information provided by the user and adds it to the EPDA-core replica and the EPDA-core proxy. After the customisation, the server binary and its database must be in-

stalled on the server node. For a robust EPDA server version the database and
the EPDA server binary must be installed in different physical nodes. In order
to perform the execution operations provided by the user in the physical nodes
of the distributed system, the customised proxies must also be installed on every
physical node of the distributed system.

The EPDA-core client has been programmed by means of GUI builder Glade[2]
and GtkAda [20] (for the graphical part) and the communication library
Group_IO (for the communication part). Regarding the EPDA-core server, it
has been implemented by means of Ada 95, the communication library Group_IO
and a binding to the *postgresql* database. The specific features of a platform for
programming distributed applications (the structure of a distributed application,
the properties of its components and management operations) are provided to
the EPDA-Modeller by means of three files in XML format. Such format is also
generated through GUI builder Glade. EPDA-Modeller parses the XML files
and extracts the necessary information to customise the EPDA-core client and
server. From this information EPDA-Modeller gets the allowed components, the
relationship rules between them and the management operations for the customised EPDA-core client. For the customisation of the EPDA-core server, the
EPDA-Modeller generates the structure of the server database along with a customised API for that database, the server replica and the proxy binaries. The
server database is a relational database, with so many tables as both component
types and interconnections between them the distributed platform has. Every
field of a component type table represents a property of that component. Fields
of relationship tables are the identifiers of the related components. The API is
an interface which provides the basic database operations (insert, update, delete,
select) for every component type of the distributed application.

7 Usage Example

This section describes an example of how to use EPDA-Modeller to get an EPDA
for the Group_IO communication library. The user provides the allowed component types (applications, groups and agents) and the relationship rules between
them to the EPDA-Modeller. Every allowed component type is provided along
with its properties. This information is given to the EPDA-Modeller by means
of two XML files. As for execution operations, in order to allow the customised
EPDA for Group_IO to support, for instance, the install operation, we must
provide the operation name, the proxy code to perform it and the necessary
information for the functionality of the replica. An example of the proxy code
can receive the message from the server with, for instance, the following data:
the necessary resources to install the agent and the location of the source binary. From it, the proxy code checks if its physical node has enough resources
to install the agent and if the local operation system is suitable for the source
binary. According to the replica, the user has to provide a XML file with the
properties which the server group must send to the corresponding proxy in order

---

[2] It is different from Glade released with GNAT for distributed systems.

to carry out the install operation: agent's target node, agent's source node and the necessary resources to install the agent.

As a result, the EPDA-Modeller provides an EPDA for Group_IO, where the allowed components are applications, agents and groups. The customised EPDA stops the user from violating the relationship rules and the unique execution operation, for our example, is called "install" in the menu bar. First, the user must create instances of the allowed components. For every component, its properties must be fulfilled by means of a form in the right area of the GUI. Every time the confirmation button is clicked, the component, its properties and its relations with other components are sent to the server which stores it in its database. Once the agents have been defined, the user can installed them through the install operation in the menu bar. Such command is sent to the server which re-sends it to the corresponding proxy (the association between proxies and physical nodes is stored in server's database). Finally, if everything goes well, the agent is installed and the server group is informed about it; otherwise, the result of the failed checks are sent to the server group.

8   Conclusions and Current Work

An environment for programming distributed applications (EPDA) has been presented for the construction, configuration, execution, monitoring and evolution of distributed applications. The environment can be installed as robust to guarantee the continuity of its service in presence of node failures. The architecture of the proposed EPDA is suitable for several distributed applications platforms, like Glade and Group_IO. From the EPDA, we have extracted those elements which are common to every distributed application platform and we have built a tailorable EPDA called EPDA-core. An EPDA-Modeller tool has been briefly presented in order to customise the generic EPDA to different distributed application platforms.

Although the EPDA-Modeller has been checked to provide EPDA for either Glade or Group_IO library, we think it can be suitable for other platforms. We plan to test both the EPDA and EPDA-Modeller for other platforms like Ensemble, Electra, Transis, Totem, etc. At the moment we are evaluating the performance of the tailor-made proxy for different distributed application management operations and in different situations, such a proxy which is in the same physical node of an EPDA replica.

References

1. J. Kramer. Configuration Programming - A Framework for the Development of Distributable Systems. In *Proceedings of the Int. Conference on Computer Systems and Software Engineering (Compeuro 90)*, pages 374–384, Israel, May 1990.
2. M. Hayden. *The Ensemble System*. Faculty of the Graduate School of Cornell University, 1998. Doctoral Dissertation.
3. D. Dolev and D. Malki. The Transis Approach to High Availability Cluster Communication. *Communications of the ACM*, 39(1):65–70, April 1996.

4. F. Guerra, J. Miranda, A. Álvarez, and S. Arévalo. An Ada Library to Program Fault-Tolerant Distributed Applications. In *1997 Ada-Europe International Conference on Reliable Software Technologies*, pages 230–243, London, June 1997. Springer-Verlag.
5. M. Barbacci, C. Weinstock, D. Doubleday, M. Gardner, and R. Lichota. Durra: a Structure Description Language for Developing Distributed Applications. *Software Engineering Journal*, 8(2):83–94, March 1993.
6. J. Magee, N. Dulay, S. Eisenbach, and J. Kramer. Specifying Distributed Software Architectures. In W. Schafer and P. Botella, editors, *Proc. 5th European Software Engineering Conf. (ESEC 95)*, volume 989, pages 137–153, Sitges, Spain, 1995. Springer-Verlag, Berlin.
7. L. Pautet and S. Tardieu. *GLADE User's Guide. Version 3.13p*. GNAT, May 2001.
8. K. Ng, J. Kramer, J. Magee, and N. Dulay. The Software Architect's Assistant - A Visual Environment for Distributed Programming. In *Proceedings of Hawaii International Conference on System Sciences*, Hawaii, January 1995.
9. Gargaro, Kermarrec, Nana, Pautet, Smith, Tardieu, Theriault, Volz, and Waldrop. *Adept (Ada 95 Distributed Execution and Partitioning Toolset)*. Technical Report, April 1996.
10. G. Etzkorn. Change Programming in Distributed Systems. In *Proceedings of the International Workshop on Configurable Distributed Systems*, pages 140–151, United Kingdom, March 1992.
11. L. Pautet, T. Quinot, and S. Tardieu. Building Modern Distributed Systems. In *2001 Ada-Europe International Conference on Reliable Software Technologies*, pages 122–135, Belgium, May 2001. Springer-Verlag.
12. T. Batista and N. Rodriguez. Dynamic Reconfiguration of Component-based Applications. In *Proceedings of the International Symposium on Software Engineering for Parallel and Distributed Systems (PDSE 2000)*, pages 32–39, Ireland, May 2000.
13. V.C. Paula, G.R. Ribeiro, and P.R.F. Cunha. Specifying and Verifying Reconfigurable Software Architectures. In *Proceedings of the International Symposium on Software Engineering for Parallel and Distributed Systems (PDSE 2000)*, pages 21–31, Ireland, May 2000.
14. S. Maffeis. Piranha:A CORBA Tool for High Availability. *IEEE Computer*, pages 59–66, April 1997.
15. Intermetrics. *Ada 95 Language Reference Manual*. International Standard ANSI/ISO/IEC-8652: 1995, January 1995.
16. K. Birman. The Process Group Approach to Reliable Distributed Computing. *Communications of the ACM*, 36(12):37–53, December 1993.
17. F. Guerra, J. Miranda, Santos J., and J. Calero. Building Robust Applications by Reusing Non-Robust Legacy Software. In *2001 Ada-Europe International Conference on Reliable Software Technologies*, pages 148–159, Belgium, May 2001. Springer-Verlag.
18. F. Schneider. Implementing Fault-tolerant Services Using the State Machine Approach: A Tutorial. *ACM Computing Surveys*, 22(4):299–319, December 1990.
19. A. Geist, A. Beguelin, J. Dongarra, W. Jiang, R. Mancheck, and V. Sunderman. *Parallel Virtual Machine. A Users' Guide and Tutorial for Networked Parallel Computing*. ISBN:0-262-57108-0. The MIT Press, 1994.
20. E. Briot, J. Brobecker, and A. Charlet. *GtkAda Reference Manual. Version 1.2.12*. ACT Europe, March 2001.

Modeling and Schedulability Analysis of Hard Real-Time Distributed Systems Based on Ada Components [1]

Julio L. Medina, J. Javier Gutiérrez, José M. Drake, Michael González Harbour

Avda. de los Castros s/n, 39005 Santander - Spain
{medinajl, gutierjj, drakej, mgh}@unican.es

Abstract. The paper proposes a methodology for modeling distributed real-time applications written in Ada 95 and its Annexes D and E. The real-time model obtained is analyzable with a set of tools that includes multiprocessor priority assignment and worst-case schedulability analysis for checking hard real-time requirements. This methodology models independently the platform (processors, communication networks, operating systems, or peripheral drivers), the logical components used (processing requirements, shared resources or remote components), and the real-time situations of the application itself (real-time transactions, workload or timing requirements). It automates the modeling of local and remote access to distributed services. The methodology is formulated with UML, and therefore the software logic design as well as its real-time model may be represented inside any UML CASE tool. The real-time model obtained is analyzable with a set of tools that includes multiprocessor priority assignment and worst-case schedulability analysis for checking hard real-time requirements.

1 Introduction

The Real-Time Systems Annex (D) of the Ada 95 standard [1] allows users to develop single-node applications with predictable response times. Furthermore, there are a few implementations of the Distributed Systems Annex (E), that support partitioning and allocation of Ada applications on distributed systems [2]. One of them is GLADE, which was initially developed by Pautet and Tardieu [3] and is currently included in the GNAT project, developed by Ada Core Technologies (ACT) [5]. GLADE is the first industrial-strength implementation of the distributed Ada 95 programming model, allowing parts of a single program to run concurrently on different machines and to communicate with each other. Moreover, the work in [3] proposes GLADE as a framework for developing object-oriented real-time distributed systems. Annexes D and E are mutually independent and, consequently, the distributed real-time systems environment is not directly supported in the Ada standard [4]. Our research group has been working on the integration of real-time and distribution in Ada 95. We have proposed a prioritization scheme for remote procedure calls in distributed Ada real-time systems [5], and in [6] we focused on

---

[1] This work has been funded by the Comisión Interministerial de Ciencia y Tecnología of the Spanish Government under grants TIC99-1043-C03-03 and 1FD 1997-1799 (TAP)

J. Blieberger and A. Strohmeier (Eds.): Ada-Europe 2002, LNCS 2361, pp. 282-296, 2002.

defining real-time capabilities for the Ada 95 Distributed Systems Annex in order to allow the development of this kind of applications in a simpler and potentially more efficient way than with other standards like real-time CORBA.

From another point of view, Ada has been conceived as an object-oriented language to facilitate the design of reusable modules in order to build programs that use previously developed components. To design component-based Ada real-time applications it is necessary to have strategies for modeling the real-time behavior of these components, and also tools for analyzing the schedulability of the entire application, to find out whether its timing requirements will be met or not. With the possibility of distribution in real-time applications development, we also need to address issues like the modeling of the communications, or the assignment of priorities to the tasks in the processors and to the messages in the communication networks. On these premises we can think about identifying and modeling basic Ada components that can be useful in the development of real-time distributed programs and for which the schedulability analysis tools can be applied.

This paper proposes a methodology for modeling and performing schedulability analysis of real-time distributed applications, built with basic Ada logical components. The methodology has been designed to facilitate the development of systems written in Ada 95 and using Annexes D and E. The main aspects of the methodology are the following.

- It is based on independently modeling: the platform (i.e., processors, communication networks, operating systems, peripheral drivers), the logical components used (i.e., processing requirements, shared resources, other components), and the real-time situations of the application itself (event sequences, real-time transactions, workload, timing requirements) that provide the elements for the analysis.
- It models the real-time behavior (timing, concurrency, synchronization, etc.) of the Ada logical entities in such a way that there is a complete parallelism between the structure of the code written and the real-time model obtained.
- It allows extracting a model of each high-level logical component, via the instantiation of a generic parameterized real-time model. When all the components are combined together and the associated generic parameters are defined, an analyzable model of the overall system is obtained.
- It automates the modeling of local or remote access to distributed services. If a procedure of a remote call interface is invoked from a component assigned to the same processor node the procedure is modeled as executed by the calling thread; but if the same procedure is invoked from a component assigned to a remote node, the corresponding communication model (with marshalling, transmission, dispatching, and unmarshalling of messages) is automatically included into the real-time situation model that is being analyzed.
- The modeling components as well as the software artifacts of the application are represented and described with UML.

The paper will be organized as follows. Section 2 presents the conceptual environment in which real-time analysis and modeling are considered. In Section 3, we describe the basic structure of the UML real-time view in which our models are hosted, the main abstractions, and the model of the Component class, which is the element with the highest modeling power. Section 4 discusses and justifies the feasibility of the approach used for mapping the Ada structures into analyzable real-time models. Section 5 presents an example of the modeling and real-time analysis of a simple application. Finally, Section 6 gives our conclusions.

2   Real-Time Analysis Process

The real-time models are based on concepts and components defined in the Modeling and Analysis Suite for Real-Time Applications (MAST). This suite is still under development at the University of Cantabria [8][9] and its main goal is to provide an open-source set of tools that enable real-time systems designers to perform schedulability analysis for checking hard timing requirements, optimal priority assignment, slack calculations, etc.

Figure 1 shows a diagram of the toolset and the associated information. At present, MAST handles single-processor, multiprocessor, and distributed systems based on different fixed-priority scheduling strategies, including preemptive and non-preemptive scheduling, interrupt service routines, sporadic server scheduling, and periodic polling servers. The following tools are already available now (✓) or are under development (-):

✓ Holistic and Offset-based analysis
- Multiple event analysis
✓ Monoprocessor priority assignment
✓ Linear HOPA (Holistic) and Linear simulated annealing priority assignment
- Monoprocessor and Distributed simulation

The main goal of the methodology is to simplify the use of well-known schedulability analysis techniques during the object-oriented development of real-time systems with Ada. In this paper we describe only the main characteristics of the modeling technique; we do not deal with the analysis techniques themselves, the least pessimistic of them can be found in [10].

The proposed methodology extends the standard UML description of a system with a real-time model that defines an additional view containing:

- the computational capacity of the hardware and software resources that constitute the platform,
- the processing requirements and synchronization artifacts that are relevant for evaluating the timing behavior of the execution of the logical operations,
- and the real-time situations to be evaluated, which include the workload and the timing requirements to be met.

In the schedulability analysis process, the UML model is compiled to produce a new description based on MAST components. This description includes the information of the timing behavior and of all the interactions among the different components. It also includes the description of the implicit elements introduced by the semantics of the Ada language components that influence the timing behavior of the system. All these elements are specified by means of UML stereotypes. The generated MAST description is the common base on which the real-time analysis toolset may be applied. Finally, the analysis results may be returned into the UML real-time view as a report for the designer. This process is illustrated in Figure 1.

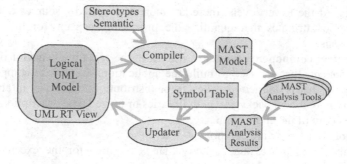

Fig. 1. Components of the real-time analysis process

3 Real-Time Model: UML RT View

The real time model is composed of three complementary sections:

The platform model: it models the hardware and software resources that constitute the platform in which the application is executed. It models the processors (i.e. the processing capacity, the scheduler, the system timers), the communication networks (i.e., the transmission capacity, the transmission mode, the message scheduler, the overheads of the drivers) and the platform configuration (i.e., the connections between processors using the different communication networks). Figure 2 shows the basic components of the platform model.

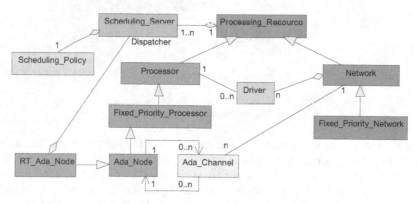

Fig. 2. Basic components of the platform model

The Processing_Resource is the root class of the platform model. It models the processing capacity of every hardware or software target that executes part or all of the modeled system activities. Each Processing_Resource has one or more Scheduling_Servers, in which the execution of the assigned activities is scheduled in accordance with a specified scheduling policy. At the highest level, the Processing_Resources are specialized as Processors, which have the capacity to execute the application's code, and Networks, which transfer messages among processors. At the lower levels, there are more specialized resources defined, which have specific attributes that quantify the processing capacity or the transmission characteristics.

The logical components model: it describes the real time behavior of the logical Ada components that are used to build the application. A software component is any logical entity that is defined as a design or distribution module in an application. A component may model packages (with libraries or tagged type descriptions), tasks, the main procedure of the application, etc.

The model of a software component describes:

- The amount of processing capacity that is required for the execution of every operation in its interface.
- The identifiers of all other components from which it requires services.
- The tasks or threads that it creates for the execution of its concurrent activities.
- The synchronization mechanisms that its operations require.
- The explicit variations that its code introduces for the value of its scheduling parameters.
- The inner states that are relevant for describing the real-time behavior of its operations.

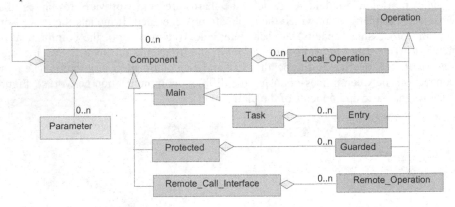

Fig. 3. The software component classes

The Component class (Figure 3) is the root class of the logical model hierarchy, It supplies the timing behavior models of each operation defined in its interface. If the operation is simple, its model is a set of attributes which describe the amount of processing that its execution requires. If the operation is composite, its model describes the sequence of operations that are executed within it. A component is also a container for other components aggregated into it, which are declared as attributes with the <<obj>> stereotype. The aggregated components are instantiated whenever the container component is instantiated. A component may also have parameters, which represent unassigned entities (external used components, operations, external events, timing requirements, etc.) that are used as part of the component's description. Parameters are declared as attributes with the stereotype <<ref>>. When a component is instantiated, a suitable concrete value must be assigned to the instance's parameters. The components and parameters declared as attributes in a component are visible and may be used in the interface, inside the operations' descriptions and inside its aggregated components.

The Component class is specialized in accordance with the kinds of operations that may be declared in its interface or with the semantics of its operations or parameters. The specialized class Main models the main procedure of the application or of any partition in case of a distributed system. Every Main instance has an implicit scheduling server that models its main thread. The Task class is a specialized kind of Main class that models an Ada task; it also has an implicit aggregated thread (inherited from Main). A Task class may offer one or more Entry type operations in its interface in order to synchronize the calling thread with the internal task thread. The Protected class models an Ada protected object. All of the operations of its interface (Local_Operations or Guarded operations) will be executed in mutual exclusion. For the execution of Guarded operations (i.e., the entries of an Ada protected object) it may be necessary for other concurrent threads to reach a specific state.

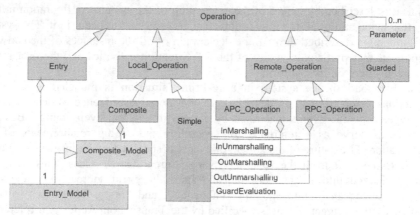

Fig. 4. Main operation classes for modeling the component interface

Every Guarded operation has an aggregated Simple Operation that models the evaluation of the guard. Finally, the Remote_Call_Interface class models a component whose operations may be invoked either from a local thread or from a thread in a remote partition assigned to another processor. Every Remote_Operation has a number of attributes that characterize the transmission parameters, and has several Simple operations aggregated, which model the marshalling and unmarshalling of the arguments of the operations. All of this information is used in the model only when the procedure is invoked remotely. The Operation class and its specialized classes model the timing behavior and the synchronization mechanisms of procedures and functions declared in a logical component's interface. Figure 4 shows the different kinds of specialized operation classes that have been defined.

Real-time situation model: it represents a certain operating mode of the system and models the workload that it has in that mode, which needs to be analyzed by the schedulability analysis tools. The analysis of a real-time system consists of the identification of all the real-time situations in which the system can operate. The analysis of each situation is performed separately.

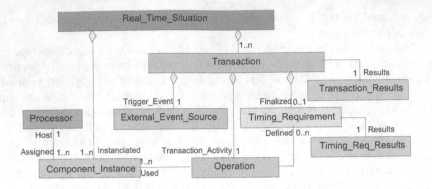

Fig. 5. Main classes of a real-time situation

Figure 5 shows the basic modeling components that constitute a real-time situation model. It is described by means of the declaration of the system configuration in that operating mode and of all the transactions that are expected to occur in it. The system configuration is described through the declaration of all the instances of the software components that participate in any of the RT_Situation activities and the declaration of its deployment on the platform.

The workload of the system in a real-time situation is modeled as a set of transactions. Each transaction describes the non-iterative sequence of activities that are triggered by the events generated by a specific external event source. Besides, these events serve as a reference for specifying the timing requirements of the RT_Situation. The nature of the stream of events is specified by an instance of any of the classes derived from the External_Event_Source abstract class. This class has been specialized into single, periodic, and aperiodic event sources. The aperiodic class specializes again into sporadic, unbounded, and bursty. The activity that is launched by the Trigger_Event is specified by the Transaction_Activity. It references an operation that is declared in the interface of an object instantiated from that activity. In each transaction we also describe the set of timing requirements that must be met. The one named Finalized is shown in the transaction declaration and stands for the final state that is reached when all the transaction activities are completed. The others are specified as arguments in the invocation of the Transaction_Activity operation; they are assigned to the operation parameters and in this way they are attached to the designated states, which were considered relevant from the timing point of view. Each timing requirement is modeled by an object instantiated from any of the classes derived from the Timing_Requirement abstract class. These classes are specialized according to the event that is taken as the reference for the calculus. They are called Global if they refer to the Trigger_Event of the transaction, and Local if they refer to the beginning of the last activity before the state to which the timing requirement is attached. They are also specialized according to other criteria like whether they represent a hard or soft deadline, whether they limit the amount of output jitter, etc.

Any object of a class derived from the classes RT_Situation, Transaction, Timing_Requirement or Scheduling_Server has an object linked, which is instantiated from the corresponding specialization of the Result class, which in turn holds the set of variables into which the results of the schedulability analysis tools can be stored.

4   Real-Time Model of the Basic Ada Structures

Even though the modeling and schedulability analysis methodology presented is language independent and is useful for modeling a wide range of real-time applications, the semantics of the high-level modeling components defined and the syntax and naming conventions proposed are particularly suitable and certainly adapted to represent systems conceived and coded in Ada.

The RT-model has the structure of the Ada application: The MAST Component instances model the real-time behavior of packages and tagged types, which are the basic structural elements of an Ada architecture:

- Each Component object describes the real-time model of all the procedures and functions included in a package or Ada class.
- Each Component object declares all other inner Component objects (package, protected object, task, etc.) that are relevant to model its real-time behavior. It also preserves in the model declarations the same visibility and scope of the original Ada structures.

A Component object only models the code that is included in the logical structure that it describes. It does not include the models of other packages or components on which it is dependent.

The RT Model includes the concurrency introduced by Ada tasks: The <<Task>> components model the Ada tasks. Each task component instance has an aggregated Scheduling_Server, which is associated with the processor where the component instance is allocated. Synchronization between tasks is only allowed inside the operations stereotyped as <<Entry>>. The model implicitly handles the overhead due to the context switching between tasks.

The RT model includes the contention in the access to protected objects: A protected MAST component models the real-time behavior of an Ada protected object. It implicitly models the mutual exclusion in the execution of the operations declared in its interface, the evaluation of the guarding conditions of its entries, the priority changes implied by the execution of its operations under the priority ceiling locking policy, and also the possible delay while waiting for the guard to become true. Even though the methodology that we propose is not able to model all the possible synchronization schemes that can be coded using protected entries with guarding conditions in Ada, it does allow to describe the usual synchronization patterns that are used in real-time applications. Therefore, protected object-based synchronization mechanisms like handling of hardware interrupts, periodic and asynchronous task activation, waiting for multiple events, or message queues, can be modeled in an accurate and quantitative way.

The RT model includes the real-time communication between Ada distributed partitions: The model supports in an implicit and automated way the local and remote access to the APC (Asynchronous Procedure Call) and RPC (Remote Procedure Call) procedures of a Remote Call Interface (RCI), as described in Annex E of the Ada standard. The declaration of an RCI includes the necessary information for the marshalling of messages, their transmission through the network, their management by the local and remote dispatchers and the unmarshalling of messages to be able to be modeled and included automatically by the tools.

5   An Example: Teleoperated Machine Tool

The Teleoperated Machine Tool (TMT) example shows how to model and analyze a real-time distributed system with the presented methodology. The system platform is composed of two processors interconnected through a CAN bus. The first processor is a teleoperation station (Station); it hosts a GUI application, with which the operator manages the tool jobs. It also has a hardware "Emergency-Stop-Button". The second processor (Controller) is an embedded processor that implements the controller of the machine tool servos and of the associated instrumentation.

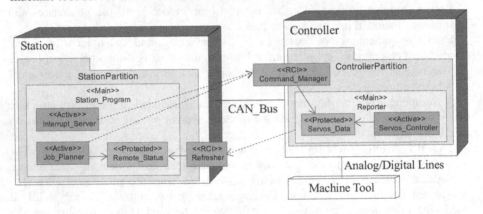

Fig. 6. TMT deployment diagram

5.1   Software Description: Logical Design

The software is organized in two Ada partitions, one for each processor. Each partition has its own Main program and offers a Remote Call Interface to the other. Each processor has a suitable implementation of the System.RPC package with guaranteed real-time features. The main components and the relations among them are shown in Figure 6.

The Controller partition's main program (The_Reporter:Reporter) acquires the status of the machine tool, with a period of 100 ms, and then notifies about it. Its active object, Servos_Controller has a periodic task that is triggered by a periodic timer every 5 ms. The RCI Command_Manager offers two procedures, one for processing the remote commands coming from the station and the other one to handle the sporadic "Halt" command raised by the emergency stop button. All the Controller components communicate among them through the protected object Servos_Data.

The Station partition has a typical GUI application plus two active and one protected objects. Job_Planner is a periodic task that monitors and manages the jobs executing in the machine tool. The Interrupt_Server task handles the hardware interrupt generated by the emergency stop button. The RCI Refresher exports a procedure that updates the remote status data sent by the controller task. Remote_Status is a protected object that provides the embodied data to the active tasks in a safe way.

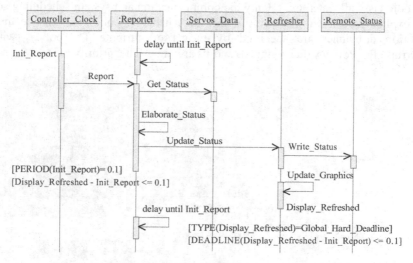

Fig. 7. Sequence diagram of the Report_Process transaction

In this example we model and analyze the normal operating state of the system, which is named as the Teleoperated_Control real-time situation. It contains four transactions with hard real-time requirements. They are all triggered by external or timed events:

- The Control_Servos_Process transaction executes the Control_Servos procedure with a period and a deadline of 5 ms.
- The Report_Process transaction transfers the hardware status data, in order to refresh the display and remote status data, with a period and deadline of 100 ms.
- The Drive_Job_Process transaction is activated each second, and its purpose is to analyze the job status and send the proper commands to the machine tool.
- The Do_Halt_Process transaction is activated by the emergency stop button. It is sporadic and has a minimum interarrival time of 5 s, and a deadline of 5 ms.

Figure 7 shows the functional description of the Report_Process transaction, using a sequence diagram.

5.2   UML Real-Time View of the TMT

The three sections of the UML real-time view will be described next.

5.2.1   TMT Platform Model

It describes the processing capacity of the three processing resources of the system: the Station and the Controller processors, and the CAN Bus network.

Figure 8 shows the platform model and a close up on the Controller partition and the CAN_Bus network. The processing capacity of the processor and all the attributes of its platform are modeled by the RT_Ada_Node MAST_Controller component. It is an embedded processor that executes the controller partition on top of a minimal real-time kernel. Controller has a periodic ticker timer, which is used for timing the periodic tasks allocated on it. Only the communication and system scheduling servers are explicitly declared. The priority and the scheduling policy assigned to the RCI partition dispatcher are specified by means of attribute The_policy (with an Interrupt_FP_Policy value assigned) and its argument The_priority (30).

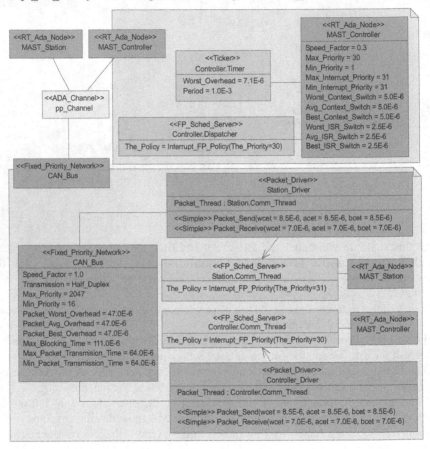

Fig. 8. Partial description of the TMT platform model

The specific values of the Controller processor parameters are:

Max_Priority= 30 Min_Priority= 1	Range of priorities allowed by the Ada compiler and MaRTE OS.
Max_Interrupt_Priority= 31 Min_Interrupt_Priority=31	Range of priorities allowed for hardware-interrupt handlers.
Worst_Context_Switch=5.0E-6 Avg_Context_Switch=5.0E-6 Best_Context_Switch=5.0E-6	Estimated context switch times between the threads of the application.

Worst_ISR_Switch= 2.5E-6 Avg_ISR_Switch= 2.5E-6 Best_ISR_Switch= 2.5 E-6	Estimated context switch times between a thread and an interrupt service routine and viceversa.
Speed_Factor= 0.3	The Controller processor has 30% of the processing capacity of the reference processor.

The CAN_Bus network is a packet-oriented half-duplex communication channel. Each packet has a frame header with 47 bits and a data field with 1 to 8 bytes. The bus transfer rate is lower than or equal to 1 Mbit/s. The packet transfer is prioritized, so a packet is never transferred if its priority is lower than the priority of any other packet that is waiting for being transferred. The real-time model of the CAN bus is described by means of the Fixed_Priority_Network component and the Packet_Drivers that run on the processors where the partitions that access the network are deployed.

The MAST CAN_Bus component has a Fixed_Priority_Network stereotype and it describes the transfer capacity of the channel. The attributes of this object that characterize its real-time behavior are:

Max_Priority= 2047 Min_Priority= 16	Priority range allowed for the messages on the CAN bus.
Packet_Worst_Overhead=47.0E-6 Packet_Avg_Overhead=47.0E-6 Packet_Best_Overhead=47.0E-6	This is the overhead due to the non-data bits of the standard CAN Bus Message Frame format. Non-data bits represent 47 bits per Data Frame (i.e., per packet).
Transmission= Half_Duplex	The transmission mode of the CAN bus is half-duplex.
Max_Blocking= 111.0E-6	The longest network's blocking time due to a packet transfer of maximum length.
Max_Packet_Transmission_Time= 6.4E-5 Min_Packet_Transmission_Time= 6.4E-5	Maximum and minimum times required for the transmission of the data bit field of a single packet frame (8 bytes/packet).
Speed_Factor= 1.0	The transmission time values refer to an implementation of the ISO 11898 standard for CAN operating at 1 Mbit/s.

5.2.2 Real-Time Model of the Logical Components

The RT Logical Model describes the timing behavior of all the logical modules that affect the real-time response of the system. As an example, Figure 9 shows the modeling elements that describe the temporal behavior of the MAST_Reporter class, which is the main program of the Controller partition. MAST_Reporter is an example of a <<Main>> component used both as a container and also as a periodic task. Its inner objects, The_Data and The_Controller, are declared as attributes of their corresponding types. Other attributes are the scheduling policy and the priority. For example the description of the composite operation Report is formulated in the aggregated activity diagram and follows the syntax proposed in [9]. The arguments of its simple operation Elaborate_Report, give value to the worst, average, and best case execution times expected for the operation. Arguments for the operations in the declaration of protected object The_Data (MAST_Servos_Data) and task The_Controller (MAST_Servos_Controller) are omitted for the sake of clarity. Notice that The_rc argument of Report is used in the invocation of the APC procedure Update_Status of the Refresher RCI, which in turn is defined inside MAST_Reporter as the Remote_Refresher referencing attribute.

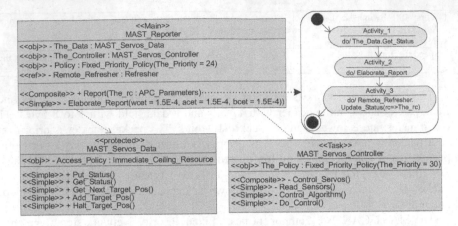

Fig. 9. TMT logical components model: MAST_Reporter description

5.2.3   Model of the Real-Time Situations

The real-time situation to analyze is formulated by means of the four mentioned transactions (Control_Servos_Process, Report_Process, Drive_Job_Process, and Do_Halt_Process). Figure 10 shows the model of the Report_Process transaction, whose functional behavior has been described by the sequence diagram in Figure 7. This real-time situation requires the instantiation of four components: The_Reporter, The_Command_Manager, The_Refresher, and The_Station_Program. In Figure 17 The_Reporter is an instance of the MAST_Reporter component and is hosted in the MAST_Controller processor.

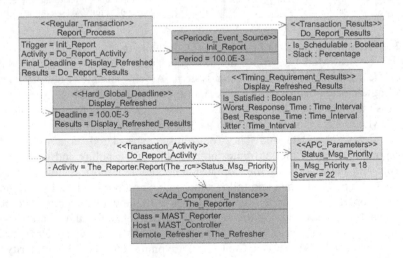

Fig. 10. Transaction Report_Process

The transaction is declared by means of a class diagram that is an instance of Regular_Transaction. Its Trigger attribute is set to the external event Init_Report, and the Final_Deadline attribute is set to the Display_Refreshed timing requirement. The external event source Init_Report is an instance of the Periodic_Event_Source class and its attribute value indicates that it has a period of 100 ms. The timing requirement Display_Refreshed is an instance of the concrete class Hard_Global_Deadline and its deadline attribute is also 100 ms. This means that the state Display_Refreshed must be reached before 100 ms after the Trigger event (Init_Report). The transaction activity is the Report operation of the component object The_Reporter. The detailed sequence of activities that constitute the transaction is obtained by recursively invoking all the operation models declared in the logical model, with the concrete values of their parameters assigned. The actions in the activities invoke the operations and the swim lanes represent the scheduling servers (i.e., the threads) in which they execute.

5.3   Real-Time Analysis and Scheduling Design of the System

The TMT example has been analyzed using the MAST set of tools [8], which let us calculate the blocking times, ceilings for PCP_Resources, optimum priority assignment, transaction slack, and system slack. We have chosen the Offset-Based Analysis method, which is the least pessimistic[10]. Table 1 shows the most relevant results obtained from the schedulability analysis tools. In this table, we have compared the worst-case response times of each of the four triggering events of the RT situation with their associated deadlines. The priorities assigned to the tasks were calculated with the HOPA algorithm integrated in MAST.

Table 1. Analysis results for the four transactions in the real-time situation

Transaction/Event	Slack	Worst response	Deadline
Control_Servos_Process	19.53%		
End_Control_Servos		3.833ms	5 ms
Report_Process	254.69%		
Display_Refreshed		34.156ms	100 ms
Drive_Job_Process	28.13%		
Command_Programmed		177.528ms	1000 ms
Do_Halt_Process	25.00%		
Halted		4.553ms	5 ms

Although the overall schedulability is interesting information, it does not tell the designer whether the system is barely schedulable, or it has margin enough for changes. In order to get a better estimation of how close the system is from being schedulable (or not schedulable), the MAST toolset is capable of providing the transaction and system slacks. These are the percentages by which the execution times of the operations in a transaction can be increased yet keeping the system schedulable or decreased if necessary. Table 1 also shows the transaction slacks obtained for the example. We can see that the execution time of every activity of the Report_Process transaction can be increased by 254.69% and the system will still be schedulable. From a global point of view, the execution time of all the operations of the system could be increased by 2.34%, since that is the system slack calculated by MAST.

6   Conclusion

In this work we have presented a methodology for modeling the real-time behavior of Ada applications, with the appropriate level of detail to guarantee that the schedulability analysis, the optimum priority assignment, and the slack calculations using the generated model, can be applied.

Its main feature is that it allows modeling complex Ada components (packages, tagged types, protected objects, tasks, etc.), independently of the application in which they are used, which in turn may serve as the basis for the support of a design methodology for real-time systems based on Ada reusable components.

The modeling power of the proposed methodology is capable of covering most of the software patterns and programming building blocks that are widely used in the development of the majority of analyzable Ada real-time applications. Of course non real-time applications may use complex synchronization structures that cannot be modeled with the proposed approach, since they don't have a predictable timing behavior. But these structures are not commonly used in the real-time application environment.

The methodology presented in this paper is currently being implemented in the UML-MAST toolset. The description and implementation of this toolset can be found at: `http://mast.unican.es`

References

[1] S. Tucker Taft, and R.A. Duff (Eds.) "Ada 95 Reference Manual. Language and Standard Libraries". International Standard ISO/IEC 8652:1995(E), in LNCS 1246, Springer, 1997.

[2] L. Pautet and S. Tardieu, "Inside the Distributed Systems Annex", Intl. Conf. on Reliable Software Technologies, Ada-Europe'98, Uppsala, Sweden, in LNCS 1411, Springer, pp. 65-77, June 1998.

[3] L. Pautet and S. Tardieu: "GLADE: a Framework for Building Large Object-Oriented Real-Time Distributed Systems. Proc. of the 3rd IEEE". Intl. Symposium on Object-Oriented Real-Time Distributed Computing, (ISORC'00) Newport Beach, USA, March 2000.

[4] Luís Miguel Pinho, "Distributed and Real-Time: Session summary", 10th.Intl. Real-Time Ada Workshop, IRTAW'01, Ávila,Spain, in Ada Letters, Vol. XXI, Number 1, March 2001.

[5] Ada-Core Technologies, Ada 95 GNAT Pro, http:// www.gnat.com/

[6] J.J. Gutiérrez García, and M. González Harbour: "Prioritizing Remote Procedure Calls in Ada Distributed Systems", ACM Ada Letters, XIX, 2, pp. 67-72, June 1999.

[7] J.J. Gutiérrez García, and M. González Harbour: "Towards a Real-Time Distributed Systems Annex in Ada", ACM Ada Letters, XXI, 1, pp. 62-66, March 2001.

[8] M. González Harbour, J.J. Gutiérrez, J.C. Palencia and J.M. Drake: "MAST: Modeling and Analysis Suite for Real-Time Applications" Proceedings of the Euromicro Conference on Real-Time Systems, Delft, The Netherlands, June 2001.

[9] J.L. Medina, M. González Harbour, and J.M. Drake: "MAST Real-Time View: A Graphic UML Tool for Modeling Object-Oriented Real-Time Systems" RTSS'01, London, December, 2001

[10] J.C. Palencia, and M. González Harbour, "Exploiting Precedence Relations in the Schedulability Analysis of Distributed Real-Time Systems". Proceedings of the 20th IEEE Real-Time Systems Symposium, 1999.

Transparent Environment for Replicated Ravenscar Applications

Luís Miguel Pinho[1], Francisco Vasques[2]

[1] Department of Computer Engineering, ISEP, Polytechnic Institute of Porto,
Rua Dr. António Bernardino Almeida, 431, 4200-072 Porto, Portugal
lpinho@dei.isep.ipp.pt
[2] Department of Mechanical Engineering, FEUP, University of Porto,
Rua Dr. Roberto Frias, 4200-465 Porto, Portugal
vasques@fe.up.pt

Abstract. This paper proposes an environment intended for the development of fault-tolerant real-time Ada 95 applications conforming to the Ravenscar profile. This environment is based on the transparent replication of application components, and it provides a set of generic task interaction objects, which are used as the basic building blocks of the supported applications. These objects provide the usual task interaction mechanisms used in hard real-time applications, and allow applications to be developed without considering replication and distribution issues.

1   Introduction

The problem of supporting reliable real-time Distributed Computer-Controlled Systems (DCCS) is reasonably well understood, when considering synchronous and predictable environments. However, the use of Commercial Off-The-Shelf (COTS) components and pre-emptive multitasking applications introduce additional problems. Using COTS components as the systems' building blocks provides a cost-effective solution, and at the same time allows for an easy upgrade and maintenance of the system. However, the use of COTS implies that specialised hardware can not be used to guarantee the reliability requirements. As COTS hardware and software do not usually provide the confidence level required by reliable real-time applications, reliability requirements must be guaranteed by a software-based fault-tolerance approach.

Traditionally, the development of computer control applications has been based on a non-preemptive computational model, where a scheduling table comprising the sequence of task executions is determined off-line (the cyclic-executive model). Therefore, the programming model for the development of these applications is simple, not requiring complex task interaction mechanisms, because it fixes the sequence of tasks' executions. On the other hand, by using the pre-emptive fixed priority model of computation, the system flexibility is increased, and the design effort is decreased. However, mechanisms for task interaction become more complex, since there is no fixed pattern for the sequence of tasks' executions.

J. Blieberger and A. Strohmeier (Eds.): Ada-Europe 2002, LNCS 2361, pp. 297-308, 2002.
© Springer-Verlag Berlin Heidelberg 2002

Therefore, it is important to provide a generic and transparent programming model for the development of pre-emptive computer control applications. The goal is to decrease the complexity of application development, by precluding the need for the simultaneous consideration of system requirements and interaction between multitasking and replication/distribution. A set of generic mechanisms must be provided, which can be parameterised with both application-specific data and application-specific configuration (distribution and replication). These mechanisms will be the basic building blocks of distributed/replicated real-time applications, providing a higher level of abstraction to developers and maximising the capability to reuse components and mechanisms in different applications.

The Ada Ravenscar profile [1] allows multitasking pre-emptive applications to be employed for the development of fault-tolerant real-time systems, whilst providing efficient and deterministic applications. Nevertheless, it is considered that further studies are necessary for its use in replicated and distributed systems [2]. The interaction between multitasking pre-emptive software and replication introduces new problems that must be considered, particularly for the case of a transparent and generic approach.

Furthermore, the restrictions of the Ravenscar profile complicate the implementation of an efficient support for replicated or distributed programming, which may result on an increased application complexity [3]. Therefore, any environment for replication support using the Ravenscar profile must be simple to implement and use, but at the same time must provide the capabilities required by the fault-tolerant real-time applications.

This paper proposes an environment to transparently support replicated and distributed Ravenscar applications. The following section presents work related to the support to fault-tolerant real-time applications. Afterwards, Section 3 presents the system model considered for the environment. Section 4 presents the framework for replication management intended for the support to the system applications, while the proposed set of task interaction objects is presented in Section 5.

2   Related Work

Fundamental for a COTS-based fault-tolerant architecture is the issue of software-based fault tolerance. Since there is no specialised hardware with self-checking properties, it is up to the software to manage replication and fault tolerance. Three main replication approaches are addressed in the literature: active replication, primary-backup (passive) replication and semi-active replication [4]. When fail-uncontrolled (arbitrary failures) components are considered, incorrect service delivery can only be detected by active replication, because it is required that all replicas output some value, in order to perform some form of voting [4]. The use of COTS components generally implies fail-uncontrolled replicas, so it becomes necessary to use active replication techniques.

As real-time applications are based on time-dependent mechanisms, the different processing speed in replicated nodes can cause different task interleaving. Consequently, different replicas (even if correct) can process the same inputs in different order, providing inconsistent results if inputs are non-commutative, thus presenting a non-deterministic behaviour.

Determinism can be achieved by forbidding the applications to use non-deterministic timing mechanisms. As a consequence, the use of multitasking would not be possible, since task synchronisation and communication mechanisms inherently lead to timing non-determinism. This is the approach taken by MARS [5] and Delta-4 [4] architectures. The former by using a static time-driven scheduling that guarantees the same execution behaviour in every replica. The latter by restricting replicas to behave as state-machines [6] when active replication is used.

Guaranteeing that replicas take the same scheduling decisions by performing an agreement in every scheduling decision, allows for the use of non-deterministic mechanisms. This imposes the modification of the underlying scheduling mechanisms, leading to a huge overhead in the system since agreement decisions must be made at every dispatching point. This is the approach followed by previous systems, such as SIFT [7] or MAFT [8], both architectures for fault-tolerant real–time systems with restricted tasking models. However, the former incurred overheads up to 80% [9], while the latter was supported by dedicated replication management hardware [8].

The use of the timed messages concept [10] allows a restricted model of multitasking to be used, while at the same time minimises the need for agreement mechanisms. This approach is based on preventing replicated tasks from using different inputs, by delaying the use of a message until it can be proven (using global knowledge) that such message is available to all replicas.

This is the approach used in the GUARDS architecture [11] in order to guarantee the deterministic behaviour of replicated real-time transactions. However, in the GUARDS approach this mechanism is explicitly used in the application design and implementation, thus forcing system developers to simultaneously deal with both system requirements and replication issues.

3   System Model

A distributed system is considered, where, to ensure the desired level of reliability to the supported hard real-time applications, specific components of these applications may be replicated. The system nodes provide a framework to support distributed reliable hard real-time applications. Since real-time guarantees must be provided, applications have guaranteed execution resources, including processing power, memory and communication infrastructure. A multitasking environment is provided to support the real-time applications, with services for task communication and synchronisation (including replication and distribution support). Applications' timing requirements are guaranteed through the use of current off-line schedulability analysis techniques (*e.g.*, the well-known Response Time Analysis [12]).

To ensure the desired level of fault tolerance to the supported real-time applications, specific components of these applications may be replicated. This replication model supports the active replication of software (Fig. 1) with dissimilar replicated task sets in each node. The goal is to tolerate faults in the COTS components underlying the application. In order to tolerate common mode faults in the system, COTS components diversity is also considered (operating system and hardware platform).

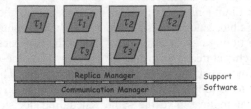

Fig. 1. Replicated hard real-time application

However, using diverse operating systems has to be carefully considered, since in order to guarantee a transparent approach, the programming environment in each node must be the same. This can be achieved by using operating systems with a standard programming interface or by using a programming language that abstracts from the operating system details. Using the Ada language in the replicated hard real-time applications provides the same programming model in all nodes, whilst diversity can be provided by using different compilers and runtimes [13].

In order to allow the use of the response time analysis [12], each task is released only by one invocation event, but can be released an unbounded number of times. A periodic task is released by the runtime (temporal invocation), while a sporadic task can be released either by another task or by the environment. After being released, a task cannot suspend itself or be blocked while accessing remote data (remote blocking).

3.1   Replication Model

As there is the goal of fault tolerance through replication, it is important to define the replication unit. Therefore, the notion of *component* is introduced. Applications are divided in components, each one being a set of tasks and resources that interact to perform a common job. The component can include tasks and resources from several nodes, or it can be located in just one node. In each node, several components may coexist. This component is just a configuration abstraction, which is used to structure replication units, and to allow system configuration.

The component is the unit of replication, therefore a component is one unit of fault-containment. Faults in one task may cause the failure of one component. However, if a component fails, by producing an incorrect value (or not producing any value), the group of replicated components will not fail since the output consolidation will mask the failed component. This means that, in the model of replication, the internal outputs of tasks (task interaction within a component) do not need to be agreed. The output consolidation is only needed when the result is made available to other components or to the controlled system. On the other hand, a more severe fault in a component can spread to the other parts of the application in the same node, since there is no separate memory spaces inside the application. In such case, other application components in the node may also fail, but component replication will mask such failure.

By creating components, it is possible to define the replication degree of specific parts of the real-time application, according to the reliability of its components. Furthermore, error detection can be provided in an earlier stage of the processing. However, by replicating components, efficiency decreases due to the increase of the number of tasks and exchanged messages. Hence, it is possible to trade failure assumption coverage for efficiency and vice-versa. Efficiency should not be regarded as *the* goal for a fault-tolerant hard real-time system, but it can be increased by decreasing the redundancy degree.

Although the goal is to transparently manage distribution and replication, it is considered that a completely transparent use of the replication/distribution mechanisms may introduce unnecessary overheads. Therefore, during application development the use of replication or distribution is not considered (transparent approach). Later, in a configuration phase, the system developer configures the application replication and allocates the tasks in the distributed system.

The hindrance of this approach is that, as the application is not aware of the possible distribution and replication, complex applications could be built relying heavily on task interaction. This would cause a more inefficient implementation. However, the model for tasks, where task interaction is minimised, precludes such complex applications. Tasks are designed as small processing units, which, in each invocation, read inputs, carry out the processing, and output the results. The goal is to minimise task interaction, in order to improve the system's efficiency.

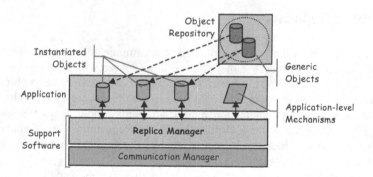

Fig. 2. Framework structure

4   Replication Management Framework

Within the presented approach, replication management is provided by means of a repository of task interaction objects (Fig. 2). These objects provide a transparent interface, by which application tasks are not aware of replication and distribution issues.

The Object Repository is used during the design and configuration phases, and provides a set of generic objects with different capabilities for the interaction between tasks. These generic objects are instantiated with the appropriate data types and incorporated into the application. They are responsible for hiding from the application the details of the lower-level calls to the support software. This allows applications to focus on the requirements of the controlled system rather than on the distribution/replication mechanisms.

This means that during the application development there is no consideration on how the application will be replicated or distributed. These issues are only considered in a later configuration phase, by replacing the task interaction objects used in the application by their equivalent that provide the required support.

Therefore, during the application configuration phase, transparency is only considered at the mechanisms level. Basically, this means that the application code is not constrained by the low-level details of replication and distribution mechanisms. On the other hand, by performing object replacement during configuration, the full behaviour of application (considering replication and distribution) is controlled and predictable. This allows the off-line determination of the real-time and fault tolerance properties of applications, which is of paramount importance in computer control systems.

The Replica Manager layer is responsible for performing the main processing of the replication mechanisms, in order to simplify the upgrade of the Object Repository generic objects. The Communication Manager [14] layer provides the required reliable communication protocols (atomic multicast and replicated data consolidation), whilst guaranteeing the predictability of message transfers [15].

5   Object Repository

In the system, application tasks are allowed to communicate with each other using the available interaction objects, either *Shared Data* objects or *Release Event* objects (which can also carry data). *Shared Data* objects are used for asynchronous data communication between tasks, while *Release Event* objects are used for the release of sporadic tasks. This task interaction model, although simple, maps the usual model found in hard real-time systems. Within the Object Repository a set of generic objects (Fig. 3) is provided, which can be instantiated by the application with the appropriate application-related data types.

Although multiple objects are available, with different capabilities and goals, during application development only three different object types are available in the repository: *Shared Data*, *Release Event* and *Release Event with Data* objects, without any distribution or replication capabilities, since at this stage the system is not yet configured.

These objects have a well-defined interface. Tasks may *write* and *read* a *Shared Data* object and *wait* in or *release* a *Release Event* object. Note that *Release Event* objects are to be used in a one-way communication, thus a task can only have one of two different roles (*wait* or *release*). *Release Event* and *Release Event with Data* objects have a similar interface; the only difference is that with the latter it is also possible to transfer data.

```
Shared Data Object

1:   when write(data):
2:       Obj_Data := data

3:   when read:
4:       return Obj_Data

Release Event Object

5:   when wait:
6:       Task_Suspend

7:   when release:
8:       Suspended_Task_Resume

Release Event with Data Object

9:   when wait:
10:      Task_Suspend
11:      return Obj_Data

12: when release(data):
13:      Obj_Data := data
14:      Suspended_Task_Resume
```

Fig. 3. Specification of development available objects

At system configuration time, the application is distributed over the nodes of the system and some of its components are also replicated. Thus, some (or all) of the used objects must be replaced by similar ones with extra capabilities. That is, with distribution and/or replication capabilities. To support such configuration, the Object Repository makes available further objects supporting either replication, or distribution or both. Furthermore different objects are also provided if the interacting tasks are within the same component, or belong to different groups of replicated components. The interested reader may refer to [16], where the specification of all these different repository objects is presented.

The interaction between tasks belonging to the same component does not require consolidation between replicas of the component. However, it may require the use of distributed mechanisms (if the component is spread through several nodes) or the use of timed messages to guarantee deterministic execution (if the component is replicated).

Remote blocking is avoided by preventing tasks from reading remote data. Hence, when sharing data between tasks configured to reside in different nodes, the *Shared Data* object must be replicated in these nodes. It is important to guarantee that tasks in different nodes must have the same consistent view of the data. This is accomplished by multicasting all data changes to all replicas. This multicasting must guarantee that all replicas receive the same set of data change requests in the same order, thus atomic multicasts must be used.

5.1   Object Implementation

In the Object Repository, all objects are implemented as generic packages. The use of generic packages allows reusing the same implementation mechanisms for objects with different data types. Even objects that do not require data instantiation (as the simple *Release Event*) are implemented as generics, since they require objects to be instantiated with extra information (for instance object identifier and ceiling priority). The use of generic packages allows parameterisation at compile time, providing significant reuse capabilities.

```
generic
    Id    : Framework_Types.Obj_Id_Type;
    Prio  : System.Priority;
package Object_Repository.Release_Event is

    type Release_Obj is private;
    function Request_Release_Obj return Release_Obj;

    procedure Wait     (Obj: Release_Obj);      -- potentially
                                                -- blocking

    procedure Release (Obj: Release_Obj);

private
     -- private interface
end Object_Repository.Release_Event;
```

Fig. 4. *Release_Event* object public interface

```
generic
    Id               : Framework_Types.Obj_Id_Type;
    Prio             : System.Priority;
    N_Replicas       : Framework_Types.Rep_Id_Type;
    with procedure    Decide (
        Instant_Values  : Framework_Types.Instant_Array_Type;
        Valid_Instants  : Framework_Types.Boolean_Array_Type;
        Rejected_Inst: out Framework_Types.Boolean_Array_Type;
        Release_Instant : out Ada.Real_Time.Time;
        Release_Ok      : out Boolean);
package Object_Repository.Inter_Group.Release_Event is

    type Release_Obj is private;
    function Request_Release_Obj return Release_Obj;

    procedure Wait     (Obj: Release_Obj);      -- potentially
                                                -- blocking

    procedure Release (Obj: Release_Obj);

private
     -- private interface
end Object_Repository.Inter_Group.Release_Event;
```

Fig. 5. *Inter_Group Release_Event* object public interface

Since the goal of transparency is to allow the simple objects to be replaced by objects with distribution and replication capabilities, the public interface for similar interaction objects is the same. For instance, Fig. 4 and 5 present the public interface for the simple *Release Event* object and for its counterpart for interaction between different groups of replicated components (the *Inter Group Release Event* object).

Although the differences between the generic parameters (the *Inter Group* object requires extra parameters: the number of proposing replicas and the procedure to be used for the decision on the release instant), the interface to the application code is the same. This approach is used in all similar objects, allowing the configuration phase to modify just the objects' declaration, not changing the application tasks' code.

Internally, the *Repository* objects are implemented as Ada protected objects, in order to provide mutual exclusion for the access to the object state and, for the case of *Release* objects, to allow application tasks to be blocked by a protected entry. As an example, Fig. 6 presents the specification of the protected type used for the *Inter Group Release Event* object.

```
generic
   -- ...
package Object_Repository.Inter_Group.Release_Event is

   type Release_Obj is private;
   -- ...
private
   protected type Release_Receive_Type (
                        Prio: System.Priority;
                        Id: FT.Obj_Id_Type) is
      pragma Priority(Prio);
      entry Wait;
      procedure Release;
      function Get_Id return FT.Obj_Id_Type;
   private
      Obj_Id: FT.Obj_Id_Type := Id;
      Released: Boolean := False;
   end Release_Receive_Type;

   type Release_Obj is access all Release_Receive_Type;

end Object_Repository.Inter_Group.Release_Event;
```

Fig. 6. Example of object private implementation

5.2   Object Configuration

In the configuration phase the simple interaction objects used during design are replaced with the appropriate objects, providing replication and distribution support. In order to demonstrate the configuration of an application through the use of different interaction objects, Fig. 7 presents an example of an implementation of some *Device_Data* type.

```
package Device_Data_Package is

   type Device_Data is ...;
   type Device_Data_Array is
   array (FT.Rep_Id_Type Range <>) of Device_Data;

   Device_Data_Replicas: FT.Rep_Id_Type := ...;
   Device_Obj_Id: FT.Obj_Id_Type := ...;
   Device_Obj_Prio: System.Priority := ...;

   procedure Device_Data_Decide (
           Values            : Device_Data_Array;
           Value_Instants    : FT.Instant_Array_Type;
           Valid_Values      : FT.Boolean_Array_Type;
           Rejected_Values   : out FT.Boolean_Array_Type;
           Release_Value     : out Device_Data;
           Release_Instant   : out A_RT.Time;
        Release_Ok           : out Boolean);

   end Device_Data_Package;
```

Fig. 7. Data handling package

The package *Device_Data_Package* specifies the type of the data and an anonymous array type. It also provides some configuration information, such as the number of replicas of the releasing group, the identifier of the object and the objects' ceiling priority. Finally, a *Decide* procedure (to be executed by a replica consolidation protocol) is also provided.

Fig. 8 and 9 present the use of this *Device_Data_Package*, respectively before and after the configuration phase. The only difference is in the instantiation of the generic package, where the *Release Event With Data* generic package only requires the identifier, priority and data type parameters. After configuration, the *Inter-Group Release Event With Data* generic package also requires the number of replicas, the data type array and the *Decide* procedure.

```
package body Example_Application_Tasks is

     package DDP renames Device_Data_Package;

     package Device_Event_Data_P is
          new Object_Repository.Release_Event_With_Data (
                         Id          => DDP.Device_Obj_Id,
                         Prio        => DDP.Device_Obj_Prio,
                         Data_Type   => DDP.Device_Data );

     Device_Event_Obj: Device_Event_Data_P.Data_Release_Obj :=
              Device_Event_Data_P.Request_Data_Release_Obj;
     -- Other Objects and Application Tasks

   end Example_Application_Tasks;
```

Fig. 8. Use of data handling package (before configuration)

```
package body Example_Application_Tasks is

    package DDP renames Device_Data_Package;

    package Device_Event_Data_P is new
        Object_Repository.Inter_Group.Release_Event_With_Data(
            Id                 => DDP.Device_Obj_Id,
            Prio               => DDP.Device_Obj_Prio,
            N_Replicas         => DDP.Device_Data_Replicas,
            Data_Type          => DDP.Device_Data,
            Data_Array_Type    => DDP.Device_Data_Array,
            Decide             => DDP.Device_Data_Decide);

    Device_Event_Obj: Device_Event_Data_P.Data_Release_Obj :=
            Device_Event_Data_P.Request_Data_Release_Obj;
    -- Other Objects and Application Tasks

end Example_Application_Tasks;
```

Fig. 9. Use of data handling package (after configuration)

6 Conclusions

The Ravenscar profile allows the use of the pre-emptive fixed priority computational model in application areas where the cyclic executive model has traditionally been the preferred approach. Nevertheless, it is also considered that further studies are still necessary for its use to support replicated and distributed systems. The interaction between multitasking software and replication introduces new problems, particularly for the case of a transparent and generic approach.

This paper presents an abstraction for application replication, intended to support the transparent replication of Ravenscar applications. This approach allows applications to be configured only after being developed, thus allowing applications to be developed without considering replication and distribution issues. A transparent support to the applications is provided through a set of generic task interaction objects, which hide from applications the low level details of replication and distribution.

Acknowledgements

The authors would like to thank Andy Wellings for his valuable support in the specification of the replication framework and to the anonymous reviewers for their helpful comments and suggestions. This work was partially supported by FCT (project TERRA POSI/2001/38932).

References

1. Burns, A. (1997). Session Summary: Tasking Profiles. In *Proc. of the 8th International Real-Time Ada Workshop*, Ravenscar, England, April 1997. Ada Letters, XVII(5):5-7, ACM Press.

2. Wellings, A. (2000). Session Summary: Status and Future of the Ravenscar Profile. In Proc. of the 10th International Real-Time Ada Workshop, Avila, Spain, September 2000. Ada Letters, XXI(1):4-8, ACM Press.

3. Audsley, A. and Wellings, A. (2000). Issues with using Ravenscar and the Ada Distributed Systems Annex for High-Integrity Systems. In Proc. of the 10th International Real-Time Ada Workshop, Avila, Spain, September 2000. Ada Letters, XXI(1):33-39, ACM Press.

4. Powell, D. (Ed.). (1991). Delta-4 - A Generic Architecture for Dependable Distributed Computing. ESPRIT Research Reports. Springer Verlag.

5. Kopetz, H., Damm, A., Koza, C., Mulazzani, M., Schwabl, W., Senft, C., and Zainlinger, R. (1989). Distributed Fault-Tolerant Real-Time Systems: The Mars Approach. In IEEE Micro, 9(1):25–41.

6. Schneider, F. (1990). Implementing Fault-Tolerant Services Using the State Machine Approach: A Tutorial. In ACM Computing Surveys, 22(4):299-319.

7. Melliar-Smith, P. M., and Schwartz, R. L. (1982). Formal Specification and Mechanical Verification of SIFT: a Fault–Tolerance Flight Control System. In IEEE Transactions on Computers, 31(7):616-630.

8. Keickhafer, R. M., Walter, C. J., Finn, A. M., and Thambidurai, P. M. (1988). The MAFT Architecture for Distributed Fault Tolerance. In IEEE Transactions on Computers, 37 (4):398-404.

9. Pradhan, D. K. (1996). Fault–Tolerant Computer System Design. Prentice Hall.

10. Poledna, S., Burns, A., Wellings, A., and Barret, P. (2000). Replica Determinism and Flexible Scheduling in Hard Real-Time Dependable Systems. In IEEE Transactions on Computers, 49(2):100-111.

11. Powell, D. (Ed.). (2001). A Generic Fault-Tolerant Architecture for Real-Time Dependable Systems. Kluwer Academic Publishers.

12. Audsley, A., Burns, A., Richardson, M., Tindell, K., and Wellings, A. (1993). Applying new scheduling theory to static priority pre-emptive scheduling. In Software Engineering Journal, 8(5):285-292.

13. Yeh, Y. (1995). Dependability of the 777 Primary Flight Control System. In Proc. Dependable Computing for Critical Applications 5, USA, pp. 1-13.

14. Pinho, L. and Vasques F. (2001a). Reliable Communication in Distributed Computer-Controlled Systems. In Proc. of Ada-Europe 2001. Leuven, Belgium, May 2001, Lecture Notes on Computer Science 2043, Springer, pp. 136-147.

15. Pinho, L. and Vasques, F. (2001b). Timing Analysis of Reliable Real-Time Communication in CAN Networks. In Proc. of the 13th Euromicro Conference on Real-Time Systems, Delft, The Netherlands, June 2001, pp. 103-112.

16. Pinho, L. M. (2001). A Framework for the Transparent Replication of Real-Time Applications. PhD Thesis. School of Engineering of the University of Porto. Available at http://www.hurray.isep.ipp.pt

Concurrency Control in *Transactional Drago*[*]

Marta Patiño-Martínez[1], Ricardo Jiménez-Peris[1], Jörg Kienzle[2], and
Sergio Arévalo[3]

[1] Technical University of Madrid (UPM), Facultad de Informática,
E-28660 Boadilla del Monte, Madrid, Spain,
{rjimenez, mpatino}@fi.upm.es
[2] Swiss Federal Institute of Technology in Lausanne, Department of Computer
Science, Lausanne, Switzerland,
Joerg.Kienzle@epfl.ch
[3] Universidad Rey Juan Carlos, Escuela de Ciencias Experimentales, Móstoles,
Madrid, Spain,
s.arevalo@escet.urjc.es

Abstract. The granularity of concurrency control has a big impact on
the performance of transactional systems. Concurrency control granularity and data granularity (data size) are usually the same. The effect
of this coupling is that if a coarse granularity is used, the overhead of
data access (number of disk accesses) is reduced, but also the degree
of concurrency. On the other hand, if a fine granularity is chosen to
achieve a higher degree of concurrency (there are less conflicts), the cost
of data access is increased (each data item is accessed independently,
which increases the number of disk accesses). There have been some proposals where data can be dynamically clustered/unclustered to increase
either concurrency or data access depending on the application usage of
data. However, concurrency control and data granularity remain tightly
coupled. In *Transactional Drago*, a programming language for building
distributed transactional applications, concurrency control has been uncoupled from data granularity, thus allowing to increase the degree of
concurrency without degrading data access. This paper describes this
approach and its implementation in Ada 95.
Keywords: transactions, locking, distributed systems, databases.

1 Introduction

Transactions [GR93] were proposed in the context of database systems to preserve the consistency of data in the presence of failures and concurrent accesses.
Transactions are also useful as a way of organizing programs for distributed systems. Their properties simplify the development of correct programs, hiding the
complexity of potential interactions among concurrent activities and the failures
that can occur in a distributed system. Transactions provide the so-called ACID
properties, that is, atomicity, consistency, isolation and durability. A transaction

[*] This research has been partially funded by the Spanish National Research Council,
CICYT, under grants TIC98-1032-C03-01 and TIC2001-1586-C03-02

J. Blieberger and A. Strohmeier (Eds.): Ada-Europe 2002, LNCS 2361, pp. 309–320, 2002.
© Springer-Verlag Berlin Heidelberg 2002

is executed completely or its effect is as it never had been executed (atomicity). If a transaction ends successfully (it commits), its effects will remain even in the advent of failures (durability). If a transaction does not commit, it aborts. In case of an abort, atomicity guarantees that all the effects of a transaction are undone, as if it had never been executed. Consistency ensures that the application state is updated in a consistent way. The effect of executing concurrent transactions is as if they were executed sequentially in some order (serializability), that is, a transaction does not see intermediate results from other transactions (isolation).

Concurrency control techniques are used to ensure the isolation property of transactions. Read/write locking is one of the most popular concurrency control techniques. Two locks conflict if they are requested on the same data item, by two different transactions, and at least one is a write lock. A lock in the appropriate mode must be requested before a data item is accessed by a transaction. Locks are released when a transaction finishes. More concurrency can be achieved by defining locks on other operations instead of just read/write locks [BHG87].

The granularity of a data item is its relative size. The concurrency control granularity is the unit to which concurrency control (locking) is applied. In general, data granularity and lock granularity are the same. Data granularity has a big impact on the performance of a transactional system. If a data item is big (for instance, a file), concurrency decreases since the probability of conflicts is higher. That is, if two transactions write the same data item, one of them will not be able to proceed even if they access different parts of the data item. Since transactions only lock those data items they access, more concurrency can be achieved with a finer granularity (for instance, records instead of files). On the other hand, the time taken to load a data item of size N from disk is less than the time needed to load N data items of size 1. Therefore, performance decreases as more disk accesses are needed to access several data items (records) of the original data item (the file). Locks in transactional languages are requested at data item level. That means that the programmer must choose either a coarse granularity to improve data access in detriment of transaction concurrency, or a fine granularity in detriment of data access efficiency.

In this paper we present the approach adopted in *Transactional Drago* [PJA98]. *Transactional Drago* is an Ada extension for programming distributed transactional applications. *Transactional Drago* offers a locking scheme where locking and data granularity have been uncoupled. With this locking scheme the programmer first chooses the data granularity to improve data access. Then, she/he decides the locking granularity for that data item. Locking granularity can vary from the coarsest level (the whole data item) to the finest (each indivisible component of a data item). Although some transactional programming languages also allow changes in the locking granularity (see Section 6), programmers must program the concurrency control, and in some cases they also have to program the recovery mechanism needed to provide the atomicity property of transactions. In *Transactional Drago* none of these error-prone tasks needs to be done. The granularity of concurrency control is declarative, and programmers just decide where locks are applied.

The paper also describes how *Transactional Drago* is translated into OP-TIMA [KJRP01], the evolution of the Ada transactional framework *TransLib* [JPAB00]. Additionally, the OPTIMA facilities for concurrency control and the implementation of lock-based concurrency control in Ada 95 are presented.

This paper is structured as follows. First of all, we present a brief description of *Transactional Drago*. In Section 3 we present how the granularity of locks is defined. The translation of *Transactional Drago* into OPTIMA is presented in Section 4. Some details about the implementation of the concurrency control in OPTIMA are given in Section 5. Finally, we compare our work with other approaches in Section 6 and present our conclusions in Section 7.

2   *Transactional Drago*

Transactional Drago [PJA98] is an extension to Ada [Ada95] for programming distributed transactional applications. Programmers can start transactions using the **begin-end transaction** statement or *transactional block*. Transactional blocks are similar to block statements in Ada. They have a declarative section, a body and can have exception handlers. The only difference is that the statements inside the block are executed within a transaction.

All data used in transactional blocks are subject to concurrency control (in particular, locks) and are recoverable. That is, if the corresponding transaction aborts, data will be restored to the value they had before executing that transaction. Data items can be volatile or non-volatile (persistent).

A transactional block can be enclosed within another transactional block, leading to a nested transaction structure. A transaction that is nested within another transaction (parent transaction) is called a subtransaction [Mos85].

Transactional Drago implements *group transactions* [PJA01], a new transaction model. One of the novel aspects of the model is that transactions can be multithreaded, i.e., a transaction can have several threads (tasks) that run in parallel. As a result it is possible to take advantage of the multiprocessor and multiprogramming capabilities. Threads working of behalf of the same transaction can cooperate by accessing the same data, i.e., they are not isolated from each other. Since locking is only intended for *inter-transactional* concurrency (logical consistency), latches [MHL+98] are used to provide *intra-transactional* concurrency control (physical consistency) in the presence of concurrent accesses from threads of the same transaction. Latches provide short-term concurrency control (they last for a single operation) in contrast with locks that are long-term concurrency control (they are not released until the transaction finishes).

In *Transactional Drago* both concurrency control mechanisms are implicitly handled by the run-time system, hiding all the complexity from the application programmer. Programs access transactional data (atomic data) just as regular non- transactional data. Programmers do not set and free neither locks nor latches. The underlying system is in charge of ensuring the isolation and atomicity properties and the physical consistency of the data.

3   Lock Granularity

Although programmers do not explicitly request neither locks nor latches, *Transactional Drago* allows them to specify concurrency control for each data item separately, thus increasing concurrency among transactions.

Let us illustrate this mechanism with a simple example. From now on we assume all data are persistent (non-volatile). For instance, if we have the (persistent) array declaration on Fig. 1(a), in transactional languages, locks are applied to the whole array. So, if two transactions update a component of the array, no matter whether they access the same or different components, one of the transactions would be blocked until the other one finishes. By default, this is the semantics of *Transactional Drago*. However, in *Transactional Drago* the programmer can define the granularity of locks to be array components (thereby uncoupling data granularity and locking granularity). In this case two transactions updating different components can be executed concurrently. The resulting effect is just as if each component of the array were separate data items. *Transactional Drago* goes even further by allowing concurrency control to be applied at each field of the record inside the array. Therefore, two transactions can update different fields of the same component concurrently. This flexibility does not induce a penalty in data access as it does in other approaches: the array does not have to be split in smaller pieces.

```
type mytype is atomic array        type mytype is array           type mytype is array
    (Array_Index_Type) of              (Array_Index_Type) of          (Array_Index_Type) of
    record                             atomic record                  record
        a: integer;                        a: integer;                    a: atomic integer;
        b: float;                          b: float;                      b: atomic float;
    end record;                        end record;                    end record;
```

(a) array level locking   (b) record level locking   (c) Field level locking

Fig. 1. Different locking granularities

The definition of the locking granularity is declarative in *Transactional Drago*. The programmer simply specifies locking granularity just using the keyword `atomic`. This keyword is used in the data item type declaration before the type declaration where locks are applied. In the previous example, if the keyword is used at the beginning of the array definition (Fig. 1(a)), locks will apply to the whole array. Because this is the normal behavior in transactional languages, the keyword can be omitted. Locking granularity at record level for variables of the `mytype` type is defined using the keyword atomic just before the definition of each component of the array (Fig. 1(b)). Field level locking is specified using the keyword atomic before the type of each field (Fig. 1(c)).

The *Transactional Drago* compiler checks for each data item (variable) whether the locking granularity has been appropriately defined by applying the following rules:

– The atomic keyword has not been used in the type declaration. By default, locking granularity is set to the whole data item (the coarsest granularity).
– The atomic keyword is used. The keyword should be found once and only once in each path from the leaves to the root of the type tree.

A type tree is built upon the type declaration of a variable. Each node in the tree is a type. The root is the type of the variable and its children are the types this type is made of. For instance, the different trees associated with the `mytype` type are shown in Fig. 2(a). If the keyword is placed before the array or record keywords (Fig. 2(b)), it cannot be placed anywhere else. All the paths from the leafs to the root will contain the keyword exactly once. If the keyword is placed before the integer type, it must also be placed before the float type (Fig. 2(c)).

Locks and latches in *Transactional Drago* are requested implicitly by the system in the appropriate mode and automatically released when the transaction finishes. To change the granularity of locks, only the type definition must be changed, since locking in *Transactional Drago* is specified in a declarative way. There is no need to modify any application code.

Pointers are considered like any other simple type (integer, boolean...), that is, they always have read/write locks. Dynamic data also have concurrency control, which is specified in the same way than for static data.

4   *Transactional Drago* Translation

Transactional Drago can be translated into Ada 95 and invocations to either *TransLib* [JPAB00] or its evolution OPTIMA [KJRP01], two adaptable OO libraries supporting transactions. Both libraries provide user-defined commutative locking. With commutative locking [GM83] two operations conflict if they do not commute. For instance, let's consider the `set` abstract data type with the following operations: `Insert(x)`, adds x to the set, `Remove(x)`, extracts an element from the set, and the membership test for x, `IsIn(x)`. The corresponding commutativity or conflict table is:

	Insert(x)	Remove(x)	IsIn(x)
Insert(y)	Yes	$x \neq y$	$x \neq y$
Remove(y)	$x \neq y$	Yes	$x \neq y$
IsIn(y)	$x \neq y$	$x \neq y$	Yes

Using commutative locking, pairs of the same operation always commute (e.g., `Insert/Insert`), and pairs of different operations commute if they have different parameters (e.g., `Insert(5)/Remove(7)`). That is, it does not matter the order in which two concurrent transactions perform insert operations, the operations commute and the final value of the set will be the same. On the other hand, if a transaction performs an insert and a concurrent one a remove operation, the operations commute if the parameters are different. Otherwise, the operations do not commute and the final value of the set depends on the order of execution of the two operations. Using read/write locks, the only compatible operations would be pairs of `IsIn` operations. Therefore, commutative locking significantly reduces the number of conflicts by taking advantage of semantic information.

OPTIMA provides the `Lock_Type` abstract class to support user-defined commutative locking. It defines two abstract functions `IsCompatible` and `IsModifier`. A concrete subclass must be derived from this `Lock_Type` class for every data item that is accessed from within a transaction. The class must provide a means to store all the information that is necessary to determine whether two operations invoked on the data item conflict or not. In the `set` example the kind of operation, i.e., `Insert(x)`, `Remove(x)` or `IsIn(x)`, and the parameter `x` must be stored. Based on this information and the commutativity table shown above, the `IsCompatible` function is able to detect conflicts. The `IsModifier` function returns true if the operation modifies the state of the object.

```
package Locks is
   type Lock_Type is abstract tagged private;
   type Lock_Ref is access all Lock_Type'Class;
   function Is_Modifier (Lock : Lock_Type) return Boolean is abstract;
   function Is_Compatible (Lock : Lock_Type;  Other_Lock : Lock_Type)
      return Boolean is abstract;
private
   type Lock_Type is abstract tagged null record;
end Locks;
```

The power and flexibility of commutativity locking can be used to implement the user-defined locking granularity of *Transactional Drago*. The mapping from *Transactional Drago* data items to OPTIMA commutative data items is performed as follows. For each data item a locking scheme must be defined. A locking scheme is defined by providing a concrete `Lock_Type` class. The constructor of the concrete `Lock_Type` class always has a boolean parameter which indicates whether it is a read or a write lock. The compatibility function is automatically generated and considers two lock values as compatible according to the following rules: (1) the constructors of the two locks have been called with different parameters; (2) the constructors of the two locks have been called with the same parameters, but both are read locks.

The array level locking type tree for the array example is shown in Fig. 2(a). For this type tree, a `Lock_Type` class with one constructor (`Array_Lock(Boolean)`) is generated. The Boolean parameter indicates whether it is a read or a write lock. Such a lock is equivalent to traditional read/write locks for that type.

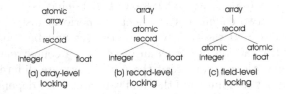

Fig. 2. Type trees for different locking granularities

If the granularity of locks is set at record level (Fig. 2(b)), a constructor with an additional parameter is generated, `Record_Lock(Boolean, Array_Index_Type)`. The new parameter is the array index. In this case, accesses (reads or writes) to different elements of the array will be compatible. Two locks only conflict if they refer to the same array component and one of them is a write lock.

Finally, the type tree shown in Fig. 2(c) illustrates locking at field level. The constructor, `Field_Lock(Boolean,Array_Index_Type,Positive)`, has an additional parameter that represents the declaration order of the field in the record. The following code shows the subclass that is created for the type tree in Fig. 2(c).

```
package Locks.FieldLocks is
   type Field_Lock_Type is new Lock_Type with private;
   function Field_Lock (Modifier : Boolean; Index : Array_Index_Type;
                        Field_Position : Positive) return Field_Lock_Type;
   function Is_Modifier (Lock : Field_Lock_Type) return Boolean;
   function Is_Compatible (Lock : Field_Lock_Type;
                           Other_Lock : Field_Lock_Type) return Boolean;
private
   type Field_Lock_Type is new Lock_Type with record
      Modifier : Boolean;
      Index : Array_Index_Type;
      Field_Position : Positive;
   end record;
end Locks;
```

The `Field_Position` parameter of the constructor `Field_Lock` represents the declaration order of the field in the record. The constructor creates a new `Field_Lock_Type` instance and assigns the parameters to the corresponding record fields. The `Is_Modifier` function simply returns the value stored in `Modifier`. The `Is_Compatible` function is implemented as follows:

```
function Is_Compatible (Lock : Field_Lock_Type;
                        Other_Lock : Field_Lock_Type) return Boolean is
begin
   return (Lock /= Other.Lock) or else
      (not Lock.Modifier and not Other_Lock.Modifier);
end Is_Compatible;
```

In general, a parameter (the array index or field position) is added to the constructor of the corresponding lock for each array/record found in the path from the root of the type tree to each node tagged atomic (not including it).

5   Locking Implementation

This section presents how the advanced concurrency features of Ada 95 have been used to implement long-term and short-term concurrency control in the OPTIMA framework.

In OPTIMA, the Lockbased_Concurrency_Control protected type implements lock-based concurrency control. One object of this type is associated to each data item during the translation of *Transactional Drago*. This protected type provides four operations, Pre_Operation, Post_Operation, Commit_Transaction and Abort_Transaction. When translating *Transactional Drago* code, every access to a data item is automatically surrounded by calls to Pre_Operation and Post_Operation of its associated concurrency control. Obviously, several Ada tasks might attempt to call these operations simultaneously. To handle this situation correctly, the concurrency control has been implemented in the form of a protected type as shown in Fig. 3. Since Pre_Operation has to be able to suspend the calling task in case of conflicts, the operation is implemented as an entry. The private part of the specification contains three private entries and some attributes, e.g. the list of currently active locks named My_Locks, and a boolean and a natural variable that are used to implement the multiple readers/single writer paradigm.

```
protected type Lockbased_Concurrency_Control is
    entry Pre_Operation (Lock : Lock_Ref; Trans : Trans_Ref);
    procedure Post_Operation;
    procedure Transaction_Commit (Trans : Trans_Ref);
    procedure Transaction_Abort (Trans : Trans_Ref);
private
    entry Waiting_For_Transaction (Lock : Lock_Ref; Trans : Trans_Ref);
    entry Waiting_For_Writer (Lock : Lock_Ref; Trans : Trans_Ref);
    entry Waiting_For_Readers (Lock : Lock_Ref; Trans : Trans_Ref);
    My_Locks : Lock_List_Type;
    Currently_Writing : Boolean := False;
    Currently_Reading : Natural := 0;
    To_Try : Natural := 0;
end Lockbased_Concurrency_Control;
```

Fig. 3 Lock based concurrency control

Before a data item is accessed from within a transaction, a Lock_Type object instance is created as described in the previous section, and Pre_Operation of the associated concurrency control is called, passing the transaction context and a reference to the Lock_Type object as parameters. The Pre_Operation code is shown in Fig. 4. First, long-term concurrency control must be handled. To guarantee isolation, the concurrency control must determine if the operation to be invoked conflicts with other invocations made by still active transactions. This check is performed in the Is_Compatible function of the Lock_List_Type (1). Successively, the new lock is compared to all previously granted locks by calling the Is_Compatible function of the new lock. If a conflict has been detected, the calling task is suspended by requeuing the call on the private entry Waiting_For_Transaction until the transaction having executed the conflicting operation ends (2). If, on the other hand, the access does not create any conflict, then the new lock is inserted into the list of granted locks (3), and the short-term concurrency control phase is initiated by requeuing on the private entry `Waiting_For_Writer` (4). The two entries `Waiting_For_Writer` and `Waiting_For_Readers` implement the multiple readers/single writer paradigm. Starvation of writers is prevented by keeping readers and writers on a single entry queue. Requests are serviced in FIFO order. Inside `Waiting_For_Writers`, the nature of the operation, i.e. read or write, is determined by calling the `Is_Modifier` (6) operation of the new lock. Read operations are allowed to proceed, until a write operation is encountered. If there are still readers using the data item, then the writer is requeued to the `Waiting_For_Readers` entry (7). This closes the barrier of the `Waiting_For_Writer` entry, since the latter requires the `Waiting_For_Readers` queue to be empty (5). After the invocation of the actual operation on the data item, the run-time automatically calls `Post_Operation`, which decrements the number of readers or unsets the writer flag.

```
entry Pre_Operation (Lock : Lock_Ref; Trans : Trans_Ref) when True is
begin
   if not Is_Compatible (My_Locks, Lock, Trans) then            [1]
      requeue Waiting_For_Transaction with abort;               [2]
   else
      Insert (My_Locks, Lock, Trans);                           [3]
      requeue Waiting_For_Writer with abort;                    [4]
   end if;
end Pre_Operation;

entry Waiting_For_Writer (Lock : Lock_Ref; Trans : Trans_Ref)
      when not Currently_Writing and Waiting_For_Readers'Count = 0 is   [5]
begin
   if Is_Modifier (Lock.all) then                               [6]
      if Currently_Reading > 0 then
         requeue Waiting_For_Readers with abort;                [7]
      else
         Currently_Writing := True;
      end if;
   else
      Currently_Reading := Currently_Reading + 1;
   end if;
end Waiting_For_Writer;

entry Waiting_For_Readers (Lock : Lock_Ref; Trans : Trans_Ref)
      when Currently_Reading = 0 is
begin
   Currently_Writing := True;
end Waiting_For_Readers;

procedure Post_Operation is
begin
   if Currently_Writing then
      Currently_Writing := False;
```

```
   else
      Currently_Reading := Currently_Reading - 1;
   end if;
end Post_Operation;
```

Fig. 4 Implementation of lock based concurrency control

Now let us go back to the first phase and see what happens to the calls queued on the `Waiting_For_Transaction` entry. Tasks queued here have requested to execute an operation that conflicts with an operation already executed on behalf of a still active transaction. Each time a transaction ends, this situation might change. When a transaction aborts, the operations executed on behalf of the transaction are undone, and hence the acquired locks can be released. This is illustrated in Fig. 5. `Transaction_Abort` calls the `Delete` operation of the granted lock list (`1b`), which results in removing all operation information of the corresponding transaction from the list. The same is done upon commit of a top level transaction (`1a`). If the commit involves a subtransaction, then the locks held so far by the subtransaction must be passed to the parent transaction. This is achieved by calling the `Pass_Up` operation of the `Lock_List_Type` (`2`). In any case, the auxiliary variable `To_Try` is set to the number of tasks waiting in the queue of the entry `Waiting_For_Transaction` (`3a` and `3b`). As a result, all queued tasks are released and requeued to `Pre_Operation`, thus getting another chance to access the data item.

```
entry Waiting_For_Transaction (Lock : Lock_Ref; Trans : Trans_Ref)
   when To_Try > 0 is
begin
   To_Try := To_Try - 1;
   requeue Pre_Operation with abort;
end Waiting_For_Transaction;

procedure Transaction_Commit (Trans : Trans_Ref) is
begin
   if Is_Toplevel (Trans.all) then
      Delete (My_Locks, Trans);                                      1a
   else
      Pass_Up (My_Locks, Trans, Get_Parent(Transaction.all));        2
   end if;
   To_Try := Waiting_For_Transaction'Count;                          3a
end Transaction_Commit;

procedure Transaction_Abort (Trans : Trans_Ref) is
begin
   Delete (My_Locks, Trans);                                         1b
   To_Try := Waiting_For_Transaction'Count;                          3b
end Transaction_Abort;
```

Fig. 5 Implementation of lock based concurrency control

6   Related Work

Argus [LS83, Lis88] was the first programming language providing transactional semantics. It provided a set of atomic types and mutexes. Atomic types have predefined concurrency control and recovery. Hence, the granularity of locks for these data types cannot be changed. Programmers can define new data types based on atomic types to increase concurrency, uncoupling data and concurrency control granularity. However, they have to implement concurrency control (using mutexes and atomic types) for those new types, which it is not a trivial task.

Hybrid atomicity [LMWF94] is used in *Avalon* [EMS91] for concurrency control to increase the degree of concurrency. However, the programmer has to program both the concurrency control and the recovery of the new type. This increases dramatically the complexity of programming.

In *Arjuna* [PSWL95] the granularity of locks applies to objects. Hence, to increase efficiency (decreasing the number of disk accesses) the state of an object should be big, but in order to increase concurrency, objects should be decomposed into smaller objects, which implies changing the code of all the applications that use the original object. [WS94] proposes a run-time clustering-declustering support for the *Arjuna* system where data granularity can be changed at run-time. However, a change in data granularity provokes a change in locking granularity.

Transactional C [Tra95] is the programming language provided by the *Encina* transaction processing monitor. Latches (or mutexes in the *Transactional C* terminology) and locks are explicitly set in *Transactional C*, which complicates programmers' task. Latches are only valid within the scope of a transaction. If a thread starts a subtransaction, the physical consistency of the data is not guaranteed.

7   Conclusions

We have presented the mechanisms for controlling the concurrency control granularity in *Transactional Drago*. The main contribution of this paper is that concurrency control granularity has been uncoupled from data granularity. This enables to increase the transaction concurrency without introducing any penalty on data access and/or recovery.

This approach contrasts with other approaches where an increase in concurrency penalizes data access and/or recovery. Furthermore, the approach of *Transactional Drago* is declarative, thus easy to use for programmers. They simply specify the data and concurrency control granularity separately. Changing the locking granularity of a data item is therefore straightforward, and does not require changing the code of the program that uses the data item.

Finally, we have shown how to map the locking granularity of *Transactional Drago* to the locks provided by OPTIMA, an Ada transactional library, and presented how the implementation of OPTIMA that handles these locks takes advantage of the advanced concurrency features offered by Ada 95.

References

[Ada95]   *Ada 95 Reference Manual, ISO/8652-1995*. Intermetrics, 1995.

[BHG87]   P. A. Bernstein, V. Hadzilacos, and N. Goodman. *Concurrency Control and Recovery in Database Systems*. Addison Wesley, 1987.

[EMS91]   J. L. Eppinger, L. B. Mummert, and A. Z. Spector, editors. *Camelot and Avalon: A Distributed Transaction Facility*. Morgan Kaufmann, 1991.

[GM83]   H. García-Molina. Using Semantic Knowledge for transaction processing in a distributed database. *ACM Transactions on Database Systems*, 8(2):186–213, June 1983.

[GR93]   J. Gray and A. Reuter. *Transaction Processing: Concepts and Techniques*. Morgan Kaufmann, 1993.

[JPAB00]   R. Jiménez-Peris, M. Patiño-Martínez, S. Arévalo, and F.J. Ballesteros. TransLib: An Ada 95 Object Oriented Framework for Building Dependable Applications. *Int. Journal of Computer Systems: Science & Engineering*, 15(1):113–125, January 2000.

[KJRP01]   J. Kienzle, R. Jiménez-Peris, A. Romanovsky, and M. Patiño-Martínez. Transaction Support for Ada. In *Proc. of Int. Conf. on Reliable Software Technologies, LNCS 2043*, pages 290–304. Springer, 2001.

[Lis88]   B. Liskov. Distributed Programming in Argus. *cacm*, 31(3):300–312, 1988.

[LMWF94]   N. Lynch, M. Merrit, W. E. Weihl, and A. Fekete. *Atomic Transactions*. Morgan Kaufmann, 1994.

[LS83]   B. Liskov and R. Scheifler. Guardians and Actions: Linguistic Support for Robust, Distributed Programs. *ACM TOPLAS*, 5(3):382–404, 1983.

[MHL+98]   C. Mohan, D. Haderle, B. Lindsay, H. Pirahesh, and P. Schwarz. ARIES: A Transaction Recovery Method Supporting Fine-Granularity Locking and Partial Rollbacks Using Write-Ahead Logging. In *Recovery Mechanisms in Database Systems*, pages 145–218. Prentice Hall, 1998.

[Mos85]   J. E. B. Moss. *Nested Transactions: An Approach to Reliable Distributed Computing*. MIT Press, 1985.

[PJA98]   M. Patiño-Martínez, R. Jiménez-Peris, and S. Arévalo. Integrating Groups and Transactions: A Fault-Tolerant Extension of Ada. In *Proc. of Int. Conf. on Reliable Software Technologies, LNCS 1411*, pages 78–89. Springer, 1998.

[PJA01]   M. Patiño-Martínez, R. Jiménez-Peris, and S. Arévalo. Group Transactions: An Integrated Approach to Transactions and Group Communication (in press). In *Concurrency in Dependable Computing*. Kluwer, 2001.

[PSWL95]   G. D. Parrington, S. K. Shrivastava, S. M. Wheater, and M. C. Little. The Design and Implementation of Arjuna. *USENIX Computing Systems Journal*, 8(3):255–308, 1995.

[Tra95]   TransArc Corporation, Pittsburgh, PA 15219. *Encina Transactional-C Programmers Guide and Reference*, 1995.

[WS94]   S. M. Wheater and S. K. Shrivastava. Exercising Application Specific Run-time Control Over Clustering of Objects. In *Proc. of the Second International Workshop on Configurable Distributed Systems*, March 1994.

An Ada Binding to the IEEE 1003.1q
(POSIX Tracing) Standard*

Agustín Espinosa Minguet[1], Ana García Fornes[1], and Alfons Crespo i Lorente[2]

[1] Departamento de Sistemas Informáticos y Computación,
Universidad Politécnica de Valencia, Spain
aespinos@dsic.upv.es, agarcia@dsic.upv.es
[2] Departamento de Informática de Sistemas y Computadoras,
Universidad Politécnica de Valencia, Spain
alfons@disca.upv.es

Abstract. Run-time monitoring tools are specially helpful in developing real-time applications. The recently approved standard POSIX 1003.1q defines a common application interface (API) for trace management. No Ada interface currently exists for the POSIX Tracing services. In this paper an Ada binding specification to the amendment 1003.1q (POSIX Tracing) is proposed, in order to be able to use POSIX Tracing services in Ada applications. This specification has been implemented in the real-time kernel MaRTE OS.

1   Introduction

Writing and debugging real-time applications is a complex and time-consuming task. Run-time monitoring tools are specially helpful in developing such applications for several reasons. First, run-time monitoring is useful in debugging and tuning real-time systems. Second, it is also useful for verifying that the system meets its timing constraints during normal operation. Finally, a monitoring system provides feedback to other components (operators, application tasks, schedulers, supervisors, etc.) at run-time. This information can be used to increase the system adaptability to changes in the environment. Great effort has been made in the POSIX project to specify a set of interfaces for the handling of event data. These interfaces have recently been approved by the IEEE Standards Board (Sep 21, 2000).

The standard POSIX 1003.1q [1] defines a common application interface (API) for trace management. This API allows portable access to underlying trace management services by application programs. These underlying services provide access to streams of event data, where the events can be generated by software and/or hardware, applications and/or kernel.

One of our lines of research consists in constructing a development environment for embedded real-time applications, and more important, to use it as

* This work has been funded by the *Comisión Interministerial de Ciencia y Tecnologia* of the Spanish Government under grants TIC99-1043-C03-02 and TAP98-0333-C03-01

J. Blieberger and A. Strohmeier (Eds.): Ada-Europe 2002, LNCS 2361, pp. 321–333, 2002.

a vehicle for research in new scheduling mechanisms for real-time. In a previous work, an implementation of 1003.1q restricted to the Minimal Real-Time POSIX.13 subset [2] was developed in RT-Linux [3].

In order to be able to make comparisons, we have also implemented this standard on the real-time kernel MaRTE OS [4]. MaRTE OS is a real-time kernel for embedded applications that follows the Minimal Real-Time POSIX.13 subset. Most of its code is written in Ada with some C code and assembler parts. It allows for software development of Ada and C embedded applications. Following the MaRTE OS design, the implementation of POSIX Tracing has been done in Ada.

Currently there is no such Ada interface for the POSIX Tracing services. In order to be able to use these services from Ada applications, an Ada binding specification to the amendment 1003.1q (POSIX Tracing) is proposed in this paper. The same guidelines used in the development of the Ada binding (1003.5c) [5] to ISO/IEC 9945-1:1996 (POSIX.1) [6] have been used to develop this binding.

In section 2, we present an overview of POSIX Tracing. Section 3 summarizes the guidelines used to develop the Ada binding to POSIX Tracing. The specification is described in section 4. Finally some conclusions are presented.

2   IEEE 1003.1q: Tracing [C Language]

1003.1q is an amendment to ISO/IEC 9945-1:1996, commonly known as POSIX.1. The purpose of this amendment is to specify a set of interfaces to allow for portable access to underlying trace management services by application programs. In this section we first describe the basic services defined by this amendment. After this, the optional services are detailed.

The main entity defined in 1003.1q is the *trace stream*. A trace stream is an object which is able to register events along with the data necessary to interpret these events. The information that is registered in a trace stream can be used for debugging purposes during the development phase, used for the maintenance of fielded systems or used as a performance measurement tool.

A *trace event* is an action executed by the system that can be registered in a trace stream. Examples of trace events can be a system service call or the execution of a certain part of an application code. 1003.1q defines two kinds of trace events, system trace events and user trace events. The system trace events are generated by the trace system without the intervention of the application. The user trace events are explicitly generated from the application code. Each event is of an individual trace event type. A trace event type is identified by a name, which is a human readable string, for example "POSIX_TRACE_START", and is referenced by the application using a trace event identifier.

A trace stream is created and associated to a specific process. A process can create several trace streams with all of them sharing the same event name space. The process that creates the trace stream is called the *trace controller process*. Trace streams created in this way are called *active trace streams*. When a controller process activates the trace stream, events are registered in the traced stream and can be analyzed by the process in a concurrent way. Since the trace stream can only be accessed by the trace controller process it is also called *trace analyzer process*. When the log option described below is used the controller and analyzer can be different processes. It is important to point out that it is not necessary to program additional code in the traced process because the creation and activation of the trace stream produces the appropriate mechanisms to register the events. In the case of small multi-threaded systems, such as real-time systems, the controller process and the traced process are the same. In this case, one or several threads assume the controller and analyzer roles, while other threads play the traced process role.

One of the options defined in 1003.1q allows the user to associate a *trace log* to a trace stream. The trace log dynamically saves the content of trace stream in a file, releasing the memory resources of the trace stream so that new events can be registered. Once tracing is concluded, it can be analyzed off-line in the same platform or in a different one. Trace streams of this kind are labeled as *pre-recorded trace streams* in order to distinguish them from active trace streams.

Another option makes it possible to associate a trace stream to more than one process. In particular, a trace stream is created for a process and it is inherited by all its descendants. In this way, a process group shares the same trace stream and the same event name space. It is not possible, however, to associate trace streams to processes which do not maintain an ancestry relation.

The event filtering is the last option of 1003.1q. A controller process can determine which events could be registered or not in a specific trace stream.

3   Ada Binding to POSIX Tracing Guidelines

The 1003.5c standard is part of the POSIX series of standards for applications and user interfaces to open systems. It defines the Ada language bindings as a package specification and accompanying textual descriptions of the application program interface (API). This standard supports application portability at the source code level through the binding between ISO 8652:1995 (Ada) and ISO/IEC 9945-1:1996 (POSIX.1). This binding is dependent on the corresponding POSIX C-language system API standards in the sense that the semantics defined in POSIX.1 must be followed by this standard.

In order to make an Ada binding to POSIX Tracing, the same guidelines used to develop the 1003.5c standard have been followed. These guidelines are described in detail in "Annex B. Rationale and Notes of [5]. The most relevant guidelines used are summarized in this section.

Data Types Opaque types defined in 1003.1q correspond to Ada private types. This correspondence is direct, since the concept of opaque type is identical to the private type.

In 1003.1q, several C struct types are defined. In this binding these C structs are converted into private types and functions returning the corresponding C struct member value.

The rest of the types that are used in 1003.1q are already defined in 9945-1 and, therefore, they already have correspondence in 1003.5c. These data types of 1003.5c have been directly used in this binding.

Name Space The style used to define the name space in 1003.1q differs greatly of the style that is usually used in Ada. Due to this fact, the names used in 1003.1q have been modified following the rules below.

- The `posix_trace_` prefix has been removed from all functions.
- Object specific prefixes, such as `attr_` and `eventid_` have also been removed.
- After prefix removal, underscores have been used to split composite words, and abbreviations have been replaced with their respective full words.
- After application of these rules, several POSIX/C functions produce several POSIX/Ada subprograms with the same name. These subprograms have different parameter-result profiles, and so overloading may be used.

In this way, a C function name such as `posix_trace_attr_get_attributes` has been substituted in Ada by `Get_Attributes`

Multipurpose C Functions Multipurpose C functions are broken down in 1003.5c into several Ada subprograms, each of which performs a single operation. This is the case of the function `posix_trace_set_filter`, which is used to manipulate the filter of events of a trace. In this binding, this function has been broken down into three subprograms: one to assign the filter, another to add events and another to remove events from the filter, as can be observed in section 24.3.11 of the package `POSIX.Trace` described in section 4.

Error Reporting In 1003.1q, all the C functions return an integer value indicating an error occurrence. In 1003.5c, the exception mechanism was considered to be the most suitable to indicate error situations. When a POSIX error is detected, the exception `POSIX.POSIX_ERROR` is raised and the specific error code can be retrieved by calling the function `POSIX.Get_Error_Code`. In this way, the C functions of 1003.1q have been transformed following the rules below:

- If the C function returns a single value in one of its arguments, the corresponding subprogram Ada is a function that returns this value.
- If the C function returns several values in its arguments, or it does not return any, an Ada procedure is generated.

In this way, a C function such as `int posix_trace_create (pid_t pid, const trace_attr_t *attr, trace_id_t *trid)`, which returns an error and a value `trid`, is converted into the Ada function `function Create (Pid : Process_ID; Attr : Attributes) return Trace_Identifier`.

Form of iterators An iterator is an operator that permits all parts of a structured object to be visited. In 1003.1q, an iterator exists which allows the user to look up the trace event type list defined in a trace stream. It is implemented by means of two functions which get the next event identifier and rewind the event type list. In this amendment, as in 1003.5c, generic procedures has been used as iterators , as can be observed in section 24.3.9 of the package POSIX.Trace described in section 4.

Interruptible Operations Some POSIX operations may return prematurely if a signal is delivered and handled. In the Ada case, the interrupted operation would propagate the exception POSIX_Error with the error code Interrupted_Operation. An additional parameter Masked_Signals has been added to all C functions that can generate EINTR error to facilitate user programming. This parameter allow the user to mask some signals when the function is in execution. The default signal set corresponds to the signals used by the Ada runtime system.

Configurable limits and options The POSIX/Ada interface involves a number of options and implementation limits. Corresponding to each option and limit there is usually a static subtype (indicating the range of implementation behavior permitted) and a runtime callable function (that returns the actual implementation behavior). In addition, corresponding to each limit there is a compile time constant that specifies the portable value for that limit. Due to the very large number of limits and options, 1003.5c introduced systematic naming rules for the constants, static subtypes, and configurable limits and options. These rules have also been considered in this binding.

4   Complete Specification

This binding takes the form from a single package, named POSIX.Trace. This package is split into sections, which correspond in name and number with the sections that appear in 1003.1q. The objective of this structure is to facilitate the identification of the correspondences between the definitions of 1003.q and those of this binding.

Primitive System Data Types (2.5)

```
type Trace_Identifier is private;   type Attributes is private;
type Event_Identifier is private;   type Event_Set  is private;
```

These four private types correspond to the four opaque types defined in 1003.1q and they respectively represent the identifier of an active or pre-recorded trace stream, the attributes defining the characteristics of the trace stream when it is created, the identifier of an event type and the sets of events.

Structures (24.2.1)

```
type Status is private;
type Operating_Mode is range implementation-defined;
Running   : constant Operating_Mode := implementation-defined;
Suspended : constant Operating_Mode := implementation-defined;

function Operating_Mode_Of (Trace_Status : Status) return Operating_Mode;
function Is_Full           (Trace_Status : Status) return Boolean;
function Is_Overrun        (Trace_Status : Status) return Boolean;
function Is_Flushing       (Trace_Status : Status) return Boolean;
```

```
function Flush_Error        (Trace_Status : Status) return Integer;
function Is_Log_Overrun     (Trace_Status : Status) return Boolean;
function Is_Log_Full        (Trace_Status : Status) return Boolean;

type  Event_Info is private;
type  Truncation_Status is range implementation-defined;
Not_Truncated     : constant Truncation_Status := implementation-defined;
Truncated_Record : constant Truncation_Status := implementation-defined;
Truncated_Read   : constant Truncation_Status := implementation-defined;

function Event_Of              (Info : in Event_Info) return Event_Identifier;
function Process_Identifier_Of (Info : in Event_Info) return POSIX.Process_Identification.
                                                             Process_ID;
function Program_Address_Of    (Info : in Event_Info) return System.Address;
function Truncation_Status_Of  (Info : in Event_Info) return Truncation_Status;
function Time_Stamp_Of         (Info : in Event_Info) return Timespec;
function Task_Identifier_Of    (Info : in Event_Info) return Ada.Task_Identification.
                                                             Task_Id;
```

The type **Status** corresponds to the current trace stream status. The trace system information associated to a registered trace event in a trace system is represented by the type **Event_Info**.

Trace Event Type Definitions (24.2.3)

```
Event_Start               : constant Event_Identifier;
Event_Stop                : constant Event_Identifier;
Event_Filter              : constant Event_Identifier;
Event_Overflow            : constant Event_Identifier;
Event_Resume              : constant Event_Identifier;
Event_Flush_Start         : constant Event_Identifier;
Event_Flush_Stop          : constant Event_Identifier;
Event_Error               : constant Event_Identifier;
Event_Unnamed_Userevent   : constant Event_Identifier;

function Filter_Of_Event_Start_Data
    (Data : Ada.Streams.Stream_Element_Array) return Event_Set;
function Old_Filter_Of_Event_Filter_Data
    (Data : Ada.Streams.Stream_Element_Array) return Event_Set;
function New_Filter_Of_Event_Filter_Data
    (Data : Ada.Streams.Stream_Element_Array) return Event_Set;
function Error_Of_Event_Error_Data
    (Data : Ada.Streams.Stream_Element_Array) return Integer;
```

The constants declared in this section represent the system event types defined in 1003.1q. These event types correspond to actions performed by a trace system, such as activating or stopping a trace stream.

Some of these system event types have associated data. The functions defined in this section convert the data collected by the subprograms of section 24.3.16 into the corresponding data types.

Trace Stream Attributes Initialization (24.3.2)

```
procedure Initialize (Attr : in out Attributes);
procedure Finalize   (Attr : in out Attributes);
```

These procedures respectively initialize and invalidate a trace stream object attribute. The initialization assigns predefined values by the standard to the trace stream object attribute. Subprograms that appear in sections 24.3.3, 24.3.4 and 24.3.5 allow the user to assign and to consult these object values.

Functions to Retrieve and Set Information About a Trace Stream (24.3.3)

```
function  Get_Generation_Version (Attr : in Attributes) return POSIX_String;
function  Get_Name (Attr : in Attributes) return POSIX_String;
procedure Set_Name (Attr        : in out Attributes;
                    Trace_Name : in POSIX_String);
function  Get_Create_Time (Attr : in Attributes) return Timespec;
function  Get_Clock_Resolution (Attr : in Attributes) return Timespec;
```

These subprograms allow the user to consult the generation version, name, creation time and clock resolution of a trace stream object attribute. The name can be assigned by the user. The rest of the values are assigned by the trace system when the trace stream is created.

Functions to Retrieve and Set the Behavior of a Trace Stream (24.3.4)

```
type Inheritance_Policy is range implementation-defined;
Close_For_Child : constant Inheritance_Policy := implementation-defined;
Inherited       : constant Inheritance_Policy := implementation-defined;

function Get_Inheritance_Policy (Attr : in Attributes) return Inheritance_Policy;
procedure Set_Inheritance_Policy
   (Attr                   : in out Attributes;
    New_Inheritance_Policy : in Inheritance_Policy);

type Stream_Full_Policy is range 1..3;
Loop_Stream       : constant Stream_Full_Policy := implementation-defined;
Until_Full_Stream : constant Stream_Full_Policy := implementation-defined;
Flush_Stream      : constant Stream_Full_Policy := implementation-defined;

function Get_Stream_Full_Policy (Attr : in Attributes)
   return Stream_Full_Policy;
procedure Set_Stream_Full_Policy
   (Attr                   : in out Attributes;
    New_Stream_Full_Policy : in Stream_Full_Policy);

type Log_Full_Policy is range implementation-defined;
Loop_Log       : constant Log_Full_Policy := implementation-defined;
Until_Full_Log : constant Log_Full_Policy := implementation-defined;
Append_Log     : constant Log_Full_Policy := implementation-defined;

function Get_Log_Full_Policy (Attr : in Attributes) return Log_Full_Policy;
procedure Set_Log_Full_Policy
   (Attr                : in out Attributes;
    New_Log_Full_Policy : in Log_Full_Policy);
```

The types and subprograms of this section manage the policies that can be selected in the creation of a trace stream. These policies control three aspects of a trace stream: the trace stream inheritance by the traced process children, the behavior of a trace stream when the allocated resources are exhausted, and the behavior of the associate trace log depending on the resource limitations.

Functions to Retrieve and Set Trace Stream Size Attributes (24.3.5)

```
function Get_Maximum_User_Event_Size
   (Attr        : Attributes;
    Data_Length : Natural) return Natural;
function Get_Maximum_System_Event_Size
   (Attr : Attributes) return Natural;
function Get_Maximum_Data_Size
```

```
      (Attr : Attributes) return Natural;
   procedure Set_Maximum_Data_Size
      (Attr              : in out Attributes;
       New_Max_Data_Size : in Natural);
   function Get_Stream_Size
      (Attr : Attributes) return Natural;
   procedure Set_Stream_Size
      (Attr            : in out Attributes;
       New_Stream_Size : in Natural);
   function Get_Log_Size
      (Attr : Attributes) return Natural;
   procedure Set_Log_Size
      (Attr         : in out Attributes;
       New_Log_Size : in     Natural);
```

The first two functions of this section assist the user in the decision of which storage space to assign to a trace stream and its trace log in order to register events. The rest of the subprograms allow the user to determine and consult the reserved storage space for the event data, the trace stream and the trace log.

Trace Stream Initialization, Flush and Shutdown from a Process (24.3.6)

```
   function Create
      (For_Process    : in  POSIX.Process_Identification.Process_ID;
       Attr           : in  Attributes;
       Masked_Signals : in  POSIX.Signal_Masking := POSIX.RTS_Signals)
      return Trace_Identifier;

   function Create_With_Log
      (For_Process    : in POSIX.Process_Identification.Process_ID;
       Attr           : in Attributes;
       File           : in POSIX.IO.File_Descriptor;
       Masked_Signals : in POSIX.Signal_Masking := POSIX.RTS_Signals);
      return Trace_Identifier;

   procedure Flush (Trid : in Trace_Identifier);
   procedure Shutdown (Trid : in Trace_Identifier);
```

With the first two functions, a trace controller process creates an active trace stream with or without a trace log for another process (or for the same one). The returned identifier can be used, for example, to control the trace stream or to recover events registered in the trace stream. Flush registers the events stored in a trace stream in its trace log and releases the resources of the trace stream. A trace stream which was previously created can be destroyed using Shutdown.

Clear Trace Stream and Trace Log (24.3.7)

```
   procedure Clear (Trid : Trace_Identifier);
```

Clear eliminates all the events registered in the trace stream as well as in the trace log associated to it, if there is one.

Manipulate Trace Event Type Identifier (24.3.8)

```
   function Open     (Trid : Trace_Identifier;
                      Name : POSIX_String) return Event_Identifier;
```

```
function Get_Name (Trid  : Trace_Identifier;
                   Event : Event_Identifier) return POSIX_String;

function Equal (Trid        : Trace_Identifier;
                Left, Right : Event_Identifier) return Boolean;
```

The name space of event types is based on strings. A trace controller or analyzer process manages this name space using the subprograms of this section. A new event type can be created or, an already existing event type can be accessed from its name. Event types can be later manipulated from the application by means of its event identifiers.

Iterate over a Mapping of Trace Event Types (24.3.9)

```
generic
with procedure Action (Event : in Event_Identifier;
                        Quit  : in out Boolean);
procedure For_Every_Event_Type (Trid : in Trace_Identifier);
```

A procedure which is executed for each system and user event type defined in the trace stream can be instantiated from this generic procedure.

Manipulate Trace Event Type Sets (24.3.10)

```
procedure Add_Event             (Set   : in out Event_Set;
                                 Event : in Event_Identifier);
procedure Add_All_User_Events   (Set : in out Event_Set);
procedure Add_All_System_Events (Set : in out Event_Set);
procedure Add_All_Events        (Set : in out Event_Set);
procedure Delete_Event          (Set   : in out Event_Set;
                                 Event : in      Event_Identifier);
procedure Delete_All_Events     (Set : in out Event_Set);
procedure Complement            (Set : in out Event_Set);
function  Is_Member             (Set   : in Event_Set;
                                 Event : in Event_Identifier) return Boolean;
```

The type Event_Set is used in 1003.1q to define sets of event types, which are used, for example, for event filtering in trace streams. The subprograms defined in this section are similar to the ones used in 1003.5c for the manipulation of sets of signals.

Set Filter of an Initialized Trace Stream (24.3.11)

```
procedure Set_Filter
   (Trid          : in Trace_Identifier;
    Set           : in Event_Set;
    Masked_Signals : in POSIX.Signal_Masking := POSIX.RTS_Signals);

procedure Add_To_Filter
   (Trid          : in Trace_Identifier;
    Set           : in Event_Set;
    Masked_Signals : in POSIX.Signal_Masking := POSIX.RTS_Signals);

procedure Subtract_From_Filter
   (Trid          : in Trace_Identifier;
    Set           : in Event_Set;
    Masked_Signals : in POSIX.Signal_Masking := POSIX.RTS_Signals);

function Get_Filter
   (Trid          : in Trace_Identifier;
    Masked_Signals : in POSIX.Signal_Masking := POSIX.RTS_Signals)
    return Event_Set;
```

An active trace stream can filter some event types. Events that are filtered are not registered in the trace stream. These subprograms allow the user to manage this filter.

Trace Start and Stop (24.3.12)

```
procedure Start
   (Trid          : in Trace_Identifier;
    Masked_Signals : in POSIX.Signal_Masking := POSIX.RTS_Signals);

procedure Stop
   (Trid          : in Trace_Identifier;
    Masked_Signals : in POSIX.Signal_Masking := POSIX.RTS_Signals);
```

These subprograms activate or stop the event registry in a specified trace stream. The execution of these subprograms generates a system event data type showing the action performed by the trace system.

Trace Functions for Instrumenting Application Code (24.3.13)

```
function Open (Name :  in POSIX_String) return Event_Identifier;

procedure Trace_Event (Event : in Event_Identifier;
                       Data  : in Ada.Streams.Stream_Element_Array);
```

These subprograms are used in the traced process to define and generate the user event types. Using the function **Open**, a traced process can define a user event type for its current or future associated trace streams. The **Trace_Event** function generates an event that is registered in all active trace streams when the event is not filtered.

Trace Log Management (24.3.14)

```
function Open (File: in POSIX.IO.File_Descriptor)
   return Trace_Identifier;

procedure Rewind (Trid : in Trace_Identifier);
procedure Close  (Trid : in Trace_Identifier);
```

The subprograms of this section allow an analyzer process to access a pre-recorded trace stream, created from an active trace stream with log.

Functions to Retrieve the Trace Attributes or Trace Statuses (24.3.15)

```
function Get_Attributes (Trid : in Trace_Identifier) return Attributes;
function Get_Status     (Trid : in Trace_Identifier) return Status;
```

These functions allow for the recovery of the creation attributes and current status of a trace stream.

Functions to Retrieve a Trace Event (24.3.16)

```
procedure Get_Next_Event
  (Trid           : in Trace_Identifier;
   Info           : out Event_Info;
   Data           : out Ada.Streams.Stream_Element_Array;
   Last           : out Ada.Streams.Stream_Element_Offset;
   Unavailable    : out Boolean;
   Masked_Signals : in POSIX.Signal_Masking := POSIX.RTS_Signals);

procedure Timed_Get_Next_Event
  (Trid           : in Trace_Identifier;
   Info           : out Event_Info;
   Data           : out Ada.Streams.Stream_Element_Array;
   Last           : out Ada.Streams.Stream_Element_Offset;
   Unavailable    : out Boolean;
   Timeout        : in Timespec;
   Masked_Signals : in POSIX.Signal_Masking := POSIX.RTS_Signals);

procedure Try_Get_Next_Event
  (Trid         : in Trace_Identifier;
   Info         : out Event_Info;
   Data         : out Ada.Streams.Stream_Element_Array;
   Last         : out Ada.Streams.Stream_Element_Offset;
   Unavailable  : out Boolean);
```

These functions recover an event of a trace stream. The Timed_Get_Next_Event function can be used with active or pre-recorded trace streams. The Timed_Get_Next_Event and Try_Get_Next_Event functions are only applicable to active trace streams.

In the case of an active trace stream, when there are no registered events, the Get_Next_Event function can stop the calling process execution. Timed_Get_Next_Event allows this wait to be temporized, while the Try_Get_Next_Event never stops the execution of the process.

The recovered event information and its associated data are obtained as a result of these subprograms.

Once the POSIX.Trace package specification has been concluded, new limits and options to 1003.5c are now considered. This is made using the following modifications.

Modifications to POSIX.Limits, POSIX.Options and POSIX. Configurable_System_Limits

```
-- POSIX.Limits
subtype Trace_Sys_Maxima        is Natural range implementation-defined;
subtype Trace_User_Event_Maxima is Natural range implementation-defined;
subtype Trace_Name_Maxima       is Natural range implementation-defined;
subtype Trace_Event_Name_Maxima is Natural range implementation-defined;
-- POSIX.Options
subtype Trace              is Boolean range implementation-defined;
subtype Trace_Event_Filter is Boolean range implementation-defined;
subtype Trace_Log          is Boolean range implementation-defined;
subtype Trace_Inherit      is Boolean range implementation-defined;
-- POSIX.Configurable_System_Limits
function Trace_Is_Supported return POSIX.Options.Trace;
function Trace_Event_Filter_Is_Supported return POSIX.Options.Trace_Event_Filter;
function Trace_Log_Is_Supported return POSIX.Options.Trace_Log;
function Trace_Inherit_Is_Supported return POSIX.Options.Trace_Inherit;
function Trace_Sys_Maximum return POSIX.Limits.Trace_Sys_Maxima;
```

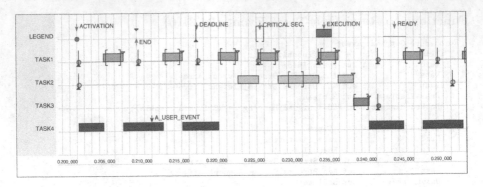

Fig. 1. Quivi Output

```
function Trace_User_Event_Maximum return POSIX.Limits.Trace_User_Event_Maxima;
function Trace_Name_Maximum return POSIX.Limits.Trace_Name_Maxima;
function Trace_Event_Name_Maximum return POSIX.Limits.Trace_Event_Name_Maxima;
```

5   Conclusions

In this paper an Ada binding specification to the amendment 1003.1q (POSIX Tracing) has been proposed. We are currently using this specification to monitor the real-time kernel MaRTE OS and the GNAT run-time system.

The 1003.1q standard has been implemented in RT-Linux and MaRTE OS. The C interface is available in both systems and the Ada binding described in this paper has also been implemented in MaRTE OS. Both systems follow the Minimal Real-time System Profile standard, which clearly restricts the POSIX trace standard in two major aspects: the system can only have one running process (with threads) and there is no general file system available. The consequences of having only one process are that the three roles defined in 1003.1q must be executed by different threads of the only process in the system, and the Trace Inheritance option cannot be supported. Having no general file system support makes it difficult to implement all the trace stream log options available in the standard, and so, only a subset of those options has been implemented. The rest of 1003.1q has been completely implemented. Relevant scheduling events (context switches, locking and unlocking mutexes, etc.) have been added as system events to both systems. These allow the user to debug and to profile the real-time application. A graphical tool called Quivi has also been implemented, which represents the trace stream log in a time chart. The trace log obtained from the example in Fig. 2 is represented using Quivi as shown in Fig. 1. This example shows a controller task which creates a trace stream with log and an instrumented task which generates an user event. Both user and system events are traced, except for Event_SCall, which is filtered out. This is a new event which has been added to the set of system events in order to trace any system call being invoked.

```
with POSIX;                         use  POSIX;
with POSIX.Trace;                   use  POSIX.Trace;
......
procedure Controller is

   Attr : Attributes;
   Trid : Trace_Identifier;
   File : File_Descriptor;
   Event_Scall       : Event_Identifier;
   Filtered_Events : Event_Set;

   task Task1;
   ......
   task Task4;
   task body Task4 is
      Null_Data : Stream_Element_Array (1 .. 0);
      An_User_Event : Event_Identifier;
   begin
      .......
      An_User_Event := Open ("An_User_Event");
      Trace_Event (An_User_Event, Null_Data);
      .......
   end Task4;

begin
   Initialize (Attr);
   Set_Name (Attr, "Test_Trace");
   Set_Stream_Full_Policy (Attr, Until_Full_Stream);
   Set_Stream_Size (Attr, 60000);
   File := Open_Or_Create ("log_file", Read_Write, Owner_Permission_Set);
   Trid := Create_With_Log (Null_Process_ID, Attr, File);
   Event_Scall := Open (Trid, "Event_SCall");
   Set_Filter (Trid, Filtered_Events);
   Start (Trid);
   delay 2.0;
   Shutdown (Trid);
end Controller;
```

Fig. 2. Example of Using the Trace Package

References

1. 1003.1q-2000 IEEE Standard for Information technology-Portable Operating Systems Interface (POSIX®)-Part 1: System Application Program Interface (API)-Amendment 7: Tracing [C Language]
2. 1003.13-1998 IEEE Standard for Information Technology–Standardized Application Environment Profile (AEP)–POSIX® Realtime Application Support Print: 186 pages [0-7381-0178-8]
3. A. Terrasa, I. Paches, A. Garcia-Fornes. An evaluation of POSIX Trace Standard implemented in RT-Linux Proceedings of the 2000 IEEE International Symposium on Performance Analysis and Software.
4. M. Aldea, M. Gonzalez. Early Experience with an Implementation of the POSIX.13 Minimal Real-Time Operating System for Embedded Applications. 25th IFAC Workshop on Real-Time Proggramming. WRTP'2000.
5. 1003.5c-1998 IEEE Standard for Information technology- POSIX® Ada Language Interfaces- Part 1: Binding for System Application Program Interface (API)
6. ISO/IEC 9945-1: 1996 [IEEE/ANSI Std 1003.1, 1996 Edition] Information Technology–Portable Operating System Interface (POSIX®)–Part 1: System Application: Program Interface (API) [C Language]

GNAT Ada Database Development Environment

Michael Erdmann

The GNADE Project,
michael.erdmann@snafu.de,
http://gnade.sourceforge.net/

Abstract. This article describes the results of the GNADE project which provides an Open Source licensed development environment for RDBMS based Ada 95 applications.

1 Introduction

The Ada 95 standard provides no interface to relational data bases management systems. As a consequence a lot different approaches have been taken to connect Ada 95 application with RDBMS products. During a relatively small project which required a data base it became obvious that there is no open source licensed software environment available which allows to integrate SQL into Ada 95 in such a way that the application does not become dependent on the used data base implementation.

The GNADE project was setup with the objective to overcome this situation by providing and maintaining over a long time, tools and support packages which make the use of SQL[1] within Ada 95 seamless in the following sense:

1. The source code should be independent of the used data base control system.
2. The tool chain should provide a migration path from other non open source products to GNADE.

1.1 Project Scope

The figure 1 shows the typical development scenario involving RDBMS products. This model assumes, that the application is implemented as a client process for one or more data base servers.

An application accesses tables (relations) in an data base control system (DBCS)[2] by means of an interface library. This library allows the application to execute SQL queries formulated in SQL on the DBCS and to retrieve the query results (so called result sets) from the DBCS.

At the same time, the structure of the tables are developed and installed in a development data base by means of SQL DDL/DML commands.

---

[1] Structured Query Language
[2] Data Base Control System

J. Blieberger and A. Strohmeier (Eds.): Ada-Europe 2002, LNCS 2361, pp. 334–343, 2002.

The output of the development process is the Ada 95 source code and the table definitions in SQL.

The scope of the GNADE project includes all issues from the support of the development of application code to the data base interface except for the data base control systems itself.

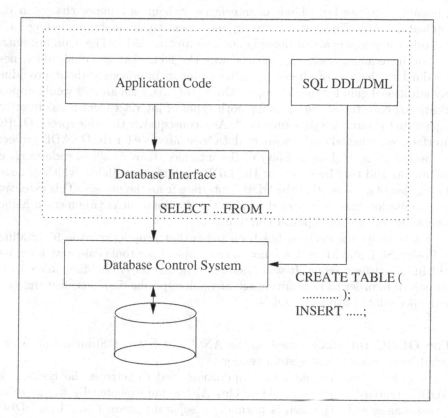

Fig. 1. GNADE Development Environment (Ref. Model)

1.2 Implementation Considerations

The following sections are presenting a short overview of the discussion and reasoning which lead to the current implementation. At the beginning of the project, three major questions had to be answered before any implementation attempt:

Q.1 - What kind interface between application and RDBMS should be used?
Q.2 - What is the best way to integrate SQL into Ada 95?
Q.3 - Which compilers and platforms should and can be supported?

1.3   Database Interfaces

There are standardized interfaces like ODBC [3] and proprietary interfaces like development libraries provided by the DBCS vendors themselves.

In order to make the application independent of the underlying interface type the first idea was to develop an abstract data base interface in order to allow applications to use both kinds of interfaces without any major change in the application code. There was a strong and intensive discussion including ACT and other developers about defining such an abstract API. The main argument for not introducing such an interface was the fact, that is would add a new standard to the zoo of already existing common interfaces without providing any additional gain for the developer. On top of this, such an API would impose additional data transformations for both types of interfaces which has negative impact on the interface performance. [4]. As a consequence the wide spread ODBC interface was selected as the primary data base interface for the GNADE project.

Beside of the high availability of the interface, there is also a wide range of documents and text books about the ODBC interface available, which removes the burden of documenting the ODBC interface from the project. This extensive documentation base is expected to give the development environment a higher acceptance in the development community.

Additionally the decision has been taken that proprietary Ada 95 bindings to PostgreSQL and MySQL are not in the scope of the tool chain any more, but still in the project scope. It was assumed that the native bindings have to be supported in order to take advantage of vendor specific data base features (e.g. high speed data path for BLOB's).

The ODBC Interface based on the ANSI and X/Open Standard [3] is provided by most data base system vendors.

In order to execute data base operations and to retrieve the results, the ODBC standard provides an API. This API is implemented by the so called driver manager (DM) which is normally a separate product (e.g UnixODBC) beside of the DBCS. The driver manager maps the ODBC API calls into the appropriate calls into the ODBC driver library provided by the installed DBCS.

In order to address databases, the ODBC provides the concept of so called data sources. A data source specifies on which host which database has to be accessed using which driver.

The binding between Ada 95 and the ODBC interface is in fact a binding between the functions exported by the DM libraries and the ODBC pack-

---

[3] Open Database Connectivity (ODBC)

[4] The performance issue has to be seen in the correct context. The interface between the application and the DBCS is normally not intended for a large throughput because the idea is that the DBCS should do the major work of reducing the data to a reasonable sized result set. Please note, if the result set becomes to large it is very likely that the application code is doing some filtering which could have already been done in the DBCS.

ages. The ODBC packages have been created manually based upon the ODBC specification[3].

1.4   Integration of SQL in Ada 95

The issue to integrate SQL into Ada 95 (or other languages) is not a new issue. In the past a lot of approaches have been taken, as for example SAMeDL [2] or SQL language bindings [1]. All these approaches may be categorized into the following classes:

1. Approaches like [1] which bind the SQL language elements like *select* * directly to Ada procedure calls like *SELEC("*")*.
2. From some kind of specification language (e.g. SAMeDL [2]) are Ada 95 packages generated which are providing methods used to access the data base by means of pre compiled queries.
3. The source code contains the actual SQL code together with Ada 95 code (e.g. [3]). A preprocessor expands the embedded SQL code into valid Ada code.

The first approach was assumed as ineffective, because it requires a lot of data transformations until the query is executed.

The SAMeDL approach based on the ISO standard requires a lot of implementation effort, because of a complex syntax of the language. But the major argument against it, was the fact that SAMeDL never became an established standard [5].

For embedded SQL solution the effort was clearly defined by the implementation of a preprocessor for embedded SQL where most of the work is left to the underlying data base system. Besides the estimated small effort, the fact that other products (e.g. Oracle, Informix) provide an embedded SQL translator was considered as a important success factor, because there is a potentially larger code base of embedded SQL code existing then for SAMeDL.

Embedded SQL and Ada 95. The GNADE implementation is based upon the ISO 92 [3] draft for embedded SQL with some commonly known extensions which have been added in order to provide a possible migration path for already existing embedded SQL code.

This standard defines the key word EXEC SQL which indicates the begin of an embedded SQL statement which is terminated by a semicolon. The syntax of embedded SQL statements resembles largely the syntax of the SQL language as shown in the example below:

```
EXEC SQL AT Company_Database
    DECLARE emp_cursor CURSOR FOR
        SELECT EMPNO, NAME, DEPTNO
        FROM EMPLOYEES
        WHERE MANAGER = :Manager_To_Find  ;
```

---
[5] The topic was dropped in 1997

Since the structure of the query is the same as for normal SQL, a large part of the embedded SQL statements can be send unchanged to the underlying data base system except for the host variables which have to be treated according to the underlying DBCS interface (ODBC). This allows to test a query manually on a test database using an interactive query tool, before it is put into the actual code.

In order to make queries more flexible so called dynamic SQL statements allow to define parts of the query at execution time (e.g. the WHERE clause).

Embedded SQL statements do communicate with the application via so called host variables. A host variable provides either the input to a query or contains the data of a column in a row of a query result set.

```
procedure Get_Manager(
    manager : in Integer ) is

    EXEC SQL BEGIN DECLARE SECTION END-EXEC
    ....
    Manager_To_Find         : INT := INT(manager) ;
    .....
    EXEC SQL END DECLARE SECTION END-EXEC
```

Host variables do follow the same visibility rules as normal Ada 95 variables which means the Manager_To_Find variable is only valid in the context of the Get_Manager procedure above.

1.5   Compilers and Platforms

The GNAT [6] compiler was selected as the primary development environment since it is available under the GNU license on the most popular platforms as Windows, Linux and Unix. Other compilers are currently not considered.

2   The GNADE Development Environment

In the GNADE environment an application is developed in Ada 95 including embedded SQL statements. As an extension to the ISO/92 standard the package may contain embedded SQL statement declaring the required tables.

The embedded SQL translator creates from this source code a compilation unit by expanding the embedded SQL statements into Ada 95 code (ref. figure 2). Optionally a file is created by the preprocessor which contains all SQL commands needed to create the data base tables in any SQL compatible data base.

The Ada 95 code generated by the translator has to be compiled and linked with the application environment to form the application.

---

[6] GNU Ada Tool chain

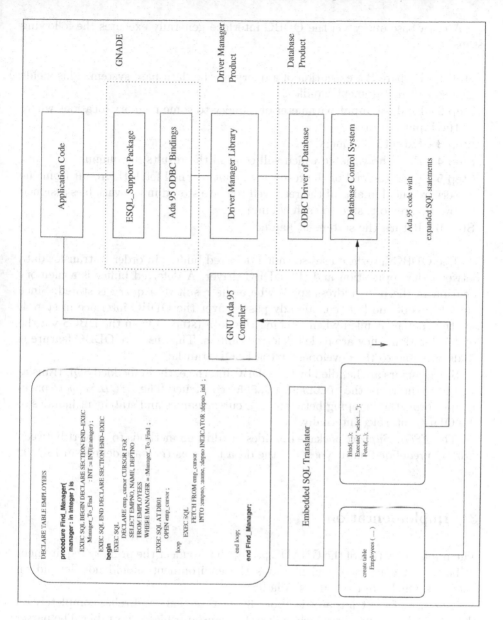

Fig. 2. GNADE Development Environment

Embedded SQL statements are expanded by the ESQL preprocessor into Ada 95 code which uses the *ESQL_Support* package. This package binds to the driver manager interface and contains the helper procedures to execute a query via the ODBC interface, set and fetch host variables.

A data base query via the ODBC interface generally executes the following steps:

Step 1 - Prepare the execution of a query on the data base system. This yields a so called statement handle

Step 2 - Bind the input parameter of a query to some memory locations where the input is stored.

Step 3 - Execute the query.

Step 4 - Bind the variable which will contain the results to columns.

Step 5 - Until the end of the result set is not reached fetch the result from the server. The domains of the retrieved row are stored in the variables assigned by the previous step to each column.

Step 6 - Return the statement handle.

The ODBC interface uses so called deferred buffers in order to transfer data between the application and the ODBC driver. A deferred buffer is a memory location in the user address space where the result of a query is stored. Since the address of the buffer is already passed over the ODBC interface in step 4, but the content is filled when fetching the data (step 5) from the DBCS via the fetch operation, they are called deferred buffers. This insecure ODBC feature is made invisible to the developer by the ESQL translator.

Since cursors are handled by the ODBC interface, the embedded SQL translator has to intercept the DECLARE CURSOR construct. The *ESQL_Support* package performs the mapping between SQL cursor names and statement handles of the ODBC interface internally.

The *ESQL_Support* package provides in addition methods to convert between Ada 95 predefined data types and the data types as they are defined in ISO/92 [3].

3   Implementation

The implementation of the GNADE project has to meet the primary requirement of being self contained, which means the environment should not depend on packages which are not part of Ada 95.

The size of the translator is about 3000 statements and relies completely on the pure Ada 95 libraries which makes the translator highly portable. The parser is implemented manually because the syntax of embedded SQL is relatively simple and in difference to normal parser's, the translator works like an editor, which reads in lines, detects embedded SQL statements, edits the result line depending on the SQL statement and writes out the result lines.

The ODBC bindings of about 6500 statements have been manually generated and do not depend on any external Ada 95 packages.

4   Portability

Application which are implemented with GNADE for the same data base vendor, are portable over platforms without any problem. This is fairly proven because within the GNADE team different operating system have been used.

Portability between database vendors is a problem because of the different implementation level of SQL and a different connect and authorization methods.

In order to achieve such portability some simple rules have to be followed:

1. Use always uppercase table and domain names.
2. Don't use any SQL extension of your vendor.
3. Use always broadly supported SQL clauses.

All the sample programs of the GNADE distribution are running correctly on three different RDBMS.

5   Migration of Legacy Code

Since there is no real migrated project known, the only experience is taken from example code of some DBCS vendors. One of the major problem in reusing embedded SQL code written for other vendors, is the fact that a lot of extension to the ISO/92 standard have been done by these vendors.

6   Experiences with Ada 95

Ada 95 did allow to bind to the ODBC interface in such a way, that the commonly available documentation may reused by the developer even on code level.

Judging from our current experiences Ada 95 encapsulates the deferred buffer handling of the ODBC interface in such a way, that the code stays portable between platforms (e.g Intel, SPARC Solaris).

The same applies for the native bindings for MySQL and PostgreSQL where Ada 95 has to interface to even more data base specific communication areas.

7   Developing Open Source Software and Ada 95

The development scenario for open source software is completely different to the daily work scenarios which are strongly bound to fixed development processes. The mechanisms which are driving the open source development is described in a very colorful way in the paper of Eric Raymond[4]. The typical boundary conditions of such projects are:

1. No budget at all.
2. Unclear responsibilities, unstable working groups.
3. The module owners are dropping out the project for personal reasons.
4. Normally no sufficient documentation.

5. A lot of platforms have to be supported, but they are not always available for testing.

Under these constraints is Ada 95 an ideal language choice because of its build in high reliability and low maintenance efforts.

8 Current Status and Future of the GNADE Project

The project has achieved its primary objective to provide stable open source licensed software which allows the integration SQL with Ada 95. The primary objectives of the future is to extend the number of supported platforms and data base products. This is supported by the fact, that the GNAT Ada 95 compiler is available for a wide range of platforms.

Table 1. Platforms supported by GNADE

Platform	Supported Database
Linux	PostgreSQL
Linux	MySQL
Linux	MimerSQL
Solaris	PostgreSQL
Solaris	MimerSQL
Windows	MySQL
Windows	MS SQL Server
Windows	Oracle 8i lite

The range of native data base bindings will be extended (e.g. Oracle Call Interface) continuously, but the long term objective is to define a common data base API and to implement native bindings on basis of this API.

This API call Ada Database Connectivity (ADBC) will provide a kernel API which contains the interface which is supported by most of the known open source and other available RDBMS products. In order to allow the use of embedded SQL in combination with native bindings it is planed to modify the embedded SQL translator in such a way that code is generated either for ODBC or the data base API interface. The first step of this initiative has been launched by distributing a draft of this API for discussion in the Ada community.

References

1. Proposed Binding Ada to Database Language SQL
   Institute for Defense Analyses and
   RACOM Computer Professionals March 1986.

2. Database Programming Language
   The SQL Ada module Description Language SAMeDL
   ISO/IEC 12227:1994
3. X/Open CAE Specification "Data Management: SQL Call-Level Interface (CLI)"
   ISO/IEC 9075-3:1995 (E) Call-Level Interface (SQL/CLI)
4. The Cathedral and the Bazaar
   Eric Steven Raymond
   August 2000.

Ada, Interfaces and the Listener Paradigm

Jean-Pierre Rosen*

Adalog
19-21, rue du 8 mai 1945
94110 ARCUEIL
jean-pierre.rosen@adalog.fr

Abstract. It is often claimed that interfaces, as provided by Java, are a must for Ada0Y. In this paper, we explain what interfaces are, and show equivalent constructs using Ada's "building blocks" approach. We focus then on one particular usage of interfaces, namely the listener paradigm. We detail various solutions to this problem, and show that interfaces are far from being the only, nor even the best, solution in many cases. We conclude that although interfaces are conceptually an interesting feature, their importance for Ada0Y should not be overestimated.

1 Introduction

We assume in this paper that the reader is reasonably familiar with Ada, but not necessarily with Java; therefore, we start by exposing what interfaces and other relevant features of Java are, then we explore the needs that are fullfilled by interfaces, and finally show how the same needs can be addressed in Ada.

This paper gives in places a view of inheritance which is quite different from what is generally considered as accepted. We understand that many people will not necessarilly agree with the ideas presented here; we only hope to provide some new food for thoughts.

2 Inheritance Revisited

When introducing the basic mechanisms of inheritance, it is customary to explain that there is a *parent* class, that provides data fields and methods, from which a *child* class is derived. The child class has the same data fields and methods as its parent; they are thus said to be *inherited*. In addition, if some of the inherited methods are not appropriate to the child class, they can be *redefined*; i.e. the child class provides a *different behaviour* for the *same* method. Incidentally, we notice that a method is either inherited or redefined, but can never disappear; all descendants of a class have (at least) the same methods as their ancestors.

This way of presenting inheritance is consistent with the so-called *delta-programming* paradigm: a child class is viewed as a slight modification in behaviour from an existing class. However, it is possible to give a different flavour to inheritance by presenting it as follows:

---

* Many thanks to R. Riehle for reviewing an early version of this paper

J. Blieberger and A. Strohmeier (Eds.): Ada-Europe 2002, LNCS 2361, pp. 344–356, 2002.

A parent class defines a set of properties that are shared by all its descendents. For example[1], all animals can eat. Therefore the class of all animals provides an `Eat` method. Then, each particular animal must define *how* it eats, by giving its own definition of `Eat`. That's why operations of a class are called *methods*: each class defines its own way of doing some basic operation. However, it may happen that all sub-classes of a given class share the same way of doing something; for example, all varieties of dogs use the same method for eating. Therefore, the `Dog` class can provide a *default implementation* of `Eat`, that will be shared by all subclasses, unless it is explicitly overridden.

In this second presentation, we focus on a *common interface* which is guaranteed to be provided by all the descendants of a class; inheritance of methods appears only as a secondary feature, a kind of default value that can, but needs not be provided by the ancestor. Actually, most OO programming languages provide *abstract methods* which are simply methods for which no default is provided, and therefore *must* be redefined by descendants.

Of these two aspects of inheritance, the guaranteed interface is clearly the most important feature; this is what allows *polymorphism*, the ability for a variable to designate values of a type that is not statically known, and still apply relevant operations to it.

3 Important Java Features

3.1 Interfaces

A Java interface is simply inheritance restricted to its first aspect: the definition of a set of provided methods, without any default values for them. A class that *implements* an interface promises to provide the methods defined by the interface. For example, a simple interface would look like this:

```
public interface Enumeration { // From package java.util
   public boolean hasMoreElements ();
   public Object nextElement () throws NoSuchElementException ;
}
```

We can now define a method which is applicable to any class that implements the `Enumeration` interface:

```
//This method prints all elements in a data structure :
void listAll (Enumeration e) {
   while e.hasMoreElements ()
      System.out.println (e.nextElement ());
}
```

---

[1] Sorry for this overused example!

In a sense, an interface is nothing but an abstract class that defines no data fields, and whose methods are all abstract. But actually, it can be argued that interfaces are not connected to inheritance at all, and are even the *contrary* of inheritance: it is just a contract that can be obeyed by several classes, *without* requiring any conceptual dependency between classes that implement a given interface. In short, inheritance corresponds to a *is a* relationship, while interfaces correspond to a *provides* relationship.

The major benefit of interfaces is that variables can be declared of an interface type, and can refer[2] to any object that implements the interface. Only the methods defined for this interface are available through such a variable. For example:

```
class DataStructure implements Enumeration {...}
   ...
Enumeration E;
   ...
E = new DataStructure ();
```

Of course, the implementation of the methods promised by `Enumeration` have full visibility on all the internals of the class `DataStructure`.

3.2   Inner Classes

Another important feature of Java, that appeared with Java 1.1, is the notion of *inner class*. An inner class is a class that is defined within another class. The constructor for such a class is actually a method *provided* by its enclosing class; as such, an object of the inner class must be created by applying the constructor to an object of the enclosing class. The newly created object is then in some sense hard-wired to the object that served to create it. The inner class has visibility to all components of this parent object.

Here is an example of an inner class, and of the creation of an inner object:

```
class External {
   public class Internal {...}
}
   ...
External ext = new External ();
External.Internal ei= ext.new Internal ();
```

3.3   Equivalence of Interfaces and Inner Classes

Any use of interfaces can be replaced by an equivalent structure that uses only inner classes. We'll show this on an example. Imagine an interface called `Wakeable` that provides a method `everySecond`. A class implementing this interface can register itself to a scheduler, that will call its `everySecond` method every second. The outline of this is as follows:

---

[2] In Java, all variables (except for elementary types) are references (i.e. pointers) to objects.

```
interface WakeableInterface {
  void everySecond ();
}

final class Scheduler {
  static void Register (WakeableInterface p) { ... }
}
```

Using interfaces, a periodic class would look like this (note that the constructor registers the current object to the scheduler):

```
class Periodic implements WakeableInterface {
  public void everySecond () { ... }
  void Periodic () { Scheduler.Register (this); }
}
```

However, the following scheme, which uses only classes (and inner classes) is equivalent:

```
public abstract class WakeableClass { // class, not interface
  abstract void everySecond ();
}

final class Scheduler {
  static void Register (WakeableClass p) { ... }
}

class Periodic {
  class localWakeable extends WakeableClass { // Inner class
    public void everySecond () { ... }
  }
  localWakeable l = new localWakeable (); // local inner object
  void Periodic () { Scheduler.Register (l); }
}
```

Note that the method `everySecond` can use the name `Periodic.this` to access the fields of the enclosing object, and has the same visibility scope, and can access the same elements, as its counterpart made from an interface. From a philosophical point of view, it is slightly different; in the interface case, the object provides the functionality (`everySecond`) itself, while in the second case the functionality is delegated to a sub-object. However, both solutions are technicaly equivalent.

4   The Ada Building-Block Approach

To understand the remaining of this discussion, it is very important to remember the basic *building block* approach of Ada. In Ada, there is no such thing as classes (in the usual sense), friends, or even interfaces defined in the language. All these usual constructs are built from the combination of basic building blocks.

The Ada approach can be understood by comparing Lego® blocks to Playmobil® pieces. The great versatility of Lego blocks comes from the fact that the same piece can be used to build very different elements; for example, the same round plate is used to build an antenna in the Space Lego, a shield in the Middle-Age Lego, or an umbrella in the Lego village. On the other hand, a piece from a Playmobil set is very specialized and cannot be used in a different context than its initial box.

Ada typically works like Lego blocks; a class is neither a package nor a tagged type. It is a *design pattern*, where a package declares only a tagged type and its associated operations. Friends (in the C++ sense) are made by declaring several related tagged types in the same package, etc. Although this approach requires a bit more effort from the programmer, it allows the building of constructs not available in other languages without new syntax.

When told about the Ada way of doing things, people often react by saying that it is only a workaround for compensating the lack of such-and-such feature in Ada; it is not. It is a different approach to building various mechanisms, that allows almost any paradigm to be used without requiring additions to the language.

5   A Design Pattern for Interfaces in Ada

In this section, we show that it is possible to define a design pattern in Ada that matches closely the notion of Java interfaces - or more precisely, the inner classes that are equivalent to a Java interface.

Since we try to mimic the way Java works, we use limited types that we manipulate through pointers. Of course, other design patterns are possible that would not require these pointers. We do not address at this point the issue of interfacing with Java, but only the one of providing an equivalent feature.

Given that:

- an interface is equivalent to an abstract class with abstract methods;
- the usual way of adding a "facet" to an Ada tagged type is through instantiation of a generic;
- generic formal parameters can already express the notion that a data type must provide a set of operations;

we can express the interface from the previous example as described in the next listing[3]. Note that the body is relatively simple, but requires some care in order not to violate accessibility rules!

The type `Wakeable_Interface.Instance` expresses the properties of the interface. An instantiation of the generic package `Implements_Wakeable` on a tagged type that provides the necessary `Every_Second` procedure will provide a

---

[3] We use here the convention advocated in [5], where the package is given the name of the class, the main (tagged) type always has the name "Instance", and the associated pointer type the name "Handle"

```ada
package Wakeable_Interface is
   type Instance is abstract tagged limited null record;
   type Handle is access all Instance'Class;
   procedure Every_Second (This : access Instance) is abstract;

   -- A type with an Every_Second operation can implement
   -- the interface by instantiating the following generic:
   generic
      type Ancestor is tagged limited private;
      with procedure Every_Second (Item: access Ancestor) is <>;
   package Implements_Wakeable is
      type Instance is new Ancestor with private;
      type Handle is access all Instance'Class;
      function Wakeable_Of (Item : access Instance)
                              return Wakeable_Interface.Handle;
      function Ful_Object_Of (Item : Wakeable_Interface.Handle)
                              return Handle;
   private
      type Inner_Type (Enclosing : access Instance) is
         new Wakeable_Interface.Instance with null record;
      procedure Every_Second   (This : access Inner_Type);

      type Instance is new Ancestor with
         record
            Inner_Instance : aliased Inner_Type (Instance'Access);
         end record;
   end Implements_Wakeable;
end Wakeable_Interface;

package body Wakeable_Interface is
   package body Implements_Wakeable is
      procedure Every_Second (This : access Inner_Type) is
      begin
         Every_Second (Ancestor(This.Enclosing.all)'Access);
      end Every_Second;

      function Wakeable_Of (Item : access Instance)
                              return Wakeable_Interface.Handle is
      begin
         return Item.Inner_Instance'Access;
      end Wakeable_Of;

      function Full_Object_Of (Item : Wakeable_Interface.Handle)
                              return Handle is
      begin
         return Inner_Type (Item.all).Enclosing.all'Access;
      end Parent_Of;
   end Implements_Wakeable;
end Wakeable_Interface;
```

new tagged type which is the original one with the addition of the interface. The function `Wakeable_Of` returns a handle associated to an object, which is usable to manipulate it as a `Wakeable` object; conversely, the function `Full_Object_Of` returns a handle to the full object, given a handle to the interface.

Here is how we would declare a class `Data1`, then use the generic to provide the class that implements this interface:

```
package Data1 is
  type Instance is tagged limited private;
  type Handle is access all Instance'Class;
  procedure Init (Item : access Instance; Value : Integer);
  procedure Processing (Item : access Instance);
  procedure Every_Second (Item : access Instance);

private
  type Instance is tagged limited
    record
      Value : Integer;
    end record;
end Data1;

with Wakeable_Interface; use Wakeable_Interface;
package Data1.Wakeable is
  new Implements_Wakeable (Data1.Instance);
```

Note that since the type `Data1` features an `Every_Second` procedure, it is automatically selected by the instantiation, but that, unlike Java interfaces, the operation provided for the implementation of `Every_Second` needs not have the same name; for example, the instantiation could have explicitly mentioned `Processing`. This can be handy in some situations, like having the same operation provided for the implementation of two different interfaces.

Finally, here is an example of a program using this data type. Note that the value is created as a `Data1`, and then manipulated as a `Wakeable`; we also demonstrate that we can go back from a `Wakeable` to a `Data1` :

```
with Data1.Wakeable, Wakeable_Interface;
procedure Example is
  use Data1, Data1.Wakeable, Wakeable_Interface;
  Handle_1 : Data1.Wakeable.Handle;
  Handle_2 : Wakeable_Interface.Handle;
begin
  Handle_1 := new Data1.Wakeable.Instance;
  Init (Handle_1, 5);

  Handle_2 := Wakeable_Of (H1);
  Every_Second (Handle_2);

  Processing (Full_Object_Of (Handle_2));
end Example;
```

With this design pattern, the *declaration* of the interface is more verbose (complicated?) than its Java counterpart; declaring that a type implements the interface just requires a simple instantiation; and *using* the data type, either normally or as an interface, is extremely simple. This is the usual trade-off with the building-block approach: the extra complexity required by not having the construct readily available is charged on the *designer* of the abstraction, but there is almost no cost to the *user*.

6   What Are Interfaces Used for in Java?

The previous section showed a design pattern that allows the same programming style in Ada as in Java. However this does not imply that all uses of interfaces in Java *must* use this pattern in Ada. In Java, interfaces are used for different purposes:

Flags. Java features some empty interfaces, i.e. interfaces that declare no methods. Classes can implement these interfaces just to flag that they allow certain operations. For example, every object features a `clone` method to duplicate itself, but the method will throw an exception unless the class specifically allowed it by declaring that it implements the interface `Cloneable`. This is clearly more a programming trick than a proper usage of interfaces: what does it mean for a class to promise that it implements... nothing?

Simple interfaces. These are truly interfaces, i.e. a promise that the class features some properties. Interfaces like `Serializable` (the class can be written to a file) or `Comparable` (objects can be compared) fall into that category. It is easy to understand that, for example, a file object can handle any object that implements `Serializable`. The above design pattern can be used in that case, although often the same effect can be achieved using simple generics.

Restricted multiple inheritance. In Java, a class can inherit from only one class, but can implement any number of interfaces. *If* we give the meaning to an interface that every class that implements it is considered as belonging to a class of objects, then this usage can be considered as an implementation of multiple inheritance. The benefits over full MI is that since all methods of an interface *must* be redefined, there can't be two default implementations for the same method at the same time, therefore avoiding the issue of repeated inheritance. Once again, this kind of usage can be achieved in Ada by using the previous programming pattern.

Listeners. This is a paradigm where there are occurrences of some events in the system, and one or several objects need to take some action in response to the event. They are said to *listen* to the event. The construct that will trigger these actions is called the *notifier*: it can be a programming object, but also a hardware interrupt for example. Typical listeners are found in the management of interrupts, mouse events, clock events, dialog buttons... The notion of *event* is not necessarily connected to an external event; it can be a simple state change in an object[3], as in OO data bases.

7   Various Implementations of the Listener Paradigm

Note first that from a conceptual point of view, listeners are *active* objects: they can have actions that are invoked asynchronously, and care must be taken about concurrent access to the methods that they offer.

Two basic mechanisms are associated to the listener paradigm: there must be a *registration* process (with the associated deregistration process), to make the notifier aware of all possible listeners, and a *delivery* process to trigger appropriate actions in each listener when the event occurs. Of course, the notifier should have no *a priori* knowledge of who the listeners are. Typically, it will maintain a linked list of listeners, and call the delivery method on each of them each time the event occurs.

7.1   Call-Backs

Historically, the first examples of the listener paradigm were for handling interrupts, or for dealing with events from user interfaces, like connecting some processing to a mouse click on a button. Most of the time, the programming language used (assembly, C) had no tasking feature. Therefore, the first mechanism was *call-backs*: a procedure is associated to the event. Registration consists in passing a pointer to the procedure to the notifier, and the notifier issues an indirect call to the procedure whenever the event happens. This mechanism is still the most common one for hardware interrupts.

Since Ada has pointers to subprograms, this solution can be used directly.

7.2   Extended Call-Backs: Interfaces

The previous solution falls short when there are several related events, with different processings that have to be registered at the same time. For example, one might want to register different call-backs depending on whether a button is clicked on with the left, middle or right button.

It is of course possible to register multiple call-backs; but a set of subprograms connected to a given entity is exactly the definition of an interface; it is therefore more convenient to define an interface, and to register the interface as a whole. For example, our `Wakeable` interface can be defined as follows, if we want various operations to be performed every second, minute, or hour:

```
interface WakeableInterface {
    void everySecond ();
    void everyMinute ();
    void everyHour   ();
}
```

It is often argued that interfaces are much better than call-backs, even when the interface features only one method. This is because *in C*, registering a call-back is done by providing the address of a function, without any kind of checking about the conformance of parameters. Interfaces ensure that the profile of the provided functions match the required profile. But of course, in Ada, pointers to subprograms must be consistent with the expected usage, so the added value of interfaces is much smaller. Therefore, it is much more acceptable in Ada to register multiple call-backs, and interfaces are not necessary in this case.

7.3 Generics

It is often the case that there is only one listener to a given event. This idiom can be very simply implemented by making the notifier generic, with the notified procedure as a generic parameter. For example, the scheduler that handles Every_Second events could be declared as:

```
generic
  with procedure Every_Second;
package Scheduler is
  ...
end Scheduler;
```

Note that we could as well provide several procedures as formal parameters, if the notifier was serving several events.

7.4 Tasking

In all the previous idioms, the processing of events was done by (aysnchronously) calling a procedure. However, as noted above, this is really an active behaviour, and it seems natural to model this with tasks. Actually, if the call-back mechanism (and variants) is in so wide-spread use, it is because at the time where GUI appeared that made an intensive use of listeners, most languages had no concurrency.[4]

Polling A first possibility is for the notifier to provide a function that tells whether a new event has arrived, or a function that returns the next event, with a special null_event if none has occurred. The listener will actively sample the notifier for events (this is how the main loop of GUIs behaves generally) :

```
task body Listener is
  ...
begin
  loop
    Event := Notifier.Get_Next_Event;
    case Event is
      ...
    when Null_Event =>
      delay 0.1;
    end case;
  end loop;
end Listener;
```

---

[4] with the notable exception of Ada, of course!

This idiom is not appropriate when there are several listeners, since the notifier would have to deliver the last event that occurred to any task that requests it; however, it would be very difficult to avoid delivering the same event twice to the same listener. In practice, the notifier will rather reset the current event as soon as it has been delivered once. On the other hand, it is easy for the listener to poll various notifiers until an event is delivered, allowing it to process multiple kinds of events.

Entries A notifier can be viewed as an event server, in which case it is natural to represent it as a task or protected object. Listeners will get events in the same way as with the previous idiom; however, `Get_Event` will typically be an entry rather than a subprogram. This implies two main differences:

- The listener will block until an event is available. This means that no active loop is necessary.
- When an event occurs, the notifier can deliver the event to all listeners that are currently queued. With a protected object, it is quite easy to ensure that no race conditions can occur if one of the listeners returns to the point where it requests an event before all listeners have been notified. With tasks, this can be ensured using `requeue` or entry families, although not as easily.[5]

8   Comparison of the Various Implementations of the Listener Paradigm

Idioms based on procedure calls are *sequential* according to Booch's taxonomy[2], i.e. there must be an external synchronization mechanism to ensure that the state of the object is not modified by another procedure while the object is being notified of an event, while idioms based on tasks are naturally *concurrent*.

Idioms based on tasking have the nice feature that there is no need for a registration mechanism: the task simply requests an event when it is in a state that allows it. The generic idiom is a purely static solution: there is no need for registration either, and the region where the listener is active is entirely determined at compile time by scoping rules.

Whether it is useful to allow more than one listener really depends on the application; although this is a must in some contexts, it can be nice in other cases to be able to ensure that an event can be processed by only one listener.

Table 1 summarizes the properties of each solution. As usual, there is no single "best" solution to the listener paradigm. Which idiom to use should be determined by the application needs.

---

[5] Sorry, the algorithm is a bit long for this paper; please contact the author if interested.

Table 1. comparison of the various idioms for the listener paradigm

Idiom	Active?	Registration	Multiple listeners	Multiple events
Call-back	No	Explicit	Yes	No
Interface	No	Explicit	Yes	Yes
Generic	No	Static	No	Yes
Task, Polling	Yes, not blocking	Automatic	No	Yes
Task, Entry	Yes, blocking	Automatic	Yes	No

9 Proposal for Ada0Y

There is a proposal for an amendment (AI-00251)[1] that would allow the equivalent of interfaces in Ada. Basically, a tagged type could be derived from several types, all of which, except the first one, would be required to be abstract with only abstract operations. The canonical example from the AI is:

```
type Stack is abstract ; -- An abstract interface type
   -- ... Operations on Stack

type Queue is abstract ; -- Another interface.
   -- ... Operations on Queue
          . . .
type Deque is abstract new Queue and Stack ;
   -- An interface which inherits from both
   -- the Queue and Stack interfaces.
   -- ... Operations on Deque
          . . .
-- An extension that implements an interface
type My_Deque is new Blob and Deque with
   record
      -- Conventional type implementing an interface.
          . . .
   end record ;
```

The proposed implementation model is very close to what is proposed in section 5: the tagged type would contain pointers to the various dispatching tables.

Note that although this would be convenient, especially for interfacing to Java, current compilers are able to recognize constructs that are "close enough" to map Java interfaces. For example, the Aonix® compiler help file explains that:

An Ada tagged limited type "claims" that it implements an interface by including in its list of components an aliased component of the interface type.

10   Conclusion

We have argued already [4] that the fact that other languages rely only on inheritance as the implementation mechanism for a number of concepts does not mean that the same should apply to Ada, given its much richer set of features. We have shown here that the fact that Java uses interfaces in various ways, and especially for all cases of listeners, should not be used to conclude that it is always the most appropriate paradigm in Ada.

Java interfaces are a useful concept, and the idea of "promised interface" is certainly an attractive feature. Moreover, since there are Ada compilers that target the JVM, it is important to define how to access Java interfaces from Ada. However, although there is nothing in Ada that maps *directly* to Java interfaces, we have shown in this paper that existing Ada constructs provide solutions to the problems that Java interfaces address. Therefore, we claim that there is no *technical requirement* for adding interfaces to Ada. It would only be syntactic sugar, since equivalent constructs can be built using current features.

But it must be remembered that sometimes, sugar (i.e. new building blocks) "helps the medicine go down"... Finding ready-to-use features in a language makes it easier to use, but having too many of them increases complexity. The real issue is therefore where to draw the line between building blocks and specialized pieces, and this is certainly not easy. Lego blocks allow much more creativity than Playmobil pieces[6], but even Lego has provided more and more sophisticated blocks over time...

In conclusion, we claim that the issue of adding interfaces in Ada0Y needs investigation, at least for interfacing with Java, but that the technical need is less important than often advocated.

References

1. http://www.ada-auth.org/cgi-bin/cvsweb.cgi/AIs/AI-00251.TXT
2. Booch, G.: Software Components with Ada, Benjamin Cummings Company, Menlo Park, 1987
3. Heaney, M.: "Implementing Design Patterns in Ada 95", Tutorial, SIGAda 2000 conference.
4. Rosen, J-P.: "What Orientation Should Ada Objects Take?", Communications of the ACM, Volume 35 #11, ACM, New-York.
5. Rosen, J-P.: "A naming Convention for Classes in Ada 9X", Ada Letters, Volume XV #2, March/April 1995.

---

[6] Admitedly, this is a personal opinion!

Using Object Orientation in High Integrity Applications: A Case Study

Alejandro Alonso[1], Roberto López[1], Tullio Vardanega[2]*, and
Juan Antonio de la Puente[1]

[1] Departamento de Ingeniería de Sistemas Telemáticos
Universidad Politécnica de Madrid, E-28040 Madrid, Spain
[2] Directorate of Technical and Operational Support
European Space Research & Technology Centre, 2200 AG Noordwijk, Netherlands
{aalonso, lopezr, jpuente}@dit.upm.es, tullio@ws.estec.esa.nl

Abstract. In this work we analyse the suitability of using object-oriented features in high integrity systems, and the interest of redesigning a system implementation to include these constructs. The analysis was based on retrofitting object-oriented programming into the pre-object oriented design of the OBOSS software package. The evaluation of the impact was measured in a number of ways. The implications of this approach, with respect to the requirements for high integrity systems are also discussed. The final conclusion is that in this particular case is not worthwhile retrofitting OOP.

1 Introduction

OBOSS (On-Board Operations Support Software) [8] is a software package that provides a reuse framework for on-board data handling systems in satellites. OBOSS was first produced as an evolution of a system used in flight and then used as baseline in several other flight projects. It was initially written in Ada 83, using special features available in the Aonix AdaWorld/ERC32 compilation system that implements some of the real-time capabilities of Ada 95.

A modified version of OBOSS was successively developed [9]. The aim was to port OBOSS to Ada 95 [7] in a form compliant with the Ravenscar Profile [2] prescriptions. This version was tested with GNAT/ORK/ERC32. As part of the revision work, recommendations were formulated, which identified areas suitable for further enhancement with object-oriented features, especially tagged types and dispatching operations.

The GNAT/ORK compilation system [5] stems from the integration of two distinct components: the open-source Ada 95 GNAT compiler, currently supported by Ada Core Technologies (ACT) [1], which constitutes the target-independent component of the product; and the Open Ravenscar Real–Time Kernel (ORK), an open-source, small-size, reliable and efficient kernel that implements the tasking model defined by the Ravenscar Profile. GNAT/ORK is currently available on Linux platforms as a cross compilation system targeting the ERC32, a radiation tolerant version of the SPARC v7 computer architecture [3].

---

* Currently at the Università degli Studi di Padova, Italy

J. Blieberger and A. Strohmeier (Eds.): Ada-Europe 2002, LNCS 2361, pp. 357–366, 2002.

The goal of the work reported in this paper was to modify OBOSS using object orientation and to investigate the effect of the changes on system predictability, execution time and storage size and management. Special care was taken to ensure that the code follows the guidelines for using Ada in high integrity systems [6].

2   Background and Approach

Our implementation work in this project is to analyse the suitability of using object-oriented features in high integrity systems. For this purpose, OBOSS was partially modified to include selected object-oriented programming (OOP) features. In particular, the work concentrated on replacing variant record type declarations, which appear to have the greatest potential for program improvement if converted to tagged types.

An important part of our work was also to analyse whether it is feasible or worthwhile to redesign, a posteriori, a system implementation to include object-oriented features. In this particular respect, we have to observe that the OBOSS design makes quite advanced and proficient use of Ada 83, but includes no provision for Ada 95 OOP. In view of this origin, the current OBOSS design exhibits some inherent limitations:

- It is necessary to modify the original code if a new packet type is required. In particular, the procedures that handle packets should be changed, which means that new bugs could be added to procedures that previously worked correctly.
- The use of case statements for the handling of variant records, which OBOSS used to handle the inherently polymorphic nature of its packet structures, makes the code more difficult to read.
- After a modification it is necessary to recompile and re-qualify a large part of the code.

In the following, we describe and discuss the OOP modifications we have made to the OBOSS design.

3   OOP Redesign of OBOSS

Satellite systems operates under the supervision of a control centre based on ground. The ground centre requests services to the satellite by sending telecommands (TC). On the other hand, the satellite sends status and verification information in telemetries (TM). The European Space Agency has developed a Package Utilisation Standard (PUS) [4] that defines a packet-based interface for the execution of a number of services by on-board application processes. These operations are performed by a so-called Data Handling Control (DHC) system.

OBOSS was developed as a software framework to promote reuse in the development of PUS-based DHC systems. The operations model is structured as a set of service providers and service users. The service providers handle a collection of PUS services. Whenever a TC is received, it is routed to the appropriate service provider, which analyses its correctness and executes the associated service operation or sub-service. Each of the TC's has a specific source packet format.

Service providers have a common structure and operation model, which effectively consists of the following logic:

- Convert the PUS packet into an internal representation. For this purpose, the packet is parsed for identifying the corresponding sub-service and internal data structure.
- Execute the sub-service. The code that corresponds to the requested sub-service is executed and the corresponding service reports are generated.
- Execute a recovery routine, if the parsing of the PUS packet failed.

The original OBOSS design defines the type `Internal_TC_Representation` for internally representing the PUS packets. This type is implemented as a variant record, in order to accommodate structural differences between different packet types, as well as different information depending on the success or failure of the packet parsing. In the case of success, another variant record (`Internal_TC_Source _Data`) is used to store in a different internal format the specific information of each available sub-service, which is the type discriminant.

The reason for this approach is that some of the functions that handle these data packets are independent of the data contents of the packet. It is therefore desirable to make them operate on the same type, irrespective of the specific packet format. On the other hand, there is an obvious need for handling differently packets of different formats. These requirements can be fulfilled by using variant records. Format-Independent functions do not care about the specific contents of the data, while data-independent format functions execute differently, depending on the variant types discriminant and based on case statements.

The analysis of the OBOSS code and documentation indicates that the most interesting advantage of using object orientation in OBOSS lies in the possibility of including new telecommands (hence, new packet formats), while minimising the changes in the code. As mentioned before, in this way the effort of regression testing could be very much reduced. The original OBOSS design does not collate in the same package the above mentioned packet types and the associated operations, which makes them non-primitive and prevents the programmer from using class wide programming. In addition, as both types were not included in the same package, the cost of code modifications is higher. In this particular situation, the benefits of using object orientation cannot be obtained simply by changing variant records for tagged types. A new design of the concerned OBOSS Ada packages is required.

The rationale of the new approach is to try to locate and collate in the same package a basic type and the associated primitive operations. In doing so, we tried to minimise the changes done to the OBOSS framework, as the overall architecture has proven to be valid.

Special emphasis in the project was placed on the internal representation and handling of TCs, so as to permit the addition of new ones, with minimum impact. The new implementation relies on the following facts:

- The available TC sub-services are described using tagged types. The root of the class is `Internal_TC_Src_Data`.
- The available TC's are described by extending the root type with the TC specific data.
- An abstract function called `Interpret_TC` is defined. It should include the code to process each of the TC sub-services. Dynamic dispatching is used for executing the proper function at runtime.
- A function called `Parse_Source_Data` converts a packet into the internal TC representation provided. Class wide programming is used to this end. Internally, this function calls operations associated with each of the TC sub-services to perform the conversion from the PUS packet into a suitable internal representation. Dynamic dispatching is not appropriate because a set of common operations have to be executed before making the actual conversion.

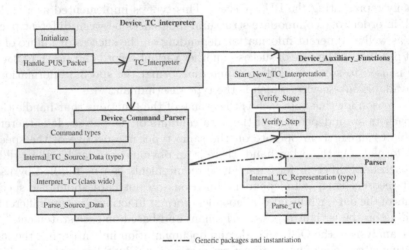

Fig. 1. System architecture

The redesigned architecture is shown in figure 1. The prototype implementation has been tested with the *Device Command Distribution Service*, which is a representative sample of the OBOSS service catalogue. The following packages are relevant:

- `Device_Auxiliary_Functions`: this package exports a set of functions required to process TC sub-services. It is included because the functions can be used from two different modules.
- `Parser`: this is a generic package. It is in charge of parsing a TC and validating it. If the TC is valid, the information stored in the record is the internal representation of the TC.
- `Device_Command_Parser`: This package converts the PUS packet information into an internal format and, later, processes it. It instantiates `Parser` and makes it visible.
- `Device_TC_Interpreter`: This package provides the visible interface of OBOSS. It is based on a sporadic task that handles each of the incoming packets.

The activity of this task is to validate the TC, convert it into an internal representation and, finally process it.

This approach facilitates the inclusion of a new sub-service. One possible way to do this is to modify the Device_Command_Parser package. In particular, the Internal_TC_Src_Data should be extended with the record that internally represents the new TC, and operations for parsing and processing it should be provided. In this way, it will not be necessary to modify a single line of code of those packages that uses Device_Command_Parser. Another possibility is to include this code in a child package. Then, the recompilation effort will be very much reduced.

4 Basic Types Modification

Package Parameter_Representation includes the implementation of a subset of the basic parameter types and structures described in the PUS definition document. In particular, there exists a type (Standard_Value) that is the union of all the supported parameter types. Its structure is a variant record, with the type (boolean, enumerated, signed or unsigned integer, ...) and the corresponding format (size or range) as discriminant. A number of common operations on this type are also defined, such as "<" ,">", Put in a data stream, and Get from a data stream.

A simplified view of the original Standard_Value definition is shown below.

```
Enumerated_16_Bit_Size : constant := 16;
Enumerated_24_Bit_Size : constant := 24;
type Enumerated_16 is range 0 .. 2**Enumerated_16_Bit_Size - 1;
type Enumerated_24 is range 0 .. 2**Enumerated_24_Bit_Size - 1;


Unsigned_Integer_13_Bit_Size : constant := 6 * Basic_Types.Byte_Size;
Unsigned_Integer_14_Bit_Size : constant := 8 * Basic_Types.Byte_Size;
type Unsigned_Integer_13 is range 0 .. 2**Unsigned_Integer_13_Bit_Size - 1;
type Unsigned_Integer_14 is new Basic_Types.DWord;
                                                                          10
type Parameter_Type_Code is range 0 .. N;
type Standard_Value
      (Type_Code : Parameter_Type_Code := 0;
        Format_Code : Parameter_Format_Code := 0) is
   record case Type_Code is
         when Not_A_Value_PTC => null;
         when 1 => case Format_Code is
               when 16 => Enumerated_Val_16 : Enumerated_6;
               when 24 => Enumerated_Val_16 : Enumerated_24;
            end case;                                                      20
         when 2 => case Format_Code is
               when 13 => Unsigned_Integer_Val_13 : Unsigned_Integer_13;
               when 14 => Unsigned_Integer_Val_14 : Unsigned_Integer_14;
            end case;
      end case
   end record;
```

This definition can be improved by using tagged types. In the OOP redesigned version, `Standard_Value` is an abstract tagged type. The same holds for representing the different types of parameters. These types are extended to represent each of the data types, as sketched in the following code fragment. The mentioned basic operations are defined as primitive, in order to use dynamic dispatching on their call.

```
type Standard_Value is tagged null record;

Enumerated_16_Bit_Size : constant := 16;
Enumerated_24_Bit_Size : constant := 24;
type Enumerated_16 is range 0 .. 2**Enumerated_16_Bit_Size − 1;
type Enumerated_24 is range 0 .. 2**Enumerated_24_Bit_Size − 1;

type SV_Enumerated_PTC is abstract new Standard_Value with null record;
type SV_Enumerated_Val_24 is new SV_Enumerated_PTC with
   record Value : Enumerated_24; end record;                          10

Unsigned_Integer_13_Bit_Size : constant := 6 * Basic_Types.Byte_Size;
type Unsigned_Integer_13 is range 0 .. 2**Unsigned_Integer_13_Bit_Size − 1;

type SV_Unsigned_Integer_PTC is new Standard_Value with null record;
type SV_Unsigned_Integer_Val_13 is new SV_Unsigned_Integer_PTC with
   record Value : Unsigned_Integer_13; end record;
```

The major advantage of this modification is the possibility of adding new parameter types or structures, without the need to modify the code of the client packages. The same holds with the package `Parameter_Representation`, if the extensions are included in a child package.

5   Analysis of the Use of Object-Oriented Techniques

5.1   Space

Type representation

The size of the type `Standard_Value`, when defined as a variant record always spans 256 bits. This is so because the compiler has to get memory to store the largest possible value. When using tagged types instead, the memory required depends on the actual amount of data to be stored, plus some memory to store the tag. In the case in question, the required memory ranges from 32 bits to 224.

Size of executable code

The size of the final executable code is expected to be larger in the object-oriented version, due to the need to include further code and routines. Table 1 shows the sizes of a program using the object-oriented version of OBOSS and the original one. There is a considerable difference in size. However, we are uncertain as to whether the compilers made all the possible optimisations, with respect to the functions to include in the final code. Further work is required to investigate the specific reasons for the considerable size increase. We plan to carry out this investigation but we are unable to report on it in this paper.

Compiler	NON-OOP	OOP
GNAT/ORK	72,744	273,932
GNAT native	58,060	229,428

Table 1. Comparison of the size of executables

5.2   Execution Time

Execution time is another parameter that is specially important to analyse. For this purpose, a number of sample programs have been coded, using dynamic dispatching or case instructions for handling variant records. Table 2 shows the results of making a number of Put and Get operations, executed sequentially. The operations transforms a PUS type into a data stream and vice versa. This table also shows the execution time of the "<" operations for a number of PUS types.

The interesting finding from this experiment is that the object-oriented version is faster. This is because with the compiler in use, the execution of dynamic dispatching is faster than a corresponding implementation based on the case statement, which is not surprising. In any case, the execution time difference is not too big.

Type	PUT/GET functions		< function	
	Non-OOP	OOP	Non-OOP	OOP
Boolean	339.2	331.9		
Enumerated_8	464.8	455.8	12.6	3.6
Signed_10	598.7	589.9	12.5	3.6
Unsigned_10	570.9	562.0	12.5	3.6
Real_1	889.0	881.8	22.5	14.5
Time	693.0	685.8	55.5	47.5
Character_String	4515.6	4508.8		

Table 2. Comparison of execution times(μs)

5.3   Dynamic Memory

Object-oriented constructs may imply the use of dynamic memory, which should be avoided in high integrity applications [2]. We have tried to detect the use of dynamic memory in the OOP version of OBOSS by setting a breakpoint in _gnat_malloc, the function that GNAT uses to reserve dynamic memory. We have not found additional uses of the heap than in the previous version of OBOSS.

The use of dynamic memory by this package, compiled with GNAT/ORK, was analysed in [9]. As mentioned in that paper, this detection technique is not fit to exhaustively catch all occurrences of allocation violation, which in fact requires full object code analysis. Hence, although we believe that the OOP features we have used do not necessary require dynamic memory, full object code analysis is required to make sure that the compiler does not insert dynamic memory calls. In any case, the most direct and efficient way to achieve this objective is to have compiler support for detecting the allocation violation. The IRTAW group agreed to include restriction No_Implicit_Heap_Allocation in the Ravenscar profile to detect this situation [10].

5.4   Time Predictability

The use of tagged types and class-wide programming in OBOSS should not give rise to the loss of predictability of execution time. In the Ada 83 version, the time to process a TC depends on its type. Case statements at application level code were used to determine the appropriate code to execute. Hence, the worst case computation time corresponds to the command that requires more processing time. Exactly the same happens with the new version. The only difference is the technique that is used to decide on the proper function to execute. In any case, it is necessary to look carefully at how dynamic dispatching is implemented, in order to make sure that it is suitable for this type of systems.

5.5   Cost of the New Design and Implementation

We find it also interesting to analyse the cost of retrofitting OOP into pre-object oriented design. The effort required to modify the Parameter_Representation package has been low, of course only after we managed to understand the code and analysed the impact of the inclusion of the selected object-oriented constructs. In the case of the redesign of the service providers, the cost has been higher, but affordable. This was due to the well structured initial OBOSS architecture.

The major advantages are related with the ease to modify and adapt an object-oriented implementation. We believe that with the new structure it is much simpler to include new sub-services. Apart from this, there are no big gains in terms of execution speed. As a downside, the size of the code has significantly increased.

In our experience, it is worth retrofitting an object-oriented approach if the system is expected to be extended with a certain frequency or if a re-design is anyway required, due to changes on the system specification or malfunction caused by a poor initial design. On the other hand, if specification changes are not expected or the system is well-designed, then arguably there is little benefit. This is the case with OBOSS, where the following facts have to be considered:

- The system is well designed.
- Addition of new sub-services is not a frequent event.
- The structure of client packages will not be significantly improved with the new interfaces.

6   Conclusions

This paper reports the experience of retrofitting object-oriented programming into the pre-object oriented design of the OBOSS software package. OBOSS is intended for use in the development of data handling control system in satellites, which are, by their nature, high integrity systems. The OOP features included in OBOSS make it more readable and easier to modify. The execution time and the storage size of the modified types are slightly improved. An important drawback is the overall size of the executable, which becomes bigger, although we believe that improvements in future versions of the compiler would diminish this difference.

The development of high integrity systems poses a number of requirements on the language constructs to be used and in the behaviour of the system. Time predictability is preserved when using OOP OBOSS. In fact, from this point of view, the temporal behaviour of the particular use of dynamic dispatching is similar to the original code, which relies on the case statement to decide the specific operations to execute. Dynamic memory is a feature to avoid in high integrity systems. The OOP OBOSS version does not seem to add additional heap claims.

A question to consider it is whether is worthwhile to retrofit OOP into non-OOP systems. The answer depends strongly on a number of factors such as the quality of the original design, the need and frequency of system modifications, and the gains of introducing OOP in the system. In the case of OBOSS, we believe that is not worthwhile to make it. The system is well designed, changes in the PUS packets are not expected, and the interfaces to client packages would not be much improved.

The OBOSS design started in 1993 with Ada 83 in mind, hence OOP was excluded because of lack of support more than by decision. Yet, the paper shows that the OOP redesign of it (in addition to striving to avoid dangerous features like uncontrolled dynamic dispatching) certainly is more elegant. The paper also shows that this improvement (which is valuable for a reusable product) is countered by a considerable size increase. It remains to be seen the impact of the increased semantic power of the OOP construct upon the complexity of the design and execution of the verification phase.

7   Acknowledgements

We would like to thank Juan Zamorano, José Ruíz, and Ramón Fernández, for the fruitful discussions that have helped to improve the quality of this paper. We would also like to thank the anonymous reviewers that have made very constructive and detailed comments.

References

1. Ada Core Technologies Inc.: GNAT web page. http://www.gnat.com
2. Burns, A.: The Ravenscar Profile. Ada Letters, Vol. XIX, No. 4. ACM Press (1999) 49–52.
3. European Space Research and Technology Centre: 32-bit Microprocessor and Computer System Development. Deliverable on Contract 9848/92/NL/FM. (1996) http://www.estec.esa.nl/wsmwww/erc32/erc32.html
4. ESA, Packet Utilisation Standard. Europen Space Agency, Noordwijk, Netherlands, PSS-07-101: Issue 1 (1994). (http://esapub.esrin.esa.it/pss/pss-cat1.htm).
5. de la Puente, J.A., Ruiz, J.F, and Zamorano, J.: An Open Ravenscar Real-Time Kernel for GNAT. In: Keller, H.B., and Ploedereder,E.: Reliable Software Technologies — Ada-Europe 2000. Lecture Notes in Computer Science, Vol. 1845. Springer-Verlag (2000), 5–15.
6. ISO/IEC/JTC1/SC22/WG9. Guide for the Use of Ada Programming Language for High Integrity Systems (2000), ISO/IEC TR 15942:2000.
7. Taft, S.T., Duff, R.A.: Ada 95 Reference Manual. Language and Standard Libraries. International Standard ISO/IEC 8652:1995(E). Lecture Notes in Computer Science, Vol. 1246. Springer-Verlag (1997).
8. TERMA Elektronik: Software System Development for Spacecraft Data Handling Control. Deliverable on ESTEC Contract 12797/98/NL/PA. (1999) http://spd-web.terma.com/Projects/OBOSS/Home_Page
9. Vardanega, T., García, R., de la Puente, J.A.: An Application Case for Ravenscar Technology: Porting OBOSS to GNAT/ORK. In: Dirk Craeynest & Alfred Strohmeier (eds.): Reliable Software Technologies — Ada Europe'01. Lecture Notes in Computer Science, Vol. 2043. Springer-Verlag (2001) 392–404.
10. Wellings, A.: Status and Future of the Ravenscar Profile: Session Summary. Proceedings of the 10th IRTAW. Ada Letters, Vol. XXI, No. 1, March 2001, 5–8.

Author Index

Lecture Notes in Computer Science

For information about Vols. 1–2275
please contact your bookseller or Springer-Verlag